The Burden of Black Religion

The Burden of Black Religion

CURTIS J. EVANS

OXFORD
UNIVERSITY PRESS

2008

OXFORD
UNIVERSITY PRESS

Oxford University Press, Inc., publishes works that further
Oxford University's objective of excellence
in research, scholarship, and education.

Oxford   New York
Auckland   Cape Town   Dar es Salaam   Hong Kong   Karachi
Kuala Lumpur   Madrid   Melbourne   Mexico City   Nairobi
New Delhi   Shanghai   Taipei   Toronto

With offices in
Argentina   Austria   Brazil   Chile   Czech Republic   France   Greece
Guatemala   Hungary   Italy   Japan   Poland   Portugal   Singapore
South Korea   Switzerland   Thailand   Turkey   Ukraine   Vietnam

Published by Oxford University Press, Inc.
198 Madison Avenue, New York, New York 10016

www.oup.com

Oxford is a registered trademark of Oxford University Press

Library of Congress Cataloging-in-Publication Data
Evans, Curtis J. (Curtis Junius)
The burden of Black religion / Curtis J. Evans.
    p. cm.
Includes bibliographical references and index.
ISBN 978–0-19–532818–9; 978–0-19–532931–5 (pbk.)
1. African Americans—Religion.   2. Black theology.
3. United States—Church history.   I. Title.
BR563.N4E9645 2008
277.3'0808996073—dc22   2007034723

9 8 7 6 5 4 3 2 1

Printed in the United States of America
on acid-free paper

Preface

In writing this book, I learned a lot about myself and how and why I have arrived at certain conclusions about the topic I have chosen to study. Self-awareness, of course, does not necessarily make the task of sorting through a bewildering array of historical evidence and offering plausible arguments for one's conclusions any easier. My intent in telling a bit about the *how* of my research is not meant to divert attention away from *what* I have written. I hope readers will be just as critical of what I have written after reading this preface as they would have if I had not included it. I believe my attempt to tell how I went about doing this project and what I hope to accomplish by undertaking it will provide deeper insight into why and how I came to certain conclusions, which will perhaps create more sympathy for my arguments, if not agreement. I think it only fair that I situate myself in relation to my subject matter because I have been trying to do the same with the many figures that I discuss in the body of this work. None of us is outside history, so we should try to give an account of ourselves as one way of informing the reader how our ideas are shaped by our personal biography and social location.

The origin of this book is probably deeply buried in my personal past and psyche. As young boys growing up in a small town in Louisiana, my brothers and I did not talk very much about race. We worked in the fields after school and spent most of the summers "chopping cotton" during the hottest parts of the day. There was not much time and energy to theorize about race. Our daily lives reflected the effects of a deeply racial Southern past, and we had a visible reminder of race when we went to town on the school bus five days a week and noticed railroad tracks that separated the black and white parts of town. As a child, I had limited contact with those who did not have my shade of melanin, though my brothers and I were conscious enough of race that we knew such things as which small towns to avoid while traveling or after dark, and we assumed that in general whites and blacks did not go to the same schools. My mother's frequent admonitions for us to love our enemies and not return racially charged epithets (though I do not recall hearing any spoken directly to us) must have been her way of trying to prepare us for a world that she believed was not so kind and loving.

My experiences as an undergraduate, master's, and doctoral student were filled with exciting intellectual discoveries. I loved history, in part because I could not quite figure out what I wanted to do with my life. As a student at the University of Houston, I found myself fascinated by an open honor's class on the Old South, taught by Cheryl Cody. The course and her feedback really made me excited about studying history, though it brought me no closer to a career. Yet it began a slow process of trying to come to terms with my personal history and our nation's racial history. I wanted to know how white Southerners used the Bible and the Christian faith to defend slavery and later segregation. I tried to understand how my history fit into the broader history of America that I was studying with such interest. I read books like Eugene Genovese's *Roll, Jordan, Roll* (1972) with eagerness, particularly his fascinating discussion of slave religion. Along the way, I was drawn to some of the most unsavory aspects of our nation's history, though it was not because of a morbid desire to revel in the underside of history, as critics may argue, but because of a persistent longing to understand or make sense of race relations. I often wondered what would be a "satisfactory" explanation for me as I continued to read and dig deeper into these sources. At what point would I know why white Southerners did what they did, and when would I feel that I had a sufficient understanding of how and why, for example, slavery was justified? What would this knowledge do to my understanding of the Bible and Christianity because I was a practicing Christian studying these things?

As a doctoral student at Harvard University, I had a rich environment in which to flourish intellectually. I prized the expansive collections at Harvard's libraries. When I entered Harvard, my stated dissertation topic was white evangelicals and the civil rights movement. This was a continuation of my master's thesis. I could tell that my advisors probably thought there was not much more to be done on that topic. My own research proved them correct. Fortunately, my advisors allowed me breathing room to explore and examine different issues. I am grateful that I had a number of excellent professors who expanded my view of the world. I was still a bit hesitant about exploring race specifically and African American history, even after David D. Hall suggested that I look at sociological studies of African American religion in the 1930s and 1940s. I wanted to work on a more "universal" topic. I was trying to move beyond the particularities of my own experience. Race was too close to me, though it was apparently so pressing that I was already dealing with it in my master's thesis. I wanted to be a scholar, and I did not want others to associate my work and interests with racial particularity and the poverty and illiteracy of my youth in the rural South. I struggled with a distorted image of becoming an expert on race and race relations. Continued research in the archives deepened my attention to race in such a way that I was irresistibly drawn to the topic, despite my concerns about how I would be perceived as an academic in the future. I came to realize that it was precisely the particularity of my personal experience as an African American growing up in the rural South that informed my writing and helped make my distinctive contribution to the writing of a particular kind of history. I owe a great deal of gratitude to Robert Orsi for helping me understand this more clearly.

Fortunately, I took David's advice and the seeds of this book germinated in my mind. I came to make the project entirely my own and engaged in a much broader analysis than what David suggested, but I owe the basic idea of this book to him. As I continued to do research and prepare my prospectus, I was struck by how black sociologists of the 1940s were so eager to prove that blacks were not "innately religious." Obviously, I wondered: What did innate religiosity mean to these interpreters? Who was claiming that blacks were naturally religious? Why was this issue so salient that it demanded analysis in academic works? These and other questions led me back in time. I kept digging until I felt that I had found the roots of these assertions of innate religiosity in the 1830s, among the romantic racialists, who I treat at length in chapter 1. I wanted to know what the cultural and political implications were of claims of black innate religiosity. Furthermore, I was interested in why the religious capacities of blacks became such an object of inquiry and how, if at all, this related to changing conceptions of their intelligence. I desired answers to how debates about religiosity and intellectual capacity evolved in relationship to discussions of the place of blacks in the nation. These questions led me farther back in time to debates among missionaries in the eighteenth century who were trying to convince slave owners to Christianize their slaves. After spending some time reading this literature, I became convinced, even after reading extensively in the secondary literature, that no one had quite approached the topic from this particular angle.

When I set out to explore the "burden of black religion," I became aware that certain issues that I examined had been explored in part. For example, George Fredrickson's *The Black Image in the White Mind* (1971) devotes an entire chapter to romantic racialism in the mid-nineteenth century. Yet Frederickson was concerned primarily with white conceptions of blacks, and though religion figures prominently in his chapter, his primary interest lay elsewhere. I became convinced that romantic racialism was the first fully articulate discourse of black innate religiosity, which had profound consequences for how blacks were imagined and the prospects of blacks flourishing in the nation. So the sociological works of the 1940s that sought to disprove innate religiosity began to make sense when placed within this broader historical trajectory. Innate religiosity was seen as a subset of racial essentialism by black sociologists. Because the nature of black religious life was profoundly transformed as blacks entered Northern cities in massive numbers beginning in 1916, black sociologists saw it as their duty to discredit assertions of innate religiosity, particularly to the extent that they had been informed by the experiences of blacks in the rural South. Claims of innate religiosity were also a reminder of a race-based assessment of black prospects in the nation, and they lingered as barriers to black assimilation because they signified permanent racial differences. Black social scientists in particular pointed to blacks entering modernity in the urban centers of the North. Their works, I argue, represented a new phase in interpretations of black religion and were crucial for assessments of black prospects in the nation in more recent history.

I have provided a cultural and intellectual history of race and religion, noting how blacks and whites responded to and shaped the ideas of each other. Perhaps social historians will not be pleased at my failure to give more detailed attention to political, economic, and social relations on the ground. Perhaps I have not paid sufficient attention to the circulation and dissemination of the ideas and books that I examine in this work. More could have been done on finding out who was reading these works and how pastors and church leaders responded to them. But the sacrifice I made in depth, I hope, was a trade-off for a more general analysis of the importance of a particular kind of discourse about black innate religiosity and how it shaped imaginings about how the nation was to be constituted and the grounds of inclusion in American culture. To limit my discussion to local and particular contexts would have unnecessarily bogged down the discussion and detracted from the historical trajectory of a persisting set of ideas and cultural images of black Americans. I tried to frame the book as a series of historical arguments and debates with a common theme that changes form over time, even though many of the same concerns are at the heart of these debates. However, I think that I have adequately analyzed and set forth the basic arguments of the persons discussed in particular social and historical contexts such that readers will have a deeper understanding of them because I have linked these discussions to a broader historical narrative about the meaning of black religion and the place of blacks in the nation. By examining many figures that are rather obscure or unknown today, I have also provided an alternative view of American history, race relations, and the study of African American religion. Seen from the perspective of persistent debates about religion and its meaning in the lives of black Americans, American history looks very different and much more tortured than even our more inclusive general histories would indicate.

As a doctoral student, I was exposed to the underbelly of American democracy in the rich archives of Harvard University. Not even that sanctuary of learning provided a completely safe space from the tentacles of race. Indeed, Harvard housed the very records of the past of some of its own professors' disturbing writings about blacks. What I discovered in these archives seemed so deeply incongruous with my more general ideas about American history, and my mother's counsel of showing love and compassion for all seemed almost irrelevant to what I was studying. I could not imagine the place of love and mercy in the midst of such a painful past of brute power relations, oppressive racism, and harsh political realities. All I saw was a huge mountain of hatred and racism that was impervious to kindness and compassion. I wanted to end my studies at Harvard. I tried to imagine an alternative path to personal sanity and a decent livelihood. I remember reading G. Stanley Hall, Howard Odum, and other writings of social scientists again and again, somehow hoping that I was misreading what they had written. Dreams of lynching and violence haunted me. I could not imagine that history could exert such a profound influence on me in the present. After all, was not the past *past* and was not all of this stuff, as some would say, *dead* history? Even when I tried to avert my eyes, I could not turn away from what was in front of me. Only by further research and writing could I exorcise this demon (or so I hoped) that had entered and now haunted my imagination.

James Baldwin once wrote that history is literally present in all that we do and that we owe our aspirations, our identities, and our frames of references to this history. Baldwin believed that it is with great pain and terror, particularly for black Americans, that one begins to assess the history that has placed one where one is, and that we must engage in a battle with at least one historical creation, namely one's self, to attempt to re-create one's self according to a principle more humane and liberating. Somewhere along the way, Baldwin suggests, one begins the attempt to achieve a level of personal maturity and freedom that robs history of its tyrannical power and thereby one changes history. I hope that Baldwin had more in mind than the individual heroically liberating him- or herself from the constraints of history, because I am not sanguine about humans' internal capacity to change themselves individually and thus defy the constraints of their upbringing and culture. I agree that careful attention to history and writing history can be a means of personal liberation, or at least a way of coming to terms with the pain and tragedy of one's own past. Working through these materials was my own way of coming to terms with my personal past and the nation's racist history, which is very much a continuing process. I suppose some of us also write history to present alternative narratives of how it looks when told from the point of view of those at the bottom. We write to complicate simple narratives of national innocence. One's view about the American nation and its failures and accomplishments, for example, could hardly be more different from what I have narrated if one read the celebratory histories of America in many home schooling curricula (to use an unusual but nonetheless important example).

Surprises, paradoxes, and ironies abound in my narrative. I have high-lighted these because they demonstrate some of the contingencies that exist in our nation's history. One moment Martin Delany, a black nationalist, is brooding about black prospects, urging blacks to leave the United States and settle in South America. A decade later, he is far more sanguine about black participation in the nation and eventually throws in his lot with the Union forces in the Civil War. Romantic racialists laud the vivacity, spontaneity, and emotion of slave religion. Immediately after the Civil War, the successors of the abolitionists and romantic racialists excoriate black communities for pos-sessing a religion of feeling and emotion that allegedly lacks morality and practical living advice. What is the basis for inclusion and laudation in one setting becomes the basis for exclusion and denigration in a different cultural and political context. Attention to these eruptions and ironic twists indicates that history takes many unexpected turns. Progress is never direct and inevi-table and has always come at an astonishing cost to African Americans.

The reader will have to judge whether I am successful in the importance that I have placed on black religion, but I have tried to bring together the concerns of traditional historical narratives with the subject matter of religious studies. In my view, mainstream historians have tended to neglect the role of religion in American history. I have attempted to supplement the research of historians by inserting a crucial and neglected element in discussions of race relations, politics, and images of blacks. I have also been attentive to the newer work in religious studies that examines religion as an object of inquiry and as a disciplining field that limited and constructed its subject matter through lan-guage, institutions, and various other means. This cultural study of religious studies as a discipline has deeply informed my thinking, though I make no explicit reference in my book to the many works that have shaped the field. This attention to the making of the study of religion and my extension of this to the making of the "black church" is a positive step toward a fuller analysis of our own place in the history of our discipline in addition to a contribution to the complexities of race and religion and their intersections in American history. I believe that debates about and images of African Americans have been crucial to how Americans have imagined themselves as a nation and that what Fredrickson calls the "black image in the white mind" has profoundly affected the development and realization of the United States as a particular kind of nation. If nothing else, it is this modest assertion that I hope will be substantiated by this book.

Acknowledgments

I thank Oxford University Press for allowing me to reprint a version of chapter 4, which appeared as "W. E. B. Du Bois: Interpreting Religion and the Problem of the Negro Church," *Journal of the American Academy of Religion*, May 23, 2007, pp. 1–30 (published online, doi:10.10093/jaarel/lfm001). Thanks to the American Society of Church History for granting me permission to reprint sections of chapter 7, which appeared as a separate essay in the December 2007 issue of *Church History*. Columbia University's Oral History Office graciously let me use quotations in chapter 4 from its collection on W. E. B. Du Bois. A fuller version of chapter 6 will appear in the Winter 2008 issue of *Religion and American Culture*. I owe thanks to the Center for the Study of Religion and American Culture for permission to publish a slightly different form of that essay.

Though it is true that books are communal projects, I have spent a great deal of time writing and thinking alone. Left alone too long, I would easily become prone to despair. Fortunately, I have been able to enjoy the company of librarians, fellow scholars, and friends who have made the writing of this book a more enjoyable endeavor. This book began as a doctoral dissertation. The entire Harvard University library system has to be thanked for allowing me to use its rich resources, and I am sure that I must have bothered them about interlibrary loans more than any other single person. Particular gratitude is extended to Widener, Lamont, Tozzer, and Andover. I offer a special thanks to Renata Kalnins and Gloria Korsman at Andover

Library. What extraordinary librarians who made my research a much more pleasant task! While at Harvard, I also made several trips to Amherst College, where David Wills opened up to me files that he had collected for a major documentary project on African American religion. Use of already copied periodical literature and newspaper articles was especially helpful given the tedious nature of plodding through serial issues of old newspapers that usually have no indices.

Once I left Harvard, this project always remained on my mind, even if I thought I was working on something entirely different. The staff at Howard University's Moorland Spingarn Research Center was so kind and helpful, especially Dr. Ida E. Jones and Joellen El Bashir. The Schomburg Center for Research in Black Culture, part of the New York Public Library System, graciously opened its doors to me. Even in the midst of renovations and loud fans, the staff provided the documents that I needed. I thank Columbia University for opening its rich Oral History Research Office to me. I shall never forget my pleasant experience at the Clark Atlanta Special Collections of the Robert W. Woodruff Library. Never have I met a staff of people so willing to help. The resources and the physical environment were excellent. I am sorry that my illness cut short my time there.

The Fund for Theological Education provided me with a dissertation fellowship, which allowed me time and finances to complete my doctorate (without which this book would not be possible). I am especially grateful to the Louisville Institute for awarding me an honorary dissertation fellowship for 2004–2005. I especially thank James W. Lewis, Kurt Richardson, and John Corrigan for either informing me about or urging me to apply for a first book grant. Louisville Institute awarded me the First Book Grant Program for Minority Scholars for fall to spring 2007–2008. This generous grant allowed me to complete this book and will give me some time to begin a new project. I owe the Louisville Institute a mountain of gratitude, and I hope that the completion of this book (and its merits) will be a small token of my appreciation.

The anonymous reviewers for Oxford University Press gave me much helpful feedback about the organization and arguments of the original manuscript. I have tried to take this advice and make this a better book. Theo Calderara, associate editor with Oxford, expressed great support and interest in my project from our very first meeting. Thanks for your encouragement and the faith you have in the value of my book, Theo. Special thanks to Daniel Gonzalez for guiding me through the process of preparing the book for publication. Enormous gratefulness is owed to Laura Poole for copyediting the book. Thanks, Laura, for such a monumental task!

Early in the dissertation process, David D. Hall provided much counsel and advice. So also did Evelyn Brooks Higginbotham, who served on my dissertation committee. Only now, however, do I realize how much I owe Robert Orsi for his trenchant criticisms and his unwavering support. I have been goaded by his extensive commentary on various drafts of the dissertation. Although all faults in the work are my own, I am confident that this work is much better because of his assistance. Bob has helped me in more ways than he realizes. Thanks go to him for his kindness and advice and for providing a safe place for me to study and develop as a person while at Harvard. I am truly grateful for all that he has done to help me along. Even when I could or would not take his advice, I am reminded of all the assistance that he provided.

I thank especially Amy Koehlinger, John Corrigan, and Amanda Porterfield at Florida State University. They provided a rich intellectual environment and unstinting support for me to begin my academic career. My conversations with Amy have especially reminded me of how important it was to keep pursuing the questions that I encountered in my work. I shall always be thankful to her for being a listening ear and for taking the time to give me feedback on a whole range of issues. Now that I am in Chicago, I will not only miss the warm weather in Tallahassee, but I will especially miss Amy's warmth and hospitality.

Friends too numerous to name have shared advice with me that has helped in some way to write this book. I apologize in advance if I forget any of their names: Thomas Donlon, Heather Curtis, Stephen Shoemaker, Mitzi Smith-Spralls, Emma Anderson, Yosef Sorett, Ginny Brereton, Christopher White, Brandon Bains, Lin Fischer, Tovis Page, Jon Roberts, David Hempton, Wallace D. Best, and Marla Frederick. Hannah Decker and Gerald Goodwin were great mentors when I was an undergraduate at the University of Houston. They incited my first love and passion for history, which sustained me in the writing of this book. Many critical comments were offered on the early drafts of the dissertation chapters at Harvard Divinity School's North American Religions colloquium. Members of the Florida State University American Religious History Colloquium gave me feedback on one chapter in its early stage. I have discussed two chapters before an excellent and attentive crowd of faculty members and graduate students at the University of Chicago's Divinity School. Their extraordinarily helpful counsel made me even more eager to improve the book's arguments.

I would like to thank the members of my church in Tallahassee, Florida. Though I do not recall discussing at any length the contents of this book with many of the members, their encouragement and support have enabled me to write and to think through many personal issues in my life. I thank Kurt

Richardson especially for his long-standing friendship since my years at Gordon-Conwell. His life of faith combined with his deep respect and passion for intellectual endeavors have provided me with an exemplary model of the scholarly life. I owe him and many others my gratitude for helping me along the way. I am especially thankful to God for granting me the grace to endure and surmount the personal pain of my past, which in so many odd ways intersected with the tragic history I have sought to narrate herein.

My wife, Janet, has probably heard more about this book than any other living person. I am sure she will be happy when it is published. I could not have done this without you, sweetheart. I love you for the person that you are. I know that your support and love helped me in those moments when I wanted to trash the entire project. Your unconditional love, your joy in living, and your indomitable spirit of optimism enabled me to do what I could not have otherwise done. Our experience together has been one of the reasons for my modest optimism. You know what I mean.

I dedicate this book to the legacy and memory of the late William R. Hutchison. I "met" Bill when I was a graduate student at seminary. He called me to let me know that I had been accepted at Harvard. He was the kind of person who lifted your spirit, challenged your intellect, and broadened your understanding of the world. After finishing this project, I could never be as optimistic about the legacy of liberal Protestants and as sanguine about human goodness as Bill was. Yet I have deep respect for the man and his work. I probably took one of the last graduate seminars in American religious historiography that Bill taught before his death. There were about six of us in the seminar room, and Bill never ceased to make us laugh and think as he told so many of those interesting stories that only he could tell. On several occasions, Bill and Jenny (his wife) invited graduate students to their home for discussions of papers and the sharing of delicious meals prepared by Jenny. Jenny was always the gracious hostess. I shall never forget when taking my general (comprehensive) exams that I emailed Bill out of panic one day because I was so worried about my response to one of the questions and began dourly requesting his assistance in choosing another career if things did not work out in academia. Later that evening, my wife told me that Bill had called and told her a story about a similar experience he had at Oxford just to let me know that everything was okay. About a week later, I saw Bill at a colloquium where David Hall announced that I had successfully completed my general exams and that I was granted ABD (all but dissertation) status. With his wry sense of humor, Bill looked at me, that distinctive crooked smile on his face, and said, "Well, I guess you got through things okay." I dedicate this book to the man and his exemplary scholarship. I made it a habit to read the acknowledgments of books when I was preparing for my general exams and I was struck by the number of authors who made reference to Bill's influence. This made me wonder about how our influence and ideas can spread and shape the lives of others in ways that we could not have imagined. Here's to you, Bill, and may this book honor your legacy in some small way.

Contents

The Burden of Black Religion

Introduction

As the honored speaker to represent his graduation class at Yale
Divinity School in 1893, Henry Hugh Proctor stood before his fellow
students and distinguished faculty members to present his address,
"A New Ethnic Contribution to Christianity." Proctor was one of twelve
black students at Yale University. Because he had written his master's thesis on the theology of the slave songs, he thought it best to talk
about the contributions of blacks to Christianity. Proctor developed
a theory of the historical development of Christianity in which race
and religion played reciprocal roles. He argued that "conversion had
involved a mutual conquest" in which religion modified "the race"
and the race, "by developing that element of Christian truth for
which it has special affinities, modified the religion."[1] So each race
brought to Christianity its particular contribution. Drawing on racial
theory that was dominant in his day, Proctor argued that the Hebrew race conveyed its genius for ethics to Christianity. Greeks supplied theology and philosophy, and the Teutonic mind offered liberty
and a love of freedom to Christianity. The Saxons brought energy,
vigor, enterprise, and thrift. Yet with all of these elements of native
genius offered to the faith, Christianity was still not complete. The
Africans would bring humility, fidelity, patience, love, and large-
heartedness to Christianity. These qualities would signal the distinct
contribution of Africans. The Saxons and the Africans, as "comple-
mentary opposites," could carry Christianity to its fullness.[2]

Proctor later served as the pastor of the First Congregational Church of Atlanta from 1894 to 1920. His church provided a wide variety of social services in the community and was instrumental in introducing social Christianity among blacks in the South. Proctor's church was one of the first black "institutional" churches in the South, which were churches that took on a variety of functions in urban centers.[3] Proctor's musings as an important black leader about the "ethnic contribution" of blacks to Christianity reflected broader speculations about the place of blacks in Western civilization and their contributions to human history. His comments about blacks represented one of several views regarding black religion. Proctor's perspective was similar to the romantic racialist view of black Christianity that was promulgated by Harriet Beecher Stowe and other white Northerners opposed to slavery in the mid-nineteenth century. Indeed, Proctor wrote, "Truth is stranger than fiction. Harriet Beecher Stowe's 'Uncle Tom's Cabin' was more than a character of fiction. He was a real representative of the Christian slave."[4] Allison Dorsey wonders how it is that Proctor, without a "trace of self-conscious irony" and with "no criticism of Stowe's racist and paternalistic images," could embrace Stowe's depiction of Uncle Tom as a reflection of blacks' "true, best selves."[5] This racialist conception of black religion involved claims about the innate religious nature of blacks, what Proctor and others called the Negro's genius for religion. Assertions that blacks were naturally or innately religious changed in relation to black's social, political, and economic situation. Being naturally religious was not a static concept, but its social and cultural meaning was profoundly affected by broader changes in discussions about black capacities and their place in the nation. Innate religiosity, for example, could mean "feeling" or "emotion" that was said to be unique to blacks and a complement to the "rational" faith of whites, as in the case of Stowe and her white romantic racialist contemporaries. Or it could mean the "degraded" practices of the native African that appeared to be what some called "religion," as white social scientists in the late nineteenth century claimed. In either case, an attempt is made in this book to historicize how this interpretive concept of what it meant to be religious was often shaped by the politics of the interpreter and evolving debates about the value of a certain kind of religion.

Black religion became the chief bearer of meaning for the nature and place of blacks in America because of questions raised by the early conversion of slaves to Christianity (in the eighteenth-century Southern colonies) and the nearly universal belief among European and American whites that Africans were lacking in intellectual capacity. What followed, through a long and complex historical process, was heightened attention to religion as the signal quality of blacks in America and as the central locus of their actual and potential contributions to the nation. Initially, the nature and function of slave religion was interrogated because of the awkward problem of possessing Africans who converted to the religion of their captors (some slave owners were being Christianized at the same time as their slaves were). Gradually, scientific concepts of race incorporated popular notions about African intellectual inferiority and theories about distinctive black religious capacity became the lens through which blacks were judged as fit or unfit for participation and inclusion in the nation. Romantic racialists' reconceptualization of religion as feeling in the nineteenth century and their focused attention on Africa as having a place among the nations by making a unique contribution in the realm of religion (as opposed to intellect) at an uncertain date in the future did much to set the terms for later variations of the debate about blacks' place in the nation. Persisting assumptions about black innate religiosity and the rancorous disputes about the role and function of black churches had their origins in these early discourses about black religion. "Black religion," whether conceptualized variously by whites and blacks as an amorphous spirituality, primitive religion, emotionalism, or actual black churches under the rubric of "the Negro Church," groaned under the burden of a multiplicity of interpreters' demands ranging from uplift of the race to bringing an ambiguous quality of "spiritual softness" to a materialistic and racist white culture.

Although concepts have a rather messy history and rarely conform to neat chronological categories, a general historical narrative of how different understandings of black religion changed over time is useful. I briefly trace how the possession of slaves spawned a host of debates about the character and fitness of slaves. Anglican missionaries in Virginia and South Carolina in the eighteenth century, for example, raised questions about the morality of owning slaves and incited further discussions about whether alien African peoples could understand or accept Christianity. To ask whether slaves could convert focused attention on the nature and meaning of conversion and distinctions between civilizing and Christianizing a black population held in bondage. This incipient concern about the function and nature of slave religion was prompted by slave owners' fears that conversion to Christianity would lead their human property to feel spiritually (and perhaps humanly) equal to their earthly masters or that slave acceptance of this new religion would hinder their labor capacity, make them arrogant, or lead to outright slave insurrections. As late as the early nineteenth century, slave owners continued to worry about the effect of Christianity on their black slaves, and this attention to the Christianization of slaves left a profound and lasting legacy on later discussions about the function and nature of African American religion. The immediate historical effects were more detailed analyses of how religious or moral capacity differed from intellectual capacity and white Christian missionaries and preachers propagating the Christian gospel as a device for slave control as they asserted that Christianity made slaves more pliable, docile, and industrious as laborers and more obedient and faithful as servants of their white earthly masters.[6]

Enlightenment figures like Thomas Jefferson argued that blacks were intellectually inferior to whites, but they made space for religious contributions by asserting that blacks possessed, as did all people, a moral sense. This widespread and lingering view that Africans were intellectually inferior to Europeans bequeathed to slave owners, abolitionists, and antislavery advocates a dichotomous notion of the African as possessing a degraded but functioning moral sense (which was a basic assertion of their humanity) yet lacking in the intellectual capacity that Europeans or "civilized" peoples possessed. Jefferson's specific view, I argue, set the terms of the later debates about black religious and cultural contributions to the nation. When white abolitionist Lydia Maria Child asserted in 1833 that white people almost universally believed that blacks were "naturally inferior in intellect," she added that belief in their "strong affections" and "moral character" coexisted with this assessment.[7] Given that blacks were deemed intellectually inferior, and given also that observers claimed to find evidence of "religion" among them, it was thought that perhaps here their humanity could be affirmed. To assert that blacks were human required some speculation about what their unique contribution to culture could be. So the romantic racialists grounded blacks' humanity in their religious sentiments to the extent that by the 1830s, as Elizabeth Clark argues, many Americans "turned for guidance to the emotions over the intellect" and identified "the moral sense more with feeling than with rational thought."[8] Northern abolitionists tried to make their case for blacks' distinctiveness, and thus their humanity, by pointing to the special feelings of their innately religious nature. Claims that blacks excelled in the "feminine" virtues, such as religion and the arts, followed from assertions that whites excelled in the "masculine" virtues of reason and enterprise because of their race.[9] Religion, then, as a natural gift or characteristic of blacks, was celebrated in part because its promoters firmly believed that blacks did not equally possess the intellectual capacities of Anglo-Saxons.

The image that naturally religious blacks would bring a softening touch to a materialistic, overly intellectualized culture was always an available option for those reflecting on blacks' place in the nation. Even some black leaders drew on this image, as is evidenced in Proctor's statements. Generally, white Northerners held this view and evoked it in times of unusual cultural stress. They found blacks a convenient symbol to point out what their society lacked, and romantic images of African Americans became a means of mediating the spiritual experience of whites. More formal interpretations of black religion were also affected by this discourse of innate religiosity. Social scientists in the late nineteenth century and beyond, for example, universally acknowledged the importance of churches in black communities. They presented scientific theories about the nature of religion in black minds and bodies and the role that black churches played as social institutions. Psychologists theorized black religion as the emotional effluvium of primitive, childlike minds. A theory of racial difference explained that blacks had slipped back into their natural selves and that this development would have terrible consequences for the South because it could lead to its Africanization.

Even as black interpreters worried about the political passivity of "the Negro Church," white interpreters, especially in the new psychology of religion, pathologized black culture by linking black religion in the South to an allegedly innate and savage African nature that erupted after years of being repressed by the "beneficent" influence of slavery. The contradictions of portraying Southern blacks as childlike (and presumably harmless) *and* as adult savages (by linking them to a putative, unchanging African propensity to criminality and violence) were never consciously resolved, though interpreters argued that slavery nurtured the "childish" side of Africans and freedom allegedly released the savage beast within. White interpreters continued to claim that blacks in the South in the late nineteenth century were in the primitive or childlike stage of cultural and religious evolution even as they portrayed them as adult savages intent on doing harm to whites. My discussion of this pathologizing of black religion, with its center in the school of G. Stanley Hall's new psychology, demonstrates that white interpreters were eager to posit that the social effect of black religion was harmful to the South and the nation and that black religion coexisted with immorality. Theories of the mind posited an immoral and criminal African character at the root of America's racial problems and functioned in part to mute claims that blacks were oppressed in a system of white supremacy in the South and were being mistreated at the hands of racist white Southerners who were lynching blacks with astonishing levels of cruelty in the late nineteenth century. The pathologizing of black religion was sometimes coupled with gendered claims, by both blacks and whites, that black culture was feminine and sickly and that blacks lacked the moral and intellectual capacity to achieve manhood, a crucial attribute of civilization as conceptualized by late-nineteenth-century theorists. The new psychology repudiated entirely romantic racialists' assertions that black religion would inject a spiritual element of feeling and emotion into a white materialistic culture. Rather, the new psychologists dissected and described black religion under the rubric of emotionalism and in the clinical language of psychopathology.

By the late nineteenth century, a new element was introduced into interpretations of African American religion by black interpreters. With the rise of the disciplines (especially the social sciences), the creation and normative description of an entity called the "Negro Church" took place. Most black interpreters, trained in or intellectually indebted to the social sciences, spelled out and articulated the theoretical and practical boundaries of the Negro Church. They sought a unified black church (or at the very least, coordinated cooperation among black churches) to address the political, social, and economic problems of black oppression in the United States. Although most black interpreters maintained that most black Americans were members of churches, we should not accept at face value that "the Negro Church" was a simple reflection of a social reality. That is to say, black churches did play an important role in the lives of blacks at the time (most of whom were Southerners), but the normative discourse of the Negro Church was descriptive and prescriptive. It articulated a particular conception of what black churches ought to do in light of the depressing situation of blacks in the South at the end of the nineteenth century. I examine in detail the work of W. E. B. Bu Bois and his contribution to what I call the creation and genealogy of the discourse of the Negro Church. The normative idea of the black church has its origins in the work of Du Bois and had profound ramifications for later discussions about whether the black church was an instrument of protest and accommodation in a racist society. Yet this debate was not entirely new because it reasserted, in different language and in a new historical context, the critiques of black religion that had been advanced by antebellum Northern African Americans who felt that black slaves had accepted a passive, otherworldly Christianity imposed on them by slave owners and white Christian preachers. Nevertheless, the function and nature of black religion acquired a new salience in the discourse of social science.

Although some black leaders were influenced by the ideas of the new psychology, it does not appear that the two trajectories of interpretation overlapped significantly. It is true that some black Northern interpreters adopted the language of emotionalism from time to time, but for the most part white interpreters provided a psychological interpretation of "Negro religion" as black interpreters often talked about the defects of the Negro Church. Even when social scientists in the 1920s and 1930s began decoupling race and culture and rejecting older notions about the "primitive" lacking in self-control and the qualities necessary for "civilization," white interpreters tended to focus on black religiosity or spirituality (now reevaluated as a positive quality of blacks) while black interpreters continued to debate about the nature and function of the Negro Church. Although I discuss in more detail the reasons for this division between black and white interpretations in chapter 5, the principal reason seems to have been the cash value offered by black attention to pooling the resources of black churches because most blacks were members of them already. Black leaders wanted to find ways to bring together black communities in a collective effort to take on the problem of racial oppression in America. No other institution besides the church offered as many potential constituents.

White interpretations of black religion or spirituality, however, rarely involved the specificity that attention to actual black churches entailed for black leaders concerned with the concrete problems of their communities.[10] In my analysis in chapter 6 of *The Green Pastures*, one of the longest-running plays in Broadway history, I demonstrate that white images of black religion had an almost ethereal romanticized quality about them and rarely touched on the actual cultural and practical work that could bring the nation closer to some semblance of racial harmony and political and economic equality. Yet the cultural work of such productions as *The Green Pastures* (and perhaps to a lesser extent, *Uncle Tom's Cabin*) was that they allowed whites to create a safe and idealized image of blacks that seldom addressed the concrete situation of black/white relations in the nation. When white interpreters were in physical proximity to blacks, they hardly ever evoked this type of romanticized language and these religious images of blacks as gentle primitives. New Englanders, for example, working among blacks in the post–Civil War South explicitly repudiated Stowe's romantic racialism. *The Green Pastures* was about black Southerners safely removed from New Yorkers and other Northerners who could indulge their fantasies within the safe spaces of a stage or theater. It was Manhattanite Marc Connelly's image of rural Southern blacks that was reproduced in the play. Small wonder that as blacks began entering Northern cities during World War II, Harvard Divinity School dean Willard Sperry could wax so eloquently about the pathos and power of black spirituals rooted in a deeply religious Southern culture even while expressing grave fears about the alleged radicalism and repudiation of "Uncle Tomism" among blacks in cities like Detroit. Blacks seemed quaintly religious and spiritual from a distance.

The terminal point of the book is the 1940s, though I make a brief comment about more recent studies of African American religion in the epilogue. Black social scientists set out to bury persisting notions of black innate religiosity in their sociological studies of black religion in the 1940s. It may now seem a curious thing to find that academic study would be devoted to determining whether people of African descent were innately or uniquely religious. Although I do not make the claim that all such studies explicitly set out with this issue as their central concern, I do argue that it was at the very least a principal subtext for most of the major studies of black life in the 1940s. The

denial of African innate religiosity in part reflected black interpreters' weariness with the psychic satisfaction that such images of black religion provided
for whites and their rather vague assertions (rather than demonstrations) that
blacks were naturally religious. But more fundamentally, the critique of innate
religiosity was about the place of blacks in the nation. Were blacks racially (and
hence essentially) different from whites? If the proponents of innate religiosity
were correct, then blacks would find it difficult to undermine segregation and
differential treatment. Some leading black sociologists like E. Franklin Frazier
made this explicit in their rejection of black innate religiosity, stating that the
end of innate religiosity would signal a beginning for black assimilation into
the nation. Innate religiosity was rejected as a persisting notion of racial essentialism and was thus regarded as an obstacle to black social, economic, and
political progress.

Yet precisely as this new paradigm that emphasized developing secularization among Northern blacks and potential black integration gained the ascendancy and became almost an orthodox view by the early 1960s, particularly
among sociologists, weariness with the progress of civil rights reform and
social scientific assertions of black pathology in the urban North (coupled with
claims that blacks needed to shed their "peculiarities" to join the putative
American mainstream) led to restatements of a unique black spirituality. This
time, however, the claim that blacks possessed a special aesthetic capacity over
and against arid and materialistic whites became a rather transmuted secular
form of older notions of romantic racialism. Critics of integration were still
critical of black churches and often denigrated the black church as otherworldly
and more generally criticized Christianity as the "white man's religion." In
some ways, the debate returned full circle to a romantic racialist conception of
black culture, except that now blacks were its leading proponents (though its
effects can be detected in some of the studies of slave religion and black culture
conducted by white scholars in the 1970s).[11]

Claims of black innate religiosity, discussions about the role of the Negro
Church, and cultural images of black religion are brought together in this book
and examined over a broad period of time. These seemingly disparate issues
have repeatedly come together in important ways, not least in their impact
on the real conditions of blacks in the nation. Although I did not set out with
Raboteau's work in mind, my work historicizes four central issues that occupied Albert Raboteau's *Slave Religion* (1978). As a product of the social, political,
and religious ferment of the 1960s and 1970s, Raboteau's book was concerned
with (1) the problem of black innate religiosity, which he briefly rendered as a
persisting claim that blacks are somehow "naturally religious"; (2) the extent to
which African cultural and religious traditions existed in African American

culture, an issue generally related to debates about the distinctive nature of black religion and the extent to which black religious expression is a rejection of white Christianity; (3) the question of the so-called otherworldly and compensatory nature of slave religion; (4) and the accommodation/protest debate often framed as: does the "black church" promote social and political reform and thus stand against institutional racism, or has it encouraged a passive resignation to the status quo?[12] These concerns were implicated in almost all the debates about black religion in the 1960s and 1970s, and they continue to impact contemporary debates. We encounter these topics again and again in my work. The question of the function of black religion, for example, emerged most prominently in discussions about the Negro Church and acquired a greater salience after the rejection of natural religiosity and the urbanization of black life. I ask how these issues came to be so important, and what the social context and implications of these debates were.

After a brief discussion of eighteenth-century Christian missionaries assuring slave owners that Christianizing slaves would make them better servants, I look at how concerns about slave Christianization led to broader debates about slave intellectual and moral capacities. These initial concerns about the nature and function of slave religion had important consequences about how blacks' capacities would be assessed. The bulk of chapter 1 is a discussion of romantic racialism, with particular attention on Harriet Beecher Stowe's views and that of other romantic racialists who formulated a theory of black innate religiosity that would in hindsight prove to be immensely influential in imaginings about the ultimate place of blacks in the nation and of what their distinctive contributions to American culture should or ought to be. I argue that the romantic racialist image of blacks harbored an ambivalence about what the "natural African" could contribute to the national character and what role blacks could have in the nation. I attend to the historical context of this view and of its original articulation by noting that it was a way of affirming the humanity of blacks, even while asserting a racially essentialist view of their capacities and future destiny.

Historians have offered different evaluations of romantic racialism, and my work attempts to take a middle ground among the existing possibilities. James McPherson regards it as extraordinary that abolitionists, even if they believed in racial differences, were able to declare their belief in the equality of blacks in a "nation where popular belief *and* scientific learning overwhelmingly proclaimed the Negro's absolute inferiority."[13] Although the abolitionists to whom McPherson refers were not all romantic racialists, his description of the broader context in which romantic racialist ideas were promulgated must be kept in mind when judgments of white antebellum representations of African

Americans are made. One must consider the dominant images of blacks to which romantic racialists were responding and the ideas of race to which they themselves subscribed. Stanley Harrold is correct when he argues that "white abolitionists never overcame their racial and cultural biases," but even Harrold asserts that the romantic racialists and abolitionists who believed in innate racial differences could still affirm that such differences were not grounds for enslavement.[14]

George Fredrickson argues that romantic racialism "occupies a curious and anomalous position in the history of American racial thinking" because it was benevolent in intent and not generally linked to an "unequivocal theory of white supremacy." At its most generous, Fredrickson observes, romantic racialism has come close to an affirmation of a pluralist conception of distinct racial "gifts" advanced by black writers like Du Bois and Kelly Miller at the turn of the century. Fredrickson concludes, however, with a harsh judgment that this view of blacks "sometimes reflected little more than a nagging sense, on the part of 'tenderminded' reformers, that their culture had its harsh and unattractive side and that white Americans lacked the disposition to conform fully to their own 'spiritual' values."[15] This assessment comes closest to my own because it recognizes that the romantic racialist image of blacks was often about what "lost" values whites projected onto blacks to reclaim them as their own and rested on a theory of racial difference. Yet a quick dismissal of romantic racialism must account for why blacks, especially blacks who had an active interest in Africa, found this romantic conception of their capacities to be so appealing throughout the nineteenth century.[16] Telling the story of the contradictions and ironies surrounding the articulations of romantic racialism forms part of the first chapter.

In the second chapter, I turn to the ways that white Northerners and Southerners converged in their critiques of African American religion in the 1870s after the Civil War. Northerners, to be sure, were generally not as pessimistic as Southerners about black capacities, even though further research into this area raises caution about the extent to which Northern and Southern views of blacks differed in theory and practice. The point here is to demonstrate that a new conception of what it meant to be naturally religious and of the meaning of black religion emerged during the Reconstruction era: Insofar as black religion was seen as a central aspect of black culture, white interpreters' claims about its "wild" and regressive nature left little room for blacks as productive and useful citizens in the nation. Northern middle-class blacks were ambivalent about the folk culture of Southern blacks. Although they rejected whites' racial interpretations of black religion as African regression, they also found much that was distasteful and culturally inferior in the religious practices of black Southerners. By the late nineteenth century, however, some black leaders, during a time of growing segregation and violence, evoked the romantic racialist notion that blacks possessed peculiar gifts and should conserve their racial energies to avoid the excesses of a white materialistic society. Perhaps this image of blacks was seen as a necessary counter to the pervasive negative images of blacks in the late nineteenth century and was a logical outgrowth of the importance of black churches because of the exclusion of blacks from so many other facets of the broader society.

My third chapter charts the growing importance of the professional disciplines and the social scientific study of black religion. I look at both black and white interpretations of black religion, with a specific emphasis on the psychological construct of emotionalism as the defining feature of black religious life. These studies were both a continuation of popular criticisms of black churches and a newer analysis of black religion that purported to be grounded in science. I trace these early studies of the primitive mind to the period when a gradual shift, not apparent until the 1920s, in views about the meaning of the primitive occurs. The implications of this newer understanding of the primitive are examined in more detail in the fifth chapter. This turn to the primitive allowed me to assess in Chapter 6 the extent to which laudatory reviews of Marc Connelly's *Green Pastures* reflected disillusionment with modern society and how the image of black religion the play presented was used to bolster critiques of American culture.

Chapter 4 looks at the origins of the Negro Church. I argue that Du Bois was crucial in setting the terms of later debates about the nature and the function of the black church. Attention is paid to the reasons for Du Bois's emphasis on what he called the Negro Church. I situate Du Bois's work and thought within the broader cultural ascendancy of social scientific interpretations of African American life and changing understandings of black religion. I argue that Du Bois never quite resolved the tensions of the older romantic racialist conception that blacks would make a distinctive religious contribution to the nation and his particular emphasis on the defects and problems of the Negro Church. I also demonstrate that Du Bois in some ways anticipated contemporary postmodernist critiques of grand narratives in his early project to provide a local and particular analysis of the lives and culture of black Americans. Yet his talk about a monolithic Negro Church has exerted a much greater influence on later interpretations of black religion, especially among African American interpreters, even as white interpreters and artists continued to promote the romantic racialist conception.

The fifth chapter also juxtaposes the critique of African American religion, particularly in the rural South, as otherworldly by progressive black leaders in and outside the black churches alongside the romanticization of black religion in the South by white admirers. Black leaders' turn to drama as an authentic expression of black life was one reason for this reevaluation of black folk culture in the South. Attention is paid to this irony of the turn to the primitive untouched by the problems of modern society at the precise historical juncture when many African American leaders were seeking to move beyond what they regarded as the backwardness and regressive religion of rural black Southerners and transplanted Southern migrants in the Northern cities. The Great Migration of blacks to the urban North, as Milton Sernett argues, was a watershed event in African American history and had profound implications for interpretations of black religion. The rise of instrumentalist conceptions of black religion, Sernett notes, was centrally about stressing the social dimensions of black Christianity and addressing the problems of an urban, industrialized society. But for many instrumentalists it also entailed assessing the progress of African American religion to the degree to which it was an "instrument" of or force for social and political reform.[17] Their interpretations of African American religion have become the prevailing view in scholarship since the Great Migration, I argue, and placed unusually heavy demands on the black churches.

Chapter 6 examines the contents of and responses to *The Green Pastures*. I explore the nature of black and white interpretations of the play and suggest that black leaders were troubled that the play's popularity was another attempt by whites to portray blacks as outcasts in the midst of a modern society. Whites, however, used the play as a way of reflecting on their own dissatisfactions with the state of religion in a modern bourgeois culture. Whites, as one critic put it, were using religious images of blacks to work through their own spiritual experiences. Connelly's re-creation of the Genesis narrative (and Jewish experience as depicted in the Bible) through his fantasy of blacks in the rural South allowed whites to experience afresh a religious world that many had lost in their move to the urban North. Black Southerners depicted as innately humorous and incurably religious made belief possible again, at least within the safe world of the theater.

My seventh chapter takes a broad view of the meaning of the urbanization of black Americans to white and black interpreters of black culture. I offer a close examination of social scientific works on blacks, primarily in the North, that claimed that urbanization undermined notions of black innate religiosity. As some blacks began to drift away from the churches in the urban North in the 1930s and 1940s, as a certain segment of the black elite lost their beliefs and as black churches began competing with various other institutions, interpreters began to reassess long-standing claims that blacks possessed a distinctive racial temperament. Urbanization was seen by social scientists such as E. Franklin Frazier, for example, as a necessary step to pave the way for black assimilation into the broader culture. But for whites, the urban North evoked images of godless and violent blacks or of lost blacks who lacked an authentic and deeply rooted culture. While both whites and blacks agreed that secularization was taking place among black Northerners, white interpreters were less sanguine about the city as a locus of potential integration.

In the epilogue, I trace how the language of cultural pathology, in part to support assertions of the damaging effects of segregation and racism, became more common by the 1950s and 1960s. Black religion was tangentially treated in these studies, even in those that tried to break away from assertions of black cultural pathology. I point out how this attention to black culture in the urban North significantly shifted the terms of long-standing debates about African American religion. I contend that religion no longer occupied a salient role in social scientific debates about the place of blacks in the nation. I also briefly note how later studies of African American religion were influenced by this renewed attention to African American cultural distinctiveness. I end with a few remarks about the ways more recent studies of African American religion continued to reassert and differ from the interpretations of black religion covered in the body of this book. I offer a mild critique of the presuppositions underlying these interpretations of black religion, urging interpreters to adopt a more chastened view of agency in their reflections on the religious experiences of black Americans.

The major task of this book is to historicize the burden that has been placed on black religion, paying particular attention to how it emerged over time and how it entered a new phase in the 1940s. I close, however, with the 1960s debates because of the crucial change in expectations of black religion that this decade brought about. Because the civil rights movement has been covered extensively by historians, sociologists, and journalists, it is not my intent to engage these works, except to make a few comments about how things have changed and remained the same (in some ways) since the 1960s in interpretations of African American religion. I do not attempt to offer an alternative narrative to the many histories and studies of black religion that are examined in my book, but I hope that a critical evaluation of the uses of "black religion" and the telling of various stories about the black church will provide some new thoughts about how more interesting narratives of African American religious practices and beliefs might be written. At the very least, my work demonstrates that African Americans and images of black religion in American culture have been crucial to the development of the nation's ideals and also reflective of its manifest failures. I hope that this book will forward newer conversations about the meaning and significance of African American religion in American culture and thereby enable readers to understand the crucial importance that blacks have played in the imagining and making of the United States as a nation.

I

The Meaning of Slave Religion

Historians have noted the significance of the 1830s and 1840s for increasingly bitter debates over slavery and deepening divisions between the North and South. Proslavery thought in the South became more systematic and self-conscious.[1] Slavery's defenders promulgated an increasingly elaborate array of arguments supporting human bondage. To justify slavery, it was seen as necessary to provide arguments about how the character or moral capacity of Africans suited them for slavery. Calls for immediate abolition and fears of slave rebellions (prompted by the bloody uprising of Nat Turner in Southampton County, Virginia, in 1831) were integral to the historical and cultural context of these discussions about the nature of black slaves. Evaluations of blacks' capacity were not new, but the forces that gave rise to the heated debates of the 1830s coincided with more precise attempts to delineate the character of slaves. Audrey Smedley argues that in the early decades of the nineteenth century a developing racial ideology, which rejected environmental explanations of racial differences, held (among other things) that outer physical characteristics were but markers of inner intellectual, moral, or temperamental qualities.[2] The notion that these qualities were heritable and the belief that racial differences were fixed and unalterable influenced ongoing discussions about slaves' capacities and their place in the nation.[3]

The basic religious claim of the common origins of humanity was rooted in the Christian tradition, which still held a significant sway over discussions about slaves and their treatment (especially up to the Civil War). The Christian argument for the common origin of humans did not, however, prevent whites from holding Africans in bondage. Jon Butler, for example, has argued that Anglican Christianity in the early eighteenth-century South enthusiastically endorsed slavery.[4] But this support of human bondage rested uneasily, in the minds of slave owners, with thoughts about the Christian doctrine of a common humanity and raised deep worries about the implications of sharing the Christian faith with a population held in bondage and deemed in practice as inferior. This tension became more acute when the advocates of monogenesis and polygenesis concentrated attention on whether Africans and Europeans were of the same species. Ethnology, however, as a developing science of racial theory, even in its proslavery context of the mid-nineteenth century, never quite elicited the cultural authority of Christianity because of its antireligious bias and its technical and elaborate arguments. It was only in the late nineteenth century that scientific racism trumped appeals to Christianity as a softening agent or humanitarian impetus in the treatment and place of blacks in the nation.

Proslavery apologists (in the South and North) were the leading figures who were adamantly opposed to assertions of the equality of blacks. Any attempt to argue for blacks' freedom or humanity had to take into account their claims. They justified the Christianization of slaves by the 1830s on the grounds that it humanized slavery and uplifted Africans from superstition and paganism. Although proslavery apologists differed among themselves about whether blacks represented a distinct species, they all affirmed that blacks were permanently inferior to whites and should remain a laboring class under white supervision. Many Northern white antislavery advocates (some of whom were abolitionists) had doubts about the intellectual capacities of blacks, but they argued that even if blacks were intellectually inferior to whites, they should not be enslaved.[5] These white antislavery leaders (whom I call romantic racialists) argued that blacks would prosper in a future when moral sentiment or religious affection was valued as highly as intellect. Black Northern interpreters of African American religion were divided over the role that religion should play in the lives of slaves and in the advancement of blacks in the nation. Although some black leaders longed for a Christianized Africa, others felt that religion in the black community deflected attention away from the real problems that blacks faced in America.

As abolitionists became more vocal in demanding immediate emancipation for slaves, their views on slaves' character became more explicit. Among the romantic racialists, who were a segment of the abolitionist movement, particularly in Massachusetts and New York, appeals for sympathy for a suffering, meek, and Christian people became more common by the 1830s.[6] Romantic racialists argued that Africans were gentle creatures of feeling who were dragged from their natural habitat by avaricious and bellicose Europeans. This emphasis on slave meekness and religiosity was in part a counter to the worries and fears of slave owners that abolitionists were inciting slaves to rebellion and slave owners' views of Africans' alleged natural barbarity and propensity for violence apart from white supervision or ownership. Romantic racialists condemned slavery because they believed it stunted the natural capacities of Africans and did not allow their religious feelings and native culture to emerge fully.

Proslavery apologists and abolitionists alike wrote extensively about the character and nature of blacks. Defenders of slavery pointed to what they saw as the peculiar psychology of slaves to demonstrate that Africans were fit for slavery. Slavery was advanced as a benevolent institution that brought Christianity to a savage people. Some leading proslavery advocates also began articulating their racial arguments in the language of ethnology by the 1840s to confirm the appropriateness of bondage for blacks. Ethnology was created as a science of race to delineate alleged differences between races and peoples. Northern antislavery proponents, however, sought in various ways to assert the readiness of slaves for freedom, but even they often grounded their arguments for emancipation in racial theories that posited innate differences between blacks and whites. Variously describing blacks as naturally religious and kindly disposed toward their oppressors, the arguments of the proponents of emancipation often converged with those of the defenders of slavery, who claimed, among other things, that the docility of slaves demonstrated their contentment under the slave system. Nevertheless, romantic racialists asserted that inferiority or innate differences were no grounds for enslavement.[7]

Romantic racialists were not very specific about the destiny of blacks. Some favored colonization because they believed that white prejudice in America was simply too strong; others felt that only in Africa could a Negro temperament flourish. More commonly, romantic racialists claimed that blacks could offer something to the nation that the stern Anglo-Saxon lacked, a "softening influence" that would be diffused throughout the community. Africans would contribute meekness and Christian grace to the improvement of the American character. Given the halting and vague affirmations of potential and actual black contributions to the life of the nation that this view offered, George Fredrickson has criticized some abolitionists for being unable "to ground their case for [blacks] on a forthright and intellectually convincing argument for the basic identity in the moral and intellectual aptitudes of all races." Fredrickson argues that this conception of blacks weakened the abolitionist struggle for equality and helps explain the persistence of racism after Emancipation.[8] Indeed, when one examines the critiques of black culture and religion by the Northern missionaries who came to the South after the Civil War, the limitations of this notion of the naturally religious African become all too evident. But perhaps it is too heavy a burden to place the principal blame on this specific segment of the population for the persistence of racism after the Civil War, even if the limitations of their legacy are clear in hindsight. Romantic racialism, with all its sentimentalism about the feelings and emotions of slave religion and the potential contributions of blacks to American culture, was certainly a step beyond dominant racial views of black inferiority in that its advocates called for an end to slavery. Their failure to imagine or prepare for blacks' entry into society after slavery was their principal flaw.

The arguments about African American religion and the developing image of blacks as naturally religious made it difficult to envision them as independent and free persons in the nation, which is why individuals like black nationalist Martin Delany rejected this image. As an alternative to the image of blacks held by proslavery apologists, which was centrally about their permanent subjection to whites and their adoption of Christianity in exchange for African heathenism and superstition, the romantic racialists found it difficult to argue for a position that did not locate religion at the center of their conceptions of blacks and black contributions. This was so because they believed that blacks were intellectually inferior to whites. Yet the rejection of colonization as it became accompanied by an unstinting call for immediate abolition in the 1830s was one step toward a faint hope for an interracial democracy. Prominent abolitionists had their doubts (justified in light of the post–Civil War period) that white Americans would ever accept blacks as equals. Perhaps this explains why some whites like Harriet Beecher Stowe and Lydia Maria Child projected their desires for black advancement into a future age of moral sentiment when they hoped to witness an African religious nationality flourish. It was a difficult task to envision that "normal" white Americans would accept blacks when the nation's leading intellectual and prominent founder, Thomas Jefferson, who pronounced in the nation's founding document those memorial words that "all men are created equal," doubted that blacks could be incorporated into the commonwealth and recommended that they "be removed beyond the reach of mixture" with white Americans.

Separating the Intellectual from the Moral Sense

Winthrop Jordan has argued that early attempts to determine black capacities reflected confusion about exactly what constituted "capacities." The conflation of mental/intellectual with religious faculties was common among those who argued about the humanity of black slaves in the early eighteenth century. The concept of human intelligence did not appear quite so distinct from attributes that we might today label religion or even wisdom. As Jordan writes:

> This absence of clearcut distinctions and interlacing of mental capacity with spiritual grace also becomes manifest in the fact that the issue of the Negro's mental ability first arose historically out of doubts concerning his ability to participate in the experience of conversion. So long as men thought of themselves as primarily spiritual creatures, no one could possibly talk about innately inferior intelligence in the sense the concept is used today. Later in the [eighteenth] century, however, the separation of mental from spiritual abilities was clearly underway, as was to become especially obvious after the Revolution.[9]

Because the Church of England had a "virtual monopoly on missionary work" among slaves in the plantation colonies of British North America in the first half of the eighteenth century, it should come as no surprise that missionaries and slave owners had doubts about Africans' ability to learn the complexities and intricacies of a foreign Anglican theology.[10] Africans would have to face a time-consuming process of religious instruction because of Anglican missionaries' conception of conversion as catechesis.[11] For cultural and linguistic reasons, slave Christianization raised questions about the capacity of Africans to understand and adopt a new worldview and system of religious discipline.

Still, it is a curious phenomenon that Christian missionaries, both Anglicans and (later) evangelicals, had to deal with doubts about slaves' ability to receive Christianity in light of long-standing assertions within the Christian tradition about the miraculous work of the Holy Spirit in the believer's heart. (This is not to overlook the consistent emphasis in Christian traditions on learning the rules of a religion through an extended process of discipline and catechesis.) Was this an implicit fear that Africans were seen as so alien by the English that not even Christianity could reduce the distance between whites and blacks? Or was it an unspoken assumption about the efficacy of a particular kind of Christianity, the religion of the Church of England, to transform others? It does not appear that these worries were specifically limited to Anglican missionaries' concerns about *their* religion's ability to convert Africans. Certainly Anglican missionaries had to engage a host of slave owners' complaints about the potential function or effect of Christianity on their slaves: that it would make them lazy, arrogant, rebellious, or presumptuous in regarding themselves as spiritual equals to their masters.[12] This attempt to assure slaveholders that Christianity made Africans more content, docile, and morally better slaves had the effect of forcing missionaries to clarify and elaborate on slave capacities. This led missionaries into all kinds of contorted and complex assertions about the effects of Christianity on slaves. George Whitefield, an Anglican minister who preached a deeply affective and revivalistic version of Christianity, knocked down the criticisms of slaveholders in Maryland, Virginia, and North and South Carolina in a 1740 published critique of their objections to slave Christianization. Whitefield, for all his complaints against slave owners, did not call for the abolition of slavery, but rather urged slave owners to persevere in Christianizing their slaves and in making them a central part of an organic hierarchical institution.[13] Whitefield distinguished between Christianizing and civilizing a slave. He maintained that civilizing meant simply imposing "outward restraints" on slave behavior. It failed to transform them inwardly. He reassured slave owners that truly Christianizing slaves would make them more obedient servants to their white masters.[14] The effect of these controversies about the function of Christianity in slave communities was to deepen attention to slave capacity and articulate more precise distinctions between the moral and intellectual faculties of slaves.

This argument over slave capacity was not limited to Anglican missionaries. Although apparently the same objections to slave conversions were being answered, Presbyterian evangelist Samuel Davies's plea for slave Christianization indicated more clearly that slaveholders defended their failure to do so on the ground that Africans were dunces or simply lacked the intellectual capacity to accept Christianity (which Davies and other evangelists interpreted as a ruse used by slave owners who sought excuses not to Christianize slaves). In 1757, Davies vigorously debated with slave owners in Virginia, assuring them that Christianity was a universal religion.[15] The defense of the universality of Christianity was a response to slave owners' fierce resistance to including Africans within the sphere of Christian conversion (for all the reasons noted and incipient notions of African "racial" differences). As Davies developed his argument, he directly confronted the objection that "Negroes are such sullen perverse creatures, or stupid dunces, that it is impossible to teach them any thing that is good."[16] Embedded in this objection was both a moral and intellectual critique of black capacities. Although Davies conceded that this was "undoubtedly the true character of some" black slaves, that some had a "low and barbarous education," imperfect knowledge of the English language, and "no opportunity for intellectual improvements," he insisted that black slaves were "generally as capable of instruction, as the white people."[17] Crucially, however, Davies argued that Christianity was "not a difficult science." If blacks did not learn it, the "fault lies in the heart, rather than in the head." Davies concluded his response to the particular assertion of black stupidity as an obstacle to slave Christianization by noting: "Some of them shew, that they have sense enough to love God, and hate Sin, though they are ignorant in other respects."[18] Davies's comment implied that Africans may very well be dull and stupid, as their slave owners complained, but they could be converted to Christianity nonetheless. Davies and others were thereby furthering this conceptual divide between intellectual capacity and moral or religious aptitude.

The demarcation of spiritual capacity from intellectual aptitude would have significant implications for understandings of black capacity. From the perspective of missionaries, the emphasis on slave religious capacity would render superfluous discussions of emancipation because it assured slave owners (or so the missionaries hoped) that Christianity made slaves more obedient and accepting of their bondage.[19] It would also bequeath to later generations a rather generalized religious notion of potential black contributions to the nation. In the specific context of late-eighteenth-century discussions, slave Christianization could proceed apace with the assumption that black religious life had no effect on their physical or outward condition (although missionaries continued to complain throughout the eighteenth century about the obstacles placed in the path of slave evangelism). A new standard of judging blacks emerged. In his *Notes on the State of Virginia* (1787), Thomas Jefferson, though not specifically concerned with slave evangelization, argued that although black slaves were seriously deficient in "the endowments of the head," they did not lack in the endowments of the heart, particularly in their possession of a moral sense. Jefferson's claim that blacks were inferior to whites in the endowments of both mind and body *and* his argument about their religious sentiments indicates the clear-cut boundaries that had separated religious experience or sentiments from intellectual capacities. Indeed, the safer claim about a moral sense was probably made because Jefferson (as he remarked in a letter to his nephew Peter Carr in 1787) felt that social and political chaos would ensue if it were argued that the moral sense was not universal, but existed only in those who possessed high intelligence. Blacks could be judged inferior in certain respects without the necessary implication that they were less than human, as Jefferson demonstrated.[20] Not only that, but blacks (and their defenders) were left with the burden of having to prove their moral equality with whites, because the assumption of intellectual inferiority became nearly universal among whites. Yet even moral equality was not a self-evident truth for Jefferson or later critics of black culture. It would have to be constantly demonstrated and reasserted before a mostly hostile white audience.

The separation of the moral sense from intellectual capacity was further evident in the thought of Benjamin Rush and other white contemporaries of Jefferson praising or commending blacks of scientific achievements but not offering a single black minister as evidence of black attainments. Rush was well acquainted with Richard Allen and Absalom Jones, important leaders in the early African Methodist traditions, but he did not put them forward as examples of black equality. Whites assumed that blacks possessed religious abilities. Doubts on this point would have denied that they were human. At stake was intellectual capacity. Black leaders and their allies were not content merely to assert the humanity of blacks; they wanted to affirm their fitness for freedom and their capacity for self-government. Even at this early stage in the nation's history, the need to vindicate the race was crucial to proving that blacks could become good citizens. The requirement of proof invariably led to measurements of intellectual, moral, and cultural capacity.[21]

Jefferson constructed a psychology of blacks that would later be adopted (in some ways) by proslavery apologists. He provided political, moral, and physical reasons why blacks could not be incorporated into the nation. "Real distinctions" that nature had made were among these reasons. Jefferson argued that blacks were characterized more by "sensation" than reflection. Though gifted in music and oratory, he maintained, blacks lacked the ability to engage in sustained reasoning. Anticipating the proslavery arguments about reversion to barbarism, Jefferson asserted that the nature of blacks (their difference of color and faculty) was an obstacle to their emancipation. Jefferson's psychology of black character offered a theory of racial difference that on one hand, affirmed the inferiority of blacks to whites. On the other hand, by acknowledging a moral faculty, space was created for a potential moral or religious contribution.[22]

Jordan argues that Jefferson's view of blacks was the "most intense, extensive, and extreme formulation of anti-Negro 'thought' offered by an American in the thirty years after the Revolution." He asserts that Jefferson also bequeathed to later generations a "prejudice for freedom" and an "egalitarian faith."[23] The tensions that Jordan sees in Jefferson's thoughts were present also in the writings of white defenders of black freedom, even if their views of black capacities were not as pessimistic as Jefferson's. Jefferson's doubts about black intellectual abilities were just as real for them, even though when they made such claims they were often coupled with assertions about the special religious qualities of blacks. Such statements about black religious "peculiarities" were at best halting attempts to affirm the humanity of blacks. But even the most ardent of black defenders articulated and sustained the dominant racial theories of their day.

Constructing the Naturally Religious Slave

Debates about African American character were ever evolving and changing their form. The environmentalist perspective on slaves' culture, by which their "degraded condition" was attributable to climate, geography, social experiences, and the horrors of slavery, began to decline in the late eighteenth century. Scientific investigations into human anatomy, growing claims of ethnologists about innate racial differences, and arguments about whether the human races were one or many species were part of this deepening conviction that black slaves were radically distinct and inferior to whites. The heated arguments about the nature of slavery, the rise of the proslavery "positive good argument" in the 1830s, and the abolitionists' agitation for slavery's end together led to an intense focus on the nature of slaves—whether blacks were "fit" for slavery, whether they could handle freedom, and what Africans had or had not done, could or could not do, apart from white supervision.

There was a new stress in mid-nineteenth-century American literature, historical writing, and science on the peculiarities of diverse peoples and national stocks. This emphasis approached a racialist explanation of society and culture. The romantic movement in Europe was in part a turn away from the universalism of the Enlightenment and an adoption of concepts of inbred national character and genius that could easily be translated into concepts of racial superiority. Johann Gottfried von Herder, a late-eighteenth-century German philosopher, was an important theorist of cultural nationalism, which tended to celebrate diversity. Herder argued that each national group possessed particular gifts manifested in the course of its historical development. In fulfilling its unique cultural or spiritual heritage, each group or *Volk* was bringing to fruition a single and laudable aspect of human character that no other people could express as well. Herder viewed these differences without making invidious comparisons between groups, an example for some Europeans and Americans who sensed spiritual inadequacies in their own heritage and looked to other peoples for the flowering of neglected human virtues.[24]

The romantic fascination with differences in peoples and nations coincided with and was influenced by large-scale immigration to the United States in the 1840s and 1850s, primarily from Ireland and Germany. In 1855, as if to challenge the more cosmopolitan thought of Herder, Frenchman Arthur Comte de Gobineau's *Inequality of Human Races* was published. Gobineau predicted the decline of the Anglo-Saxons in the United States because of an influx of "degenerate races" from Europe.[25] Variously described as Anglo-Saxons, Caucasians, and Teutons, "white" Americans were seen as possessing certain traits and qualities that were lacking in other groups. Even Northern abolitionists accepted this racialized language. Boston's Unitarian James Freeman Clarke, for example, concluded an important antislavery speech on Thanksgiving Day 1842 by admitting that blacks were inferior to whites in some faculties and superior in others. Blacks did not possess that "indomitable perseverance and will" that whites did, but blacks had a native courtesy and "almost universally, a strong religious tendency, and that strength of attachment which is capable of any kind of self-denial, and self-sacrifice." Even so, Clarke argued, whites "ought to remember the bond as bound with them."[26] The call for sympathy was advanced as claims for permanent racial differences were advanced as well.

The development of scientific classifications and rankings of human beings were gradual processes, but their impact on the romantic racialists was evident by the 1840s. Liberty, courage, and a host of positive qualities were seen as racial traits confined to the great Anglo-Saxon race. This was the beginning of a nationalistic glorification of the dominant stock, a tendency to make America's virtues racial rather than historical or environmental in origin.[27] American abolitionists sometimes made comparisons between Anglo-Saxons and Africans to understand why each occupied their various positions in world and U.S. history. In an address delivered in 1854, for example, Theodore Parker (1810–1860), a Boston Unitarian minister and a militant abolitionist, indicated both his admiration for and disillusionment with the Anglo-Saxon character by lauding the "strong love of individual freedom" that Anglo-Saxons possessed "in common with all the Teutonic family" and lamenting that they were the "most aggressive, invasive, and exclusive people on earth."[28] In a speech delivered four years later, Parker contrasted the warlike Anglo-Saxon with the docile African, concluding that the "African is the most docile and pliant of all the races of men." Because of the African's lack of aggressiveness, he lamented, "white men have kidnapped the black, and made him their prey."[29]

Abolitionists like Parker were not making the same claim for black inferiority that the proslavery advocates were advancing.[30] Although the defenders of slavery described Africans as prisoners of their emotions, docile, and incapable of living in freedom, romantic racialists lauded the alleged natural feelings and affectionate nature of blacks. They ascribed to the priority of feeling over the intellect, recalling Herder's relativism more than the hierarchical racism of other European racial theorists. Fredrickson contends that this view "was widely espoused by Northern humanitarians who were more or less antislavery."[31] They accepted that blacks were different from whites and probably would always be so, but they also sought to offer a more positive view

of differences within the context of currently accepted ideals of human behavior and sensibility.

The romantic racialist view of blacks elaborated a racial type and gender
was an important dimension of this conception. Theodore Tilton, editor of a
widely read abolitionist newspaper the New York *Independent* and an advocate of women's rights, argued that the Negro was the feminine race and that
Africans possessed a "strange moral, instinctive insight that belongs more to
women than men."[32] Romantic racialists held that blacks had more feminine
or Christ-like qualities than Anglo-Saxons: Anglo-Saxons were masculine and
bellicose, Africans emotional, sedentary, submissive, generous, and peaceful.
Africans were considered exemplary Christians in their capacity to forgive
rather than take vengeance. Anglo-Saxons were intellectual, adventuresome,
aggressive, exploitive, and warlike—less suited for the "Christian virtues"
idealized by the romantic racialists.[33] This notion of blacks also posited a future African society that would be governed by moral sentiment rather than
intellectual capacity. Hollis Read, a Northern minister, saw a noble age in
which a Christianized Africa would take its seat at the table of nations. This
political vision was coupled with claims about the naturally religious and affectionate nature of blacks.[34] On one hand, arguments about innate religiosity
assumed racial traits that were innate and thus incapable of alteration. On the
other hand, being naturally religious meant that blacks were receptive to the
Christian faith, evidenced by frequent comments in missionary reports about
the openness of blacks to the Christian Gospel. Romanic racialists' thought
was plagued with an internal tension of having to explain why blacks needed
Christianity if they already possessed such natively Christian virtues.

As abolitionists increased their attacks against slavery in the 1830s, they
sought in various ways to point out the evils of the slave system, assert the
humanity of blacks, and show the readiness and capacity of blacks to be free
persons. One way to demonstrate the inherent evil of slavery was to prove how
harmful it was to those in bondage and emphasize their undeserved suffering.
Some early abolitionists pointed to the "horrible ignorance" and "barbarism" of
slaves as an example of the brutalizing influence of the institution of slavery
rather than as a demonstration of inherent characteristics of the race or individual slaves. Blacks ultimately became a symbol for what was tragically lacking
in white America. Disillusionment with politics provoked by the wars in Texas
and Mexico in the 1840s and other national problems apparently made the
figure of a nonacquisitive and religious black slave more appealing.[35] Religious
feeling and sentiment, with emphasis on the home and its comforts, were
regarded as viable alternatives to the harsh world of politics and commerce.

Colonization and Romantic Racialism: Probing the Connection

William Ellery Channing (1780–1842), a Unitarian leader who offered a moderate stance against slavery, was one of the first antislavery advocates to make use of the stereotype of the affectionate, docile, and naturally religious slave. Channing served as the pastor of the Federal Street Church of Boston from 1803 to 1842. Deeply concerned about the problem of slavery, he was still unable to bring himself for many years to associate with abolitionists, whom he found shrill and fanatical. At the urging of friends, Channing decided to commit to print his thoughts on slavery. His work, *Slavery* (1835), was more influential than its short length might indicate, because many conservative gradualists and proslavery advocates found it necessary to answer his critique of slavery years after his work was published.[36] Channing was especially at pains to evoke sympathy for the slave. His description of the harmful and deleterious influences of slavery on slave life, morality, and physical health and his impassioned and moving remarks about the cruelties of slavery represent a high mark in the attempt to elicit compassion and fellow feeling for slaves. Channing sought to invert the standard claim that slavery's benevolence was evident in the slaves' attachment to their masters. Instead, he argued, "Of all the races of men, the African is the mildest and most susceptible of attachment. He loves, where the European would hate. He watches the life of a master, whom the North-American Indian, in like circumstances, would stab to the heart. The African is affectionate. Is this a reason for holding him in chains?"[37]

Channing also demonstrated that the very characteristics of Africans that were previously used to commend and approve of slavery were those that could be used to prove its cruelty and injustice. Why should any humane and Christian person wish to enslave these deeply affectionate and religious persons? "Let not this manifestation of a generous nature in the slave be turned against him," Channing proclaimed, and then went on: "Religious instruction should go hand in hand with all other means for preparing the slave for freedom. The colored race are said to be peculiarly susceptible of the religious sentiment. If this be addressed wisely and powerfully, if the slave be brought to feel his relation and accountableness to God, and to comprehend the spirit of Christianity, he is fit for freedom." The Boston Unitarian believed that Africans and black slaves were indeed peculiarly susceptible to religious sentiment, and he decried using this unique aspect of their culture as a defense for enslaving them.[38]

Two points in Channing's work appeared again and again in the writings of other white romantic racialists: that black slaves were peculiarly susceptible to religion and that this religious sensibility was in some way an indication of their fitness for freedom. These contentions about a special religious quality were more fully developed by colonizationists who called for an African nationality that would be permitted to unfold without white interference. This latter argument became especially prominent in the 1850s when colonization was revived in the antislavery movement.[39] This close connection between colonizationists' rhetoric about blacks being naturally religious and the language of romantic racialists has not been previously noted. This connection indicates that there is evidence that romantic racialists were deeply indebted to colonizationist sentiments and that they never really abandoned the belief that free blacks could not flourish in America. Perhaps, too, romantic racialists made such claims about the naturally religious African because they were wedded to notions of racial solidarity, which would explain why they could wax eloquently about black capacities emerging in Africa but say little about concrete issues regarding black and white relations in America in the event of the emancipation of black slaves. The deeply religious elements of colonization provide support for this view.

Arguments for colonization developed in the post-Revolutionary period as a way of dealing with the presence of free blacks in the nation. Colonization was seen as a means of ending slavery in America, Christianizing and civilizing Africa, and confronting the problem of whites' refusal to accept blacks as equals.[40] As Northern states began abolishing slavery in the late eighteenth century, increasing concerns about potential conflicts between free blacks and whites emerged.[41] The rise of colonizationist sentiment went hand in hand with the growth of the free black population. Colonizationists presented a depressing portrait of degraded and wretched free blacks who simply were not able to cope in a white society. Such defenders of colonization asserted that Africa was the natural habitat of blacks, and it was humane and just to send American blacks to Africa.[42] Colonizationists claimed that by sending American blacks, the recipients of Christianity and civilization, to Africa, slavery would be vindicated by the inscrutable providence of God. Americans, both the North and South, could pay off the moral debt that they owed for transporting thousands of Africans from their original home.[43]

Many of the same arguments about the benefits of colonization that blossomed in the 1850s had already been advanced as early as the 1780s. Samuel Hopkins, pastor of First Congregational Church in Newport, Rhode Island, proposed sending two free blacks from his congregation to Africa in 1773, with the intention of these black missionaries bringing Christianity and uplift to Africa. As Winthrop Jordan notes, "Christianization of Africa was primarily a logical extension of converting American slaves."[44] Although

Newport had served as one of the most important slave markets in the British North American colonies in the 1750s and 1760s, a gradual abolition law was finally passed in Rhode Island in 1784.[45] But by then, Hopkins had begun to support a plan to colonize all black Americans to Africa because he despaired of whites ever granting blacks freedom or according them equality.[46] His vision of a Christianized and civilized Africa with republican institutions and flourishing commerce was deeply appealing to missionaries and found strong support among some of the founders of the American Colonization Society.

In 1816 the American Society for Colonizing Free People of Color in the United States was founded (later more commonly known as the American Colonization Society). This effort to colonize free blacks grew out of the work of Robert Finley, a Presbyterian pastor in Basking Ridge, New Jersey. Finley took note of the growing number of freed blacks in his neighborhood and searched for a religious solution to prevent them from falling into vice, infidelity, and pauperism. He concluded that everything about them, including their color, was against free blacks and recommended colonizing them to Africa. Finley wrote that his desire was to give free people of color an opportunity to rise to their "proper level," provide a powerful means of putting an end to the slave trade, and send blacks as missionaries of civilization and Christianity to Africa.[47] Henry Sherwood once wrote that it is difficult to explain how colonizationists like Finley could argue for the removal of a dangerous and wretched element from the population that was also seen as the means of bringing uplift and civilization to Africa.[48] William Hamilton, a prominent black New Yorker who presided over the 1834 National Black Convention, noticed this same contradictory stance of the American Colonization Society. Hamilton chided the society for sending forth mixed signals that on one hand lauded blacks as "kind, meek, and gentle" and on the other hand regarded them as "ignorant, idle, a nuisance, and a drawback on the resources of the country." Hamilton called attention to the irony of this stance: "As abandoned as we are, in Africa we shall civilize and christianize all that heathen country. And by thus preaching continually, they have distilled into the minds of the community a desire to see us removed."[49] In an attempt to explain this apparently contradictory stance of the American Colonization Society, Sherwood rightly noted that arguments for colonization were intended to appeal to various segments of the country and to different social classes at different times. To slaveholders and the white South, removing free blacks was obviously a desirable goal because of their anomalous position among enslaved blacks and white fears that their very presence would challenge claims of blacks' suitableness for bondage.

Civilizing and Christianizing Africa was also a goal advanced by churchmen and religious bodies. Some advocates of colonization expected that blacks who attended schools in America would serve as willing leaders to other blacks. Colonizationists also held that the existence of a settlement in Africa would deter slaveholders from securing cargo in human beings, although one effect of the U.S. ban on the importation of new African slaves in 1808 was an increase in the price of slaves, making them even more valuable commodities.[50] Ultimately, the colonizationists believed that blacks needed contact with whites to acquire certain virtues, especially Christianity, so that they could return to the land of their forebears and bring commerce, civilization, and true religion.

By proposing to remove free blacks, as Paul Goodman writes, colonizationists "formally conceptualized the American republic in racial terms and offered a program for purifying the nation, North and South."[51] Even if we take seriously the elevated language that blacks' sojourn in America was part of a providential plan to bring Christianity and commerce to Africa, the colonizationists did not see any long-term place for free blacks in the nation. This was made abundantly clear when the American Colonization Society sent a memorial to Congress in 1820, warning about the perils of the growth of the free black population. The memorial held that free blacks could never be happy or useful in America and that it was necessary to remove them because their increase in number did not translate into an increase in the "physical strength" of the nation.[52] In the view of these colonizationists, no future in America was envisioned for blacks, and even the conceptualization of black capacities was tied to an African future.

Romantic racialists, as white Northerners uncomfortable with slavery, simply had their doubts about black capacities and their inclusion in the nation as free persons. Some of them had been former colonizationists, though they began to reject this option once they learned how Northern free blacks reacted to such proposals. To be sure, romantic racialists argued that slavery should end and that blacks had unique gifts. Only haltingly, however, did some of them contend that the flourishing of such gifts would take place in the United States. We see these contradictions and tensions in the thought of Alexander Kinmont, a leading exponent of this deeply racial view of black capacities.

Kinmont's *Twelve Lectures on the Natural History of Man* (1839) took this argument of natural religiosity one step further than Channing. Kinmont identified specific alleged black virtues with Christianity. Kinmont's works were later widely cited by abolitionists. Born in 1799 in Scotland, Kinmont set sail for New York in 1823 and later settled in Cincinnati, Ohio (where he died in 1838). He gave a series of public lectures in 1833–1834 that became the basis for his book (published posthumously). While in Bedford, Pennsylvania, he began examining the doctrines of the Jerusalem Church and became a convert to the religious system of the great Swedish mystic Emanuel Swedenborg. This conversion may explain Kinmont's distrust of what he regarded as a ratio-nalistic approach to Christianity. For him, the Caucasian mind preferred a philosophical, analytical approach to faith. This was not, in his view, neces-sarily a fault but rather an outgrowth of their enterprising spirit, roving dis-position, inquisitiveness of mind, and their haughty, proud, and overbearing character. Caucasians, Kinmont believed, investigated and analyzed truth, but the Ethiopian (used interchangeably with *Negro* and *African*) narrated rather than reflected on truth. Kinmont's mild critique of the domineering aspects of the Caucasian mind led him to a more favorable evaluation of the religion of blacks (or at least his idealization of a naturally religious black character). He condemned what he called "the Grecian intellect" for having an excessive desire to define and expound the mysterious points of the Christian faith, while lauding the "tranquil mind" of the Africans, which was more likely to accept the impressions of the Christian faith. The "excited understanding" of the Caucasian intellect tragically sought to grasp truth through reasoning.[53]

Kinmont believed that each race had its particular contribution to make to civilization. Only in Africa, he averred, could blacks' temperament flourish and "display in their native land some very peculiar and interesting traits of char-acter, of which, we, a distinct branch of the human family, can at present form no conception."[54] The African contribution would not be marked by science but by a refined, exalted, and "lovely theology" that would characterize the African's unique gift to human civilization. This African theology would be a "reflection of the light of heaven more perfect and endearing than that which the intellects of the Caucasian race have ever yet exhibited."[55] This distinction between Af-rican theology and the Caucasian intellect was a logical corollary of Kinmont's theory that human beings possessed a "moral sense" and an "intellectual sense," either of which could be improved but both of which were distributed by nature differently to racial groups. For Kinmont, then, culture was a product of race and social environment, but historical forces operating over an extending period of time could make differences between peoples become nearly per-manent.[56] So he believed that blacks were losing their ability to fully express their endowment of the moral sense because whites had torn them from their natural environment. It was a "sad error of the white race, besides the moral guilt which was contracted," Kinmont proclaimed, "when they first dragged the African, contrary to his genius and inclination, from his native regions."[57]

The hope of the African race rested in its light-heartedness, Kinmont maintained, and "natural want of solicitude for the future," natural talent for music, and willingness to serve, "the most beautiful trait of humanity, which we, from our innate love of dominion, and in defiance of the Christian religion, brand with the name of *servility*, and abuse not less to our own dishonor than their injury." Referring to the African as a religious, affectionate, mild, and docile race, Kinmont contrasted him to the Caucasian, who was almost (he believed) constitutionally unable to be a Christian. "All the sweeter graces of the Christian religion," Kinmont charged, "appear almost too tropical and tender plants to grow in the Caucasian mind; they require the character of human nature which you can see in the rude lineaments of the Ethiopian, to be implanted in, and grow naturally and beautifully withal." Kinmont cast the flowering of the Negro religious temperament in the distant future, when the Negro nature could flourish in the tropical land of its birth and ancestry. The African race, in his estimation, would reach millennial perfection long before the domineering white race would reach its pinnacle. The burden of Kinmont's lectures was to demonstrate that although the Negro race possessed the very characteristics posited by slaveholders—willingness to serve, improvidence, musical giftedness, light-heartedness, and docility—these traits were no grounds for enslaving them. Indeed, the gentler and milder virtues that owed their origin to divine beneficence were those that blacks possessed in abundance, he asserted, and these would flourish in a noble African civilization in the future.[58]

Kinmont's conception of Africans was deeply gendered. In his view, Africans were domestic creatures who preferred to stay at home and not wander far from their local habitations. Africans were a race more tender and feminine than Caucasians. They possessed the virtues that Caucasians lacked: sweetness, a "gentle beauty of the Christian religion," and a mystic, quiet, and humble spirit. They were more like children of nature than the European (a term he used interchangeably with *Caucasian*), who was manly and proud. Europeans felt compelled to dominate and rule over such weaker peoples. While the Caucasian was migratory and roaming, Kinmont maintained, the African was provincial and confined by "natural inclination" to one quarter of the globe. Yet he warned Caucasians that their stage in history was temporary and they might be overtaken by another race in the future. He wrote: "Who shall regret it, if the reign of goodness shall at last supercede the supremacy of truth, and feminine prevail over the masculine virtue?"[59] Kinmont left space for a future age when African affection and gentleness were just as valued as the Caucasian intellect.

This coupling of the feminine African and the manly European did not lead Kinmont to recommend racial amalgamation. Interracial sexual relations were an "unnatural mixture" that he abhorred. Kinmont argued that the Caucasian was a single race that exhibited several distinct and permanent varieties, which should mix among themselves to improve the "general race." Germans, Britons and "those tribes from which they have sprung, whether in Germany or Gaul" should mix to develop the best qualities of the race. But

Africans, Kinmont argued, had yet to exhibit their "splendor of the divine attributes." Though Africans had "fewer vivid manifestations of intellect" than the Caucasian, perhaps they, too, would develop a future civilization that would reflect their "complexion" and "natural temperament." These two races of distinct origins, in Kinmont's view, would each flourish in their respective locales, though he never indicated on what basis he felt that Caucasians, given their natural migratory instincts, would settle for a definite locale to develop their special talents without invading the space of other groups.[60] Yet this joining of the "superior" feminine qualities of the African with a proposed future age of moral or religious sentiment would become the central quality of romantic racialists' conceptions of the distinctive contributions of blacks to *American* society and rested on a firm belief in blacks' intellectual inferiority.

Feminine Emotions and a "Feeling" Religion

Elizabeth Clark argues that by the 1830s "many Americans turned for guidance to the emotions over the intellect, identifying the moral sense more with feeling than with rational thought."[61] This changing understanding of the role of emotions would have important consequences for reflections on slave religion. Historians have argued that ethical sentimentalism, which placed an emphasis on sympathy and feeling, and evangelical revivalism, which gave priority to the heart or affective religion over the intellect and rationality, served as sources of antislavery thought.[62] Women made particular contributions to this emphasis on the emotional and affective in interpretations of blacks. Their ideas were disseminated through a growing genre of sentimental literature and domestic fiction, of which antislavery novels constituted one important part. By making strong appeals to emotion and seeking to evoke sympathy for slaves, romantic racialists mapped onto blacks increasingly feminine theories about slave religious capacities and natural religiosity. To the extent that black religion was equated with emotion and feelings, blacks were said to be naturally religious in a way that whites were not. The appeal to slaveholders to liberate their slaves, who were seen as creatures of emotion who could experience and deeply feel pain, became a standard trope in this literature, both in fictional accounts and antislavery pamphlets. The association of slaves with the feminine occurred on two fronts: First, slaves were regarded as feminine in that they were seen as creatures of feelings and emotions, qualities that were regarded as peculiar to women and children. Second, women played an important role in disseminating this literature and became enormously successful as the public voices behind these now-dominant portrayals of blacks. Harriet

Beecher Stowe's *Uncle Tom's Cabin* was the most important disseminator of these ideas of blacks as naturally religious. Stowe's book became the first American novel to sell over a million copies.[63] Though her work may have been the most important and well known, she was not the only significant female leader to promote these views about blacks.

In 1832, Lydia Maria Child (1802–1880), William Lloyd Garrison, and thirteen others founded the New England Anti-Slavery Society. Although Child was urged on by her husband, David, to devote herself to the antislavery cause, it was her first contact with Garrison that, in Child's words, "got hold of the strings" of her conscience and pulled her into various reforms. However, as early as 1824, with the publication of her book *Hobomok*, Child had already shown sympathy for Indians, slaves, and others oppressed by her own culture.[64] But her important book *An Appeal in Favor of That Class of Americans Called Africans* (1833) was responsible for converting many future leaders to the antislavery cause, among them Channing, orator Wendell Phillips, Unitarian Thomas Wentworth Higginson, and Massachusetts Senator Charles Sumner. *Appeal* propelled Child to the forefront of the abolitionist movement. A remarkable woman and prolific author, Child was a Unitarian who both fought for women's rights and advanced the antislavery cause. By the late 1830s, she was a central figure in the antislavery movement. Although she spent most of her life in Massachusetts, she displayed in *Appeal* a deep fund of knowledge of African history and cultures that was matched, according to her recent biographer, Carolyn Karcher, only by Martin Delany among her African American contemporaries and by Mary Lowell Putnam and Herman Melville among whites.[65]

In *Appeal,* Child noted that the "opinion that negroes are naturally inferior in intellect is almost universal among white men; but the belief that they are worse than other people" was much less extensive.[66] Although the frequency of the claims of whites that blacks were morally degraded should not be minimized, Child's point demonstrated the persistence of this view of distinguishing between blacks possessing a religious or moral sentiment over against their alleged lack of intellect (in a relative sense). Child also indicated that many whites, "who were by no means admirers of the colored race," were willing to concede that blacks were remarkable for their "kind feelings" and "strong affections."[67] This discussion of feelings took place in her chapter on the "Moral Character of Negroes." In the chapter on the "Intellect of Negroes," Child rejected the common claim that blacks were naturally inferior to whites and maintained instead that "artificial causes" produced their "present degraded condition."[68] Child concluded, however, "even if the negroes were, beyond all doubt, our inferiors in intellect, this would form no excuse for oppression, or contempt."[69] Although she was fiercely opposed to colonization and labored to show that blacks once possessed a great civilization in ancient Egypt to prove that they were the intellectual equals of whites, there are indications that Child was a romantic racialist at heart and that she had doubts about the intellectual capacities of blacks. These doubts seemed to have led her to look elsewhere, beyond the intellect, to affirm the potential and actual contributions of blacks to the nation and, indeed, to human history.

By 1841, as editor of the *National Anti-Slavery Standard*, the official organ of the pro-Garrison American Anti-Slavery Society, Child quoted approvingly the works of William Ellery Channing and Alexander Kinmont, particularly those sections that expounded the image of blacks as naturally religious. She had been attracted to the teachings of Swedenborg and became just as dissatisfied by the "cold intellectual respectability" of her brother's Unitarianism as she had been repelled by the Calvinism of her youth.[70] Perhaps Kinmont's ideas on race and his acceptance of Swedenborg's mystical teachings appealed to her own religious sentiments. Child had joined the Swedenborgian New Church in 1822 but began looking beyond its teachings by 1836. By the early 1840s, she was visiting a variety of churches, but the Swedenborgian influence seemed still resonant in her reflections on race. In an article in *Anti-Slavery* in 1841, Child wrote that she came across an idea that was "so long familiar" to her mind in the writings of Kinmont. Those thoughts led her to conclude with Kinmont that Africans were more the children of nature than were Europeans and that their future, unlike Europeans, would be marked by a "new and lovely theology," not by science. Africans would develop a civilization that would be marked by a "certain beautiful nature," a "reflection of the light of heaven, more perfect and endearing than that which the intellects of the Caucasian race have ever yet exhibited."[71] She added, "Above all the people in the world, the African race are probably most susceptible of religious feeling, and have the strongest tendency to devotion. Swedenborg speaks of them as being near to Christians in the spiritual world than any other heathen by reason of their docility and reverence."[72] Although Child was ambivalent about how to interpret Swedenborg's claim, she had been sure of one thing for a long time: "that a very prominent place among the nations must be assigned to the African race, whenever the age of Moral Sentiment arrives." She granted preeminence to blacks in a misty millennial age to come. "Creatures of affection and of faith," she wrote, "everything marks them peculiarly appropriate to represent a religious age, as the Anglo-Saxons were to represent an intellectual one."[73]

By the 1840s and 1850s, the belief among romantic racialism that blacks were intellectually inferior to whites was well established. The attempt to find the unique contributions of blacks was the next task. Much attention, as indicated already, was focused on the religious capacities of blacks, or more generally, the peculiarities that were innate to their feeling natures. It is not clear precisely what *feeling* meant except that it was often contrasted to intellect as a healthy ideal or an alternative to a calculating, analytical approach to life and social forms of existence that inevitably involved oppression of "weaker" peoples. When romantic racialists stated that blacks were intellectually inferior to whites, they were quick to indicate that this was not an apology for slavery and that blacks did possess gifts and unique characteristics of their own.

Harriet Beecher Stowe (1811–1896) gathered up all of these notions of Africans as creatures of sentiment and affection, infused them with a specifically Christian meaning, and widely popularized them. Her most recent biographer suggests that Stowe may have been exposed to Kinmont's ideas while she was living in Cincinnati (which may be one of the sources for her attribution of deeper feeling to blacks).[74] Stowe's influential work, *Uncle Tom's Cabin* (1852), while obviously important for its role as an antislavery polemic, was filled with descriptions of blacks as naturally susceptible to religion.[75] Her book must be understood in the context of the move away from Calvinism by Stowe and other New England Protestants who adopted in its place what William McLaughlin calls a "romantic evangelicalism" that emphasized the intuitive perception of truth through the feelings or emotions of the heart and that sentimentalized women and children (and blacks, a point that McLaughlin does not mention) as means of grace.[76] Stowe's emphasis on the naturally religious intuitions of black slaves in *Uncle Tom's Cabin* in contrast to a stifling and abstract theological system bolstered her critique of unattractive features of Calvinism with which she was familiar.[77]

Stowe began her novel by contrasting the character of Uncle Tom, introduced as a pious, reliable, and loyal black slave who "got religion" at a camp meeting, to the profane and hardened Haley, a white man who lacked all the softer sentiments and emotions and was only interested in buying and selling slaves. This is one of the central divides in the novel in regard to the distinction Stowe draws between blacks and whites. Religion characterized Tom's virtue, whereas money animated the soul of Haley. Uncle Tom, said Augustine St. Clare, Tom's kindly first master, had a natural genius for religion. Stowe also paired blacks, women, and children, all of whom she said were able instinctively to see the "true state" of things.[78] Speaking of Aunt Chloe's resigned comments about her hard lot in life, Stowe wrote: "In order to appreciate the sufferings of the negroes sold in the south, it must be remembered that all the instinctive affections of that race are peculiarly strong. Their local attachments are very abiding. They are not naturally daring and enterprising, but home-loving and affectionate." This domestic conception of a black temperament was thoroughly gendered and resembled Kinmont's ideas about the native qualities of the African race. For Stowe, Africans were naturally sedentary and timid. In her view, they lacked the naturally aggressive and inquisitive qualities of An-glo-Saxons, and their local attachments made the separation of their children in the slave system especially painful.[79]

In a crucial passage that illustrates the appeal of the naturally religious Negro, Stowe contrasted Cicero, the ancient Roman statesman, to Uncle Tom, the poor but humble Negro. Cicero, a symbol for the modern Anglo-Saxon, apparently could not have accepted the simple truths of the Bible had they been presented to him. Instead, "he must first fill his head with a thousand ques-tions of authenticity of manuscript, and correctness of translation." But to Tom, unconcerned with historical and critical questions about the Bible, reli-gious belief was so "evidently true and divine that the possibility of a question never entered his simple head."[80] For Stowe, the African temperament was more naturally receptive to religion, yet there was something about the Anglo-Saxon temperament that made them despise this affectionate quality of the Negro. Stowe agreed with Kinmont who argued that there was something about the Anglo-Saxon mind that resisted the tender plants of Christianity.[81]

Stowe and other romantic racialists combined humanitarian sympathies with strongly held beliefs about permanent racial differences.[82] *Uncle Tom's Cabin* was the central text to spread the ideas of the romantic racialists and the notion of a naturally religious black slave in the popular American imagina-tion. This makes it all the more important to underscore the issues left un-resolved by Stowe and her like-minded contemporaries. As an allegedly unenterprising and affectionate race, it is not quite clear what Africans could contribute to American society in the future. These romanticized religious blacks were seen as creatures so bound by climate and a state of dependency that the options seemed to be either colonization (where their supposedly latent religious capacities could flourish) or a hazy condition of submission in the United States (a situation that was rarely given specificity). Thus it is no surprise that in her grand vision for the future of Africa, Stowe wrote:

> If ever Africa shall show an elevated and cultivated race . . . the negro race, no longer despised and trodden down, will, perhaps, show forth some of the latest and most magnificent revelations of human life. Certainly they will in their gentleness, their lowly docility of heart, their aptitude to repose on a superior mind and rest on a higher power, their childlike simplicity of affection, and facility of forgive-ness. In all these they will exhibit the highest form of the peculiarly *Christian life*, and perhaps, as God chasteneth whom he loveth, he hath chosen poor Africa in the furnace of affliction, to maker her the

highest and noblest in that kingdom which he will set up, when every
other kingdom has been tried and failed; for the first shall be last,
and the last shall be first.[83]

Here Stowe's narrative commentary was strikingly similar to the language of
the colonizationists who expressed hope for a Christianized Africa with ex-
patriated blacks who would impart to Africa a Christian nationality. Constru-
ing biblical passages corporately or racially that could be construed individually
("God chasteneth whom he loveth"), Stowe demonstrated her commitment to
racial essentialism. As Arthur Riss argues, Stowe's belief that Africans possessed inherent racial characteristics was foundational to her conception of a
communal identity generated by race.[84] Stowe posited that "the race" would
flourish in Africa, not that the rights of individual blacks in America were to be
realized.

At the end of her novel, Stowe echoed a sentiment common among romantic racialists: that the reports of missionaries testified that "none have
received the Gospel with such eager docility as the African." Africans were
purportedly naturally receptive to religion, and their unquestioning faith
shamed the "higher and more skilful culture" of whites. Colonization to Africa
seemed to be the ideal condition for the flourishing of the Negro temperament,
as related in the novel's conclusion.[85] Later, Stowe protested that she was not
a colonizationist and traveled to England in 1853 as an "antislavery activist."
Despite her protestations, others continued to criticize the novel for advocating
colonization as the solution to the problem of slavery in America.[86]

An often overlooked aspect of Stowe's depiction of black religion was her
attempt to demonstrate the varieties of religious experience among blacks and
ground them in Africans' reputedly unique physiological and psychological
makeup. In her *Key to Uncle Tom's Cabin* (1853), she provided a number of
examples of black conversions and black religious experiences to support her
depiction of Uncle Tom's vision of the suffering Jesus (the scene in which Tom
experiences extreme pain as a result of being cruelly beaten by Simon Legree,
his slave master). To be sure, Stowe did not cease using blacks as religious
exemplars to shame literate whites about the alleged patience, meekness, and
Christian gentleness that a despised and lowly African people had been capable
of demonstrating under great suffering. Yet she elaborated in more detail on
the scientific or psychological reasons behind Uncle Tom's religious experience
in her *Key*. She pointed to "a curious chapter of psychology" to explain the
peculiar religious practices of "the negro race." Her appeal to the "psychologist"
in the novel and the "mesmerists" in the *Key* suggests that she used the terms
interchangeably. In both cases, Stowe relied on the science of the human mind

to bolster her argument about blacks' religious experiences. Stowe was conversant with the mesmerists' claims about deeper levels of consciousness and inner sources of feeling, which in part opened the door for speculations about a subconscious or unconscious realm of human experience. Mesmerism, imported from Europe into America in the early nineteenth century, had sought to demonstrate that there were human experiences well beyond the five physical senses. By Stowe's time, it was regarded as a science of the mind and quite widely accepted for its curative value. It has been argued by one historian that mesmerism was an early form of psychotherapy because of its emphasis on mental and emotional healing rituals.[87]

Stowe attributed blacks' religious expression to their "nervous organization" that was "peculiarly susceptible and impressible" to the "powerful stimulant of the Christian religion." She noted that mesmerists had "found that the negroes are singularly susceptible to all that class of influences which produce catalepsy, mesmeric sleep, and partial clairvoyant phenomena."[88] Stowe felt that blacks possessed an "oriental character" that was tropical in origin and more akin to the Hebrews of old and modern Oriental nations than to the religion of whites. Her extended discussion of the different religious experiences of blacks led her to conclude in the *Key*: "The negro race is confessedly more simple, docile, child-like and affectionate than other races; and hence the divine graces of love and faith, when in-breathed by the Holy Spirit, find in their natural temperament a more congenial atmosphere."[89] This was the crucial point that Stowe and other romantic racialists continually made when attempting to explain why black slave Christians differed from white Christians. Yet Stowe took all of this evidence from the psychology of black religion to be a demonstration of "how very different" blacks were from "the white race" more generally.[90] Just as important was her reliance on an emerging scientific or psychological interpretation of black religious capacities. In her case, however, a psychological study of black religion confirmed the distinctive contributions of blacks and was not seen as a denigration of their unique religious practices. (Psychological theories of black religion in the late nineteenth century would not be so celebratory in their analyses.)

Although Stowe's Uncle Tom has often been caricatured as a passive figure who meekly submitted to slavery as God's will, her emphasis on Tom's refusal to grant Simon Legree authority over his soul or spiritual life was a powerful critique of Southern evangelicals' claim that the system of slavery as it existed in the South was not in conflict with the slaves' spiritual freedom. Stowe exploited this argument by demonstrating that it did nothing to prevent the master from cruelty toward slaves, but she also created space for slave agency by demonstrating that it was Tom's allegiance to God, his heavenly master, which enabled him to disobey Legree's earthly commands. So though Tom did indeed long for another world to be with Jesus, and it can be rightfully said that he possessed an otherworldly religion, Stowe reworked one classical religious defense of slavery (its claim that slavery did not detract from the slave's relationship with God) to demonstrate its crucial flaw. Even if slave owners did not possess the slave's soul as defenders asserted, Stowe intimated that this limited agency of slaves was fundamentally incompatible with slavery because it would invariably lead to extreme cruelty or the death of slaves at the hands of their masters because of slaves' claims to a higher authority than their earthly masters.[91] In the end, however, Stowe's Uncle Tom possessed freedom only in another world.

We may sum up the central features of the naturally religious slave as imagined by Stowe and other romantic racialists as follows: docility, receptiveness to the divine, unquestioning faith, and an intuitive sense of the transcendent.[92] The creation of this religious temperament served several functions. It evoked sympathy; it was presented as a moral alternative to the cultivated, domineering, and refined Anglo-Saxon's alleged racial temperament; and it suggested that only in Africa could a Negro religious temperament truly flourish. But all of these scenarios left unanswered the question about how the naturally religious black, when freed, would fare in American society.

Proslavery Apologists and the Benefits of Slavery

Defenders of slavery also constructed a black character that coincided in important ways with that of the romantic racialists. The docile, loyal, and contented slavery, posited by proslavery apologists and depicted in plantation novels, was eerily similar to the submissive, gentle, and affectionate slave of the romantic racialists. This was so because pro- and antislavery arguments alike were part of this broader discourse about innate racial traits, which became increasingly popular with the rise of the new science of ethnology in the 1840s. Romantic racialists attempted to affirm racial variety without necessarily making negative judgments about blacks. Proslavery apologists, however, unequivocally asserted the inferiority of blacks. Though some proslavery theorists argued that blacks were receptive to Christianity and naturally religious, more often they decried what they saw as the emotionalism and superstition of black religion. Slavery was in part justified because (its defenders maintained) it brought Christianity to a savage people who were incapable of self-government. Yet to assert that blacks were creatures of feeling and affection, as the romantic racialists did, was but a more positive assessment of what proslavery apologists regarded as simply emotionalism that needed to be eradicated and replaced with "true Christianity." *Feeling* could very easily become unrestrained and dangerous *emotion*, depending on the politics of the observer. Thus it is no surprise that by the end of the Civil War, the affectionate and naturally religious slave had become the superstitious and emotionally extravagant freed person in the eyes of Northern missionaries to the South.

Proslavery apologists offered a racial theory about the destiny of black Americans that went as follows: Black slaves were morally and intellectually unfit for freedom. They were idle, improvident, depraved, and immoral. Therefore, it would be folly to free them. Blacks in bondage to white Southerners had found a refuge from the idolatry, cannibalism, and vice of Africa. Slaves had been Christianized, civilized, proslavery defenders argued, and made useful under the benevolent tutelage of their white masters. A psychology of the slave temperament was offered by those proslavery apologists more interested in ethnological findings: indolence, lasciviousness, imitative capacity (and thus no creativity or originality), lack of judgment and foresight, a child-like attachment, filial affection for and loyalty to their masters, a superstitious and reverential disposition that made them susceptible to religious impressions, and a passive and obedient nature, which made them easily governed. In 1854, in an extended analysis of the character of black slaves, Thomas R. R. Cobb, a lawyer in Georgia, concluded,

> This inquiry into the physical, mental, and moral development of the negro race, seems to point them clearly, as peculiarly fitted for a laborious class. Their physical frame is capable of great and long-continued exertion. Their mental capacity renders them incapable of successful self-development, and yet adapts them for the direction of a wiser race. Their moral character renders them happy, peaceful, contented, and cheerful in a status that would break the spirit and destroy the energies of the Caucasian or the native American.[93]

For Cobb, blacks benefited from their reception of Christianity under benevolent white masters, and their labor for slave owners was simply one small task in exchange for a much greater good. Defenders of slavery had a fixed and definite place for blacks in the nation.

Kenneth Paul O'Brien has argued that as Southern thought matured in its defense of slavery, two discrete images of blacks developed: the savage and the child. The savage black was always a reality to the Southern mind. Many Southern whites claimed that blacks, released from the civilized oversight of white masters, would revert to a state of barbarism and savagery. Yet the image of the child, helpless on his own but capable of functioning under the supervision and direction of his superiors, was also prominent in the thought of proslavery apologists.[94] Proslavery advocates sought to demonstrate that not only were blacks fit for slavery but their docile nature was evidence of their contentment as slaves. Black rebellion or slave revolts were attributed to the pernicious philosophy of the abolitionists. As John Blassingame writes, "Facing the withering attacks of the abolitionists, they [Southern writers] had to prove that slavery was not an unmitigated evil. The loyal contented slave was a *sine qua non* in Southern literary propaganda . . . [this stereotype was devised] to relieve [whites] of the anxiety of thinking about slaves as men."[95] The need to reassert this claim, however, was not merely a response to abolitionists but was probably a continuing worry among slave owners about the potential effects of Christianity on slaves. The specter of Nat Turner's rebellion haunted the minds of many Southern whites years after the event occurred.

The denigration of blacks' character functioned as a defense of their enslavement and Southerners reiterated again and again a perfect fit between black character and their enslavement by whites. In his *Inquiry into the Law of Negro Slavery*, Cobb unequivocally affirmed the physical and mental/intellectual inferiority of blacks. He asserted that the "mental inferiority of the negro has been often asserted and never successfully denied." Ironically, he quoted Theodore Parker's arguments extolling the active qualities of the Caucasian (Anglo-Saxon) as an illustration of and additional evidence for black inferiority to whites. Though he denigrated the religious traditions of the "barbarous" tribes of Africa, Cobb conceded that blacks in America were "very susceptible of religious impressions, exhibiting, in many individual instances, a degree of faith unsurpassed, and a Christian deportment free from blemish." He concluded that slaves were "passive and obedient, and consequently easily governed."[96]

Apologists for slavery found themselves perforce advancing the notion of a docile black temperament if only for the sake of maintaining a particular image of slavery as being ideally suited for childish blacks, and in this way, they contributed to the image of blacks as naturally religious, though few of them romanticized the "natural Negro" in Africa (as some romantic racialists did). Southerners were more apt to describe the idolatry and heathenism of Africa in the most unflattering terms while lauding the benefits of bringing Christianity and slavery to a benighted and savage people. Cobb made this point with stark clarity:

> in mental and moral development, slavery, so far from retarding, has advanced the negro race . . . While, by means of this institution, the knowledge of God and his religion has been brought home, with

practical effect, to a greater number of heathens than by all the combined missionary efforts of the Christian world. But remove the restraining and controlling power of the master, and the negro becomes, at once the slave of his lust, and the victim of his indolence, relapsing, with wonderful rapidity, into his pristine barbarism.

But even while belittling slaves, Southerners were locked into this battle over the nature of the slaves because they realized that it behooved them to demonstrate how slavery had uplifted or elevated the slave. Thus, although Albert Taylor Bledsoe, a professor of mathematics at the University of Virginia and a staunch defender of slavery, found it necessary to lambaste Channing for referring to Africans as "one of the best races of the human family," he angrily pointed out that the affectionate, meek, and religious blacks that Channing described were not to be found flourishing in Africa but in bondage in America under the benevolent tutelage of whites.

Bledsoe's unstinting defense of slavery, however, should not blind us to the point he made about what was at stake in debates over the nature of the slave's character (though the same type of argument he made against the abolitionists could have been used against proslavery defenders). He wrote:

The truth is, the abolitionist can make the slave a brute or a saint, just as it may happen to suit the exigency of his argument. If slavery degrades its subjects into brutes, then one would suppose that slaves are brutes. But the moment you speak of selling a slave, he is no longer a brute,—he is a civilized man, with all the most tender affections, with all the most generous emotions. If the object be to excite indignation against slavery, then it always transforms its subjects into brutes; but if it be to excite indignation against the slaveholder, then he holds, not brutes but a George Harris—or an Eliza—or an Uncle Tom [all, in their own way, exemplary characters in Stowe's *Uncle Tom's Cabin*]—in bondage. Any thing, and everything, except fair and impartial statement, are the materials with which he works.[97]

Proslavery apologists argued that an Uncle Tom, if he existed, could flourish in the South precisely because Africans had been exposed to the benefits of Christianity, civilization, and a stable home life. Nehemiah Adams, an ardent defender of slavery, put it this way: "SLAVERY MADE UNCLE TOM. Had it not been for slavery, he would have been a savage in Africa, a brutish slave to his fetishes, living in a jungle, perhaps; and had you stumbled upon him he would very likely have roasted you and picked your bones."[98] For the defenders of slavery, what was natural about the African was savagery and superstition. The affectionate qualities that romantic racialists professed to find had been developed and nurtured by the institution of slavery, proslavery advocates angrily asserted. Linked to this argument was the claim that if released from slavery blacks would relapse to their natural selves into a state of animal-like depravity and heathenism. Claims of white supervision were therefore justified on the grounds that this social arrangement was socially and politically beneficial for blacks and whites. It also masked white fears of angry blacks' chafing under a system of inhuman bondage.

Tensions between Christianity and Scientific Racism

By the late eighteenth and early nineteenth centuries, monogenesis (the view that all humans had the same origin and were members of the same species) was the dominant idea about the origin of human differences and was bolstered by Scriptural authority, science, and an Enlightenment philosophy that emphasized natural rights and human equality.[99] When polygenesists began insisting on a separate origin for the races, they usually denied the biblical account or did not give it much attention. Though they and monogenesists agreed that blacks were inferior to whites and should be held as slaves, clergymen in particular were troubled that the polygenesists were undermining the authority of Scripture. They declined the support of scientists and found themselves generally opposed to the findings of the new science of ethnology, which emerged in the 1840s. However, they did make selective use of this developing science, especially as it provided theoretical support for slave labor, differences between the races, and the alleged lack of an African civilization worthy of notice.[100]

Audrey Smedley writes that by the early decades of the nineteenth century, the concept of race had taken on definite features. This "singular paradigm" included the following elements: (1) a universal classification of human groups as exclusive and discrete biological entities based on assessments and value judgments of phenotypic and behavioral variations, (2) the imposition of an inegalitarian ethos that required the hierarchical ranking of these groups, (3) the belief that outer physical characteristics of different human populations were but surface manifestations of inner value-laden realities (behavioral, intellectual, temperamental, moral, and other qualities), (4) the notion that all of these qualities were inheritable, and (5) the belief that each exclusive group (race) was created unique and distinct by nature or God, and that their imputed differences, believed fixed and unalterable, could never be bridged or transcended.[101] New sciences—ethnology, anthropology, craniometry, anthropometry, and phrenology—arose to theorize the relationship among the world's peoples. These new sciences were also implicated in questions of social and public policy, especially the debate over black slaves and their role in the life of the nation. They did not arise as purely disinterested sciences that interpreted the real world "out there," but rather arose squarely within and as a product of racial conflicts and the holding of blacks in bondage.[102]

The growing importance of ethnologists and their influence created tensions for both proslavery advocates and abolitionists. There emerged a growing concern by defenders of slavery like James Henley Thornwell, a prominent Presbyterian divine in South Carolina, and George Fitzhugh, proslavery theorist in Virginia, that science was not tethered to a religious or Scriptural worldview and that disparaging remarks about the Genesis record could ultimately unravel the Christian social order of the South.[103] For Northern abolitionists like Stowe and Child, however, the aggressiveness they found in American society coincided with what they saw as a growing emphasis on the intellect as the final arbiter of value and meaning. Their attempt to elevate the religious feelings of Africans over and against whites was one response to this problem. A desire for an infusion of a religious sensibility into a power-hungry and intellectualistic culture was evident in their writings. This generally coincided with white Southerners' calls for a deeply religious society with slavery as a central part of its structure. A religiously infused slave home and society were seen as the antidote to the "godless" -isms of abolitionism, socialism, and Jacobinism (a reference to the violence and excesses of the French Revolution). The nature of the slave therefore played a crucial role in both idealized and romanticized conceptions of the American nation.

On July 12, 1854, before an audience at Western Reserve College, Frederick Douglass found it necessary to give his views on recent ethnological theories of race. The speech was delivered the same year that Josiah C. Nott and George R. Gliddon's *Types of Mankind* was published, a massive work that elucidated the meaning of "ethnology," defined by the authors as a "science which investigates the mental and physical differences" of humans.[104] *Types* was also an apology for slavery, grounding its argument about differences in scientific data and the "natural" capacities of races. It was an important text in disseminating negative ideas about Africa, propounding once again the idea that Africans were incapable of producing a civilization.[105]

Douglass began his speech by arguing for the basic humanity of blacks. Though concerned with the massive ethnological support amassed by Nott, Gliddon, and others as evidence for the inferiority of slaves, his central concern was to defend the humanity of blacks. Douglass also affirmed the unity of

humanity in contradistinction to the theory of separate human species advanced by Nott and Gliddon. He was appalled that "there should arise a pha-
lanx of learned men—speaking in the name of *science*—to forbid the
magnificent reunion of mankind in one brotherhood." Douglass's speech had
a moral fervor and righteously indignant tone to it. Though he clearly understood the "science" of his opponents, he chose to hone in on the moral and
religious bases for human equality and unity. Clearly impatient with the intricate and seemingly dispassionate scientific writings that produced support
for the inferiority of Africans and infuriated with what he knew to be the social
and political power of the entire ethnological enterprise to sustain and construct racial differences, Douglass chose to emphasize the moral dimensions of
his topic.[106] Perhaps Nancy Stephan and Sander Gilman help explain Douglass's motives when they assert that African Americans "continued to infuse
discussions of race with theological, moral, and political concern" even as a
"purely factual" science was appealed to by whites. Douglass's appeal to morality and human rights stood as a powerful expression of resistance to "scientific silence" on questions of value and meaning.[107]

White Southerners throughout the antebellum period continued to elaborate, with or without the explicit support of the new science of ethnology, on
the slave character and what slavery "offered" the slave. White Southerners
universally held that blacks were inferior to whites. Although Fitzhugh professed to abhor the notion that blacks were members of another species, an
argument advanced by the polygenesists, he wrote that Southern slavery relieved blacks from "a far more cruel slavery in Africa, or from idolatry and
cannibalism, and every brutal vice and crime that can disgrace humanity."
Fitzhugh argued that slavery "christianizes, protects, supports and civilizes"
blacks. Slavery imposed external control over a people who lacked self-control
and who were supposedly dominated by impulse, passion, and physical appetites.[108] The elucidation of an elaborate defense of slavery was therefore based
on a massive denigration of the character of black slaves and did not require
ethnology or "racial science" per se to make the case for black inferiority (at least
not prior to the Civil War).

Longing for a Christian Negro Nationality: America or Africa?

African American leaders joined in this debate about black character. Leonard
Sweet suggests that even before the Civil War blacks claimed as part of the
heritage of slavery a moral and spiritual superiority to their white oppressors.
Sweet contends that this was seen as a "superiority of practice" in relation to

the professions of white American Christians. Some black leaders also argued, he maintains, that slave suffering opened blacks to the workings of divine grace. In the first half of the nineteenth century, though, few black commentators would have claimed that avarice (seen as the animating power behind slavery) or other vices were constituent racial traits of Anglo-Saxons. Assertions of the moral or spiritual superiority of blacks were grounded on environmental conditioning rather than racial characteristics: Blacks were deemed superior not because of inherent moral virtues or racial traits but because they had endured the horrors of slavery and had relied more fully on God because of their oppressed condition. Some quoted various Scriptures, indicating that the meek and lowly would be blessed and inherit the Earth. Blacks felt a group affinity that was based on shared experiences and similar conditions of oppression. The notion that blacks shared an essential, distinctive racial genius (similar to the romantic racialism of white Northerners) was at best latent in the thought of black leaders in the early nineteenth century.[109]

Wilson Jeremiah Moses has argued that the first full-blown expression of black nationalism emerged in the 1850s, partly as a result of disillusionment with the course of political events in the nation. The claims of the black nationalists resembled those of the romantic racialists in important ways. Martin Delany, Alexander Crummell, and other early nationalists advocated a form of racial chauvinism that lauded the moral and aesthetic capacities of blacks. Delany and Crummell in particular were intent on Christianizing and civilizing the continent of Africa. They supported colonization, even though both thought that blacks had much to gain from proximity to the virtues of Anglo-Saxons. The notion of inherent traits and native characteristics appeared throughout their writings. This was a move away from previous environmental depictions of black capacities, which had dominated black thought. After the Civil War, Crummell offered a theory of providential history in which their "aboriginal traits" suited blacks for morally superior work in the future. Crummell explicitly acknowledged his indebtedness to William Ellery Channing and Alexander Kinmont, but by then his theories had begun to resemble the thinking of racial theories of that time, which posited radical distinctions between blacks and whites.[110]

This debate became even more intense as sectional divisions over slavery turned more acrimonious during the 1850s.[111] That decade witnessed a series of important changes in American society that incited major debates about the future of blacks in America. The Fugitive Slave Law of 1850 and the *Dred Scott* decision of the Supreme Court in 1857 evoked deep disillusionment for abolitionists and black leaders. The Fugitive Slave Law, which was part of the Compromise of 1850, denied alleged slaves a jury trial or the right to testify on their own behalf. It also provided for the enforcement of the act by newly appointed federal commissioners as well as federal marshals, and the U.S. military if necessary. Stowe exclaimed that she could not bear the thought of "Christian and humane people actually recommending the remanding of escaped fugitives into slavery."[112] Much resistance to the law ensued in the North.

Even more disturbing for many abolitionists, the *Dred Scott* decision of 1857 carried the imprimatur of the highest court in the land, the U.S. Supreme Court. Chief Justice Roger Taney held that blacks, even if they were free, could never be considered citizens of the United States and thus did not have a right to sue in federal courts. Reflecting on his opinion of the founder's frame of thought respecting blacks, Taney wrote: "They [Negro slaves] had for more than a century before been regarded as beings of an inferior order, and altogether unfit to associate with the white race, either in social or political relations; and so far inferior, that they had no rights which the white man was bound to respect." Taney also held that Congress lacked the power to prohibit slavery in any federal territories. The Missouri Compromise, which had banned slavery in the vast territories north and west of the state of Missouri, was declared unconstitutional. Sectional disputes became increasingly bitter. Discussions of emigration and colonization revived, and the question of a black nationality flourishing in Africa became even more salient. It is no surprise, then, that Stowe's *Uncle Tom's Cabin* ends with George Harris writing about the future of blacks in Africa. According to Stowe's own testimony, the Fugitive Slave Law was a major factor in her decision to write her work. This revival of talk about colonization, however, should not obscure the fact that the prospect of colonization had brought together the free black community much sooner than the sectional and political problems of the 1850s. From its very founding, the American Colonization Society had become an object of criticism by free blacks. As Sweet writes: "The commotion over the meaning, methods and motives of the American Colonization Society did more to generate black solidarity and engender a sense of identity among the black community than any other single issue in the first half of the nineteenth century."[113] Articulate black responses to claims of black inferiority became more common as colonizationist plans attracted greater attention from 1816 onward and organized black protests culminated in the formation of the National Negro Convention movement in 1830.[114]

However, black opposition to colonization should not be overemphasized such that the desire of some free blacks, especially those disillusioned at the depth and virulence of racism in America, for a Christianized Africa and a Negro nationality (as it was labeled in the nineteenth century) is minimized. As

James Campbell writes, "The idea that they had been ordained to carry Christianity and civilization back to the land of their foreparents struck a cord with many black Christians."[115] Even among blacks who were hostile to the American Colonization Society, emigration was not entirely rejected as long as it was voluntary and initiated by blacks.[116] Among those blacks who favored emigration, such as Massachusetts seaman Paul Cuffe, the desire to bring Christianity to Africa and the benefits of civilization were the dominant motives. But such sentiments for emigration were not very popular with most black leaders during the 1830s and the 1840s, in part because of their opposition to the plans of the American Colonization Society.[117] During the 1850s, however, a revival of emigration sentiment occurred, due in part to political events that brought great disillusionment to the prospects for free blacks in the United States.

Still, black Northerners were skeptical about white assertions of romantic racialism and began associating it with schemes for colonization. In an open letter to Frederick Douglass, written in 1852, William G. Allen, an African American professor of rhetoric and belles-lettres at Central College in McGrawville, New York, defended Horace Mann, known as a friend of blacks, from the criticisms of blacks in New Bedford, Massachusetts. Mann, an educational reformer in Massachusetts and then a member of the national House of Representatives, had sent a letter to the Colored Convention in Cincinnati in which he argued that Africans were inferior in intellect to Caucasians but superior in sentiment and affection. The New Bedford members of the Colored Convention construed Mann's comments as favoring colonization to Africa. Allen defended Mann's "sincere love" for blacks, even though he wrote that he differed from Mann, particularly in his argument that Mann regarded black Americans as an "African race." Allen wrote that blacks were a composite group in America. Mann did not, Allen asserted, intend to support colonization, as blacks in New Bedford believed. But according to Allen's report, Mann's comments were a welcome support of Allen's beliefs that the "heart is king of the head" and the African would stand "at the head of a true civilization" in the future when "calculating intellect" was not the sole determiner of value and meaning in American society. Allen also commended Mann for suggesting that Africans were superior in affection and sentiment to all "races," Mongolian and others, not just Caucasians. Allen gave Mann the benefit of the doubt. While he could not be sure if "Mann has outgrown fully the prejudice of color which he learned in his youth," Allen believed that it was not wrong for Mann to offer a theory that was "considered scientifically."[118] Although Allen indicated that other blacks were willing to acknowledge that Mann meant no harm to blacks by his remarks, it is difficult to believe that Mann's comments, given as they were by a respected leader who had engaged in extensive educational reform and worked with immigrant groups, were not viewed with some alarm by other blacks, as was seen in the protests of the New Bedford Colored Convention.[119] Linking Mann's comments about blacks' alleged affectionate nature with worries about his alleged support of colonization is also an indication that colonizationist sentiment was connected in the minds of blacks with this particular religious image of Africans.

Though Douglass may have been certain, as he wrote to Stowe, that the "truth is, dear madam, we [blacks] are *here*, and here we are likely to remain," the same could not be said for other literate and free Northern blacks who wrote about black prospects in America.[120] The same year that Stowe's book was published (1852) and a year before Douglass wrote these words, his long-term associate and fellow publisher, Martin Delany, had become utterly disillusioned at the prospects of blacks living peacefully in America. Writing to William Lloyd Garrison, Delany gloomily concluded, "I must admit, that I have no hopes in this country—no confidence in the American people—with a few excellent exceptions—therefore I have written as I have done. Heathenism and Liberty, before Christianity and slavery!"[121] Although Douglass and other black Northerners had a favorable view of Stowe's *Uncle Tom's Cabin*, Delany not only criticized her for promoting colonization but argued that she did not really know free blacks and that she manifested "no sympathy whatever with the tortured feelings, crushed spirits and outraged homes of the Free Colored people."[122] Delany wrote to Douglass, "Although Mrs. Stowe has ably, eloquently and pathetically [that is, with great feeling] portrayed some of the sufferings of the slave, is it any evidence that she has sympathy for his thrice-morally crucified, semi-free brethren any where, or of the *African race* at all?"[123] Delany felt that Stowe and other whites could not envision living among free and independent blacks, though Douglass vigorously dissented from this view. From Delany's vantage point, the romantic racialist evocation of sympathy for blacks had its limitations. It did not extend to free blacks.

Martin Delany (1812–885) was the leading advocate of black nationalism in the mid-nineteenth century. After spending one term studying medicine at Harvard College, he was forced to leave because of student protests. Delany was one of three black males who applied to Harvard's Medical School during the academic year 1850–1851 under the auspices of the American Colonization Society. They were allowed to attend for one semester and then dismissed after student protests. Student protests contained the following arguments: that the presence of an inferior race was socially offensive, that the presence of blacks would cheapen a medical degree, and that they had not been informed of the decision to allow black students admittance to the medical school. The faculty decided that it was "inexpedient" to admit these three black students to the medical school, though there were a few opposed to this decision.[124]

Delany became ever more pessimistic about the destiny of blacks after the Fugitive Slave Law took effect. In his influential book, *The Condition, Elevation, Emigration, and Destiny of the Colored People of the United States* (1852), he urged blacks to leave the United States but not the continent because "the continent of America seems to have been designed by Providence as an asylum for all the various nations of the earth." He also exhorted blacks to elevate themselves and overcome those faults of their own that hindered their success. Delany thought the religious temperament of blacks was one chief obstacle to their progress. He believed that the colored races "are highly susceptible of religion; it is a constituent principle of their nature, and an excellent trait in their character. But unfortunately for them, they carry it too far."[125] This statement is consistent with Delany's comments in the *North Star*, an influential black newspaper he coedited with Douglass. In an open letter to Douglass in 1849, Delany had criticized blacks for neglecting meetings and lectures that did not directly pertain to religious matters. He was not heartened that among "our people generally, the church is the Alpha and Omega of all things." Delany complained that young blacks "had no interest in anything but religious meetings." He declared this to be an "error arising from the miserable blunders of our former teachers, instilled into them by their pro-slavery and slaveholding oppressors, thereby the easier to degrade us, and keep us in wretched servility and subjection."[126] He asserted that black churches distracted from meetings and lectures that attacked slavery and brought attention to the wretched conditions of blacks in the country.

In Delany's view, the church was the "only acknowledged public body" among blacks. It was a surrogate state legislature and blacks' only source of information. But for Delany, this was not a good thing because "that which does not emanate from the church, may not expect to interest the people to any considerable extent." During his trip to Lancaster, Pennsylvania, Delany found a general apathy among blacks regarding the problem of slavery. He castigated black leaders for preaching "stale and miserable doctrines, such as the necessity of the colored people being low, humble, dejected, low-spirited, sorrowful, miserable beings, suffering a life of sorrow in order to get to heaven."[127] Delany rejected any religion that hindered a vigorous assault against slavery and that counseled blacks meekly to accept their oppression.

While not explicitly citing the work of the romantic racialists, Delany was reacting against the widespread notion of a religiously submissive black and at the same time advancing similar notions of innate traits of an aesthetic, moral temperament into his black nationalist ideology. He ruefully noted "the secret of the white man's success with all of his wickedness, over the head of the colored man, with all of his religion."[128] Delany disputed the notion that blacks should peacefully submit to slavery. He urged them to realize that God does not expect them to wait for Him to act. Blacks must do for themselves what God has given them the ability to do. In Delany's view, the argument that "man must pray for what he receives, is a mistake, and one that is doing the colored people especially, incalculable harm." Prayer and requests for divine aid have their place, but because of grave misunderstandings, their misuse was bringing great harm to blacks. Delany contended that it was not necessary to be religious to live on Earth and that one glance at the contrast between blacks and whites should have made this clear. He wrote, "It is only necessary, in order to convince our people of their error and palpable mistake in this matter, to call attention to the fact, that there are no people more religious in this Country, than the colored people, and none so poor and miserable as they." This was convincing proof for him that "God sendeth rain upon the just and unjust." Black people must learn that their success in life does not depend on their "religious character." This simple truth should forever dispel from blacks' minds, Delany maintained, that their oppression was a result of God's displeasure. If this were so, the widespread wickedness of whites would have resulted in a curse far worse than what blacks had suffered.[129]

Although Delany rejected the specific attributes usually ascribed to the naturally religious slave (docility, submissiveness, and meekness), his arguments were inextricably bound to the broader discourse of black innate religiosity. In an address before the National Emigration Convention of Colored People, held at Cleveland, Ohio, in 1854, Delany asserted that it was undeniable that blacks possessed the "highest traits of civilization." Blacks were, he maintained, "civil, peaceable and religious to a fault." But like the French, Irish, Germans, and English, they possessed native or "inherent peculiarities." Though "the white race" excelled in mathematics, sculpture, and architecture "as arts and sciences," blacks would "yet instruct the world" in languages, oratory, poetry, music, and painting "as arts and sciences." Compared to whites, who were also gifted in commerce and "internal improvements as enterprises," blacks would make their mark in ethics, metaphysics, theology, jurisprudence, in true principles of morals, "correctness of thought," religion, and law or civil government. Delany wrote that the inherent traits of blacks ought not to be denied but developed and cultivated "in their purity, to make them desirable and emulated by the rest of the world."[130] He felt that the unique gifts of blacks would have to flourish in South America, the West Indies, or Central America because the United States only wanted to keep them enslaved. Delany, at least at this point in his career, held out little hope for a black future in the United

States and therefore counseled blacks to meet the domineering Anglo-Saxon on his own terms, not with prayer but with cannon shot, prepared for the worst but hoping for the best.[131]

Delany's call for black militancy and aggression was given a broader hearing during the 1850s. Stanley Harrold shows that by the late 1850s even some white abolitionists had begun to attack the foundations of romantic racialism. They grew impatient with the submissive, feminine, Christ-like qualities said to be typical of black slaves. Thus in 1858 Theodore Parker out of apparent exasperation claimed that blacks lacked the courage and "instinct for liberty" that were so strong among Anglo-Saxons. Because of the strength of their "affectional instinct," which attached them to others by "tender ties," blacks did not lash out against their oppressors. If they had, Parker averred, the "stroke of an axe would have settled the matter long ago." But alas, blacks would not strike![132] So they continued to suffer under their white oppressors. As sectional disputes grew more bitter and rancorous and many braced for a divided nation, the "necessity" of opposing slavery by force became the only real option for some abolitionists. John Brown's raid on Harper's Ferry in 1859 even moved some of the most peaceable abolitionists to laud slave insurrections. So it does appear that on the eve of the Civil War some leading abolitionists no longer found it helpful to advance the notion of the naturally religious and feminine slave character. But this was obviously a complicated issue for African American abolitionists, and even some white antislavery advocates continued to evoke the notion of a naturally religious slave, hoping that a Christian Negro nationality could some day flourish in America or Africa.[133]

In the midst of these debates by blacks, the romantic racialist conception of blacks still persisted among some whites opposed to slavery, but even among those who held this image of blacks radically different directions for the future of blacks were proposed. Colonization to Africa or an uncertain future in the United States represented the two basic options. Colonization among whites whom Moses labels "benevolent conservatives" reflected a deep disillusionment with the political events of the 1850s; the growth of slavery in the Western territories, particularly Kansas and Nebraska; and the depth of racial prejudice and oppression in America.[134] Hollis Read, a white Congregationalist minister in Cranford, New Jersey, and a former missionary to India, reflected the long-standing Christian defense of colonization when he suggested in 1864 that the Negro problem could be solved only by blacks emigrating to Africa and developing a "Christian negro nationality." Read envisioned an Africa with an "enlightened commerce" bolstered by an extensive scheme of colonization, with a Christian government, laws, and institutions "all baptized in the spirit of Christianity." Read called on missionaries, philanthropists, and Christians to do their duty by assisting in this great task so that Africa would have a place among the nations. As the "exiled sons" of Africa, blacks in the United States would bring to this vast continent "all the good things" they had learned in the land of their bondage and in the "school of a rigorous discipline" they had gone through. All of this, in Read's view, would help the oppressed children of Africa recover some of what they had lost and make partial sense of the long night of sorrow that American blacks had endured.[135]

Read had mixed feelings about the place of blacks in the United States. He acknowledged that they had every right to remain in this country. It was their country just as much as it belonged to whites. Nor did he offer colonization as an adequate remedy for slavery, though he quickly noted that it would have "legitimate bearings on that whole system of bondage and degradation." Yet Read did urge blacks in America to feel a duty to their fatherland and to their "race." He advised them to go forth, "even if it be at a personal sacrifice," as agents who will "rescue a continent from the low depths of social, civil, and moral debasement." American blacks possessed the privilege to go their fatherland and to raise up the African continent. Though Read called for universal, unconditional emancipation as the first and immediate solution to the Negro problem (he also held that slavery was *the* cause of the raging Civil War), he believed that the final destiny of blacks was to attain a full nationality in Africa. He wrote, "We feel safe in connecting the highest and best destiny of the colored man with his fatherland."[136] In his mind, God was bringing freedom to American blacks and would restore them, like the ancient Israelites, to their homeland.

Read's descriptions of Africa and its tropical wonders were remarkably similar to Stowe's narrative comments in *Uncle Tom's Cabin* about the gorgeousness and splendor of that vast land. Stowe's vivid images of an Africa with gold, gems, and waving palms were linked to a psychological portrait of a Christian and meek people made pliable and gentle by a tropical environment and centuries of oppression.[137] Similarly, Read presented Africa as a land of rich soil, forests, and mines waiting to be cultivated by "an inviting capital, enterprise, intelligence, skill, civilization, and Christianity," which had been acquired by her transplanted children.[138] Deeply shaped by a tropical environment, the African, Read wrote, was humble, gentle, docile, grateful, and given to a forgiving spirit. Unlike Europeans, they were not ambitious and easily aroused. Like Kinmont, Read believed that blacks possessed a more childlike and "unsophisticated nature" than whites, which made them peculiarly susceptible to Christianity. It was Read's view that Christianity was a mild, peaceful, and softening religion that would "ultimately find in Africa, and in eastern climes, a soil congenial and peculiar to itself." Perhaps as part of their distinctive temperament, Read maintained, "religious susceptibility and moral dispositions are the more marked characteristics of the negro family." This religious sensibility made blacks very different from whites. Wherever whites went, Read asserted, they were likely to build first a bank or a trading house, but the first effort of blacks was to construct a meeting house to worship.[139]

Read insisted that it was in the interests of blacks to go to Africa because the prejudices against them in America, whatever their causes, were so deep that no law could repeal them. So profound were the differences between whites and blacks, Read claimed, that whites would never change their negative sentiments about black people. No sensible person, Read argued, would plead for amalgamation in the face of this deep aversion to blacks. Apparently, God, "by giving different constitutions and complexions to great branches of the human family," intended blacks and whites to be kept separate. The slave trade violated this divine allotment and dragged Africans to America, where they simply did not belong. God had prepared a better home for them in Africa.[140]

Read was happy to report that he found support for his views in the writings of Edward Wilmot Blyden, then a professor at Liberia College. Blyden was born in the West Indies, came to the United States in 1850, and settled in Liberia in 1851. He became a leading spokesman for African colonization. Blyden's emphasis on Africa as the center where "the race" could develop its physical, spiritual, commercial, and intellectual strength held deep appeal to white romantic racialists like Read.[141] Yet for all his enthusiasm for a Negro nationality, Read concluded that in Africa this nationality should be "fashioned after the Anglo-Saxon mould and vitalized by a living Christianity." What Africa needed, Read insisted, was Christianity, civilization, industry, enterprise, education of the masses, and all the "higher departments of learning." All of these qualities comprised the "Anglo-Saxon type of life." Only the redeemed children of Africa, who had benefited from the virtues of the dominant Anglo-Saxon in America, could bring to Africa what she lacked. Read was careful to add that a Negro nationality had to be vitalized by the religion of the New Testament because this was the "only living, enduring element of a nation's life." As important as commerce, learning, wealth, industry, and enterprise were, they were "mere adjuncts" to the life of a nation.[142]

Read left unresolved his critique of slavery, which was coupled with a belief in its benefits to blacks, and the development of a Negro nationality, though he argued that freed blacks in America had the greatest responsibility in uplifting fellow blacks and bringing to Africa the benefits of a Christian civilization. He gave no indication of how he would sell his plan to free blacks who adamantly rejected colonization to Africa and who identified America as their home. But unlike the romantic racialists who posited a hazy future for blacks in America, Read was clear about the meaning of what he saw as the deep racial differences and the distinctive religious sensibility of Africans. For him, God had not appointed a place for blacks in the United States. Blacks' natural environment was Africa and the U.S. Negro problem could only be solved when blacks were allowed and encouraged to go to Africa to develop their own Christian civilization.

Romantic racialists who envisioned a future for blacks in America were not sure what that future would or could be. One work in particular in these years sought to predict and influence future relations between blacks and whites. It was prepared by Robert Dale Owen, a reformer from Indiana who had served as a member of the U.S. House of Representatives from 1843 to 1847.[143] Owen was a member of the three-man body set up by President Lincoln to recommend policy for the newly emancipated slaves. Their Final Report, under the imprint of the American Freedman's Inquiry Commission, appeared in 1864. The section written by Owen was reprinted in *The Wrong of Slavery; The Right of Emancipation; and The Future of the African Race in the United States.*

Owen's book examined the various obstacles that blacks would face as freed persons and provided an examination of the ways that blacks and whites could work together to form a democratic society. While calling racial amalgamation a great evil, Owen offered a rather general analysis of what blacks and whites had to offer each other and in the process presented one of the most full-blown descriptions to date of the alleged racial distinctions between blacks and whites. He wrote:

The Anglo-Saxon race, with great force of character, much mental activity, an unflagging spirit of enterprise, has a certain hardness, a stubborn will, only moderate geniality, a lack of habitual cheerfulness. Its intellectual powers are stronger than its social instincts. *The head predominates over the heart. There is little that is emotional in its religion.* It is not devoid of instinctive devotion; but neither is such devotion a ruling element. It is a race more calculated to call forth respect than love; better fitted to don than to enjoy. The African race is in many respects the reverse of this. *Genial, lively, docile, emotional, the affections rule;* the social instincts maintain the ascendant. Except under cruel repression, its cheerfulness and love of mirth overflow with the exuberance of childhood. *It is devotional by feeling.* It is a knowing rather than a thinking race ... It is not a race that will ever take a lead in the material improvement of the world; but it will make for itself, whenever it has fair play, respectable positions,

comfortable homes. As regards the virtues of humility, loving-kind-
ness, resignation under adversity, reliance on Divine Providence,
this race exhibits these, as a general rule, in a more marked manner
than does the Anglo-Saxon.[144]

Clearly, three decades of public discourse about the naturally religious slave
found expression in Owen's work. Present in it were the strong and virile
features of the Anglo-Saxon as identified by Theodore Parker in the mid- to late
1850s. Owen's hope that with time the "Christian graces of meekness and long-
suffering [as exhibited by black slaves] will be rated higher than the world rates
them now" recalled Child's desire for Africans to have a prominent place in the
coming "age of Moral Sentiment" and Stowe's longing (in the mouthpiece of
George Harris) for a Christian age when the African race would take a prominent station at the table of nations. Owen expected that blacks would be able
to bring a "softening influence" that would "make itself felt as an element of
improvement in the national character." The African race, he hoped, would also
"gain much from us." He believed freed men and women would profit from
their contact with whites' "force of character, in mental cultivation, in self-
reliance, in enterprise, in breadth of views, and in habits of generalization."
Owen envisioned a peaceful future for blacks in American society, though
clearly he believed that blacks needed the virtues of the Anglo-Saxon more than
whites needed the virtues of blacks.[145] Even so, no specific political or economic
program was spelled out in this policy recommendation for the president,
which is quite surprising because Owen had years of practical political experience in one of the nation's highest political offices. Nothing was said about
blacks and whites sharing power, which partly reflected his belief that blacks
would never take the lead in making a "material improvement" to the world.
Apparently it was unthinkable to move beyond vague generalizations about the
religious sentiments and domestic attachments of an African alien in the midst
of a putatively Anglo-Saxon civilization.

A Dissenting Voice

There was one major dissenting voice among white opponents of slavery in the
antebellum period whose views of slave religious practices prefigured the
representations of black religion advanced by Northern missionaries and
teachers after the Civil War. Frederick Law Olmsted, noted travel writer and
landscape architect, provided one of the most thorough contemporary evaluations of slave life in the South. Unlike certain travelers who lived for one or two

months in the South, Olmsted spent fourteen months spread over two separate trips in 1852–1853 in the seaboard slave states and in 1853–1854 through Texas and the back country. He published a number of articles as a special correspondent for the *New York Daily Times* from 1854 to 1857. After doing substantial research in New York libraries and reading widely in Northern and Southern newspapers and agricultural journals, Olmsted's first book of his trilogy was published in January 1856 as *Journey in the Seaboard Slave States.* This was followed in 1857 by the second volume, *A Journey through Texas.* The final book, *A Journey in the Back Country*, appeared in 1860. *The Cotton Kingdom*, an abridgement and substantial revision of the trilogy, was published in 1861, when Olmsted accepted an offer to become executive secretary of the U.S. Sanitary Commission. Although he was not an advocate for immediate abolition, Olmsted considered slavery a moral evil and hoped to keep it from expanding. So his writings were inevitably and inextricably involved in the debate over slavery. A great deal of his work sought to demonstrate that slavery was economically unprofitable because of its demoralizing influence on labor, and this point was especially crucial in Olmsted's evaluations of black religious life under slavery.[146]

Olmsted found much to criticize in his journeys, and the religion of blacks was a specific object of his criticism. In a *New York Daily Times* article published in 1853, he doubted that an Uncle Tom character was "natural" or "altogether consistent" under the conditions of slave life. None of the language about a naturally affectionate and religiously exemplary slave found its way in Olmsted's work, in marked contrast to the writings of the romantic racialists. He asserted that the "mind and faculties of the negro are less disciplined and improved in slavery than in the original barbarism of the race." This was a direct refutation of the claims of proslavery apologists who argued that the civilizing and Christianizing influence of slavery lifted Africans from their barbarism and paganism. Olmsted insisted that slavery forced blacks into a "stupid, unmanly, and animal" existence. Rather than lifting them to manhood, he maintained, slavery instead reduced blacks to mere babes. Slavery, in his view, was the cause of the degraded condition of slaves.[147]

Olmsted argued that it was doubtful that as many slaves were converted to Christianity as was often claimed by those who defended bringing the faith to African "savages." He asserted that a profession of faith among the slaves was founded on the "exhibition of certain phrensied states of imagination, excitable at will in any mind not habitually disciplined to the control of reason, and in the direction of words and actions according to certain precepts and formulas." Among these religious practices of black slaves, Olmsted wrote, were delirium, madness, and even catalepsy. "Blind obedience to certain rules of conduct," he claimed, "which they have been taught to consider of supernatural importance, and slavish reverence to certain days and words and things, are as habitual among the Fetish worshippers of Africa as among their transplanted cousins, the baptized and enrolled church-members of America." Although black slaves in America had a "better" morality and "superstition" than their African ancestors, and reflected something *"more like* [what] Christianity prompts a man to," their religion was not to be equated with true Christianity. It was "no more the same thing than a rush light is a sunbeam."[148]

This characterization of the religious practices of slaves led Olmsted to compare slave religion to his normative vision of true Christianity. He argued that true Christianity can only be defined practically as a principle of the heart which "manifests itself in the constantly progressive, moral elevation of the individual." The religion of the slaves, Olmsted continued, hardly fit this description. It degraded their manhood; trained them in cowardice, imbecility, and duplicity of mind; and destroyed a sense of "high individual responsibility." For this reason, he insisted, the Christianity brought to the slaves could hardly be a compensation or "palliation" for the wrongs that they had endured under slavery. After all, Olmsted argued, slavery could not be shown to have produced any substantive Christianity among blacks because by its very nature slavery was "most strongly opposed to the reception in the hearts of its subjects anything that can be reverently dignified with the holy name of Christianity."[149]

Olmsted expressed surprise at the "crazy jocular manner" in which slaves talked of the religious ecstasies into which they often fell and noted with amazement the "frequency with which the slaves use religious phrases of all kinds" and the "readiness with which they engage in what are deemed religious exercises." These frequent religious conversations, he wrote, gave one the initial impression that genuine Christianity existed among the slaves. But alas, their "religion," Olmsted declared, was but a strange mixture of superstition and fanaticism, attested to by the frequent conversations that slaves alleged that they had with Jesus, the apostles, or the prophets of old. He was horrified that some slaves accounted for some of their actions by attributing them to the direct influence of the Holy Spirit or the devil. Olmsted contended that there was nothing meek or gentle about these slaves; rather, they were susceptible to revolt if another intensely religious figure like Nat Turner came along to incite them.[150] Here Olmsted had returned full circle to the worries of eighteenth-century slave owners who feared that slave Christianization could lead to insurrection rather than docility, but he proposed a deeper study of the Bible and more education for the slave population to counter the dangers he perceived in their incomplete conversion to Christianity as he understood it. Olmsted ominously wrote:

It seems to me that this state of mind is fraught with more danger to their masters than any to which they could possibly have been brought by general and systematic education, and by the unrestricted study of the Bible, even though this involved what is so much dreaded, but which is, I suspect, an inevitable accompaniment of moral elevation, the birth of an ambition to look out for themselves. Grossly ignorant and degraded in mind, with a crude, undefined, and incomplete system of theology and ethics, credulous and excitable, intensely superstitious and fanatical, what better field could a cunning monomaniac or a sagacious zealot desire in which to set on foot an appalling crusade?[151]

Olmsted insisted that slavery and its harsh environment had degraded blacks, but at times his arguments mirrored prevailing concepts of innate racial differences that accounted for the "peculiar" religious practices of black slaves. Although Olmsted professed that blacks were capable of "indefinite elevation" and offered an environmentalist argument for differences between blacks and whites, he propounded theories of racial types to explain slave religious practices.[152] For example, he argued that the "African races, compared with the white, at least with the Teutonic, have greater vanity or love of approbation, a stronger dramatic and demonstrative character, more excitability, less exact or analytic minds, and a nature more sensuous, though (perhaps from want of cultivation) less refined." These racial differences, he continued, clarified why blacks took pleasure in bright, "strongly contrasting colors" and in music ("in which nearly all are proficient to some extent") and why blacks were less adapted for steady, uninterrupted labor than whites. Yet, Olmsted asserted, blacks were superior to whites "in feats demanding agility and tempestuous energy."[153] Still, he held that education would help them overcome the handicaps under which they suffered because of slavery.

In a vivid description of a slave church service in New Orleans, Olmsted recorded his account of shouts, groans, "terrific shrieks," and "indescribable expressions of ecstasy." Feet stamping, jumping, and clapping hands roused him to heightened curiosity and fear. Olmsted noted that the "tumult often resembled that of an excited political meeting; and I was once surprised to find my own muscles all stretched, as if ready for a struggle—my face glowing, and my feet stamping—having been infected unconsciously, as men often are, with instinctive bodily sympathy with the excitement of the crowd."[154] He surmised that the preaching was so "wholly unintellectual" that its effect must have been the "action" of the preacher rather than the "sentiments" (i.e., rational discourse) that imparted meaning or instruction to the mind. Olmsted noticed the ritual aspects of slave religious practice in this particular instance and did not regard them as debased imitations of white Southern religious practices. In fact, he reported with a special keenness on the various aspects of the worship service that dramatized the communal nature of ritual action as it was recip-rocated between the preacher and the church members.[155]

As a critic of slavery, an astute observer, and a serious student of Southern culture, Olmsted provided one of the most complete reflections on black re-ligion during the antebellum period. His negative assessment of slave religion prefigured the critiques of black religion that proliferated after the Civil War. Olmsted's lucid and detailed writings contained some of the most vivid de-scriptions and interpretations of black religion from a white Northerner. He had many interests in his travels to the South, and pointing out the problems of labor in the slave system was one of the most prominent. His psychology of the slave temperament, however, is most relevant to our discussion. Olmsted's emphasis on the African temperament and his focus on what he regarded as the lack of reason in black religion and its alleged failure to promote self-discipline were themes that would begin to dominate white Northerners' cri-tiques of black religion after the Civil War.

Conclusion

It was curious that white Christians, who presumably believed that all humans had a common spiritual nature, adopted the argument that blacks were pe-culiarly religious. The desire to evoke sympathy for the benighted and op-pressed slave was laudable and seems to have become the principal force in the creation of the naturally docile, gentle, and religious slave. But assumptions about racial variation and permanent racial differences, which only deepened in time, were also crucial to the promulgation of this image. Not only that, but the longing to find in blacks what was seen as lacking in the specific historical and social contexts that certain white Americans found themselves in was so strong that they projected onto blacks those virtues that could seemingly de-liver the needed spiritual, psychological, and moral goods. Blacks had become the pivot for the critique of modern bourgeois culture, a theme that would recur in later cultural depictions of black religion.

The contention about natural religiosity was so inextricably wrapped up in the language of race that it was strongly rejected by the social scientists of the twentieth century, who repudiated such notions as a racial genius or innate religiosity. Its link to assertions of black intellectual inferiority and claims about the aggressiveness of Anglo-Saxons were indications that it was a product of its time and had limited historical usefulness. Romantic racialists described *and prescribed* idealized naturally religious blacks as sacrificial lambs for the sins of America, especially in Stowe's *Uncle Tom's Cabin*. The romantic racialist notion of blacks was a symbol of a racial destiny that was never quite specified in terms of its actual features in a historical time and place. Its expectations and plans for black flourishing in the nation were tentative and shallow and easily wilted under the forces of scientific racism and the massive moral critiques of black culture that emerged in the post–Civil War period and later in the nineteenth century.

2

Black Religion in the New Nation: Outside the Boundaries of Whiteness

Reevaluations of black religion were under way as soon as Northern missionaries came into sustained contact with freed persons. The affectionate and naturally religious Negro imagined and constructed by the romantic racialists became the emotionally extravagant Negro to white missionaries (and even to some black missionaries). The social, cultural, and political forces that sustained sympathy for the weak and genial slave had passed. A new era had dawned, and new conditions prevailed in which a different kind of religious temperament was theorized for blacks. Criticism of black religion certainly existed in the antebellum period, as noted in chapter 1, but the dominant way of speaking about black slaves by a number of influential Northern abolitionists was the romantic racialist claim about innate religiosity, a relatively benign view constructed over against racist conceptions of blacks. Among the successors and legatees of the abolitionists, this discourse of romantic racialism fell out of favor and was transmuted into a negative reinterpretation of black religion. Feelings became unruly emotions, and innate religiosity now meant the possession of a primitive or culturally inferior form of bodily religious expression. What developed by the late 1870s was a convergence of Southern and Northern interpretations of black culture, except that the latter believed that progress was possible through education and exposure to "higher" culture, whereas the former argued that blacks were racially inferior to whites and would remain indefinitely in a subordinate position to whites in the South.

Thomas Gossett notes, "The difference in attitude toward the Negro before and after the Civil War is striking ... The lofty strain is not generally found in the literature concerning the Negro which followed the Civil War—not in the South, and increasingly not in the North ... What replaces [the benevolent image of blacks] is an undisguised hatred of the Negro which portrays him as little if any better than a beast."[1] These more negative characterizations of African American Christianity corresponded with the following: (1) more sustained contact with blacks by missionaries to the South; (2) cultural differences between the freed persons and the Northern missionaries; (3) newer (Victorian) expectations for a religion of decorum and propriety, which inculcated habits of industry, discipline, and self-control; and (4) evolving discussions in the language of social science about primitive dark-skinned peoples and their alleged inability to fit into the new nation.

Reflecting in 1874 on his work among a black regiment in the Sea Islands, South Carolina, during the Civil War, abolitionist Thomas Wentworth Higginson indicated that he "was prepared to see much more degradation than ever showed itself" among the blacks with whom he worked.[2] White and black missionaries anticipated encountering blacks who were degraded and scarred—physically and psychically—by a lifetime of bondage and in desperate need of "regeneration and civilization," and black culture was seen in terms of what it lacked: refinement, culture, discipline, and industry. Northern whites held that blacks deeply needed instruction in frugality, temperance, honesty, and the dignity of labor. James McPherson argues that criticisms of black churches by the legatees of abolitionism after the Civil War were common. Protestant missionary societies, the American Missionary Association (AMA) the most prominent among them, portrayed black religion as an "amalgam of camp-meeting emotionalism, amoral pietism, and pagan occultism."[3] As Eric Foner writes, freedmen's education aimed simultaneously to equip blacks to take advantage of citizenship and to remake the culture that they had inherited from slavery, as this culture was understood by Northern whites.[4] The "excesses" of black religion were viewed as one of the main problems of black culture. By paying close attention to how black religion was imagined and reinterpreted, we encounter a negative assessment of black prospects in the new nation. This emphasis on interpretations of African American religion therefore leads me to qualify Edward Blum's recent claim that white Northern Protestants in the 1860s espoused a civic nationalism that advanced a "racially egalitarian ideology that viewed former slaves as full American citizens."[5] Because blacks attached so much importance to their churches (as white Northerners themselves testified), it is highly unlikely that they could be incorporated into the new nation if a radical reconstruction (or overthrow, as some Northern whites desired) of their religious practices was the precondition of their active participation. My conclusion, however, bolsters Blum's general narrative, which demonstrates that more radically racist notions of blacks, particularly as white Northerners coincided with and reinforced Southern views, become more fully articulated and enforced by law by the late nineteenth century.

Although initially pleased that many black Southerners were Christians, Northern white teachers and missionaries found much that deeply disturbed them in the religious practices of the ex-slaves. Some 5,000 Northern teachers, most of them from New England, made this trek to the South during and after the Civil War.[6] By 1869, over 9,000 teachers, black and white, were employed in the freedmen's schools, and over half of them were women.[7] Motivated by deeply rooted religious and humanitarian impulses, the religious biases of these teachers and missionaries led them to call for a radical reconstruction of black culture and religion. As Lawrence Levine writes, these missionaries "rarely wavered in their conviction that their pupils had to be reconstructed in almost every particular from the rudiments of learning to their style of worship, from their habits of cleanliness to the structure of their families, from their moral fiber to their manner of speaking and pronunciation."[8] Efforts to purify the religion of the freed persons were a major part of this attempt to reconstruct the fundamental basis of their culture. Purifying the religion of blacks entailed pointing out the "heathenish" customs of black religion, instructing the freed persons in the proper interpretation of the Bible, and admonishing Southern blacks about what white Northerners saw as their ubiquitous vices: sexual immorality, theft, lying, and lack of punctuality.[9] Apart from Northern white influence, black religion was deemed by Northerners a failure in inculcating morality and self-control in the black masses and was thus judged as impractical in preparing blacks to become fit citizens of the new nation.

White Northerners Reevaluate Black Religion

In May 1866, Charles Stearns took up residence in Columbia County, Georgia. Having spent much of his life in Massachusetts, Stearns was known as a radical abolitionist. In 1854, he went to Kansas, abandoned his pacifism, and took up a Sharp's rifle. After the Civil War, he argued for education, voting rights, and landownership for black Americans. Stearns purchased a 1,500-acre plantation in Georgia and there formed a cooperative commonwealth, where he intended to share the profits with his black employees. Stearns insisted that blacks possessed all of the natural capacities that whites possessed. By 1872, however, Stearns's views about blacks had begun to change. After years of close encounters with blacks, Stearns expressed deep disappointment at black progress. He claimed to witness a lack of punctuality among black workers and long worship services that vied for the freed persons' time and interest in physical labor. Stearns especially lamented the "failure of the black peoples' religion to make them into obedient laborers." His defense for criticizing black Christianity was that a moral religion was essential to the nation. Stearns contended:

> First and foremost in the regeneration of any nation or people, must their religious institutions be moulded into the forms of morality, or else it is in vain to preach morality to the *people*. If the saints of a nation can be immoral, of course its sinners will be doubly so, or at least they will never be any better than the sanctified ones are. In proof of this assertion you have only to look at the character of all nations where an immoral religion prevails. Therefore, if you would reform the freedmen of the South, you must commence with their religion, and no efforts corresponding with the mighty interests at stake, will ever be put forth to accomplish this task, until the Northern people are made fully acquainted with the hideous evil here exposed.[10]

Stearns warned that if white Northerners did not do their duty thoroughly and quickly, within twenty-five years the South would be awash with black immorality. He invoked horrid visions of the future in which "fearful waves of social vice engendered and taught by the *religion* of the *Southern negroes*" (emphasis in original) and a "mighty engine" of black immorality would sweep over the South, unless white Northerners would take up their solemn responsibility to reform the freed persons.[11] Stearns felt that the transformation of black religion should be a central priority for the nation and for black progress in and incorporation into the new nation.

Stearns was not making the simple claim that the religion of the freed persons contained a few excesses. Rather, he argued that blacks' religion made them totally unfit for productive citizenship in a reconstructing nation. He argued that black "saints," for example, were of all blacks the most dishonest and lazy. They lacked any interest in education, he insisted, and practiced every conceivable vice. Their "religious exercises," Stearns continued, began around nine o'clock in the evening and lasted until midnight (and until the break of day, in some instances). Until their benevolent white friends came to them, Stearns argued, the freed persons were apparently never taught that their religion should regulate their daily lives. Religion for them was merely about praying, dancing, and singing in religious meetings. Stearns recalled asking a young girl named Priscilla, who claimed to have had a religious experience, if she had ever been taught that genuine religion would make her a better girl *and* cause her to do her work more faithfully. She responded, "I never knew that religion had any thing to do with my work."[12]

What appeared to be religion among blacks, Stearns claimed, was a mass of "heathenish observances," "insane yellings," and violent contortions of the body that provided proof that the race was "thoroughly demented." Such religious "mummery" and unhallowed performances deeply offended Stearns. As painful as it was, he asserted, it was necessary "to show the utter falsity of the pretentions [*sic*] of the blacks to be in possession of the religion taught by our Lord and Saviour Jesus Christ."[13] One way of demonstrating this point was to show that blacks practiced a religion that was entirely unknown to white Christians in the South or "any other class of people" in the United States. The foundation of these weird religious practices, Stearns surmised, lay in Africa. He recounted a conversation with a "Northern gentleman" who told him that he had witnessed something similar to Southern black religious "all night meetings" on the coast of Africa, where he had spent the past two years. Stearns recalled a discussion with "another Northern gentleman" whose time in the Fiji Islands made clear to him that the religious services of blacks in the South "resembled, very nearly, those of the cannibal-worshipers on those ill-fated Islands, only that ours [black worshippers' religious services] were not followed by a feast on human flesh, as he had witnessed in the case of the islands mentioned."[14] Perhaps, too, Stearns intimated, this connection explained why blacks seldom had a conviction of sin or a "deep sense of having wronged a holy God" even after they professed to have had a religious experience. Stearns's search for the reasons behind the defects and the distinctiveness of black religion led him to posit that the blackness of Africa was probably what darkened the souls of blacks in the South.[15]

Although Stearns said that he was convinced that blacks were educable and potential intellectual equals with whites, he tallied what he regarded as their distinctive characteristics. Some of these traits were so prevalent, he maintained, that they were inherent to the nature of blacks. These included (1) extreme forms of self-esteem or unlimited confidence; (2) unwillingness to obey any order, (3) lack of vindictiveness, (4) mirthfulness (they "sing eternally in their religious meetings"), (5) love of approbation, (6) lack of punctuality, (7) wastefulness and carelessness, (8) lack of perseverance, (9) conservatism (clinging to old forms and ways of doing things), (10) stealing, and (11) lying.[16] These characteristics were remarkably similar to those posited by proslavery advocates as innate to black character and by those who had doubts about blacks' ability to flourish in a free society. Perhaps Stearns realized this when he noted that common claims like his that blacks were unwilling to work for or obey whites were being made by white planters who hailed the arrival of the Ku Klux Klan. To be sure, Stearns deplored the actions of the Klan and presented an unvarnished account of their violence against blacks. Yet he suggested that planters agreed with him that blacks would not take orders, and therefore they had recourse to the Klan to force blacks to work. There was a deep irony here in that Stearns, a Northerner exposing the "recent outrages" of the Klansmen and other violent white Southern vigilante groups, unwittingly provided support for one of the central defenses of slavery: that blacks, when freed from white control or supervision, would refuse to labor.[17]

Stearns's critique of African American religious practices illustrates the ambiguities of whites who were sympathetic to blacks. Describing and decrying black religion as "enthusiasm" and unbridled emotionalism became even more common as the 1870s wore on. Although constructions of black religion were one part of a complex matrix of ideas about black culture, there is evidence that black religion was a central object of concern partly because of the legacy of romantic racialists of the antebellum period who so frequently wrote about the natural religiosity of blacks. Moreover, as black churches became almost completely separated from white churches in the Reconstruction years, the center of black life became even more crucially expressed in these religious meetings and social spaces that were no longer under direct white supervision.

A reconceptualization of innate religiosity was under way. In the aftermath of the Civil War, natural religiosity came to be regarded as a negative primitive quality that required refinement and discipline, otherwise it could descend into mere religious feeling and emotionalism devoid of practical utility. This new way of looking at the religion of the freed persons was especially evident in the experience of Elizabeth Kilham. Kilham was among the number of Northern teachers who made the trek to the South immediately after the Civil War to bring education, uplift, and civilization to the ex-slave population. In her work among freed persons in Richmond, Virginia, Kilham witnessed the excitement generated by the coming of General Oliver Otis Howard, commissioner of the Freedman's Bureau, to organize a local freedman's bureau and speak to blacks at a local church about the duties and privileges of freedom. What followed Howard's address especially attracted Kilham's attention. She was astounded by the religious worship services of the blacks and the preaching style of the local pastor. The black pastor's "peculiar" interpretation of the Scriptures puzzled Kilham, in part because he found teachings in the Bible which had not been "brought to light by the researches of any commentator."[18] Witnessing scenes that appeared to be the products of a "disordered imagination," she was shocked by the excitement and physicality of black worship. These activities, she wrote, left "an impression like the memory of some horrid nightmare—so wild is the torrent of excitement, that, sweeping away reason and sense, tosses men and women upon its waves, mingling the words of religion with the howlings of wild beasts, and the ravagings of mad men."[19] The emphasis on black religion sweeping away reason is similar to Frederick Law Olmsted's pre–Civil War claims that it was not "disciplined to the control of reason." Northerners in the immediate post–Civil War context, with their emphasis on emotionalism, frenzy, and the loss of reason and self-control, were inching toward the language of psychopathology in their understandings and moral diagnoses of the problems of black worship. For the most part, however, they continued to write and speak as moral critics (that is, as Northern Protestant Christians) in most of their evaluations of the deficiencies they perceived in black Southern religion.

Although Kilham was deeply offended by the worship practices of blacks, she was surprised by her own reaction to the religious aura of their meetings. She sensed an "invisible power" that seemed to hold her and others in its grasp as they were gathered in this church where they were nearly suffocating from the heat and wild excitement. Kilham confessed that the "excitement was working upon us also [other Northern whites?], and sent the blood surging in wild torrents to the brain, that reeled in darkened terror under the shock." A few moments more, she related, even she would have "shrieked in unison with the crowd." Kilham struggled to explain how, on one hand, the physical dominated the mental at these meetings, and yet, on the other hand, for both the "impressionable" ignorant persons and the enlightened and self-controlled, there was a power, terrible in its impact, that made itself felt in these meetings. In her view, it would take another generation before most black worshipers could withstand the pressure to engage in these wild exercises and to begin a more sober and proper form of worship.[20]

Kilham noted that Northern teachers of the freed persons were commonly asked if blacks were universally religious. Most answered "yes," but she felt compelled to dissent. Kilham acknowledged that blacks attended church regularly; they did not deny the faith. But the content of their beliefs and practices and the particular manner of their religious expression deeply troubled her. Kilham's experiences among the freed persons changed her opinion of the value and meaning of their religion. She wrote:

> Before going among the freedmen, I held in common with others,
> the idea that they were naturally religious, and that there was
> both reality and depth in their religious life. "Perfect through suf-
> fering," "purified in the fires," were in our minds; and we judged that

they who had so greatly suffered must needs be thereby greatly purified, and raised to a higher plane of religious life, than we had attained. . . . And so thinking, we forgot that faith is born of knowledge, and this was withheld from them; we forgot that their inability to read made the truths and teachings of the Bible a dead letter to most of them; that the only instruction they received was from men, ignorant as themselves, who jumbled together words and phrases only half caught and not at all understood, in one mass of senseless jargon; and that all their ideas of religion were gathered in noisy meetings, where those who shouted the loudest and jumped the highest, were the best Christians.[21]

Kilham regretted that she and other white Northerners had allowed their sympathy for blacks to overrule their best judgment. While teaching the freed persons in all other branches of learning, she maintained, it was the greatest tragedy that she and other teachers had allowed themselves to be learners instead of teachers in the most important of tasks, instilling religion in blacks. Kilham attempted to mitigate the gravity of her error by attributing it to humility and reverence. Nevertheless, she maintained, an error it was and one that could not now be remedied because the "molding stage of freedom, when these [black] people were as wax in our hands, has passed." The self-confidence of blacks stood as a reproof to the silence of whites to point out the extravagance and error of their worship practices.[22]

Kilham contended that an ignorant religion could never become a "high type of religion." Sincere as blacks may have been, most of them were as "ignorant as heathens of the objects and foundations of our faith." Kilham could not bear observing the confidence that the freed persons possessed about their salvation. Her religious sensibilities assured her that "easy assurance is the perfect fruit of utter ignorance, and one of its surest proofs." She found bodily movements and physical displays that in her estimation had no connection with true religion. Communal excitement and emotional intensity were no substitute for a righteous life or a genuine Christian experience in which Christ actually dwelled in the heart of the believer. Kilham observed that blacks constantly used religious expressions in contexts and settings completely unrelated to the conversation at hand. Little children on their way to school made such statements as "I ain't late dis mornin', bress de Lord" because of force of habit not because such expressions were proof of "real religion." So although the freed persons and their children used religious terms often, Kilham charged, they continued to steal, swear, and fight, even when they had attended a religious meeting the night before.[23]

Kilham's strongest proof against the notion of blacks being naturally religious was the evidence she cited that "religious feeling" decreased as blacks became more educated. "Indifference" replaced "excitement." She was searching for another conceptual category in which to place black religious expression. To assert that blacks were not naturally religious was to say that either they were not religious in the same way that white Northern Protestants understood the term (which equated morality or ethics of a certain kind with religion) or that their religious feeling was a product of a defective education or social experience (this religious feeling would presumably decline as they become more educated or accepted the proper form of Christianity). Kilham noted that those blacks who had been free for many years exhibited none of the wild religious excitements of the former slaves. Though she expressed sympathy for those educated blacks who abandoned or never expressed any of the religious behavioral patterns of the former slaves, she lamented a "strong tendency to infidelity" among them. This was understandable, Kilham noted, because these educated blacks had been forced by unpleasant circumstances to refrain from church attendance. She quoted one "highly educated colored woman" to prove her point:

> I don't know whether I believe in anything or not. So far as I hear anything about religion, I don't see much to believe in. If I went to church, I might; but I am shut out from that. I won't go to the colored churches, for I'm only disgusted with bad grammar and worse pronunciation, and their horrible absurdities; I can't go to your [white] churches, for if I am admitted at all, I am put away off in a dark corner, out of reach of everybody, as if I were some unclean thing, and I will not voluntarily place myself in such a position.[24]

Kilham also observed that as a result of the education of the younger blacks, extravagant preaching, "meaningless hymns," and noisy singing were being ridiculed. Young blacks in the cities formed choirs and "adopted the hymns and tunes in use in the white churches."[25] From Kilham's perspective, the plight of educated blacks in such situations posed serious questions about the wisdom of segregating them within white churches, though she did not in any way press this as a major concern. Her musings on the role of white churches in addressing this problem merely appeared as a one-sentence conclusion about the possibility of segregation being questioned in heaven "when shades of distinction are invisible in the light of eternity."[26] Ultimately, blacks would have to reform their own communities with the help of some outside intelligent leadership, though Kilham hardly expected educated blacks to provide such leadership.

Several of Kilham's objections to African American religious practice would become common among white critics of black religion. The romantic racialist language of blacks as naturally religious, gentle, and affectionate all but vanished. Though Kilham and others acknowledged that blacks were capable of changing under the influence of white Northern educators, doubts about the educability of Africans in America often emerged in such conversations. Even statements about the ability of blacks to develop and grow were found alongside assertions of traits that were said to be inherent or native to the African temperament. "Superstitions," which meant religious practices of an African heritage, were criticized by whites as antithetical to a normative true Christianity and often their presence raised doubts about blacks' fitness to be incorporated as active citizens in the new nation. The author of an 1875 article in the *American Missionary Magazine* told of his experience among blacks in Augusta, Georgia. He argued that blacks were controlled by a "grotesque idealism" and an "ethnical tendency to material religious practices." Emancipation left blacks, he claimed, in a condition that required the "wisest Christian guidance." Much black worship preserved traces of the "barbarous ritual of its Congo ancestors" and "tendencies which the civilized associations of more than two centuries have failed altogether to arrest." "Black enthusiasts" had been unfortunately left to themselves, the author continued, and their condition of ignorance, authorized and enforced by law, was not likely to improve any time soon. Blacks had been left to the guidance of the blind.[27]

Racial difference was the dominant theory to explain black behavior, even though Northern whites theoretically believed that black progress was possible. The idea of slavery as a formative influence was now minimized and blacks' temperament or disposition became the key to explaining their distinctive religious practices. One writer for *Harper's Weekly* wrote in 1872 that the "negro mind has an insatiable craving for excitement, which finds its gratification chiefly in the varied scenes of the camping ground."[28] In 1874 a writer for *Harper's New Monthly* argued that the Negro mind was weak in the "exact sciences" and "characteristically susceptible to religious impressions." He asserted that "emotional services of praying and singing" were among the "highest enjoyments" of blacks. Blacks were more controlled by their "religious professions" than the average white person. They possessed untrained and undeveloped minds.[29] Specific racial temperaments were continually evoked to explain the peculiar religious expressions of blacks. So though the evaluation of feelings and emotions had changed, white Northerners in the post–Civil War context shared the racial theories of the romantic racialists. In this new social setting, however, black religion was deemed defective and lacking in morality. The genial and naturally religious slave had become the immoral, emotionally unstable, and fanatically religious freed person.

A few dissenting voices were heard, however. In 1875, Reverend H. S. Bennett observed that "certain [white] Northern writers" now believed that black religious life in the South was so low and degraded that blacks' only hope lay in the "overthrow of the colored churches now in existence and the establishment of those with a higher type of morality." Bennett claimed that writers for the *Congregationalist* and the *Independent* (two papers thought to be radical by Southerners in their call for black rights) had concluded that black ministers and church members were committing gross immorality, lacked chastity, and rarely experienced discipline in their churches. He agreed that petty stealing, lying, immorality, Sabbath-breaking, and frequent violations of the ten commandments were common among blacks. Bennett affirmed that most blacks in the South "have an indistinct idea of what constitutes a Christian walk and conversation." He concurred that their meetings were places of "wildfire" and shouting, and that in their religious life "they dwell more upon churchgoing and having a rousing time than upon conformity to the ten commandments." Bennett lamented that "no one can appreciate their low moral condition until he has spent years in a situation where it grows upon him." However, he acknowledged, after so many dour concessions, that the power of the Christian religion had a positive influence in the lives of black Southerners and they owed "everything good and lovable and promising in their natural traits to the power of the religion of Christ." The language of romantic racialism made its way back into Bennett's laudation of black religious strengths. The familiar commendation of blacks for being an affectionate, gentle, humble, forgiving, and law-abiding people was made without any awareness of how it contrasted so sharply with all of the vices that Bennett had just enumerated as rampant among blacks.[30]

Bennett attributed the religious life and the "passive virtues" (patience, fortitude, and endurance) of black Southerners to their experience in slavery. He wrote, "That these traits of character are the result of their religious life, as affected by their experience in slavery, and not their natural disposition, may be abundantly shown by the way in which the whole race is moved upon by the religious ideas and experiences which are current among them." He maintained that religion entered into the daily thoughts and feelings of blacks and that "religious conversation" was heard even as blacks met one another on the streets. Their picnics, benevolent societies, and celebrations centered around their churches. Even their Fourth of July celebrations had a religious character. "No people," Bennett claimed, "could be so profoundly stirred as they are by their weekly meetings, without showing the effects of the forces which work upon them in their lives."[31] Bennett's denial that religion was a product of blacks' "natural disposition" indicates that there were those who defended this proposition: This is why Bennett blamed slavery for the "special" sins of blacks. He placed his hope for black moral and mental elevation in general education, especially the work of the AMA. Bennett urged white Northerners to be patient with blacks and not elevate one denomination above another. He thought it folly to overthrow the black churches because such a drastic measure would bring rapid disorganization and chaos among black Southerners. Schools and churches should work in collaboration to bring about the elevation of a degraded and struggling people.[32] Yet Bennett's voice was a minority among Northern whites, as he conceded in his essay. Negative assessments of black religion were now the dominant ones.

Black Missionaries Offer a Different Path

Educated black missionaries also expressed surprise and sometimes revulsion at the religion of the freed persons, though black missionaries tended to regard the freed persons' religious practices more favorably after extended contact with them. Henry McNeal Turner's visit to Roanoke Island, North Carolina, in 1865 is usually cited as an example of a black missionary responding critically to what he saw as the heathenism, emotionalism, and barbarism of black religion in the South.[33] Turner claimed that he encountered black Methodists who worshiped under a "lower class of ideas" and entertained a "much cruder conception of God and the plan of salvation." "Hell fire, brimstone, damnation, black smoke, hot lead, [etc.]," he complained, "appeared to be presented by the speaker as man's highest incentive to serve God, while the milder and yet more powerful message of Jesus was thoughtlessly passed by." But Turner's critique was primarily theological in nature, and otherwise he went on to say that these same black Christians had a deep zeal and determination "in their efforts to serve God." He also praised Southern blacks for embracing the truths of the Bible with an "undeviating determination," which drew out a "signal majesty" from the Scriptures.[34] This was a very different conception from white critics, such as Lucy Chase who insisted that blacks "must find out that their way is not the best way" and found little of value in the religion of the freed persons.[35] Or the criticisms of Stearns and Kilham, who saw virtually nothing worth retaining in the religion of Southern blacks.

Yet educated Northern blacks were ambivalent about the religious practices of the Southern black masses precisely because of their awareness of white criticisms of the distinctive folk practices of black Southerners and black Northerners' own desire for a more refined faith. But at least throughout the

1870s, Northern black criticisms of black Southern folk practices were more moderate than those of whites and sought to strike a balance between praise and criticism. Benjamin Tanner's views of white criticisms of black Southern religious practices clarify this point. By 1875, Tanner, a leader in the African Methodist Episcopal Church, noted ruefully, though with obvious hyperbole: "The Religion of the Negro! Why, the years are but few since it was proclaimed worldwide to be the ideal religion of the land—so simple, so pure, so practical?... But alas! The Negro is no more the typical religious of the Republic that he used to be." Now, he continued, the religion of the Negro is considered "but a single remove from Paganism." Even Northern liberals saw black religion as the "sorriest mixture of heathen superstition," the "most rudimentary of the teachings of Christianity," and "abominable in the extreme." Tanner was especially upset that the *Independent*, usually friendly toward blacks, carried an article that was exceedingly critical of their religious practices in the South. He could not bring himself to engage in the radical critique of black religious practices as did white missionaries from the North. Tanner presented his own experience among blacks in the South as evidence of his observance of their sincere faith.[36] He noted that the formerly benign view of black religion was disappearing and that even Northern interpreters of black religion found little if anything to praise. In this new account of black religion a convergence between southern and northern interpretations of black religious practice as emotionalism and extravagant frenzy emerged. Both white northerners and southerners also agreed that the nature of their religion made blacks totally unfit for labor, the central quality of freedom deemed necessary for participation in the new nation.

The Convergence of Northern and Southern Views of Black Religion

Paul Buck notes in his classic work on the reunion of the North and South that after the trauma of the Civil War, newspapers, magazines, and publishing houses poured forth a flood of articles and books on all phases of Southern life and problems. The major Northern magazines and periodicals, such as *Harper's*, *Lippincott's*, and the *Atlantic*, vied with *Scribner's* in reporting on the Southern scene. A new sympathy for the South emerged.[37] Especially in reports on the situation of blacks in the South, one finds a convergence of Southern and Northern sentiments in the journals of the time. The deteriorating social condition of blacks, the enormity of the race problem, and the desire to let Southerners handle blacks in their own way are prominent in this literature of the late 1870s. For one example of this change in attitude, Edward King, a

Massachusetts journalist for *Scribner's*, spent 1873 to 1874 touring the South.[38] King devoted a chapter to the moral character of blacks in the South in an important and widely circulated book published in 1875. He argued that about one-third of blacks in the South were in a hopeful condition, another third were in a "comparatively stationary attitude," and the other third "is absolutely good for nothing." This final portion of the population, King maintained, had made no progress in morality, education, or refinement of any kind since the war. He was convinced that the "religion of the negroes in many parts of the South appears pretty completely divorced from morality," so much so that it was difficult to persuade "one's self that blacks as yet deserve recognition as a moral race." Even their best friends, King noted, would admit that although blacks are "very religious, they are also very immoral." Adultery, though a mortal sin to "Northern and Southern white religionists, is simply venial to the black man," he confidently asserted.[39]

King wrote that he observed a radical difference in the practice and meaning of religion between blacks and whites. Anglo-Saxons possessed a "tough moral fibre," but neither this toughness nor a building of conscience had developed in blacks as a result of their "conversion to the religion of the Lord." Whereas whites believed that salvation could only be attained through faith, self-denial, and hard work, for many blacks religion made them unfit for their daily duties.[40] Shouting, visitations from angels, hearing voices from heaven, and seeing great lights were the only things that seemed to bring peace to blacks and to make religion real for them. King wrote, "Men and women foam at the mouth, wander about the fields and forest half distracted, a spasm of spiritual insanity having taken possession of them." All of this camp-meeting revivalism and enthusiasm "sometimes totally unfit the negroes for labor during the whole week." These meetings often descended into orgies, where "whiskey and licentiousness do their work." Because most of these blacks had "reached only the confines of real Christianity," King averred, their religion was only a form of "Fetichism with a Christian cloak."[41]

King thought of his views as moderate. He criticized white ministers and others who felt that blacks were making no progress: In his view, moral growth was a slow process, and he believed that with the help of the teachers from the Freedmen's Bureau and the AMA, as well as "Southern people of high character," blacks would gradually move forward.[42] But if their religion, which was seen as their most striking quality, was defective, what could they contribute to the developing nation? There was a cruel irony in the pleadings of Thomas Wentworth Higginson in 1874 on behalf of blacks in a letter to the editor of the *Nation*, one of the most influential journals in the country.[43] Higginson responded to an editorial article that accused blacks in the Sea Islands of South

Carolina of having an intelligence that was so low that they were deemed slightly above the level of animals. He jumped on this editorial, denouncing its rash conclusions and pointing out its flaws based on his own experience serving as a colonel of a colored regiment in the Sea Islands during the final years of the Civil War. To vindicate blacks' humanity, Higginson pointed to their "religious sentiments" and the power of their "unfaltering faith" to sustain them under so many years of oppression. Surely their uprightness, their spirituals, and their religious values, he persisted, made them superior to animals and therefore members of the human family.[44] Higginson's claim that religion was the signal quality of blacks' humanity occurred at the time when other white Northerners like Stearns, Kilham, and King maintained that it was precisely black religion that disabled them and prevented them from advancing. These critics of black religion certainly did not share Higginson's assertion that lying, stealing, drunkenness, and lack of chastity were as common among whites as they were among blacks. His statement that the "religious sentiment is an essential part of their [blacks'] temperaments" was precisely the problem with blacks in the eyes of Northern whites like Stearns, Kilham, and King. For them, black religion was not an exemplification of blacks' nobility but a manifestation of their degradation and descent into their worst selves.

The upshot of these discussions of African American religion was that white Northerners acquired a new appreciation for the putative sordid mess that white Southerners had on their hands. As Buck writes, "A note of pathos, some pity, and understanding of what burden the white South was carrying, also entered for the first time in the Northern outlook."[45] These various portrayals of black religion must be seen within the context of the broader national weariness with the race problem and the Northern desire to allow Southerners to handle *their* Negro problem.

Southern Theories of Black Religious Retrogression

After the withdrawal of federal troops in 1877, Southerners were left to control their own affairs. The Negro problem was theirs to solve again. White Northerners were anxious to be relieved of this burden. Southern whites, in part to explain and rationalize the deteriorating social and political condition of blacks in the South, produced a vast literature on the Negro problem. The reality of lynching, political disenfranchisement, and segregation was given detailed justification. Though dissenting voices were sometimes heard, the dominant claims of black savagery descended like a dark cloud over the South.[46] As blacks lost their right to vote, were thrust off their property to make way for white owners, suffered at the hands of lynch mobs, and lost any significant political and economic power in the South, white Southerners justified these developments by arguing that it was a defective African nature that explained the worsening situation of blacks in the South. Few Northerners came to blacks' defense.

Herbert Gutman has written that "retrogressionist beliefs" about black Southerners gained increasing popularity in the 1880s and 1890s. These retrogressionist ideas, which essentially argued that blacks were reverting to African barbarism, especially in their sexual and religious practices, saturated the early twentieth-century popular media, historical writing, and academic social science. These writings made the case that the essential "restraining" influences on unchanging Africans had ended with emancipation, causing a moral and social retrogression among the ex-slaves.[47] Although Gutman notes that retrogressionist arguments often focused on the black family and sexual behavior, black religion played a crucial role in these negative characterizations of southern blacks. White Southern Methodist clergyman Atticus Haygood, for example, pointed to reforming black religion as the key to helping improve blacks' situation in the South. Haygood conceded that black religious "notions may be in some things crude, their conceptions of truth realistic, sometimes to a painful, sometimes to a grotesque, degree." Still, although African Americans "may be more emotional than ethical," Haygood wrote, and "show many imperfections in their religious development," religion was surely their "strongest and most formative" characteristic.[48] Moderate churchmen like Haygood were disturbed by what they regarded as a loss of religious values among black ministers and a rise of dangerous emotionalism among the black masses.[49] These religious values included fidelity, cheerfulness, deference, simplicity, and a childlike disposition. This lament for the good old days was inextricably linked to a longing for a past when whites ruled over an allegedly inferior and child-like race.[50]

The claim that blacks were regressing was an updated form of the proslavery argument that blacks would revert to African barbarism once freed from the "benevolent tutelage" of slavery (an argument that had been advanced by Thomas Jefferson in the late eighteenth century). George Stetson, a white traveler (from Boston) to the South in 1877, wrote: "It is thought that they are deteriorating in every way; physically from want of care and proper parental management; mentally and morally, because not controlled as in slavery times."[51] This notion of retrogression as an expression of a black culture freed from the supposed restraining influences of slavery became the core of the radically racist mentality that swept over the South in the 1890s.[52]

Two important works of the 1880s illustrate the different ways that the same conclusion was reached by Southerners who pathologized black culture and justified the deterioration of conditions among blacks in the South by pointing to the alleged defects of their minds, morals, and bodies: Joseph Tucker's *The Relations of the Church to the Colored People* (1882) and Philip A. Bruce's *The Plantation Negro as Freedman* (1889). Tucker, rector of St. Andrew's Episcopal Church in Jackson, Mississippi, presented a powerful speech before the Church Congress in Richmond, Virginia, in October 1882 that dealt with the "relations of the [Episcopal] Church to the colored race." A Northerner by birth, Tucker had fought in the Confederate army and later settled in the South.[53] During a vigorous debate at this Congress of Episcopal Churches, Tucker argued that the Church should relate differently to blacks and whites because of the "vast mental and moral differences between the races." Tucker was particularly adamant that Northerners stop interfering in the South and permit white Southerners to settle their own racial affairs. He argued against blacks controlling their own churches and holding positions of leadership in the churches.[54]

Much of Tucker's speech was a despairing and prejudicial account of the "pathologies" of black religion, which were educed to justify the need for segregated dioceses in the Episcopal communion. Leaders in the Episcopal Church wanted to retain black members, Tucker noted, but they also sought ways to segregate black and white churches while putting blacks under the authority of a local white diocesan bishop. This concern with blacks in the church was particularly salient in Mississippi because black net migration to the state from the agricultural districts of the upper Southeast between 1870 and 1880 was nearly equal to the state's net loss of whites. Blacks comprised a majority in many counties of Mississippi.[55] Fears of the Africanization of the South combined with more specific and local worries about blacks obtaining leadership positions in the churches.[56] While decrying the alleged reversion to savagery in black churches under black ministers, Tucker and other religious leaders did not object to segregation of the races, but they demanded that blacks be put under the supervision of whites so long as they were a part of their denomination. Tucker indicated that his speech was given so that "those who do not know the race experimentally may be able to perceive something of the difficulties which lie in the way, and which have caused such apparent apathy of Southern Christians concerning the moral and religious condition of the negro race."[57]

To sharpen the contrast between the benefits of slavery and the degraded condition of emancipated blacks, Tucker turned to the freed persons' distant

African past. This was the key, he argued, to understanding their degenerate religious practices. Tucker claimed that human life held no value for Africans and that they murdered men, women, and children as though they were animals. He described Africans as emotionless, unable to feel pain and sympathy in the presence of human suffering. They were cannibals, Tucker asserted, who feasted on the flesh of those slain in battle and who killed off the weak and infirm.[58] Their religion contained no notion of a future state and was only a "mixture of witchcraft, bloodshed, fiendish orgies, and terror-driven superstition." All travelers to Africa agreed, Tucker argued, that there were no words among the tribes of Africa to express the ideas of gratitude, generosity, industry, truthfulness, honesty, modesty, gentleness, and virtue. Morality as it guided relations between the sexes, Tucker maintained, or as it instructed society in principles of truthfulness and honesty, had "no lodgment whatever in the native African breast." This African background, Tucker concluded, shed light on the "roots and causes out of which have grown their [blacks'] ideas and practices as regards morality."[59]

Slavery provided blacks with an "outward restraint," Tucker contended, and enabled them to learn elements of civilization, points of marriage, truthfulness, and honesty. The discipline and punishment of slavery were necessary to instruct such "absolute barbarians." Unfortunately, such punishment led to rampant dissembling among blacks and merely outward expressions of honesty, virtue, and truthfulness, whereas in reality, the "phraseology of righteousness" served as a cover for various incidents of wrongdoing and thus made the slaves into unintentional hypocrites. Slaves had the form of righteousness but not the substance. This was the key to unlocking the current hypocrisy and immorality among Southern blacks, according to Tucker. Stealing, lying, cheating, adultery, and other vices became common among slaves because they realized that they could avoid punishment simply by concealing what they had done. Because the native African had no idea of a "moral difference between truth and falsehood," Tucker asserted, he had to learn that certain acts that elicited punishment from his owners could be continued only if he could "use words in such a way as to cover himself." It was a slippage of meaning between word and act such that only enough of the meaning of words was learned so as to keep slaves safe. Blacks were therefore able, Tucker maintained, to continue engaging in concealed acts of wrongdoing without any sense of guilt or wrongdoing.[60]

The slaves avidly accepted, Tucker continued, the "person and errand" of Jesus Christ from the whites who taught them, because there was "something in the story of the Cross [which] appealed to them with a force unknown to those who live easy and comfortable and self-indulgent lives." But this belief made no effect on their daily lives. "They could grasp the vague ideas of pity and of hope, but could not grasp the sense of duty," Tucker charged. "Duty always came to them under the sternness of oppression, and they could not connect the idea of love with that of duty."[61] Tucker believed that the duties of slavery caused blacks to chafe, and as they reacted to the restraints of slavery, they rejected all "constraints upon desire." When they were taught that certain acts were contrary to the commands of Jesus or the Bible, "they thought that white people were trying to make them believe that the Lord Jesus was a slave driver too." They simply could not understand how any obligation could be separated from a state of slavery. Tucker argued that freedom for the slaves meant absence of all constraint, positive or negative. As he put it, "And so the religion which they did accept from the white people grew to be a matter of emotion only, having no constraining force upon their conduct. Religion meant love, and love meant freedom, and freedom meant absence of duty, moral or physical." Their religion degenerated into a form of antinomianism that promised freedom from any legal restraints and recommended only God's love for the sinner.[62]

Tucker also maintained that the end of slavery brought about a relapse into "many practices of African barbarism." The "removal of the constraint of slavery" led to a resurgence of witchcraft (which, he asserted, had never lost its hold on blacks). Such superstitious practices among blacks, "which are really remnants of African devil worship," increased in force after the Civil War. These old customs of African barbarism were grafted on the Christianity presented to the slaves and were very difficult to discard.[63] In the growing black population, Tucker and other whites were deeply fearful that in the South "we have Africa over again, only partially restrained,"[64] meaning a degeneration of moral and religious conditions and a resurgence of amorality. The savage religious customs among freed persons, Tucker insisted, produced a "strange obliquity of moral vision, a strange perversion of judgment, a curiously conglomerated religion—which it is exceedingly difficult for any white people to understand, and utterly impossible for those to understand who had no practical experience with the race."[65] What was left was an "outward form of Christianity with an inner substance of full license given to all desires and passions."[66]

Though Tucker believed that there were exceptions, he indicated that his statements were true for the mass of blacks in the South.[67] The effect of freedom was a "great subsidence into evil" for most blacks. Freedom meant rest and cessation from labor and new sins arose. Negro churches were springing up everywhere, in part because of northern money, but they were primarily about "shouting, praying, singing, all manner of excitement, hysterics, trances, [and] loud calls upon God." Lacking was the true religion, which produced a "holy, humble, and obedient walking before God."[68] Black religion, in short, had deteriorated into a "false religion" since the Civil War, and only a "Hampton in Mississippi" could probably alter the situation.[69]

Tucker's reference to Hampton indicates how white Southerners perceived the essential religious element of this institution. Hampton Institute was founded in 1868 in Virginia by Samuel Armstrong, a veteran brigadier general for the Union in the Civil War. Hampton held a regimented twelve-hour schedule for its students, who were trained in industrial education, which included training in a specific trade and agriculture combined with broad moral principles rooted in the Christian tradition. Armstrong believed that morality and industry worked together and were especially appropriate for blacks and other "indolent" and "weak tropical races."[70] Tucker apparently hoped that a school like Hampton in Mississippi would help correct the "false religion" of blacks, instill in them a proper regard for labor, and enable them to adjust to their subordinate role to whites in the South.

Tucker identified three obstacles to carrying a "pure gospel" to blacks: (1) the reluctance of whites to work among blacks, (2) blacks' "profound distrust" of white teachers and "white teaching," and (3) the existence of religion among blacks that already suited them. He suggested that a white parish already working among blacks should be encouraged to continue its work. This would provide, Tucker hoped, a center from which positive influences would radiate, most prominently in teaching blacks "better things" about religion. He argued that building chapels for blacks was not the answer because blacks would quickly occupy them, "out-talk" the whites who came to preach to them, and labor under the false notion that they knew more about Jesus than whites. But for all of their religious talk, Tucker averred, they "will not therefore forsake one sin or practice one virtue." In imagining how Northerners and the "very young and innocent" might react to blacks and to black religion, Tucker believed that such people would "come to the conclusion that these [black] people have been greatly maligned and abused, and that they are more devout and more religious than whites."[71] Tucker was willing to concede that blacks were religious and, indeed, that religion was "natural" to them, but the point was that they were religious in a very different way than whites were religious. Tucker insisted that practical religion was simply nonexistent among blacks. Virtue, truth, and honesty were lacking, and thus their religion was virtually useless.[72] This meant that blacks were "religious," but in a way that rendered them useless as citizens of a new and emerging nation.

Such accounts of black religion were calls for closer white scrutiny and control of black life even as the South moved toward stricter racial segregation in the legal realm. As a reaction to a Northern "sentimental" view of black religion, Tucker and others were urging white Northerners to allow them to proceed with their own work among blacks (without romantic visions of what was possible for them). If blacks' conceptions of their religious duties differed as profoundly from those of whites as Tucker and others asserted, then white fear of independent black churches alongside a move toward legal segregation and disenfranchisement is more easily understood. To the extent that blacks were said to be reverting to African savagery, a call for white inculcation of religious and civic duties was deemed to be absolutely essential for "peaceful" and "harmonious" relations between the races. Blacks could not be allowed to be so isolated that they were able to hatch diabolical plans that could be harmful to the larger society, and this made sense to those Southern whites who harbored deep fears of black anger and resentment because of the oppression of slavery and contemporary hardships imposed on blacks. Tucker and others painted a dour picture of black religious life in part because it was thought that if blacks were shown to be making practically no advance in morals, despite their fervent religious practices and their "boasted emancipation," then they certainly could not be trusted with the franchise and those civic and political responsibilities that befitted citizens who earned them.[73] Black religion made blacks' unfit for freedom and political participation, Tucker asserted. It did so by squandering their time and energy, giving them a cover and support for their immoral behavior, and granting them a clear conscience even when they engaged in the most criminal actions.[74] Segregation, white supervision, and paternalistic oversight were the suitable social arrangements urged by Tucker.

Tucker's views were disseminated broadly. His speech and its "endorsements" were collected in a pamphlet. H. H. Chambers, a Presbyterian lay member and the chief justice of the Supreme Court of Mississippi, praised Tucker for noticing the "indisputable fact that religion and morality are wholly dissociated in the minds of the bulk of the negro population" and welcomed his address, permitting his name to be used as an endorsement of Tucker's views on black religion.[75] Tucker was also more than happy to include in his pamphlet the endorsements of a few black ministers in the South whose sentiments accorded with his own. Among these were the comments of Reverend Isaac McCoy Williams, described as a "colored Campbellite minister" of Jackson, Mississippi.

But Williams's interpretation of black religion diverged in important particulars from Tucker's. While asserting that few blacks were equipped to vote, Williams still blamed the nation for allowing so many black citizens to remain in ignorance. Unlike Tucker, Williams held slavery accountable for the "semi-barbarous condition" of most blacks. Williams's portrayal of the appalling situation of blacks in the South ended with an appeal to "the Church" (which can be read as an address to the churches of the North and South) to send more missionaries and educators to the South, even though Tucker himself had urged white Northerners to stop meddling in Southern affairs and to allow white Southerners to handle blacks as only they knew how. Williams held with Tucker that the moral condition of blacks was very low, but even here he used a sordid depiction of moral decline to call for aid, education, and uplift from those inside and outside the South. Still, his name appeared on Tucker's pamphlet.[76]

Black Leaders Dissent

Two prominent African American Episcopalians, Alexander Crummell and Anna Julia Cooper, also felt it necessary to enter this debate about black religion in direct opposition to Tucker. Crummell (1819–1898) was one of the most prominent black leaders in the late nineteenth century to wrestle with the problems of depicting and interpreting the black experience. Born free in New York City, reared in a family that held membership in St. Philip's Church, New York's leading black Episcopal congregation, educated at Queen's College in Cambridge, and having served as a resident missionary and educator in Liberia from 1853 to 1872, Crummell's experience as an African American was certainly unique. Nonetheless, he was deeply interested in the religious lives of African Americans and emerged as one of the leading vindicators of black progress in the late nineteenth century.[77] After Crummell returned to the United States from Liberia in 1872, he became rector and priest of St. Luke's Episcopal Church in Washington, D.C.[78] After requests from black ministers, Crummell published a response to Tucker's speech.

The full title of Crummell's address gives a sense of his feelings about Tucker's speech: "A Defence of the Negro Race in America from the Assaults and Charges of Rev. J. L. Tucker, D.D., of Jackson, Mississippi." He interpreted Tucker's address as a "gross and exaggerated charge of deterioration against the entire race" that amounted to a "disguised attempt" to demonstrate that Emancipation was a failure.[79] Crummell was particularly disturbed that Tucker had attributed gross immorality, dishonesty, hypocrisy, and general lewdness as "Negro peculiarities" that were "constitutional" to blacks. He drew on his own work in Africa to refute Tucker's claims about the degraded African character. He wrote, "I have lived nigh twenty years in West Africa. I have come in contact with peoples of not less than forty tribes, and I aver, from personal knowledge and acquaintance, that the picture drawn by Dr. Tucker is a caricature."[80] He granted that there were weaknesses and "degradation" among blacks, but he attributed it to their being a "victim race" who had suffered from years of slavery.

Any peculiarities exhibited in black life were to be seen as "American characteristics" that were the "legitimate outcome of the pernicious system of bondage
which has crushed this race for than two hundred years now."[81]

Crummell indicated that he would, for the sake of argument, "make large
concessions" about problems in black southern religion. He acknowledged that
ignorance was prevalent, that a "taint of immorality" affected black religion
(which he attributed to the heritage of slavery), and that frenzy, hysteria, and
superstition were problems in black churches. Crummell and other middle-
class Northern blacks were generally wary of the worship styles and religious
folk ways of black churches in the South. Among these blacks, for example,
William Wells Brown, a noted author and reformer, visited the South from
1879 to 1880 and recorded his impressions in a book of travels, *My Southern
Home* (1880). Brown was critical of the revival meetings that he witnessed
among blacks in Tennessee. Like white Northerners such as Stearns and King,
Brown believed that such revivals were "injurious to both health and morals"
because of the hours they ended and the amount of time they consumed. He
was deeply disappointed that black Southerners thought that shouting and
outward demonstrations were "necessary adjuncts to piety." Brown argued that
the only remedy for these problems lay in an educated ministry, even though he
acknowledged that it would be exceedingly difficult to convince the "uneducated, superstitious masses" to support them.[82]

Perhaps because of the growing gulf between middle-class Northern blacks
and Southern blacks, mostly in the rural South, the criticism of black religion in
the South by Northern blacks was also becoming harsher.[83] Crummell's defense of black religion in the face of Tucker's critiques indicates that Northern
blacks, however, were not willing to engage in a wholesale denigration of
Southern black religion. Even after making concessions to Tucker's reproach of
black religion, Crummell maintained that black Christianity was genuine and
true, that it had produced "fruits of righteousness," and that it engendered
"astonishing self-sacrifice for the glory of Jesus." He was bewildered that
Tucker could consign an "immense multitude" of Christians to spiritual ruin
and "sit in judgment upon the character and piety of multitudes of people
whom he has never seen, and of whom he knows nothing!"[84]

To Tucker's claims that Northerners should stop interfering in Southern
affairs with respect to blacks, Crummell angrily responded: " 'We Southern
people know the Negro better than you do!' This is the old claim which the
American people have heard *ad nauseum*. Alas, for all their knowledge they
never knew them well enough to treat them as men!"[85] He rejected the claim
that Southerners possessed a special knowledge of blacks that somehow made
them particularly fit and disinterested in their efforts to confront the Negro

problem. Crummell asserted that Northerners were just as invested in the slave trade as were Southerners, that Northerners were just as willing to employ blacks in their houses and on their farms as slaves, and that white Northern missionaries since the Civil War had done extensive work among Southern blacks, all of which added up to Northern experience and knowledge of black culture.[86]

Likewise, in a paper read before a convocation of colored clergymen of the Protestant Episcopal Church at Washington, D.C., in 1886, Anna Julia Cooper chose to take on, in part, Tucker's critique of black religion and his negative views of the black family and sexuality. Cooper, who was born near Raleigh, North Carolina, was at the time of her address an educator at St. Augustine's College in Raleigh. As a black woman who was born in slavery, an Episcopalian, and one who had trained and worked with Southern blacks, Cooper was uniquely positioned to answer Tucker's charges. Although the bulk of her speech was an attempt to prove the importance of black women in regenerating the race, our interest lies in her specific emphasis on black religion.[87] Cooper noted that leading black men (no doubt with Crummell in mind) held fast to the hope that the Episcopal Church, with its high liturgy and solemn worship, might be "eminently fitted to correct the peculiar faults of worship—the rank exuberance and often ludicrous demonstrativeness of [black] people."[88] She chastised the Church for causing blacks to leave its communion and find fellowship in others, a failure she attributed to the Church's refusal to consider the views of black men and women about their own betterment. Cooper objected to the tendency of the Episcopal Church (and white churches more generally) to expect blacks to be content with a "perpetual colored diaconate, carefully and kindly superintended by the white clergy."[89]

Each denomination would have its specific debates about missionary work among blacks in the South. What is important for our purposes is the precise way in which the broader discourse about black religion emerged within a specific social and political context of the nation. The central themes of degeneration, black progress or retrogression, innate religiosity, and the controversy over the extent to which black religion exercised a positive or negative influence on the character of blacks and their place in the nation were constants in these types of discussions. Black leaders, as expected, generally offered a more favorable interpretation of black religion, but throughout the late nineteenth century, black and white commentators alike gradually began to manifest in their writings the growing influence of social Darwinism and anthropological theories about sociocultural evolution of race groups, and their significance for ranking the religion of the races. By the 1880s, immigration to the United States from southern and eastern Europe, calls for exclusion of

Chinese immigration, the continuing shrinkage of the Indian frontier, and the growing interest in the scramble for Africa (by both missionaries and colonizers) heightened concerns with racial rankings and claims about the racial superiority of white Anglo-Saxons.[90] Within this context, the attempt to rank religions hierarchically within a sociocultural schema became more pressing. Interpreters increasingly turned to science to ground their arguments about the nature of black religion, though even these scientific assessments were extensions of popular prejudices and were articulated (later) in the moralizing and clinical language of psychology rooted in a liberal Protestant tradition.

Groping for a Science of Black Religion

The other major critique of black religion in the 1880s came from Philip A. Bruce, a white historian in Virginia. John David Smith argues that in 1895 Bruce published the best early book on the economic and social aspects of slavery in the colonial period. Bruce was plantation born and bred, the scion of a long line of Virginia plantation aristocrats who embodied the values and symbols of the Old South. He grew to manhood surrounded by many slaves on a 5,000-acre tobacco plantation in Charlotte County. Educated at the University of Virginia and Harvard Law School, Bruce worked first as a Baltimore lawyer, then as manager of Richmond's Vulcan Iron Works, and finally as a journalist. He eventually chose the life of the gentleman scholar. In the years 1895–1910, he contributed three major works on the economic, social, and institutional history of his native state in the seventeenth century. Bruce's more popular study, *The Plantation Negro as Freeman* (1889), was directly addressed to the Negro problem.[91] Herbert Gutman writes that this book "served as perhaps the most important connecting link between the 'popular' views of Afro-American 'decline' common in the 1880s and the detailed 'scientific' works published between 1890 and the First World War."[92]

Bruce dealt with various aspects of black life (for example, family and schools), but I am primarily concerned with his analysis of black religion.[93] Though claiming to state his conclusions "impartially and dispassionately," Bruce proposed radical changes in the communities of black Americans and in how they were treated. His depiction of black culture as pathological and criminal was specifically related to debates about the fitness of blacks to vote, the widespread image of the vicious black male intent on raping white women, and the civil rights of the freed persons. Bruce was quick to distinguish between the "passionate religious feeling" of blacks and the "sober and godly conduct" of true religion. He argued that "as an abstract hope and naked aspiration, it [a passionate religious feeling] colors his whole nature as much as his most impetuous appetites do."[94] The black male was said to be "as much open to religious impressions and as much dominated by his religious emotions" as the black female, though "their influence does not cause him to act as wildly and hysterically as she does." It is not clear from this statement that he posited an inherent difference in religious practices for black men and women, though he added that black men generally exercised more self-control in their religious ecstasies than did black women.[95]

Bruce maintained that within the black psyche there had to be a distinct moral and religious "sense."[96] In this attempt to separate the "moral sense" (which blacks allegedly lacked) from the "religious sense" (which he asserted that all blacks possessed), Bruce was refining conceptual categories that had significant meaning for understandings of black capacities and black destiny in American society. We recall how another Virginian, Thomas Jefferson, had argued that black slaves were given by nature a bountiful supply of endowments of the heart, though he added that they lacked the endowments of the head (intellect). When defending this proposition, Jefferson argued against those who claimed that slaves "had a disposition to theft," noting that theft should be "ascribed to their situation, and not to any depravity of the moral sense."[97] By linking the moral sense with endowments of the heart, Jefferson had paved the way for the association of feeling and emotion with "religious capacity." But he went further by arguing that the moral sense consisted of basic principles of right and wrong, which all peoples possessed at a basic intuitive level.[98] The moral sense was about religious capacity and ethics or morality. The two were intrinsically related in Jefferson's formulation, and this conceptualization of religious capacity was advanced by romantic racialists who merged the moral sense and religious capacity in their discussions of slave religion.

Although there is no evidence that Bruce was directly responding to Jefferson's and other thinkers' arguments about the moral sense, clearly his attempt to sever the moral sense from the religious sense was a further development in the refining of conceptual categories of human capacity in direct relationship to whites' real-world experiences with blacks. With Jefferson, the moral sense was possessed by all, and it "was as much a part of man as his leg or arm," he wrote to his nephew.[99] The separation of religious capacity from intellectual capacity coincided with and reflected a different evaluation of blacks' potential contribution to the nation. This dichotomy between the moral and intellectual senses, particularly with respect to interpretations of blacks' capacities, remained basically intact up to the Civil War. Northern white critics were moving toward Bruce's analysis in their complaints that black religion was divorced from ethics (though Bruce never expanded in detail on intellectual capacity as a separate conceptual category because he assumed that it was settled that blacks were intellectually inferior to whites). His separation of the religious sense from the moral sense was a crucial development in assessments of black prospects in the nation and as a newer "scientific" analysis of black religion. Black religion was theorized as effluvium or a noxious extraneous emanation from a disordered mind and a defective brain. Utterly rejected was the romantic racialist conflation of the moral sense with religious expression.

For Bruce, however, this was not merely an abstract theoretical debate. His theories on black religion gave direct support for widespread Southern white beliefs that blacks were very religious and morally degenerate. The implication of his theorizing was that blacks really did not share a religion with whites. They were no longer converts to Christianity. They were reverting to their natural African selves. Their "religion" had nothing whatsoever to do with ethics and morality. It was simply emotionalism and feelings arising from the physiology of black bodies. Bruce argued that "strong religious feeling [was] apparently consistent with the lowest instincts and the most unbridled passions." This explained why even the "most pious" blacks were often those who were the "most unrestrained in their ordinary deportment." If anyone wondered what to make of Bruce's ideas, he argued that a "religious sense" was "frequently seen to be as fully developed in a negro imprisoned for murder, or arson, or burglary, or even rape, as in those who are comparatively blameless." Convicted felons had just as vivid a sense of heaven, the afterlife, and "the religious sentiment" in their hearts as those who were not criminals.[100]

Religious skepticism was thus impossible for blacks, Bruce averred, because they lacked the capacity for speculative thought. Blacks would sooner make enemies of skeptics or scoffers than of those who belonged to a different political party. Infidelity was so "wholly foreign to the intellectual leaning" of blacks, that they could not countenance the rantings of those who subscribed to it. Bruce asserted that the key to blacks' divorce of "religious faith" from "true piety" was the fact that their minds were unable to "appreciate and measure the practical relations" between belief and conduct. Like children who lack logical power and cannot understand certain connections between their words and actions, Bruce insisted, blacks were unable to recognize that their religious faith ought to produce moral behavior. Their religion was so deeply rooted in their biology, he continued, and thus so natural to them that it impelled them blindly forward, not allowing them to reflect on why they act as they do. As Bruce wrote, "It [the religion of blacks] has all the force of an appetite which cannot control whether he desires to do so or not. He follows unquestionably wherever it leads, and it never relaxes its hold upon him, being associated with a free indulgence of instincts that are apparently in conflict with it, because it is as much an instinct as these are." So the religious instinct had no force in regulating physical appetites. Rather, Bruce argued, the religious impulses of blacks ran hand in hand with their lewdness (or other sinful appetite) because the black mind could not imagine that there was an incongruity between religion and lewdness. Religious degeneracy was a product of a defective mind and imagination, Bruce proclaimed, and black religion was therefore a product of bad biology.[101]

Bruce asserted that Christian conversion among blacks, "as a rule" did not mean regeneration or a change in their character but "only a burst of enthusiasm, a temporary state of intellectual drunkenness that has no practical bearing on the general spirit" of their lives. Though this divorce between religion and morality might strike observers as hypocrisy, Bruce doubted that this was the case. Hypocrisy would require an "unswerving steadiness of will" that would be impossible for the black mind. Such an intricate process of pretending conversion and living in sin would require too much logical thought for most blacks. Because of their "innately devotional" temperament and their inability mentally to sustain hypocrisy, blacks "cannot be charged with religious cant and pretense, however immoral or criminal" they might be.[102] But this temperament explained why the religious emotions that swayed blacks at funerals, at revivals, and in churches were merely expressions of "physical drunkenness." Bruce diagnosed such religious ecstasy as a product of an unstable, susceptible nature. Such "religious emotions" were a "species of excitement" that resembled the effects of overindulgence in alcohol: Just as "fumes" from alcohol rise to the brain and produce a pleasurable sensation, so the religious feelings worked up by blacks in various settings result in "vehement movements of the body, ecstatic laughter, and boisterous singing." Once the fumes are exhausted, the excitement subsides. These transitory emotional peaks, according to Bruce, were merely forms of sensual gratification, not true religious feeling as whites understand it.[103]

Bruce backhandedly praised "the church" among blacks because it was the "only form of organization that blacks have been able to sustain with a steady and unchanging concurrence of mind." Black churches served as social and religious institutions, he contended, discounting the fact that such churches contradicted the commonly held notion that backs were "unable, usually, to work soberly and persistently together for a common object" by asserting that these churches served no practical goals. Practical goals in the churches were subordinated to "pleasure and religion," Bruce declared, and therefore blacks' weakness for cooperation was still evident. In other words, they were able to sustain churches only because they gave vent to the pleasure and sensations that were pent up in the black mind, not because they were able to work together and accomplish goals (Bruce never specified what goals he had in mind). The churches merely reflected "various inclinations" among blacks and should not be seen as a product of cooperative endeavor and foresight.[104] Even black peoples' faith in witchcraft and what Bruce saw as their varied superstitions were testimony to the "inherent tenacity of the fundamental qualities of the race" and what happens when they were "entirely at liberty to follow their natural inclinations."[105]

Bruce concluded his work with a somber warning about reversion, predicting that within a few generations the Negro would become "an exact physical image of his African ancestors."[106] Even worse, intellectual reversion would make the Negro a "more dangerous political factor, because it will increase his inability to grasp enlightened ideas of public policy." Moral decadence could not be arrested by schools and churches, so the swift and severe punishment of the law would be required to deal with rampant black crime.[107] Bruce even fantasized that the entire South could be "relegated to its primeval condition with a view to its being settled again exclusively by a white population."[108] He believed that only something of this sort could save the white South from Africanization.

Such notions of black retrogression became so widespread that the aged Frederick Douglass despaired. In a speech delivered in 1888, Douglass noted that this portrayal of black life was "not confined to the South. It has gone forth to the North. It has crossed the ocean; I met with it in Europe."[109] He continued that it is said that the Negro's "honesty is deceitful," "that his morals are impure," "that his domestic life is beastly," "that his religion is fetishism," that "his worship is simply emotional," and "that, in a word, he is falling into a state of barbarism."[110] Douglass conceded that emancipated blacks had indeed made little progress, and in many ways the condition of blacks in the South was worse than when they were slaves. But he placed the blame squarely on the shoulders of whites and the forces arrayed against blacks, not on an innate African nature.

African Americans and the Critique of the Black Ministry

Hightower T. Kealing, a college professor and the first president of the AME Church's St. Paul Quinn College in Texas, wrote in 1884 that blacks in the South were in a transitional state. The older people in the churches demanded an "emotional discourse," whereas the younger members demanded a rational form of preaching. Those who demanded a rational style of preaching sought a preacher who presented his message with "good thought in chaste language, without the musical intonation." Kealing argued that the younger people, "schooled in the new order of things," were opposed to preaching that was filled with "all sound and no sense." He proposed that a compromise would be necessary in such a fluid situation, in which a "ratio-emotional discourse" would combine the best of both traditions.[111] Particular attention was paid to black ministers and their defects, especially in the pages of *AME Church Review*.[112] In 1887, T. B. Snowden, an African American professor at Centenary Biblical Institute in Baltimore, Maryland, stressed the need for an honest and moral church ministry, writing that black churches needed "more teaching ministers, who will not try to excite the feelings of the people," but who will instruct, exhort, and reprove church members.[113] In 1890, Booker T. Washington entered this debate by castigating the poor morals of black ministers in a widely reproduced essay.[114]

This critique of the black ministry touched on questions about the moral fitness of blacks to run their own affairs and the quality of black churches under such leaders. Both blacks and whites argued that the black ministry was in need of serious moral overhaul, but neither was quite sure what to do, because it was widely acknowledged that black church members preferred their own black ministers. Education and uplift were recommended, though Southern whites like Tucker were more inclined to call for some form of white supervision of black ministers.

In 1888, Francis Grimké, pastor of the fashionable Fifteenth Street Presbyterian Church in Washington, D.C., added his voice to this debate about the role of black ministers. Grimké had been trained at Princeton Seminary from 1875 to 1878 under the influence of the influential Presbyterian divine Charles Hodge. Visitors to Grimké's church wrote about the presence of black schoolteachers, doctors, lawyers, and dentists.[115] Grimké spoke of the major challenge "intelligent ministers" faced as they tried to lead blacks in the South. He complained of those "utterly unfit" to be ministers and urged those "better qualified" to take their rightful place in the ministry. Immoral, selfish, and blind guides calling themselves ministers and preachers, Grimké asserted, were tragically "leading" blacks in the South. He proposed higher educational standards for ministers, a more rigid exercise of discipline in the churches, and a greater emphasis on Christian character. Grimké insisted that the "time has passed, or at least should be, when any and every ignoramus can mount into the ministry on a plea of a supposed divine call to preach."[116] This was a direct challenge to the older ministers whose influence was in part based on their understanding of and rootedness in black folk culture.

In her work on black Baptists, Evelyn Brooks Higginbotham argues that educated ministers were attempting to subvert the power of illiterate black leaders by privileging the written word, the Bible, and other published writings.

Texas Baptist minister Sutton Griggs urged that for blacks to succeed, they must "move out of the age of the voice." Literacy, correct doctrine, rational discourse, and strict moral standards were offered as the remedy to the emotional, "immoral," and expressive culture of Southern blacks.[117] Theophilus Gould Steward, pastor of the Union AME Church in Philadelphia, wrote in 1885 that the era of "Mumbo Jumbo, fetishism, and Voudouism [sic] has passed away" and that the time had come for the "African race" to claim its equal recognition among the "Caucasian races."[118] Each of these ministers believed that they were witnessing an important transitional stage in black life and felt it was their duty to hurry history along.

At the time when black ministers were being scrutinized, black women began claiming their own authority in church life, education, and race progress. In 1888, Ida B. Wells, who would later become the leading black spokesperson against lynching, wrote three articles for the *Christian Index*, a newspaper published in Jackson, Tennessee, for the Colored Methodist Episcopal Church. She criticized the black ministry in all three articles. Wells accused black ministers of being too often intellectually and morally unfit to hold their positions. She called for ministers who were dignified, noble, cultivated in intellect, and consecrated in their work. She also demanded community accountability, suggesting a stronger role for women.[119] She was joined by other educated African American women in the black churches who challenged traditional notions of a "woman's place" within the churches and in the broader racial struggle.[120]

Booker T. Washington in 1890 was among those black leaders outside the ministry who entered this contentious debate. Washington was consistently critical of black churches and especially black clergymen. He was the foremast black leader in the country from 1895, when he gave his now-famous speech at the Cotton States and International Exposition at Atlanta, Georgia, until his death in 1915. Northern whites (and some Southerners) regarded him as the leading expert on black life in the South, and it was largely through his role as an exponent of industrial education at Tuskegee Institute that philanthropic largesse was channeled from the North into various black organizations and educational institutions.[121] August Meier has noted that prior to Washington's promotion of industrial education at Tuskegee, the AMA was the "most influential single agency fostering industrial education." But it was Samuel Armstrong, by founding Hampton Institute (originally under the auspices of the AMA), who really gave industrial education a big boost during the Reconstruction period. The very notion of industrial education as promoted by Armstrong rested on an understanding of blacks as slothful, backward, and lascivious people who needed to learn the values and skills of civilization.

Armstrong shared the view of missionary teachers and Freedmen's Bureau agents about blacks' need for moral education, industry, work habits, and discipline. He urged blacks to eschew politics and the demand for civil rights. These would come, he claimed, in the distant future when blacks had acquired high moral standards and property.[122]

Washington recalled with fondness in his autobiography, *Up from Slavery* (1901), the first meeting he had with Armstrong at Hampton in 1872, when Washington arrived fresh from the "degrading influences of the slave plantation and the coal mines" of Virginia. This "superhuman" man appeared almost perfect to the young sixteen-year-old ex-slave. Washington recounted images of students at Hampton "worshipping" the late general; in Washington's estimation, Armstrong truly was a "type of that Christ-like body of men and women who went into the Negro schools at the close of the war by the hundreds to assist in lifting up my race."[123] As a student at Hampton, Washington spent hours drinking in the general's wisdom and his ideas about industrial training and education for blacks in the South. One of Armstrong's central beliefs, taken up by Washington, was that the "old-time" religion of blacks hindered the development of industry. Armstrong argued that blacks emphasized the "emotional" aspect of their religion more than the moral and that their religion failed to check their "evil tendencies." In Armstrong's view, black ministers were lazy "demagogues" who shunned hard work by seeking "easy" calls to preach.[124] His ideas on black religion and blacks' place in the South found their most ready acceptance in his pupil, Washington.[125]

Washington became the principal of the newly formed Tuskegee Normal School for blacks in Macon County, Alabama, in 1881. His central philosophy was that through industry, thrift, and Christian character, blacks would eventually attain their constitutional rights.[126] True to his adoption of Armstrong's criticisms of black ministers as an obstacle to black industry, Washington did not hesitate to denounce the moral failures of blacks, especially ministers, before white audiences.[127] Washington first attracted wide attention from blacks outside of the educational field in 1890, when he delivered a scathing critique of the black clergy at the Fisk University Commencement. The speech was published in the *Christian Union*, an influential New York religious journal edited by Lyman Abbot, minister in the Plymouth Congregational Church in Brooklyn.[128] Washington asserted that after having come into contact with black ministers for eight years "in the heart of the South," he could state with certainty that three-fourths of the black ministers generally and two-thirds of the Methodists in particular "are unfit, either mentally or morally, or both, to preach the Gospel to anyone or to attempt to lead anyone."[129] He said that most black ministers made everything else subservient to their salaries and designed services in such a way to get more money from church members. Black ministers, Washington asserted, were not trusted by those who knew them best, especially in matters of finance and "general morality." He included a story of a black preacher who was at work one day in a cotton field in the middle of July, when he suddenly stopped, looked upward, and declared, "O Lord, de work is so hard, de cotton is so grassy, and de sun am *so* hot, I bleave dis darkey am called to preach."[130]

Washington believed that the black South was a vast mission field because even though most blacks were church members, few of them were really Christians. There was "no evidence," he argued, "that a large proportion of these church members are not just as ignorant of true Christianity, as taught by Christ, as any people in Africa or Japan, and just as much in need of missionary efforts as those in foreign lands."[131] Ministers were simply untrained and not equipped to make Christian disciples in Washington's view. Preachers' messages were "emotional in the highest degree," and were only considered successful to the extent that they "set people in all parts of the congregation to groaning, uttering wild screams, and jumping, finally going into a trance."[132] To rectify this problem, Washington proposed a nondenominational Bible seminary or training school that would teach students the Bible, how to prepare sermons, how to study, how to read a hymn, and how to reach and help people outside the pulpit "in an unselfish Christian way."[133]

Daniel Payne, a senior bishop in the AME Church, agreed with Washington. Payne was a tireless promoter of education for black ministers. He wrote congratulating Washington for having the courage to speak about such a pressing problem. Payne indicated that for "nine winters" he made his residence in the South and that for twenty-five years he had operated in "Southern fields," which provided him with ample opportunity to observe the "great defects" that Washington found among black ministers. He confirmed that there were "scores of cases" of cotton fieldhands leaving behind their work for an "easier way to get a living." Payne was convinced that Washington "understated the facts" regarding the number of those morally unqualified for ministry. He felt that Washington's "relation to the South as an educator" entitled him to a respectful hearing.[134]

As Washington's status grew, his opportunities increased to speak before white audiences, especially in the North. In a speech delivered in 1894 before the National Unitarian Association in Saratoga, New York, Washington urged his audience to help lift Southern blacks out of darkness into light and "out of degradation into civilization." Ever the pragmatist who carefully studied his audience and never a stickler for denominational labels, Washington stated, "You may label their regeneration Methodism, I care not, label it Presbyterianism, I care not, or a Baptist belief, I care not, I know what it is: it is American Christian manhood, something above creed or denominational labels." Well aware of common white complaints about black rapaciousness, Washington "defended" blacks by noting that no matter how much they go to church or shout and get happy, if they found themselves going to bed hungry, one could be sure that they would be "tempted to find something before morning." Blacks needed intellectual and moral training and the money that funded schools to support this training. Though blacks could "feel more in five minutes than a white man can in a day," Washington quipped, they needed training to strengthen their intellects.[135] The "emotional side" of their religion caused them to live in the next world, and this often distracted from their performance of practical duties. Washington asserted that blacks were fond of singing religious songs and of crying out, "give me Jesus." But at Tuskegee and conferences sponsored by the school, blacks were urged "to mix in some land, cotton and corn and a good bank account; and we find, by actual experience, that the man who has Jesus in this way has a religion that you can count on seven days in the week."[136]

Washington repeated his criticisms of black religion in many other speeches. His work confirmed the ideas of those who believed that black religion divorced ethics and Christian profession, and that the moral progress of the race was going to be a long, tedious process. Of course, he was eminently practical and used his rather dour predictions of blacks in the South to solicit aid for Tuskegee and his other projects for industrial education. Moreover, he was indebted to the currents of modernist religious thought that were influential at the turn of the century. He criticized black ministers for adhering to "worn-out theological dogmas," chided black church members for their emotionalism and their excessive emphasis on heaven and the world to come, and emphasized a practical religion that "sanctified" labor and efficiency.[137] In one instance, Washington stated, "Nothing pays so well in producing efficient labor as Christianity."[138] In an article in 1905 in the North American Review, his ideas seemed to have mirrored those of Tucker. Though Washington blamed slavery rather than emancipation for the moral defects of blacks, he did agree that slavery's "one great consolation" was that it gave Christianity to slaves. Slavery delivered blacks, he averred, from African fetishism, a "merely childish way of looking at and explaining the world." But like Tucker, he believed that blacks learned a form of Christianity under slavery that was "totally detached from morality."[139] Now blacks needed to learn personal responsibility and the relationship between ethics and religious belief. Washington insisted that at the annual Negro conferences sponsored by Tuskegee attendees be instructed to get rid of immoral schoolteachers and ministers and to "draw moral distinctions within the limits of their own communities." Regarding African American religion, he noted, "It has been said that the trouble with the Negro Church is that it is too emotional. It seems to be me that what the Negro Church needs is a more definite connection with the social and moral life of the Negro people."[140] Washington also called the Negro Church "from its apocalyptic vision back to earth."[141]

James Anderson argues that the Tuskegee model of education espoused by Washington represented a social philosophy. Leading businessmen, politicians, and most Northern philanthropists came to view Tuskegee and Hampton as the way toward a solution to the Negro problem.[142] Washington's emphasis on the backwardness and immorality of black preachers in the South and his insistence on industrial and agricultural education to produce a docile black labor force had great appeal to Northern and Southern whites who were seeking a way through the knotty Negro question. The degeneration of black religion, whether attributed to slavery or emancipation, was the dominant discourse. Even Northern liberal Henry Field, traveling the South in the late 1880s, longed for pleasant pictures from his childhood of affectionate and deeply religious blacks over against the alleged "dead level of mediocrity" that he found among blacks in his day.[143] So whether from the North or South, whites felt that their beliefs about black degeneration were confirmed. Even prominent blacks like Washington assured them that their views were correct.

Blacks Conserving Their Racial Gifts

David Blight asserts that slavery for blacks carried a social burden of shame.[144] Nathan Huggins, focusing on a period later than that under consideration, concludes that shame of the past led blacks to deny aspects of their culture that reminded them of their former condition, and of these he lists "enthusiastic religion."[145] Charting the "progress of the race" was one way of demonstrating how blacks had fared since slavery. Constant and heroic attempts by blacks to "vindicate the race" were other means of accomplishing the same end.[146] Alexander Crummell expressed this sentiment well. Although he had little love for the religion of the black masses, as a black leader he found himself in the unenviable position of defending black culture. Though he lauded English culture, his own proud heritage led him to elevate the special qualities of blacks in America. For those who urged blacks to forget their special grievances and focus on the fact that they are "American citizens," Crummell asserted at his annual Thanksgiving sermon in 1875, "We are just now a 'peculiar people' in this land; looked at, repulsed, kept apart, legislated for, criticised in journals, magazines, and scientific societies, at an insulting and intolerable distance, *as a peculiar people*; with the doubt against us whether or not we can hold on to vital power on this soil; or whether we have the capacity to rise to manhood and superiority."[147] For Crummell, blacks had to focus not only on their heritage from slavery but on their dual roles as blacks and American citizens. African Americans needed to tend to their special needs and troubles, and this imperative became increasingly urgent as blacks were legally segregated by the end of the nineteenth century. Thrust on their own resources, blacks had to rethink their responsibilities to themselves and find ways to reform and shape their own institutions. Meier has shown that as disenfranchisement grew and office holding decreased, blacks gradually became disillusioned with politics and increasingly turned to moral and economic development as a "substitute for and as a prerequisite to political activity."[148] In this context, greater attention to the role of black churches and the meaning of black religion became by necessity more pressing.

The social necessity of black churches was in part explained as a reflection of the special qualities of black people. In other words, blacks were not in separate churches simply because whites did not want them but because they had a special style of worship and a "distinctive racial character" that could find its proper outlet only in the company of other blacks. In a paper read before the Minneapolis Ministerial Association in November 1886, L. H. Reynolds, a layperson in the African Methodist Episcopal Church, argued that races have distinctive temperaments and habits, which must be taken into account in social affiliations. For example, Reynolds said that Italians were nervous, irritable, and vengeful in comparison to the "average American," who was said to be inquisitive and astute. Employers should modify their methods to "suit the peculiar temperaments and habits" of such different groups. He asserted that there was a law of race affiliation that drew blacks together in their churches (as a result of race antagonism among whites!), but he also believed that a "higher law of race assimilation" would eventually create a composite race in America and supersede this temporary "law of race-affiliation." All of this was to say that each race was best suited to reach its own people, but hope was held out that eventually race antagonism would be overcome.[149]

Reynolds was not a theologian or minister, but his ideas reflected contradictions within black social thought at the time. Blacks were forced to form their own churches, and, in the words of Bishop Daniel Alexander Payne, thrown on their own resources.[150] But virtue was made of necessity. Although Reynolds could laud the black churches for fulfilling the unique interests of blacks, he could scarcely conceal his desire that blacks would one day have mixed churches with whites. A situation that was imposed on blacks by whites was given a "racial" interpretation. Blacks were not in their churches just because they were driven from white churches but because they possessed a peculiar racial character that could only find fulfillment within their own religious associations. For Payne, the segregation of the churches turned out to be a good thing. It forced blacks to support and govern themselves. It made them responsible to themselves, and it gave them "an independence of character" that they could not attain under the supervision of whites.[151] Though Payne did not offer a racial interpretation of black church affiliation, he, too, found it necessary to make a virtue out of necessity. Racial pride, vindication of the race, psychic affirmation, and countering the claim that blacks lacked the capacity for self-government were all a part of these series of defenses about what was peculiar in the black churches.

Crummell was just as critical as whites of what he saw as the rampant emotionalism and immorality in black churches. But he was not willing to fix religious emotionalism and other "excesses" in biology. He pointed instead to education and "true godliness" as the antidote to the defects in black religion. Still, Crummell maintained a romantic racialist conception of black Christianity for most of his life, especially in his reflections on the unique contributions of blacks to America. In a sermon delivered in 1890, Crummell denounced the "hysterical pietists" who eschewed morality in the name of feeling and emotion. Although he argued that emotion played a limited role in true religion, he insisted that it was in no way opposed to true godliness. True godliness, Crummell asserted, meant a reconstruction of our humanity, our deepest need because of the original fall of humanity and its attendant moral ruin.[152] Much of this exposition was standard Christian doctrine. Although Crummell did not put a "racial" angle on his sermon, it is clear that he was directing it to black preachers who he believed sought to stimulate the emotions of their hearers. As Wilson Jeremiah Moses puts it, Crummell's position "placed him in opposition to the majority of black American preachers."[153]

His critique of emotionalism notwithstanding, Crummell lauded what he regarded as the special religious qualities of blacks. In a speech delivered in 1895, he asserted that blacks possessed "aboriginal qualities" that not only enabled them to survive the ordeal of slavery but gave them a special capacity to be religious. He put it this way: "There are certain constitutional tendencies in the race which are, without doubt, unique and special. A high moral altitude is a primitive quality, antecedent to the coming of Christianity; and which has developed into more positive forms, in Christian lands, under the inspiration of Christian teaching."[154] Drawing on the thought of Alexander Kinmont, William Ellery Channing, and romantic racialist ideas, Crummell concluded that the Negro "race is essentially religious."[155] By affirming innate religiosity for blacks, he could confidently assert the nobility of the race's future and its place in world history. Unlike the romantic racialists, however, Crummell had no doubt about blacks' future. He emphatically denied that blacks would be stuck in manual labor and believed that their future would be thrown wide open so long as the nation did not insist on caste distinctions and racial suppression.[156]

Conclusion

When white Northern missionaries and educators scurried about the South after the Civil War, they expressed dismay at what they saw. Black churches that were thought to be filled with vibrant spirituality and true religion (at least in the literature they had read) were instead havens of "heathenish observances," superstition, insane yellings, and gross immorality. The African was not so naturally religious after all, or, perhaps more accurately, whites argued that blacks' natural religiosity was all wrong and required a radical transformation. Although Northerners generally blamed slavery for the defects of black religion, they and Southerners agreed that rampant immorality and a lack of ethical codes coexisted with much religion among blacks. The problem became how to explain and rectify the situation. Northerners generally argued that education and white influence (from the North and from the "liberal" South) would be of inestimable value in helping blacks shed the deadweight of their slave-ridden past. Southerners were much less interested in solutions, but generally saw this as a confirmation of oft-stated claims that blacks would revert to African savagery once freed from the beneficent supervision of slavery. African American religion in the South, especially in rural areas, came to be regarded by the 1870s and 1880s as a vestige of a savage and degraded past, and few whites found anything to compliment in it.

Black leaders felt compelled to respond to these criticisms. Although many of them conceded that moral reform was necessary in black churches, they could not accept assertions of a static African past as adequate explanations for current black religious defects. Although they generally blamed slavery, some of them began to view black religion as an expression of the distinct racial character of black Americans, and though in need of purification, as something that needed to be treasured. Some black leaders, of course, were still deeply influenced by the romantic racialism of the antebellum period, and one wonders to what degree other viable options of affirmations of black culture were available. To be handed this image from mostly Northern white abolitionists did not seem to cause any conscious discomfort for black interpreters of African

American religion, perhaps because they came to accept it as their own creation. The interpretation of what it meant to be naturally religious was being transformed and refined even as blacks held onto the relatively benign romantic view of African American religion. By the turn of the century, innate religiosity had been radically redefined. Social scientists, deeply influenced by racial theories of sociocultural and biological evolution, located religion in black brains and physiology. Blacks may have been naturally religious, they argued, but their religion was as different from "true religion" (that is, religion as practiced by white "civilized" Europeans and Americans) as science differed from magic. By locating black religion in biology, racial differences and peculiarities could be further naturalized to support an unjust social order. Segregation, disenfranchisement, and menial labor, not active citizenship or participation in the nation, were rationalized as being especially fit for a primitive people who simply did not possess the intellectual and moral equipment to compete in a modern industrialized nation. The emotional qualities of the primitive mind, according to these interpreters, made blacks archaic outsiders in a modern American society.

3

The Social Sciences and the Professional Discipline of Black Religion

By the late nineteenth century, the developing disciplines of history, sociology, anthropology, and psychology drew heavily on previous discussions about "the races" and created a new discourse of race and religion. Early evolutionary anthropology (in the post–Civil War period) in Britain and the United States accepted the notion of a hierarchy of human races. Human history was seen as a single evolutionary development through a series of stages (usually construed as savagery, barbarism, and civilization). The pinnacle of human development was deemed to be that of white Western European civilization.[1] This formulation became crucial to evolutionary psychological theories of religion.

The social sciences, and the psychology of religion in particular, were the key cultural authorities in pathologizing the religious experiences of blacks in the South. This professional disciplining of black religion has been overlooked by scholars who have ably documented, for example, the crucial role that psychological tests played in buttressing scientific racism in the 1920s. The new psychology that arose in the 1890s, particularly the psychology of religion, more vocally asserted the moral and cultural inferiority of blacks in part because black intellectual inferiority was assumed. But as George Stocking notes, by the 1920s psychological tests reflected a professional commitment to a system of instrumentation that seemed to place psychology on a much firmer scientific footing that could assure critics that race differences could be quantified.[2] The bases of black inclusion and participation in the civic life of the nation changed, but the same conclusions were advanced, namely, that blacks were unfit (morally, at first, then intellectually) to enjoy basic rights as American citizens. Yet the new psychology was just as eager as the later, more quantitative psychology of the 1920s to demonstrate that it was a science, and it served as a powerful tool in the critique of black religious life. The shift from a critique of blacks' moral or religious life to their intellectual capacities occurred in the post–World War I period partly because of heightened attention to black migration to the North, growing rates of educational achievements for blacks, and a newer respect and need for technical skills in an increasingly urban and industrial society. As William Tucker argues about the quantitative psychology of the 1920s, "In a society marked by increasing vocational complexity and consequent specialization of talent, psychology promised to rationalize the allocation of human resources by quantifying an individual's psychological traits."[3] Stated pointedly, the new psychology pathologized black religious life in the South by asserting that blacks lacked morals or an ethical life, hence the concomitant assertion of their alleged unfitness for the franchise and justifications of harsh treatment at the hands of Southern whites (which also extended to apologies for lynching). The psychologists of the 1920s lent professional support to claims that blacks in the urban North, even though some of them may have scored higher on intelligence tests than Southern whites, lacked the intellectual capacity to participate equally in a modern industrial society. Emphasis on the social scientific disciplines' growing aspirations for scientific status, though important, should not obscure their ideological function in their construal of black prospects in the nation.

Social science became the ultimate authority in the late nineteenth century (especially in the North), and religious or sentimental assessments of blacks were deemed ostensibly irrelevant to scientific matters. This gave more cultural authority to claims of black inferiority because it was no longer articulated solely by "backward" and racist Southern demagogues who obviously had a vested interest in making these arguments. Yet behind these scientific and seemingly clinical analyses of African American religion stood a massive moral argument against blacks, which was rooted in a normative liberal Protestant religious tradition. The new social sciences provided academic support and a university-based ideology (particularly in the North) for assertions that blacks were unfit to vote and incapable of participating in the civic life and governance of the nation. "Emotionalism," which emerged as the principal discourse of black religion in the new language of psychopathology, was then a clinical and seemingly dispassionate way of dissecting and denigrating black life so as to absolve interpreters of appearances of animus toward blacks and to set these academics apart from the popular prejudices and emotional outbursts of their "primitive" Southern white brethren who were lynching blacks with astonishing levels of cruelty.

The construction of the primitive was important for representations of blacks because it legitimated their deteriorating social, political, and economic condition in America by portraying them in relation to their "debased" African cousins. Images of Africa provided retrospective defenses of slavery and support for the oppression of blacks in the South by claiming an affinity between crime and sexual immorality in the black South and in Africa. On one hand, early black sociologists and interpreters of African American religion constructed the Negro Church and sought ways to make it more effective and efficient in the fight against racism and political and economic oppression. Generally, studies that initiated the discourse of the Negro Church grounded the study of black religion in *social* science rather than in theories of the mind or psychology. This gave a social dimension to black religion, and the authors of these studies explicitly and implicitly urged blacks to exert their power in the social and political realm through one of the few institutions that they owned and controlled (the church). On the other hand, white academics, especially G. Stanley Hall and those influenced by his ideas, sought to render a psychological and naturalistic interpretation of black religion. This was part of a more general trend in academic studies of religion, where emphasis was placed on the natural origins and evolution of religion and its function in the broader social order. By emphasizing theories of the mind, blame could be placed on perceived defects in blacks' character or personality, hence linking an essential African character to moral degeneration and cultural degradation.[4]

Within the context of late-nineteenth- and early twentieth-century scientific racism, such studies of black religion gave professional and theoretical support for popular claims (initially Southern) about the "immorality," "emotionalism," and "degeneracy" of black religion to explain why harsh measures in the South were required to discipline blacks. Lynching, political disenfranchisement, and segregation were discussed in these analyses of black life and sometimes explicitly regarded as understandable responses to black religious degeneration. In his influential *Race Traits and Tendencies of the American Negro* (1896), Frederick Hoffman, a statistician for the Prudential Insurance Company of America and a member of the American Academy of Medicine, argued that an increase in black churches (as well as more education) since Emancipation could not raise blacks from their low and "anti-social" condition. Race and heredity, in his view, explained the diseases, suicide, immorality, and criminality of blacks in America. In the racial struggle for existence, blacks would either deteriorate further and eventually become extinct, he maintained, or lose many of their weakest members and acquire their rightful place among the Anglo-Saxons.[5] For Hoffman and other white social scientists, science offered the key to deficient black behavior, and conditions in the biology of blacks and "race" explained their failure to adapt to a free society.

The Emotional Traits of the Primitive Races

Richard Hofstadter, in his now classic work, *Social Darwinism in America*, has argued that English philosopher and social theorist Herbert Spencer had a profound and lasting influence on American social thought in the last decades of the nineteenth century. Besides the influence his ideas had on professional social science, Spencer was read by the self-educated and by those who "were plodding their way out of theological orthodoxy."[6] Even if there may be doubt about Hofstadter's specific arguments about Spencer's influence, it is certain that Spencer's work was important in the American context because of its support for conservative social philosophies that deplored state intervention. So, too, was his emphasis on a naturalistic social science that refused to incorporate theological or religious interpretations of society and social ethics.[7] The writers whose works are examined in this chapter were desirous of providing a scientific analysis of black religion and explicitly sought to distance their work from a theological framework. For all their protests to the contrary, however, their works contained implicit theological and moral critiques of black religion. While these were theological critiques shorn of orthodox or creedal formulations, they nonetheless evince a residual Christian analysis that reinstated some of the older theological arguments against African American religion (especially in the claims that religion and ethics were separate in black religion and that blacks were deficient in Christian practice).

George Stocking argues that Spencer's sociological thought "structured the thinking of two generations of American social scientists before 1920."[8] Spencer's depiction of the "primitive mind" was crucial to anthropological studies of nonwhite peoples and had special relevance for interpretations of African American religion in this period. Spencer's work offered a sociological analysis of social development and a psychological interpretation of the mind. His theories of the primitive mind were influential in formulations of black religion by G. Stanley Hall, Frederick Morgan Davenport, and Howard Odum, all influential social scientists whose studies of black culture posited biological explanations for what they saw as black pathology and defective religious practices.[9]

Spencer devoted a section of his *Principles of Sociology* to the primitive mind, in which he argued that lighter-skinned races were "habitually the dominant races."[10] In this section, "The Primitive Man-Emotional," he set out his theory of the emotional qualities of the primitive mind. He claimed that primitive man's emotions differed from civilized man: Primitive emotions consisted of sensations and the "simple feelings directly associated with them." They possessed less of the involved "representative feelings." Among the emotional traits of the primitive mind, Spencer noted irregularity, impulsiveness, improvidence, and imitativeness. "Improvident" primitives, he argued, such as Indians, Africans, and other "exotic" people, were unable to plan for the future because they simply had an "inadequate consciousness of the future," their mental capacity lacking and disorganized. They exhibited "childish mirthfulness," had an "undeveloped proprietary sentiment," and did not have any notion of "individual possession." Their "fixity of habit" led to conservatism in an "extreme degree," which meant that they continued to do things the same way as their ancestors did without conscious thought or any particular regard for the future. Primitives were so ruled by emotions, Spencer asserted, that they lacked the discipline and self-control of civilized humans. "Governed as he is by despotic emotions that successively depose one another, instead of by a council of emotions shared in by all," as he put it, "the primitive man has an explosive, chaotic, incalculable behaviour."[11]

Positing emotionalism as the basis of primitive life was one way of denigrating "primitive culture" over the "advanced culture" of white Western Europeans, because self-control and inhibition were seen as the crux of civilization. It was also an apology for imperialism and the taking of the lands of "primitive" peoples, who were said to be backward, lacking in concepts of private property, and unable to bring about the advances that would be beneficial to their society. Unjust and discriminatory treatment of native peoples was thus justified on the basis of their biological and cultural "weaknesses," and social Darwinist propagandists argued that the fittest would survive such encounters between Europeans and primitive folk. Emotionalism as a way of describing black religion was one part of this discussion of primitive dark-skinned peoples and their role in the advance of civilized society.

"Getting the Negro before the Assembled Nations"

The phrase comes from a black visitor of the Chicago World's Columbian Exposition.[12] Reflecting on the depiction of blacks at the fair, held from May 1 to October 31, 1893, aging former abolitionist and U.S. minister to Haiti Frederick Douglass lamented that the "spirit of American caste against the educated Negro was conspicuously seen from start to finish." He was deeply disappointed that here, when there was a chance to show the world a "grand ethnological lesson" about humanity's diversity and varied cultures, the Negro was excluded and humiliated by the arrangement of the fair. Dahomean peoples of Africa were displayed, but Douglass felt that this was all a ruse because what was exhibited was their "barbarism" so as "to shame the educated Negro of America" who "ought to have been there, if only to show what American slavery and American freedom have done for him."[13] The meaning of the placing of the Dahomean village among other nonwhite villages at the Midway Plaisance, which was not a site for national exhibits, was not lost on Douglass. For all its boast of being a "Pentecost," Douglass judged the exhibition to be a sham. He declared,

> What a commentary is this upon the liberality of our boasted
> American liberty and American equality! It is a silent example to be
> sure, but it is one that speaks louder than words. It says to the world
> that the colored people of America are not deemed by Americans
> as within the compass of American law, progress and civilization. It
> says to the lynchers and mobocrats of the South, go on in your hellish
> work of Negro persecution. You kill their bodies, we will kill their
> souls.[14]

Douglass's comments and reaction to the fair shed light on the racial views of those responsible for the exhibition and the ambivalent feelings of educated African Americans about their own culture and heritage and about its representations in public discourse in the United States in the late nineteenth century. The Midway Plaisance, which contained the villages of primitive peoples, was deliberately set off from the magnificence of the White City. Guidebooks encouraged visitors to walk through the Midway and view the exhibits only after they had seen the edifices of modern civilization. The "grand ethnological lesson" was to ground American racial attitudes on "ethnological bedrock." The science of human culture enabled the exhibit to be "one vast anthropological revelation" of the superiority of the Anglo-Saxon over primitive races.[15] Douglass's comments raise questions about how ensnaring the discourse of civilization and savagery could be. Representing the race proved to be risky, because the price entailed a desire to display the prominent and educated Negro who, it was hoped, would bring favorable views of blacks. So blacks found themselves in the unenviable position of having to represent American blacks and Africans, all the while denigrating the "savage" culture of the latter to distance themselves from their superstitions. Though Douglass indicted white Americans for bringing the Dahomeans—whom he believed "were there to exhibit their barbarism"—to Chicago to gaze on them, his comments about them reinforced white perceptions of other nonwhite, non-Christian peoples.[16]

When the World's Parliament of Religions opened on September 11, glowing comments about its future role as a "new Mount Zion" were uttered, and high hopes abounded about the "crowing glory" of the conference of the world's religions coming together on America's shores. The Parliament met from September 11 to September 27, 1893. In hindsight, absences are conspicuous. No tribal religions were represented, and there was no significant representation from South America or Africa. Still, this was truly an extraordinary event. Forty denominations were part of the Congress of Religion, which overlapped with the Parliament. One hundred ninety-four papers were presented as the various delegates met in the Memorial Art Palace (now the Chicago Art Institute), and ten world religions were represented. The Parliament has been variously described by historians as (1) an attempt to define the relationship of Christianity to other religions and come to terms with the nature of Christianity's claims to superiority and ultimate truth;[17] (2) a liberal, Western, and American quest for world religious unity; (3) a symbol of the ultimacy of the Greco-Roman and Christian West;[18] (4) a world picture, an image revealing mainstream Christian America's image to itself and its image of the rest of the world; (5) a catalyst in the objectification of religion as a field of study and analysis;[19] and (6) an expression of a newfound readiness to recognize and include other non-Christian religions.[20] But perhaps most important, the Parliament, as part of the larger exhibit, reflected normative contemporary anthropological views about sociocultural evolution with Africans and African Americans at the bottom of the evolutionary scale. The depictions of blacks and Africans on Colored Day, at various parts of the exhibition, and in the various cartoons during and after the fair, demonstrated this anthropological view.[21]

African Americans had especially high hopes for the Exposition and Parliament, but it quickly became clear that their hopes for "getting the Negro before the assembled nations" (or the image or kind of representative blacks that they desired) would not quite materialize. Only two blacks presented speeches at the Parliament—Benjamin William Arnett, a bishop in the AME Church, and Fannie Barrier Williams, a prominent Unitarian and member of the Chicago Woman's Club. Arnett delivered two speeches at the Parliament, one ("Africa and the Descendants of Africa: A Response in Behalf of Africa") on the opening night (September 11) and another ("Christianity and the Negro") on the twelfth day (September 22). Perhaps because of his political connections as a Republican and a supporter of William McKinley through the latter's march to the White House—he delivered the invocation and benediction at the

1896 National Republican Convention—Arnett was chosen for his role as speaker at the Parliament.[22] Although he tried to bring a touch of humor to the proceedings by noting that he was "announced to give color" to the Parliament, he found himself in an awkward position representing Africa as an American. He began by noting that he welcomed the "redemption of Africa" and held high hopes that Africa "in the future is to bring forth a Jefferson, who will write a declaration of independence of the dark continent." Perhaps, too, a George Washington would arise, or even a Toussaint L'Ouverture (a leader of the slave revolution that brought Haiti independence from France in 1804) who would deliver his people. Arnett envisioned such a leader bringing a "republican form of government, whose corner stone will be religion, morality, education, and temperance, acknowledging the fatherhood of God, and the brotherhood of man; while the ten commandments and the golden rule shall be the rule of life and conduct in the great republic of redeemed Africa."[23]

Such themes of unity and brotherhood resonated with the Parliament's rhetoric about a new Pentecost. Paul Carus, a scientific naturalist who played a significant role in introducing Buddhist philosophy into the United States, wrote two months after the Parliament that Arnett's presence and the contents of his speech were an example that "races were represented" at the Parliament. Carus regarded this "spectacle" (that is, the grand display of the religions represented) as the "dawn of a new religious era." He noted that Arnett's comments about giving color to the Parliament were "interrupted with a storm of merriment." He interpreted Arnett's claim that the Parliament was "very well colored" as a remarkable acknowledgment from a black man that the Parliament was indeed racially diverse.[24] In the opening address on the origins of the Parliament, Charles Carrol Bonney, a Chicago lawyer and layman in the Swedenborgian church, rejoiced that even in "their temporary camps, the children of fetichism, wide-eyed and speechless, have gazed here upon this multitude of believers bearing palms, trooping hither from the uttermost parts of the earth and the islands of the deep." Bonney was responsible for organizing the various Congresses at the fair, and he went on to extol the fact that diverse peoples could forget their differences and "in unison" raise their voices to the most High.[25] Bonney's and Carus's lauding of the fair expressed their desires more than the reality of racial unity and religious harmony.

Arnett's speech about Africa's role in the future was welcomed, even though as he spoke Europeans were carving up the continent. He held out hope that the African could indeed acquire the traits of civilization and morality that whites regularly accused them of lacking (note, for example, his remarks about the ten commandments in light of long-standing critiques of black religion). Arnett also magnanimously welcomed the opportunity to speak on behalf of

America's Negroes. He concluded that by the providence of God and "the power of the religion of Jesus Christ, [we Negroes] have been liberated from slavery."[26]

Walter Houghton, editor-in-chief of *Neely's History of the Parliament of Religions*, one of the two authoritative published editions of the Parliament's speeches, edited and abridged Arnett's extensive comments about African topography, imports and exports, and Africa's deliverance from foreign powers. The remark about L'Ouverture remained, but none of Arnett's statements about a redeemer with "African blood in his veins" can be found in this collection. Excised, too, were his remarks about Africa as the cradle of civilization, the home of Moses, and the asylum of the infant Redeemer. Completely gone were the favorable statements about John Brown and his soul marching on to bring freedom from crime, sin, and ignorance to every nation. In light of such glaring omissions, we are not surprised to find missing Arnett's statements about blacks toiling in the cotton fields, laboring in mines, "suffering cruelties in the Mississippi delta," and "dying under the oppression of the rice swamps of the Carolinas and the everglades of Florida" during their long sojourn under slavery.[27] Apparently, Houghton did not think such remarks fit in well with the overall positive tone of the Parliament and its emphasis on unity and peace.

In his second speech, "Christianity and the Negro," Arnett sought to answer a question posed and answered in the affirmative by one of his fellow church members: Can the descendants of Ham (Africans) do anything great?[28] Arnett returned to his theme of past African greatness by noting that blacks were "older than Christianity." He went on to describe Africa as a "cradle of art and science," noting along the way biblical figures whom he believed were black. He expressed his hope that the Parliament would "change some of the Christians of this land" and help bring about "the brotherhood of man." Amidst all of the sentiments about peace and unity at the Parliament, Arnett injected a note of realism that was hard to ignore. His pleas for black liberty, justice, and citizenship in a "Christian commonwealth" were intended to provoke reevaluations of what constituted "true Christianity."[29] He would not allow speakers to be satisfied with a philosophical or general conception of religion or Christianity that did not entail a specific commitment to rectifying the lived experience of blacks in the nation. He concluded his address with a stinging indictment of white Christianity. Arnett argued that Africans had been stolen from their native land in the name of Christianity and that "when the slave trade was abolished by the strong hand of true Christianity, then false Christianity had no interest in souls at all." He insisted that any talk of Christianity must be done with an awareness of the evil that had been carried out in its name, especially against black Americans.[30]

Fannie Barrier Williams's speech was in many ways a similar indictment of white Christianity. Williams, however, was more attuned to black "womanhood" and what she saw as its ability to bring Christian uplift and a stable home life to blacks in the South. While lauding blacks for making the best out of the Christianity handed to them, she presented a critique of how whites had practiced the faith. "The hope of the negro and other dark races in America," she proclaimed, "depends upon how far white Christians can assimilate their own religion." But white Christians had failed.[31] Both Williams and Arnett distanced themselves and their black brothers and sisters from the "fetiches and crudities of the Dark Continent" (though Arnett was much more favorable in his general views of Africa). Williams manifested a strong attachment to a Victorian ideology of gentility, culture, and moral purity, even though her Unitarian faith led her expectedly to denigrate theology and "church."

Blacks had the special burden of demonstrating how far they had come from African paganism and the extent to which they had imbibed Western Christian culture. By doing so, they lent credence to claims about Western superiority and cultural evolution. Furthermore, as John Burris observes, blacks represented not a religious body but an ethnic group at the Parliament, and this reality was reflected in the ambivalent content of their speeches.[32] By appealing to whites to live up to Christian ideals, while celebrating the contributions of Africa to Christianity and civilization, and apologizing for black Christian failings by pointing to the defective Christianity of the whites from whom they received it, Arnett and Williams made visible the tensions in and the tenuousness of their positions. Burris correctly notes that African Americans at the Parliament "lived in a kind of netherworld between various religious and cultural realities."[33] Blacks contributed little in the end to forging a common discourse for a global society.[34] This was in part because their social reality belied the very presence of such a gathering based on common religions and human unity.[35] After all, as Ida B. Wells and Frederick Douglass constantly reminded whites, blacks were being lynched in the South by Christian people, and Christian sentiment had done little to inspire whites to accept blacks as equals. Blacks like Arnett and Williams had ambivalent attachments to both the United States and Africa, having to choose an identity that inevitably meant the denigration of the other. Though they spoke out strongly against racism and the deteriorating conditions of blacks in the South, their voices were partly muted because of the selective reporting of their speeches (few as they were) and the visceral appeal of spectacle and visual imagery (transmitted through cartoons, the set-up of the exhibitions, and the varied representations that followed the fair itself) over written and spoken words.[36]

Images of Africa and Black Religion

There was a basic lesson to be learned from the Columbian Exposition, stated clearly in a souvenir book of photographs published shortly after the fair: "Perhaps one of the most striking lessons which the Columbian Exposition taught was the fact that African slavery in America had not, after all, been an unmixed evil, for of a truth, the advanced social conditions of American Africans over that of their barbarous countrymen is most encouraging and wonderful."[37] The "Africans" in America were to be regarded not in terms of their rights as American citizens but in terms of how far they had come from the jungles of savage Africa.

By the turn of the century, historical and social scientific works regularly described slavery as having been beneficial to blacks. These studies also served as an apology for the deteriorating conditions of blacks in the South by attributing them to a resurgence of African customs and behavioral traits. This is evident in the writing of Joseph Alexander Tillinghast, a professor of social science at Converse College in Spartanburg, South Carolina. Tillinghast published a study for the American Economic Association in 1902 titled *The Negro in Africa and America*, which claimed to answer the question whether uncivilized people may be lifted (or may lift themselves) to the "plane of advanced civilization." He argued that more than slavery, the African ancestry of American blacks accounted for their degradation. The son of a South Carolina slaveholder, Tillinghast acknowledged that careful attention to the characteristics of the ancestors of American blacks should lead to a more impartial judgment of slavery and of the Negro character under slavery. The author slipped into the language of qualitative judgments so often that he hardly seemed to notice it in this work, which he labeled scientific and ethnological. Tillinghast argued that the "psychic nature of the West African exhibits more of those immaturities so common among uncultured savages, and analogous to childish thought and emotion in more developed races." Africans lacked strength of will, stability of purpose, and self-control in emotional crises. He asserted that Africans were dominated by a passionate love of music and rhythmic motion: Fitful, passionate, cruel, sensuous, and lacking dignity, they easily accepted governance at the hands of others. Africans lacked the reasoning powers of civilized races, Tillinghast proclaimed, although they could learn to imitate their white superiors in some ways.[38]

Tillinghast depicted West African religion as a crude mixture of witchcraft, cannibalism, and delusion. Continuous with a long-standing critique of

African and African American religious practices, Tillinghast was confident that West Africans' code of behavior toward their gods had no bearing on issues of social morality and that their religion had nothing to do with relations between humans. Black religion, instead, was simply a primitive "science of nature." Although civilized people have ("for the most part") differentiated their religion from science, a scientific conception of natural processes was foreign to the Negro mind. (Tillinghast alternately used the terms *Negro, African,* or *West African.*) Africans simply could not imagine "impersonal forces" such as "gravity or electricity" because they grounded their actions in the volition of some great being, visible or invisible.[39] Hence their beliefs in varied spirits and the many means of dealing with them. Tillinghast argued that Africans, like civilized people, hoped to be healed of diseases, desired good weather, and wished for freedom from harm, but they went about such efforts by sacrificing human beings, buying charms, and engaging in various other superstitious or magical actions. For Tillinghast, all of this was evidence of Africa's false science.[40]

Locating their low cultural capacities in their smaller and less complex brains, Tillinghast argued that African children were stuck in a prolonged state of immaturity, which made them unable to participate in the "higher faculties of abstract reasoning." This was a kind of arrested mental puberty, where sexual relations were freely engaged in, but the mental faculties failed to mature.[41] This view of arrested development was quite common among psychologists and social scientists who wrote about blacks in the early twentieth century. Spencer had argued in his *Principles of Sociology* that precocity was found among blacks, but for some reason it was soon arrested.[42] Philip Bruce said essentially the same thing, remarking that the "precocity of the child is remarkable" and that at the age of puberty the black child's mind became "sluggish, narrow, and obtuse" as though the "development of the physical frame absorbed what should go to the support and enlargement of the brain." Bruce speculated that because blacks belonged to a "tropical race," their mental and physical capacities ripened earlier than inhabitants of temperate zones (Spencer intimated as much in his speculations about primitive races). Bruce conjectured that this condition of arrested intellectual development had been slightly modified among American blacks, though he insisted that the mental "cloudiness" that black children allegedly experienced during puberty remained until old age.[43] G. Stanley Hall was even more specific in his views, indicating that studies showed that black children were as bright as white children until age twelve. He claimed that the sexual "instinct" developed in blacks earlier than in whites and with such suddenness that it was "far more likely to permanently retard mental and moral growth." He concluded that the "virtues and defects of the negro through life remain largely those of puberty." Hall pointed to the "emotional" and "volatile" nature of blacks to demonstrate that this overpowering influence, rooted in sexual passion, arrested mental development.[44]

Tillinghast's reflections on the "psychic nature" of blacks confirm what John Corrigan has argued about white views of blacks in another historical context (Boston in the mid-nineteenth century). Corrigan contends that whites constructed black minds as deficient on two contradictory fronts: They were said to be emotionally passive and overly passionate. This apparently contradictory criticism, Corrigan observes, ensured that blacks would be found inferior to whites.[45] On one hand, assertions of emotionality meant that blacks lacked self-control and practiced a religion that was devoid of morality, civility, and ethics. Their religion was seen as all feeling and shouting. On the other hand, claims of emotionlessness or the inability to experience feeling or pain served as defenses of blacks laboring long hours under harsh conditions. Blacks, it was said, did not become sorrowful after great losses and did not experience pain the same way as whites when it was inflicted as a result of breaking the law (a veiled apology for lynching). So for Tillinghast, blacks were described as "violently excitable" and extremely demonstrative. They could not bridle their passions, keep to a fixed purpose, or steady their emotions. This infirmity of will led to a weakness at the very root of their lives. Intense emotions, erratic impulses, greed, and strong sexual passions continually disrupted any semblance of control in their lives.[46] Yet while claiming that blacks were too emotional, Tillinghast also believed that they were incapable of empathizing with the suffering of others and were quickly forgetful of sorrowful events.[47] A theory of racial difference obscured the harshness of this conception of blacks as impassive brutes who could not experience pain, sensitivity, or kindness.

Tillinghast saw slavery as a "vast school, in which a superior race drilled an inferior one into useful civilized life." Although slavery was motivated by profit, control over blacks was necessary to handle a "physically mature but mentally and morally childish people."[48] Qualities evident among black slaves such as indolence, carelessness, brutality to animals, and aptness in deception were character flaws caused not by slavery but by products of African ancestry. Tillinghast argued, "Every characteristic just named we know to have been an integral part of the West African's nature long before any slaver ever touched our shore."[49] Race heredity, "obscurely but irresistibly dominating Negro life at every point," was thus responsible for these "elements of undeveloped character."[50]

Tillinghast maintained that the religion of blacks under slavery, though not entirely stripped of its African superstitions, underwent a revolutionary transformation. Unlike their African ancestors, whose religion had nothing to do with moral conduct, the slaves were taught the need to live by a moral code. For the African there was "no inconsistency between his piety towards the gods and cruelty or crime against human beings," but slaves were at least taught that one's relationship to God must affect how one treats other human beings.[51] Though religion among the slaves was mixed with superstitions and varied African customs, it was certainly better than the religion of their African ancestors. Christianity through white missionaries taught the slaves the "lofty ideals and exacting moral code of Christianity," even though these were but feebly grasped by the race. It brought about a revolution in their orientation to the world and their understanding of ethics.[52]

In his discussion of black social and religious development since the Civil War, Tillinghast noted that blacks *must* have some kind of religion because their temperament "calls for abundant sociability and religious excitement."[53] He attributed the existence of black churches to differences in temperament and racial instincts. Blacks, like all groups, sought satisfaction in "associated life" with those similar in appearance, tastes, and traditions. "The kind of religious services acceptable to most whites does not attract most negroes,"[54] Tillinghast claimed, and as a result of this growing separation of the races, blacks had lost much of their sense of parental responsibility, family life, and monogamous marriage.[55] Tillinghast asserted that black men raped white women because of their "primitive savage passions, which master the criminal's whole being."[56] A survival of "racial traits and customs" was evident in their religious life; their church life resembled "in its main outlines the group life of West Africa."[57] Village or church life had now taken over the function of family or home life. Tillinghast averred that this was not because slavery destroyed family life but because the "ancient racial habit of gregarious communal life is growing to-day at the expense of private home life."[58] Blacks sought social pleasures and enjoyment in their churches that whites sought in their private homes. This was, according to Tillinghast, because an "impulse from within, working with other forces, is sending the race along lines divergent form those of national development as a whole."[59]

Tillinghast, like Bruce, detected an inability on the part of blacks to see any relation between religious profession and moral conduct, which he attributed to the survival of an African racial heritage that never associated religion with morality.[60] The emotional sermons of the preachers were further evidence of the influence of Africa. Worshipers worked themselves into a frenzy until they were in a "half-demented" state. Such meetings resembled a "West African religious service."[61] The emotional temperament and imaginative mind of blacks caused them to fall under the spell of music and oratory. Tillinghast went on, "This is but an extreme expression of a cast of mind, which under the stimulus of fear, moves insensibly over the hazy line that divides the natural from the supernatural, and falls under the spell of immaterial images."[62] Because only a few blacks have escaped the superstitions and witchcraft practiced by the masses, "they cannot be cited as arguing a capacity in the mass of the negroes to attain American civilization at a pace in harmony with our national progress."[63]

Tillinghast's study sought to synthesize the century's accumulated scientific evidence of race differences in a way similar to Hoffman's work in 1896, which summarized for that time medical and anthropological studies of blacks (both studies were published under the auspices of the American Economic Association). Although Tillinghast's study was one of many that examined the prospects of blacks in a "free" society, he gave more attention to religion than most of these. Tillinghast's book was also concerned with linking "defects" and problems within black communities to their African heritage and thereby regarded slavery as having been beneficial to blacks because it supposedly arrested their moral and cultural degeneration. Although discussions of contemporary problems such as lynching and disenfranchisement of blacks appeared in the book, it does not seem that Tillinghast felt an urgency to enter these debates. As John Haller writes, Tillinghast insisted that blacks were unable to harmonize their hereditary instincts with American social organization and reverted to their African character under this condition of strain.[64] In sum, no real proposals for black improvement were offered, only a bleak picture of probable black extinction in the future because the traits inherent to the race could not flourish in America. An African heritage was therefore posited as the culprit for the plight of American blacks.

A young African American professor of economics and history at Atlanta University, W. E. Burghardt Du Bois, commended Tillinghast for attempting to study the "vital connection between the Negro in his own home and the Negro in his foster land," and he welcomed more attention to the African past of American Negroes.[65] Du Bois was disappointed that Tillinghast was so quick to settle the current Negro problem after trying to provide an "interesting social study of African customs." He disputed Tillinghast's assertions that black family life was dissolute, that crime among blacks was "threatening wholesale race deterioration," and that the younger generation of blacks was "going wholesale to the devil." Du Bois was especially troubled that Tillinghast's haste in using his study of Africa to deal with the present situation of blacks might detract from "our faith in the scientific accuracy" of his work. Methodology and scientific analysis were crucial for Du Bois. His chief objection to Tillinghast was that he was so desirous to prove a thesis that blacks had benefited by slavery that his "scientific aim" was overwhelmed. Tillinghast's lack of a broad knowledge of "savage life," Du Bois insisted, and his tendency to make comparative judgments of "primitive" life in Africa and the current conditions of civilized nations marred his work. For Du Bois, thinkers like Tillinghast simply did not possess the "mental equipment" and the necessary understanding of "race development" to undertake such an important study with scientific accuracy.[66]

Although Du Bois's study of the connections between African religions and the religious life of black Americans was part of his overall project to present a scientific study of black life and give a more balanced understanding of African cultures, white interpreters of black religion were not so sanguine about the influence of Africa. These authors, who were familiar with the work of Du Bois, found little that was useful in studying African culture, save for its explanation of the current degradation of blacks in the South. In 1904, Walter Fleming, a white historian at West Virginia University, reviewed Du Bois's *The Negro Church* and noted that historians, contrary to Du Bois's position, found little that was durable in African culture that remained intact in the American context. Fleming also argued that blacks were in white churches for a "necessary period of probation," which was a direct attack on Du Bois's view that blacks had to have their own churches because whites did not treat them as equals and did not allow them to participate in church government.[67]

But no matter whether white interpreters agreed with Tillinghast or Du Bois on the specific views they advanced about the connection between Africa and American blacks, they were certain that Africa was the "point of departure" for blacks' development in America. John Spencer Bassett, a professor at Trinity College (later Duke University) in Durham, North Carolina, though he wrote that Tillinghast's work was not as scientific as he desired, was hardly less critical of what he saw as blacks' defective heritage from Africa. All the characteristics that Spencer and Tillinghast found among primitive peoples and Africans appeared in Bassett's work: "animal emotions," improvidence, and impetuosity. Bassett argued that Africans lacked invention, enterprise, reflection, and sublimity. American blacks, he maintained, inherited from Africa a "propensity for sensuality." Slavery helped blacks adopt monogamy and enabled them to have some semblance of sexual morality, though it was admittedly still low, Bassett asserted. African religion was devoid of "sublime ideas," he continued, and had "nothing to do with morality: no god avenges lying, theft, or unchastity." Human sacrifice, personal nudity (which led to promiscuity and left little sense of modesty), and crude beliefs and practices abounded, he maintained.[68] Essentially all that was good in black religion and culture was a product of blacks' experience in America.[69] Even among white academics like Bassett who did not offer a retrospective defense of slavery, Africa was the land of darkness and moral degradation from which American blacks had been delivered. To the extent that African American religion was linked to an African past, more sinister interpretations about its nature and meaning proliferated.[70]

The Professional Disciplining of Black Emotionalism

With the rise of the new psychology in the 1890s, a particular attempt was made to offer a scientific and naturalistic explanation of black religion. The new psychology replaced the older mental and moral philosophy taught by clergymen professors in college prior to the 1890s. Nonclergy faculty taught psychology as part of the social science curriculum. Psychology was divorced from theology (at least in theory and as an academic discipline) and sought to render a natural or nonreligious account of religious practices.[71] By the early twentieth century, a fairly broad consensus on African Americans had emerged in the social sciences: As primitive peoples who were in the emotional or childhood stage of their development, blacks would have to undergo years of industrial labor and live in deficient conditions before they could in any measurable sense bridge the gap that existed between them and white Americans. Yet even as the new psychology claimed scientific status, its moral critique of black religion was scarcely hidden. In 1908, for example, in a major text on the psychology of religion, *The Psychological Phenomenon of Christianity*, the liberal Protestant Baptist minister and professional psychologist George Barton Cutten (who obtained his doctorate at Yale University) argued that "religion had nothing to do with moral conduct" among blacks in the South. Cutten wrote that Africans saw no inconsistency between piety toward their gods and crime against their "companions." He maintained that "we find the negro to-day the most religious and the most immoral of men."[72] The connection between black religion and ethics (or the moral sense) was completely severed in the new psychology.

The implicit and normative claims of academic interpretations of black religion at the turn of the century rested on certain intellectual foundations that were not always stated directly. First, a stage theory of religion was advanced, usually articulated as religion evolving from the primitive/emotional (that is, the religion of blacks and dark-skinned peoples) to the rational/spiritual (that is, the religion of white Europeans and Americans). Second, this normative liberal Protestantism denigrated bodily movement or ecstatic religious experience and physical displays of various kinds. Third, it was a religion that was deemed scientific and hence modern. All of these qualities of this implicit religion were articulated by Charles Eliot, president of Harvard University, in his address before the Summer School of Theology in 1909. The address, titled "The Religion of the Future," was immediately published in Boston by the American Unitarian Association and was soon translated into French and German.[73] Interestingly, Eliot's talk proceeded by way of negation. As with other theorists, it required an imagined other that was regarded as threatening or a vestigial reminder of the primitive in the midst of the modern world. Eliot argued that the religion of the future would not be based on spiritual or temporal authority. It would not involve personifications of the primitive forces of nature. There would be no worship of dead ancestors, teachers, or rulers. Gone were all those tribal, racial, or tutelary deities. Perhaps we might say that the adolescent races and their primitive religions would vanish in the future, if Eliot was correct. Eliot insisted that this religion of the future would not be a selfish religion, but rather a religion that was in service to others and humanity in general. No more propitiations, sacrifices, or expiation. These were barbaric conceptions of the deity, the Unitarian proclaimed. No more anthropomorphic conceptions of God. The religion of the future would not be gloomy and ascetic, and it would believe in no malignant powers.[74]

Eliot's predictions about what the religion of the future would not be substantiates Robert Orsi's claim that "religion" as it took shape in the academy was explicitly imagined in relation to the winds of religious madness that howled outside its walls. From the perspective of these interpreters, just beyond the civilized confines of the university, there were the emotional masses, superstitious relics of barbarism, and free-floating remnants of primitives in a civilized country.[75] Southern educators were quick to spell out the implications of these ideas for black life in the South. In an address on September 21, 1903, John Carlisle Kilgo, president of Trinity College, spoke to the students and the citizens of Durham, North Carolina, about the obligations of whites to black Americans. In the course of his speech he briefly paused to consider the "natural qualities" of the Negro that would enable his hearers to understand better how to help blacks. In his rather folksy style, Kilgo gave a somewhat positive Southern spin to dominant social scientific theories about black religious practices. He said:

> It is easy for the negro to be religious. He has no tendency toward any of the forms of infidelity and scepticism. Much of what many negroes call religion has in it all the qualities of superstition, especially is this true of the extreme religionists among them; but it is to the credit of the negro that he becomes over-religious instead of becoming skeptical. Judging from the standpoint of psychology the negro is evidently in the emotional period of his evolution, and it is

well that his chief emotions are the singing, whistling, dancing, and shouting emotions.[76]

Similarly, Robert Bennett Bean (originally from Virginia), an instructor of anatomy at the University of Michigan, Ann Arbor, located the "affection-ate, immensely emotional" nature of blacks in the "racial peculiarities of the Negro brain." In his view, blacks simply lacked the mental and cranial equip-ment to exercise the self-control and self-government that was found in Anglo-Saxons.[77]

These specialists and professionals agreed that blacks were creatures of emotion and that they lacked discipline and self-control. This lack of self-control was said to be especially evident in the putative loose sexual behavior of blacks and in the emotional, sensual expressions of their religious practices. These alleged natural features of blacks were variously described as peculiar, physiologically based, pathological, and criminal. Thus the very biology of blacks, described as defective and anomalous, was seen as the basis of their peculiarly emotional form of religion. G. Stanley Hall, developmental psy-chologist at Clark University in Worcester, Massachusetts, was so struck by what he perceived to be the ineradicable differences between blacks and whites that he once exclaimed in exasperation,

> No two races in history, taken as a whole, differ so much in their traits, both physical and psychic, as the Caucasian and the Afri-can. The color of the skin and the crookedness of the hair are only the outward signs of many far deeper differences, including cranial and thoracic capacity, proportions of the body, nervous system, glands and secretions, vita sexualis, food, temperament, disposition, charac-ter, longevity, instincts, customs, emotional traits, and diseases.[78]

The social scientists of the early twentieth century were answering in the affirmative Thomas Jefferson's query as to whether nature had indeed pro-duced what he saw as the vast differences between blacks and whites and the moral and intellectual inferiority of the former. "Further observation" by social scientists seems to have amply verified Jefferson's conjectures and suspicions, except that they extended his formulation of black intellectual inferiority by adding that black religious life was morally deficient and pathological (and that blacks lacked the moral sense). To extend the Jeffersonian analogy, social scientists of the early twentieth century argued that blacks were deficient in the endowments of the head and the heart. A bleaker scenario could hardly have been imagined and the dehumanization of African Americans had reached its nadir, which in part explains how prominent leaders like Hall, Davenport, and

Odum could lend their social scientific expertise to partial justifications of the shameful practice of lynching blacks.

The early studies of the twentieth century can be summarized, despite minor variations, as trying to find scientific answers to several persistent questions that are implicit in the works: (1) What was the psychological and physiological basis of black religion? (2) Why did more blacks compared to whites attend church? (3) What effect did black religion have on their moral and ethical life? (4) In what way was religion a "natural" attribute of Africans? (5) What were the genealogy, function, and meaning of emotionalism in black religion? Hall and Southern educator Thomas Bailey demanded that the new scientific study of the Negro be taken out of the hands of politicians and sentimentalists and placed where they thought it belonged—with economists, anthropologists, and sociologists. In short, they believed that the study of blacks belonged with the social scientists. Hall and Bailey did not deny that their findings would affect philanthropy and legislation, but they were confident that the social scientific study of Southern blacks would put the problems of race on a more solid and intelligent foundation and shed more light on what was possible for blacks in America.

Constructions of black emotionality were crucial to attempts to address and find a suitable explanation of the Negro problem in the United States. The "Negro problem" at the turn of the century was defined by white Southerners as their unfortunate lot in living among a mass of inferior and criminal Negroes. Fears of "Negro domination" had become widespread by the 1890s. The move to disenfranchise blacks in the South after 1890, as Joel Williamson argues, was only one part of a broader process to deprive blacks of any political power, to separate them from whites, and to ensure their subordination to whites.[79] Books, pamphlets, articles, and essays proliferated on how to solve the Negro problem. George T. Winston, president of North Carolina College of Agricultural and Mechanic Arts, expressed the sentiments of many other white Southerners in his 1901 address before the American Academy of Political and Social Science. Winston spoke of white fears of the black brute "lurking in the dark, a monstrous beast, crazed with lust." He went on, "Since the abolition of slavery and the growing up of a new generation of Negroes, crimes that are too hideous to describe have been committed every month, every week, frequently every day, against the helpless women and children of the white race, crimes that were unknown in slavery." Winston spoke affectionately of the older Negroes whose honesty and virtue, in his view, were missing in the new generation. He recalled with fondness his childhood days of playing with happy Negro slaves.[80] The contrast between the new and dangerous Negro and the older, affectionate Negro found confirmation in academic studies. To restore friendly relations between the races, Winston recommended the withdrawal of blacks from politics (without Northern interference) and "increased efficiency" by black laborers. Only with the help of white superiors, Winston contended, would this "child race" in the distant future subdue its "animal passions," cultivate its "gentler emotions," and attain "mature manhood."[81]

Winston also spoke of the "dismal and awful night of Reconstruction" that had spoiled blacks with false hopes of social and civil equality. Winston expressed hope that some day would come when the historian would make Reconstruction the "saddest picture in the annals of the English-speaking race," and his wishes were soon realized. A revisionist history of Reconstruction historiography was already under way. In his *History of the United States from the Compromise of 1850* (1892), historian James Ford Rhodes characterized the Republican scheme of Reconstruction as "repressive" and "uncivilized" in part because it pandered to ignorant Negroes, "one of the most inferior races of mankind." Rhodes came to be recognized as the first real authority on slavery at a time when slavery just had become a major topic of historical inquiry. Rhodes's work challenged proslavery views that were so prevalent in American historical thought from Reconstruction to World War I. But his antislavery stance in his historical writings did not mitigate his harsh views of blacks. Rhodes argued that only the Teutonic race was capable of developing American democracy and that it was a terrible blunder to have conferred the franchise on sensual and childish blacks.[82]

By the early twentieth century, a group of young Southern scholars gathered at Columbia University to study the Reconstruction period under the guidance of Professors John W. Burgess and William A. Dunning. Burgess and Dunning taught that blacks were children utterly incapable of appreciating their newly conferred freedom after the Civil War. They argued that granting blacks suffrage was a "monstrous thing" and that "a black skin means membership in a race of men which has never of itself succeeded in subjecting passion to reason."[83] Sensuality and emotional instability were seen as the basis of black life and were constantly invoked by white Southerners to justify the disenfranchisement and segregation of blacks in the South. Academics provided a ready supply of scientific data to confirm these views.

John Love, a member of the American Negro Academy, argued that the Reconstruction era served as the "whipping boy" of those who used it as an example of blacks' unfitness for the franchise. The American Negro Academy was founded in 1897 under the leadership of Alexander Crummell. Black intellectuals gathered under the auspices of the organization to defend blacks against attacks by white intellectuals and to work out solutions to problems that confronted black Americans.[84] The depiction of blacks in histories of the

Reconstruction period could not be avoided by academy members. Regarding Reconstruction histories, Love wrote,

> The period of Reconstruction has served as the text for discrediting Negro Suffrage and is always the apt illustration that gives point to the argument of those who attempt to prove the incapacity of the Negro to exercise the right of suffrage. There is no doubt that the effort to mould public sentiment away from Negro Suffrage has been generally successful and this success has been achieved very largely through misrepresentation in regard to the facts of Reconstruction.[85]

Love also noted the "endless refrain" in such histories of Reconstruction about blacks' ignorance, criminal tendencies, inferiority, and the threat that they posed to Anglo-Saxon society. All of these portrayals of blacks as savages incapable of living in freedom, Love insisted, had as their aim the "poisoning" of the mind of the North, the perfection of Southern white "home rule," and the disenfranchisement and political subjugation of blacks.[86]

By dissecting blacks' emotional and other alleged racial traits, social scientists hoped to alert those concerned with the Negro problem about the "real" nature of blacks to prevent "sentimental" and simplistic proposals to solve this intricate social problem. Walter Willcox, chief statistician in the U.S. census office and a professor at Cornell University, read a paper on the morning of September 6, 1899, before the American Social Science Association, urging his listeners to disabuse themselves of the notion that education and religion could prevent blacks from descending into crime. Willcox insisted that for blacks, education and religion were regarded as "fetiches, that is, something external, the possession of which guarantees the possessor a charmed and happy life here or hereafter." He recommended an informal educational system that would inspire blacks to support themselves by "legitimate industry" and to train themselves for a subordinate position in the South where they would labor without political or social power.[87]

For all its claims to objectivity, this new scientific study of blacks provided a university-based ideology for popular racist discourse about the emotional and immoral traits of Southern blacks. It lent support to Southern practices of segregation, lynching, and disenfranchisement by positing a biological basis for the alleged vast differences between blacks and whites (to the obvious detriment of blacks). Hall's proposals, for example, rested on a series of unbridgeable distinctions between blacks and whites, from skin color to susceptibility to disease. "All these differences," Hall argued, "as they are coming to be better understood, are seen to be so great as to qualify if not imperil every inference from one race to another, whether theoretical or practical, so that what is true and good for one is often false and bad for the other."[88] The new science could easily be used (as it indeed was) to show how segregation was socially beneficial for such vastly different people.[89]

Hall offered his assessment of the Negro problem in a speech, "The Negro in Africa and America," delivered at the University of Virginia in July 1905. Blacks had been disenfranchised in Virginia in 1902, and worries about its effects and the violence of the white lynch mob seemed to have been the immediate backdrop to Hall's address. He cited Bruce's and Tillinghast's works to defend his claim about the "evils of wholesale negro suffrage." In deference to his Southern audience, he publicly repented of being an "abolitionist by conviction and sentiment" because, he stated, he could not anticipate how "negroizing" the South would lead to so many problems and that granting blacks the right to vote would bring such harm to themselves and others.[90] Hall relied on the findings of recent studies of Africa by missionaries and travelers to show how "few of his aboriginal traits the negro has lost." His project was to base a study of black Americans on a close scientific analysis of their African heritage. Regarding blacks and religion, Hall argued:

> The negro has a tropical imagination, a very keen sensitiveness to nature and an over-mastering tendency to personify not only animals but natural objects. This has given birth and currency to the rankest growth of superstition to be found among any race and which often controls daily life. Some of these, like Obi worship, sorcery, voodooism, witchcraft, can be traced back to Africa and directly connected with fetich worship. The negro's intense emotionality predisposes him to believe in supernatural agencies; the good to be worshipped, the evil to be adverted or propitiated.[91]

However, it was Hall's emphasis on emotionalism that proved crucial to future discussions of black religion. Emotionalism was first and foremost a quality of childhood, Hall and others argued. In his massive two-volume book, *Adolescence* (1904), Hall argued that psychoses and neuroses abounded in early adolescent years more than at any other period of life.[92] He interpreted black culture through the lens of this theory and discussed African American religion in his appended chapter titled "Ethnic Psychology and Pedagogy, or Adolescent Races and Their Treatment." In other variations of this chapter, Hall claimed that the "virtues and defects of the negro through life remain those of puberty."[93] For Hall, blacks represented a child race who suffered from all of the problems of adolescence, principally in the realm of religious excitement, which he regarded as one cause of insanity. Hall maintained that in reality "disease expresses itself" through the "highly emotional, religious nature" of blacks. He contended that blacks, because they lived in their emotions, were susceptible to a demonstrative type of insanity rather than a state of depression.[94] All of this rested on his posting of a distinct emotional disposition of blacks.

The noted developmental psychologist argued that the Negro's nature was a kind of "diathesis," or a psychic and physical disposition that was "erethic, volatile, changeable, prone to trancoidal, intensely emotional, and even epileptoid states."[95] This pathological condition, Hall contended, was said to help whites understand why blacks were so sexually licentious and why their men raped white women: Because arrested development in black children occurred around the age of twelve, the children failed to grow intellectually and morally as did white children, but their sexual development went forward and exercised an overpowering force over black men's lives. Since the end of slavery, Hall grimly asserted, blacks had acquired a new sense of equality and idleness that destroyed the restraints imposed by slavery, which had held their "imperious lust" in check. With this external restraint removed, blacks now found themselves at the mercy of their emotions and sexual impulses.[96] The boldness and barbarity of raping white women seemed not to impress itself on them as it did on white men. Blacks needed to take responsibility for their crimes and stop protecting their criminals. Hall said he was troubled by lynching as a solution to this problem, but he admitted that "when such a crime comes home to one's wife, daughter or mother, none of us know what we should do." Hall's primary objection to lynching was its brutalizing influence on the young white men and boys who engaged in it.[97]

Hall believed that religion had a vivid and palpable reality to the black mind. Africans invested the natural world with "immediate religious meaning." Like children, Hall maintained, Africans were compelled to endow animals with human traits and to feel the "immediate presence of a supernal power" in storms, clouds, and thunder. Their belief in another world seemed to flow naturally from their conceptions of this world, and so the next world was "merely a sensuous thing." Hall wrote, "If the feeling of dependence is the root of religion no race has ever been so predisposed to it. Submission, obedience, renunciation, have been his dumb, unwritten philosophy."[98] These native traits of the African mind were revealed in a fatalism that was illustrated in the character of Uncle Tom. This predisposition to believe and accept a religiously fatalistic view of reality made the transition to Christianity smoother. Religion was necessary for blacks. At some period of their lives, nearly all blacks were church members, Hall asserted. Communication with God "in abandon, in vision and in trance" and a vivid connection with another world appeared to be the features of their minds that enabled them to experience a reality that was unknown to other races. For these reasons, Hall noted that especially for "the negro of the lower type religion is a kind of Pythian frenzy [in which] the devotee becomes mad with supernal joy. Depravity, damnation, ecstasy, goodness, heaven, and hell, are a simple and forcible creed."[99]

Though much of his work focused on African religious customs and their connection to black religion in the South, Hall's speech was chiefly about the place of blacks in the South and in the nation. He recommended that they address themselves to the solution of their own problems. Hall insisted that the Negro "make his own social life as he has made the life of his church" (the center of his life and "its most characteristic expression"). He counseled the Negro to "accept without whining patheticism and corroding self-pity his present situation, prejudice and all," and respect the "unique gifts" of the race. Blacks should not desire to be "a brunette imitation of the Caucasian."[100] Ultimately, blacks must come to realize and celebrate their gifts. Hall concluded:

> His race has gifts that others lack,—such as an intense and large
> emotional life, an exquisite sensitiveness to nature, gifts in the field
> of music and oratory, a peculiar depth of religious life (connected
> in part with the sense of dependence, which is its psychic root),
> a strong belief in invisible powers, a certain sense of fate (which
> in Africa predisposes the natives to Mohammedanism, which is
> said to be growing as fast as any religion ever spread and which
> some think a kind of next step above fetishism), rare good humor,
> jollity, patience, etc.[101]

Ann Taves argues that Hall's influence was spread as his students took up positions in psychology in various universities and colleges.[102] What follows is an examination of a specific set of individuals whose ideas were influenced by and deepened Hall's attempt to offer a psychological explanation of black religion. Taves has done much to help us situate Frederick Morgan Davenport's work, *Primitive Traits in Religion Revivals* (1905), within the context of the studies of religion by academic psychologists, but she does not address the crucial role of race in these works. Davenport's *Primitive Traits*, which originated as a doctoral dissertation in political science at Columbia University, functioned as a crucial text in the psychology of religion, and his theory of religious evolution was cited and appealed to by a number of later psychologists. Davenport was a professor of sociology at Hamilton College when his book was published, but he later left professional life for politics (he had also served as a Methodist pastor in Yonkers, New York). Mental evolution was the bedrock of his theory of religious revivals. Davenport regarded religion as being in a process of development from the animal and primitive to the rational and spiritual. Revivals for him were dominated by harmful religious emotions. Davenport made it clear what his intentions were in writing his book. He wrote, "I have undertaken not simply to discriminate spurious and genuine revivals, but to show that in genuine revivals themselves there are primitive traits which need elimination or modification in the interest of religious and social progress."[103] Though he treated a series of religious revivals, including the ghost dance among North American Indians and the Scotch-Irish revival in Kentucky and Ulster, I focus on his chapter on the "Religion of the American Negro."[104]

A deep-seated fear of emotion and a concomitant insistence on self-control were central features of social scientific critiques of black religion in the early twentieth century. Construction of African American religion as emotionalism is thus a key to understanding how ostensibly dispassionate social scientific works could situate religion in relation to lynching, interracial sexual relations, granting blacks voting rights during the Reconstruction years, and segregation in the South. Following Spencer's construction of the primitive mind closely, Davenport argued that the primitive mind was credulous and peopled by a world of spirits. Lack of control, few inhibitions (which were regarded as the crux of civilization), opinions as beliefs based on imagination and emotion (which led to impulsive action)—all of these were seen as symptomatic of the primitive mind. Appearance of sensory and motor automatisms, a lack of normal rational consciousness, and a mass of superstition dominated the primitive mind. The connection between the nervous instability of the primitive mind, the association of sensory and motor automatisms with the subconscious, and the suggestibility of the crowd, as Taves notes, formed the theoretical basis that allowed Davenport to identify the primitive traits in religious revivals that needed elimination or modification to further religious and social progress.[105] This followed from his argument that primitive relics existed in civilized societies and needed to be purged from religious revivals before "true religion" could emerge. As a former pastor and current university professor, Davenport had a particular interest in religious pedagogy and articulating the best form of a good and proper religion.

Davenport did not hesitate to call on blacks as examples of primitives with a crude imagination and religious thought that was "very frequently one long stretch of astounding images."[106] Blacks in the South were "enveloped in a cloud of superstition" and engaged in various forms of magic.[107] Apparently without any concern for the negative effect of his theories on the lives of millions of blacks living in the South, Davenport pathologized and trivialized the religious experience of blacks. What is so astonishing about his writing is the careless use of anecdotes and darky stories, especially for a man who had just completed a doctorate at Columbia University. He told the story of spending an evening on the top of Lookout Mountain in Georgia, listening with a company of friends to an "old hermit darky's account" of his religious conversion. The man, described by Davenport as a powerful giant of a black man, was sixty-seven years of age and spoke to them on the porch of their hostess's residence in the darkness of the late evening. The very choice of words revealed Davenport's attempt to create an "other" in this black man: The man, we are told, reached the "climax" of his recital of his story and was in a state of ecstasy as he concluded his narrative. While putatively seeking to impress Davenport and other whites with his spiritual experience, suddenly a dog barks, causing the man to lose his train of thought. Davenport related that immediately a "dash of savagery" came into the black man's face as he turned "with flashing eye and foaming lip upon that canine intruder." This startling intrusion was a revelation for Davenport that "primitive passion" was just below the "crust of religious culture and nurture" of black Americans.[108] They were religious savages with only the accoutrements of civilization. Pressing his point further, Davenport argued that no one doubted that the Negro people, whether in Africa or America, were members of a child race. He wrote: "Dense ignorance and superstition, a vivid imagination, volatile emotion, a weak will power, small sense of morality, are universally regarded as the most prominent traits of the negro in those sections of the black belt, where he appears in his primitive simplicity."[109] All of the clinical terms for religious pathology in the new psychology made their way into Davenport's scientific interpretation of black religion.

Davenport was deeply troubled by the fits and passions of religious groups on the American landscape. Indeed, he thought that such religious behavior posed a threat to the very foundations of the nation. Self-restraint was crucial for a free people: Emotional excess meant a loss of rational control.[110] Thus the emotional Negro embodied all that was threatening to the nation. By allowing the recently freed persons to exercise political power, the radical Republicans demonstrated that they, too, were under the sway of emotions. They had become like those—the emotional Negroes—whom they supposedly sought to help.[111] Instead of trying to exercise the powers of the "developed Anglo-Saxon," blacks needed to learn their place. Davenport wrote: "The last thing that the superstitious and impulsive negro race needs is a stirring of the emotions. That is easy and meaningless: What they need is a strict, religious discipline that will keep their passions in check and build them up in chastity, industry, and integrity."[112]

Political and social problems were all topics of discussion in this scientific analysis of religious evolution. Davenport coupled his critique of blacks as given over to emotion with an expression of his alarm over women dominating the churches. Like blacks, women represented creatures of intuition and emotion rather than intellect and rational inhibition. Davenport took comfort in the fact that a time would come when women would be less suggestible and impulsively emotional.[113] Evolution would apparently do its work in this case. But no such hope was held out for blacks. Lynching occurred in the South, in Davenport's view, because of the "reign of lust" among blacks. Their "over-powering propensity to petty theft" was testimony to the "great gulf fixed" in their consciousness between religion and morality. Unlike Jefferson, however, Davenport did not attribute this to deficient external conditions for blacks; instead, his argument implied that the "moral sense" (as did Philip Bruce) was completely separate from "religion" among blacks.[114] He asserted that blacks lived in "ages before morality," unlike the modern age, when religion and ethics were separate. Blacks therefore had an "undeveloped ethical sense," and this led Davenport and other social scientists to give their religious practices a new name, such as emotionalism, religious feeling, or something that was other than "religion" as whites understood it. A new category was created for black religion as something "other" than religion.[115]

The critique of emotionalism and the attempt to render a scientific analysis of the emotional basis of black religion deepened in studies of black life in the early twentieth century. The published dissertation *Social and Mental Traits of the Negro* (1910), by Howard Odum, represented the culmination of such aca-demic studies. Odum received his bachelor's degree from Emory in 1904 and began teaching at a rural school in Toccopola, Mississippi. Located just twenty-one miles from Oxford, home of the University of Mississippi, Odum fre-quently made the commute as a teaching fellow to collect local folklore and record information about black life in the area. In 1906, he earned his master's degree in classics at Ole Miss. As a student from 1906 to 1908, he came under the influence of Thomas Bailey, a native of South Carolina who was a professor of psychology and education at Ole Miss. Bailey had received his doctorate in psychology from Clark University, where he worked with Hall. Bailey was deeply impressed with the power of the new social sciences, and he influenced Odum in this regard. Under this influence, Odum's interest changed from the classics to social science. He ended up completing two doctorates: one with Hall at Clark in 1909 in folklore and a second in 1910 in sociology with Franklin H. Giddings at Columbia University.[116] Unable to find a teaching position in the South, Odum spent the next two years working for the Philadelphia Bureau of Municipal Research, studying the status of blacks in the public schools.[117]

Evident influences in Odum's work are Bailey's valorization of social sci-ence and Hall's emphasis on the emotional basis of black religion. Odum indicated that he had three purposes in writing his book: (1) to contribute a "scientific knowledge of the Negro"; (2) to present the "beginning" of a "scientific but practical study" of blacks in the South; and (3) to interpret the Negro problem and the means by which "the heart of the problem may be reached." He and others were groping for what he described as "the improvement and the development of the negro race" and "the establishment of relations between the races which shall be permanently satisfactory."[118] He intended to penetrate the "inner qualities of the Negro's nature" and examine the "essential causes of his conduct."[119] Only by such a scientific, detailed assessment could a reasonable solution to the Negro problem be proposed. Odum's work was thus cast as a major contribution to progressive social analysis and designed for those interested in how to deal concretely with blacks in the South.

Odum examined what he called the race traits, tendencies, and prospects for black Southerners. He undertook an extensive study of towns and cities in the South to see how blacks lived, exploring their schooling and educational prospects, churches and religious practices, fraternal organizations and benevolent societies, home life, sexual practices, diseases, morals, crime rates and legal offenses, and property ownership. In this section I primarily examine Odum's examination of African American religious beliefs and practices and his chapter devoted to "the emotions of the Negro and their relation to conduct" in the broader framework of his analysis of black culture and society.

Perhaps more than any other social scientist of his day, Odum interpreted African American religion and life through the psychological construct of emotionalism. The "function of the negro Church," he wrote, "is rather to give expression and satisfaction to social and religious emotions than to direct moral conduct." The question was whether the church could be "used effectively" to help blacks overcome their weaknesses, which he identified as criminal propensities, drunkenness, sexual immorality, "bad personal habits," a debased home life, and a host of other characteristics.[120] Given that Odum and others felt that the "negro Church" was the center around which black life revolved, it was only natural that questions about its effectiveness and its usefulness would be asked. But because he believed that black churches did little to lift the moral standards of blacks and only gave vent to their emotions, he placed little hope in them as instruments of reform.

Odum sided with those who argued that black religion was different from what whites and social scientists normally called religion. He wrote, "In spite of pretensions and superficiality, there is nothing so real to the negro as his religion, although it is a different 'reality' from what we commonly expect in religion."[121] Odum argued that religion for blacks meant pleasure, satisfaction, emotional stimulation, and arousal.[122] Because black religion was so firmly based in emotionalism, he argued, and corresponded to their actual psychic nature, it was "almost a natural acquirement." Odum theorized that blacks were in some sense naturally religious. Their religion was primarily "pleasurable excitement." It was not necessary (or even possible) for religion to be grounded in knowledge for it to become real to blacks, he maintained. For Odum, this explained why black religion lacked practical application or moral content. It was based on stimulation and emotion, and as a result "a scarcity of thoughtfulness and will-power is everywhere predominant."[123] This form of religion, Odum contended, was not conducive to the development of a social conscience. The criminal instinct so overpowered blacks' consciousness, he asserted, that they felt righteous even while committing criminal or immoral acts.[124] Here Odum was repeating the arguments of Joseph Tucker, Philip Bruce, and other white Southerners who pathologized black religion by asserting that it not only failed to inculcate ethics into black religious practitioners but also promoted criminal behavior by granting murderers and rapists a clean conscience in offering them forgiveness for their unlawful actions. In some ways, this critique went even beyond the clinical language of psychopathology.

The relation of emotions to the development of "primitive" peoples was a major concern for early twentieth-century social scientists. As we have seen, blacks were said to be primitive peoples in the emotional stage of their development. Odum contended that "primitive emotions" were dominant among Southern blacks. These emotions were "largely physiological [but] with little objective content." Odum believed that emotions constantly swept over blacks' physiological "currents," forcing them to act on impulse and seek psychic and physical release. As he put it:

> The Negro reveals himself a mass of physiological reactions and reflexes. His whole being is volatile, without continuous or stable form, easily disturbed, as easily quieted. With all this there is yet a persistency and intensity developed by the constant flow of emotional currents along the tracts of least resistance. With the passing of the immediate stimulus, therefore, the emotion is likely to cease; likewise the feeling lasts only while the process of immediate stimulation and reaction is going on. A strong physical organism with powerful sensuous capacity thus gives the Negro a rich emotional nature, which together with habituation and facility, with little inhibition save that of conflicting emotions, renders him pre-eminently subject to the feeling states. Add to this fact that the Negro is unable to attend intellectually to other things when the feelings are aroused and the result may be understood.[125]

Odum was convinced that blacks' emotional nature was responsible for their alleged frequent sexual crimes against white women.[126] He asserted,

> The chief traits which lead to the committing of offenses are thought to be the emotional nature of the negro with his sensual proclivities. ... Nurtured with some hatred toward the whites, taught no morals, *with a fanatical religion, itself leading to erratic actions*, with little regard for common decency, and bred in filth and adultery, the negro is considered peculiarly liable to crime."[127]

Because allegiance to religion and churches was deemed powerless to uphold and purify the lives of most blacks, Odum urged stricter laws against black criminal behavior.[128] Because black religion was viewed as pure emotionalism and had no ability to restrain the lawless conduct of blacks, it was judged defective and pathological. Odum maintained that blacks' strong sexual impulse was so overpowering that it left little energy for moral and mental regeneration, thus leading him to conclude, "their thoughts are most filthy and morals are generally beyond description."[129] Dominated by the animal impulses in the religious and moral realm, blacks could hope for little improvement until they learned how to control them.[130]

Odum's work was by no means the end of social scientific constructions of African American religion as defective or pathological emotionalism. Yet the strong connection between race and emotionalism in the social sciences began to face criticism, particularly in the field of anthropology under the influence of Franz Boas and his students. Notions of the primitive mind as under the sway of emotion began facing serious challenges.

Rethinking the Primitive Mind

A number of developments within the academic community and within black communities were slowly undermining long-standing notions of race and culture, and these had direct and indirect impacts on depictions and interpretations of African American religion. Many of these changes, however, were not evident until after World War I, and some of them did not have a significant impact until the 1920s. Though much clearer in hindsight and hardly noticed at the time, some of the most salient developments can be identified.

The reconceptualization of the primitive would have a profound impact on representations of African Americans and analyses of black religion, especially the psychological construction of pathological emotionalism. As early as 1901, anthropologist Franz Boas began to subject to critical scrutiny a number of generalizations that Herbert Spencer made about primitive mentality.[131] Boas was especially intent on revising Spencer's assertions of primitive peoples' lack of inhibition and self-control. Regarding the primitive mind's alleged lack of control over emotions, Boas argued that emotional control "is exerted on occasions which depend upon the character of the social life of the people." He provided an example of an "Eskimo community" that was on the point of starvation because their religious proscriptions forbade them from killing seals "basking on ice." Boas noted that the specific situations that required self-control differed vastly in various societies, and direct comparisons were pointless in such situations.[132] A notion of cultural relativism was implicit but not fully enunciated in this early essay.[133]

Related to rethinking conceptions of the primitive was a different view of Africa. Although there is no evidence to suggest that Hall altered his view that emotions formed the psychological basis of the black mind, he did begin to change his emphases on race because of his disappointment with America's foreign policy toward nonwhites and his growing familiarity with the ideas of Boas. In 1910, he noted that Boas and others had led social scientists to "regard the superiority of civilized over uncivilized man as far less than we have been wont to think it, and as perhaps offset by still greater disadvantages." Hall insisted that the time had come when "science and even a broadly based economy should teach us that primitives have certain inalienable rights to life, liberty and the pursuit of happiness, and that ruthless interference with customs that have worked well for indigenous races should cease." He argued that if left unspoiled by the "so-called higher races," primitives were generally good-natured, frank, and virtuous. He suggested that "it would be possible to-day without any [Jean-Jacques] Rousseau–like idealization of savagery, to compose from the life of many tribes a curriculum of conduct, regimen and culture that would constitute a splendid environment for any boy" in America.[134] Although these comments about the primitive reflected Hall's worries about over-civilization endangering American manhood, they also indicated a slight shift in his views of race.[135] After lamenting the policies of the United States toward Native Americans and blacks, he urged that an "African bureau" be erected in Washington, D.C., to house artifacts, exhibits, and literature to demonstrate the "best things" Africans had achieved in the past and present. All of this, Hall believed, would inspire self-confidence in blacks and teach them to understand "the magnificent emotional endowments nature has given them that has kept their spirits more or less buoyant under infinite hardships." Only an appreciation of their folklore and traditions could help them attain true freedom, Hall averred.[136]

A year later, Hall's colleague at Clark University and a former student of Boas, anthropologist Alexander Chamberlain, wrote an essay that showed a broad knowledge of ancient African cultures and was a direct attack on theories of Anglo-Saxonism. The essay's importance lies in its unequivocal assertion of the oneness of humanity and the "innumerable" contributions of Africans to human civilization. Chamberlain's claims about a future reunified humanity was a direct assault on racial theories that posited the superiority of whites to blacks and that frowned on racial amalgamation. He regarded "our own race" (whites) as a selfish race, but hoped for whites' ultimate transformation.[137] Chamberlain's use of blacks' mistreatment in America as a way of both pointing out the contributions of Africans and the deficiencies of American culture became far more common and explicit in the writings of whites in the post–World War I period. Blacks, in such writings, would become the "noble primitives" used as a weapon to critique a bourgeois and decadent white culture.

A growing interest in black folklore was part of this process of rethinking the primitive mind. Hampton Institute organized the Hampton Folklore Society in 1893 to ensure knowledge of blacks' past and their contributions to "civilization."[138] The professional *Journal of American Folklore* included several articles on Negro folklore and "superstitions" in the South.[139] Black folk songs, especially the spirituals, were viewed as the special gift of blacks to America, even by some whites who had very few positive things to say about black religion. Even Hall claimed that blacks possessed "gifts" in the field of music.[140] Odum's work, which was essentially a litany of what he regarded as pathologies within black culture, referred to black spirituals as "beautiful" and "plaintive." Although laced with expressions of their "simple" nature, his descriptions of black church music were mostly complimentary analyses of what he regarded as blacks' profound "native expression."[141]

Black leaders began to reconsider what was distinctive about black culture and sought to value the unique contributions and gifts of black Americans. In 1908, Kelly Miller, dean of the College of Arts and Sciences at Howard University, lauded the "artistic gifts" of blacks: the "lowly" spirituals, oratory, ragtime, art, and poetry.[142] In 1913, William Ferris, a member of the American Negro Academy and a graduate of Harvard and Yale, urged blacks not to "blot out the precious traits of the race." Ferris was deeply influenced by the ideas of Crummell and Du Bois. He argued that blacks possessed spiritual and emotional qualities that could "soften" human nature and "spiritualize" religion and music. Those special qualities included a lovable nature, spiritual earnestness, and musical genius. Though blacks, he insisted, "must cease imitating the vices of the Anglo-Saxon race," they should, however, acquire the "aggressiveness and tenacity of purpose" of Anglo-Saxons, even as they developed all that was precious in the "Negro genius." Ferris believed that blacks could supply what a materialistic white society lacked.[143] August Meier rightly notes that these black leaders were groping toward a form of cultural nationalism, which was accompanied by the notion of innate racial differences.[144] But this was also their way of affirming the value of what were seen as the particular cultural achievements of blacks in an American context of racial oppression.[145] In many ways, however, they restated romantic racialist conceptions of black religion and culture in a new social and political context.

A confluence of forces that reinforced and undermined the idea of racial traits came together to reshape images of the primitive, traditional ideas about African history and cultures, and the gifts or contributions of blacks to American culture. After World War I, a deep disillusionment with Victorian values of self-control, propriety, decorum, and order set in and had a major influence on characterizations of primitive peoples and folk cultures.[146] Monroe Work, director of Records and Research at Tuskegee Institute, was no radical, but by 1916 even he voiced the question: Why don't blacks through music, art, history, and science make their own special contributions to the progress of the world rather than simply pattern their lives and achievements after what whites had done? Work called on blacks to draw inspiration from their African past and "not despise the rock from which they were hewn."[147] The rehabilitation of the image of Africa went hand in hand with a different conception of blacks' current role in the United States. Searching for a distinctive contribution was a form of cultural rehabilitation.

Conclusion

Reformulations of theories of race by Boas and his students from the 1920s onward, significant changes in the communities of African Americans (Northern migration and growing educational opportunities), and more positive views of the emotions and primitive peoples and cultures were among the major changes involved in the theoretical separation of race and culture. The pervasive fear and dislike of emotionalism experienced a significant decline. The contrast, for example, between the litany of claims about emotionalism and superstition in black religion in church historian Richard Reed's paper before the American Society of Church History in 1914 and the longing for a heartfelt emotional religion found in William Warren Sweet's *Revivalism in America* (1944) are striking.[148] Sweet, professor of church history at the University of Chicago, lamented the denigration of emotion that had long held sway in the field. Unlike Davenport, he argued that excessive fear of emotion was detrimental to the life of the church. He wrote, "In certain realms of life emotion is a better guide than reason."[149] Although still critical of an "overemotionalized religion," Sweet's work contained a wistfulness for a revival of a vibrant, Methodistic personal religion of emotion and feeling. He blamed the "new psychology" for having discredited the "old emotional revivalism." On this point, one can hardly doubt his conclusion. Sweet mourned the loss of the personal element in religion over a social gospel that emphasized the impersonal and institutional nature of the church. He noted that "emotion has been so completely squeezed out of present-day Protestant worship that the people are becoming emotionally starved." Sweet suggested that motion pictures were perhaps so popular because they may have been filling this void.[150] It is not surprising that his contemporary, Willard Sperry, dean of Harvard Divinity School, also found something wrong with the modernist Protestantism of his day and sought its emotional and otherworldly antidote in his romanticization of the religion of poor blacks in the rural South. Things had changed considerably by the 1940s.

Discussions and interpretations of African American religion were changing, however, because of various developments within the social sciences and events on the cultural landscape. Perhaps one of the most signal changes in black life was the emergence of a small but highly educated group of intellectuals who took up the task of representing the race and providing their own studies of black life and culture. Though the question of emotionalism did not entirely go away, there was a parallel discussion (alongside psychological theories of the mind) about how to harness and redirect the power of an entity called the Negro Church. The pressing urgency of the plight of African Americans and the negative images of blacks in the broader culture and the academy were crucial factors in the vehemence of the debates about the nature and function of the Negro Church.

4

The Creation and the Burden of the Negro Church

In some ways, W. E. B. Du Bois anticipated contemporary postmodernist critiques of essentialism and master narratives. His professional career from 1896 to 1910 in many ways forced him to wrestle with these issues that occupy modern theorists. I am particularly interested in Du Bois's fears about grand narratives, overly general accounts about the lives of black Americans, his apprehensions (often muted) about Western science's claims to universality, and his attempt to offer a local and particular interpretation of the meaning of African American religious communities. Du Bois never made a clean break from his veneration of Western notions of objective social science. He was a deeply conflicted person, and these internal conflicts became rather explicit in many of his early studies of black culture. In the social and political context of the lynching and disenfranchisement of black Southerners, Du Bois's work on black communities in the South and North demonstrated that he, like other black leaders, wrestled with holding in tension a social scientific dispassionate approach to one's subjects and the older romantic racialist conception of blacks as naturally religious and gifted with special artistic capacities. Although Du Bois was centrally responsible for the creation of "the Negro Church," a comparison of his work with other black interpreters indicates that black leaders were struggling to articulate older notions of a unique spirituality alongside the new social scientific notion of "the black church" as the principal social institution in black life. None of these tensions was resolved, and in fact we find in the social thought of some of these thinkers a mix of romantic racialist ideas, a social scientific analysis of the Negro Church, and a psychological interpretation of black religious conversion and morality. The harsh circumstances of black life and the compelling power of the social sciences to define and dissect it pulled and tugged black interpreters in various directions as they sought to offer a positive program of uplift and racial development for black life. It was a difficult task indeed.

Du Bois made important contributions to early American sociology and the study of local black communities. Between 1897 and 1910, when he was professor of economics and history at Atlanta University, he put out scores of studies on almost every aspect of what he called "Negro problems." Du Bois also directed and heavily edited most volumes of the ten-volume Atlanta University studies. Though they were not given the funding that he hoped for, they nevertheless were some of the best and most objective studies done on black communities at that time. Du Bois's *Philadelphia Negro* (1899) was a crowning achievement that gained him recognition as a leading sociologist and a keen interpreter of the peculiar problems that blacks faced in a rapidly industrializing and urbanizing nation. With the vast corpus of Du Bois's sociological work on record, much of it in peer-reviewed journals and reputable newspapers, he was recognized as an expert on race relations and in the field of pioneering sociology, though white theorists often disregarded his complaints about the problems of racism and oppression in the South.

In the early twentieth century, grand sociological theories had little use for the data obtained from a careful study of African Americans. Blacks served as primitive backdrop to normative theories about contemporary "civilized" religion and nothing more for most theorists in Du Bois's day. English philosopher Herbert Spencer's schema of cultural evolution from primitive to advanced societies is crucial to the type of sociological work that Du Bois reacted to in his day. In his (first) autobiography, Du Bois wrote:

> Social thinkers were engaged in vague statements and were seeking to lay down the methods by which, in some not too distant future, social law analogous to physical law would be discovered. Herbert Spencer finished his ten volumes of Synthetic Philosophy in 1896. The biological analogy, the vast generalizations, were striking, but actual scientific accomplishment lagged.[1]

In Du Bois's view, vast generalizations and unsystematic study were the enemies of scientific social analysis. He proposed instead a comprehensive social analysis of black communities based on constantly updated studies of particular African American localities. Du Bois attempted to place the study of black life on a more solid foundation by conducting local studies that allowed one to make cautious generalizations about black life. In theory, however, this was no different than G. Stanley Hall's proposal that the study of black life should be taken out of the hands of unskilled sentimentalists and politicians and instead be placed in the hands of social scientists, who would presumably present a fuller and more accurate understanding of African American culture.

Du Bois, however, recognized the limitations and the impossibility of a strictly dispassionate scientific account of African American religion (or the culture of blacks in America more generally) when he constantly encountered racially charged reflections and pejorative references to blacks in the monographs authored by white social scientists in his day. But this did not stop him from attempting to find a method to study the lived experience of blacks in the South. In an interview late in his life, Du Bois stated, "I was a young man emotionally encompassed by problems of the Negro and the future of the Negro and the freedom of the Negro. Now, I go to Harvard and Germany, and I am trying to get the tools to accomplish this. The tools must be exact science, so that I followed that and I steeped myself in that."[2] Yet he was very much interested in an engaged approach to his study of black life. In his *Souls of Black Folk*, he criticized scholars for "having already reached conclusions" about the nature of black life. Du Bois insisted that if we wish to know more about the daily lives and longings of blacks, "we can only learn by intimate contact with the masses, and not by wholesale arguments covering millions separate in time and space, and differing widely in training and culture."[3]

There were two major issues that pushed Du Bois away from the local and particular, which were wedded to his notion of scientific accuracy and fact accumulation: violence against blacks, especially in the form of lynching, and his warring internal desires to be both an artist and an objective social scientist. Du Bois expressed these problems in several ways. He once stated: "The great object is this emotional freedom that I want. I feel distinctly, while I am in Harvard, that I am having my impulse to soar into the blue cut down and made reasonable and understandable by scientific methods." So instead of collecting factual data for his historical seminars, he would rather "like to be writing poetry and hearing music and making it, and that sort of thing."[4] In reality, the ivory tower of academia served as a form of escape from the harsh reality of the "outside" world. He noted years later that he tried to isolate himself "in the ivory tower of race." Du Bois wrote, "I wanted to explain the difficulties of race and the ways in which these difficulties caused political and economic troubles."[5] In the end, he believed he was saved by a judicious combination of thought and action, by which he meant continuing his work as scholar, but using it to address directly the problems of racism in American society. For Du

Bois, a study of the local idioms and religious practice of blacks divorced from social and political action was not only irresponsible but immoral in the face of blacks' being lynched and disenfranchised. Furthermore, he became convinced that amassing accurate data was simply unable to make a dent in the deep racial prejudices of most white Americans. For the sake of moral integrity and personal sanity, Du Bois slipped through the constraints of the academy, embraced the life of a "propagandist," and entered real-world debates about race, religion, and culture. However, his impatience with the racism in American culture led him not only to criticize white scholars and their biased interpretations of black religion but also engage in a normative religious assessment of the very people that he had sought to help. Du Bois's implicit and sometimes explicit normative religious critique of African American religion was steeped in many ways in the social scientist discourse of primitive races that he set out to refute.

Assessing Du Bois's Legacy

A careful contextual and historical analysis of the social context and disciplinary mechanisms of social science in Du Bois's day helps us develop a greater appreciation of his contributions. Although he allowed his subjects' real-world concerns and conditions to push against the boundaries of his theories, in the end his Enlightenment rationality and narrower functionalist conception of religion won out. Du Bois's own biases were revealed in an 1897 speech when he urged black churches to stick with strictly religious or moral duties. Here he was mapping an academic theory onto the actual experiences of blacks. As Robert Orsi argues about this period in religious theorizing, religion was seen as "epistemologically and ethically singular."[6] Du Bois's implicit view of a limited or specific role of religion that dealt only with "spiritual" issues led him to regard black churches as peculiar or anomalous. He was writing at a time when social scientists inextricably linked religion and morality, and almost uniformly asserted that they were separate in African American culture (though morality was rarely defined by social scientists who had inherited moral and racial biases against black religious practice). "Religion" was what made people more moral human beings. Put crudely, to the extent that African Americans' morals (almost invariably sexual practices were in mind) did not "improve" as their churches increased in number, questions abounded as to the extent to which they possessed a "religion" or at least the proper kind of religion. Defining a religion that so contradicted the ethically normative liberal

Protestant paradigm that was making its weight felt in the academy became a problem that was partially "solved" by pathologizing black religion.

Time and again Du Bois compared the Negro church to white churches and noted that the former was more than "simply an organism for the propagation of religion."[7] Unstated in this seemingly innocent scientific observation is the conviction that churchly activity has a limited or special sphere. We see this in Du Bois's testimony before the U.S. Industrial Commission when he was queried as to whether he thought black churches in Albany, Georgia, that functioned as meeting places devoted only to "religious meetings" were an improvement over those that hosted social events. He asserted that in some ways this was an improvement because it meant that once black churches lost or gave up their function of being the social centers of black communities, they could perhaps survive as the "moral center" of the community. The presupposition was that a model of the "purified" church, perhaps on something like a Puritan model of Du Bois's native New England, was what produced "true religion" or morality and that to the extent that black churches served as social centers they could not represent the "highest morals" of black people.[8]

This created a double bind for Du Bois's descriptive and normative analysis of the function of black churches. On one hand, he inveighed against them for imposing puritanical and ascetic restrictions on black life (as in his lambasting of their restrictions on dancing). Du Bois was opposed to black churches offering various types of moral prohibitions and wanted them to limit themselves to "religious" issues, presumably uplift or "human inspiration," as he once vaguely wrote. On the other hand, he constantly apologized for "moral failings" within the black community, noting that one should not expect black churches to be religious centers first because they represented the entire community and were not modeled after a purified church. Yet in his testimony before the Industrial Commission, Du Bois seemed to indicate that perhaps it would be desirable if black churches became moral centers and divested themselves of varied social functions. At times, it is not clear precisely what role he envisioned for black churches.

Du Bois's criticisms of the Negro Church have to be placed alongside his call for detailed studies of local black communities and his more positive racially essentialist claims about black spirituality. One of the ironies of Du Bois's work on African American religion is that on one hand, he was very critical of broad overarching assertions about the nature of "black life" or "the Negro community." His remedy was to provide a close, extended analysis of local communities (which he hoped to repeat over several years to measure social development) and build up such analyses as the basis for cautious judgments about African American life. So his chief emphasis was on par-ticularity and the local. On the other hand, Du Bois was a crucial figure in the creation and genealogy of the Negro Church, which was described by him and later interpreters as a singular institution or group organization that had cer-tain responsibilities in uplifting the race, bringing about political empower-ment, and organizing and pooling the resources and talents of blacks to face the hardships of economic, racial, and political oppression in the United States. Yet he never quite resolved these tensions in his thought and bequeathed to interpreters these very deeply conflicted ways of studying African American religion.

The Search for an Adequate Methodology

A pioneering sociologist, historian, and prolific writer on the culture and re-ligious institutions of African Americans, Du Bois was a seminal figure in what I call the genealogy of the discourse of the Negro Church. Du Bois re-ceived a bachelor of arts from Fisk University in 1888, a second bachelor's degree from Harvard University in 1890, a master's degree from Harvard in 1892, and after two years of study at the University of Berlin, he received his doctorate at Harvard in 1895 (the first African American to do so). Du Bois later noted that when working on his master's degree he had studied history and political science and "what would have been sociology if Harvard had yet recognized such a field."[9] From1894 to 1896, he taught Latin, Greek, German, and English at Wilberforce University, which was a leading African Methodist Episcopal denominational school. Although he wanted to teach sociology, the administrators saw no need for such a course. The fervent religious environ-ment at the school deeply troubled Du Bois. He left the school after a number of problems with the administration. He was able to secure a rather tenuous position at the University of Pennsylvania during the summer of 1896. In an oral interview, Du Bois later recalled that he was hired to prove, "on an aca-demic basis," that blacks were the chief cause of bad government, prostitution, and criminality that was then plaguing Philadelphia.[10] His task was to study the seventh ward of Philadelphia, where most blacks in the city lived. Du Bois remained in Philadelphia for fifteen months working on his study (which became *The Philadelphia Negro* [1899]), except for two months in 1897, when he traveled to Virginia to collect data for related research.

Crucial to Du Bois's attempt to find an adequate methodology to study black life were the changing social circumstances in which he worked, the deteriorating nature of race relations in the late nineteenth and early twentieth centuries, his responses to white scholars writing about the Negro problem, and his continuing interactions with African Americans in specific contexts. After moving to Philadelphia, for example, Du Bois suffered the humiliation of not having his name in the university catalog for his first year. He was not even offered a temporary professorship. In 1897, following his fifteen-month stay in Philadelphia, Du Bois was hired by Atlanta University as a professor of economics and history and as director of the Sociological Laboratory and the Atlanta University Conferences (annual conferences devoted to the systematic study and analysis of various aspects of black life in America). Throughout his professional career from 1896 to 1910, Du Bois constantly encountered problems of lack of funds for his research projects; lack of interest by leading universities in the kind of scientific study of blacks that he proposed to undertake; deteriorating race relations in the South, where blacks were being lynched, disenfranchised, and increasingly segregated; and the struggle to find a methodology in the midst of these painful lived realities.

Du Bois wrote often, in both academic and autobiographical terms, about his search for a methodology to study black culture and social problems. In his first professional review, as a young twenty-eight-year-old working among blacks in Philadelphia, he criticized Frederick Hoffman's *Race Traits and Tendencies of the American Negro* (1896) for vast generalizations, uncritical use of faulty statistics based on the 1890 census, and pessimistic conclusions about African American prospects in the United States. Hoffman, a statistician for Prudential Life Insurance, argued that in the struggle for race existence, blacks were becoming extinct and that neither religion nor education would cancel the deleterious effects of their "race traits."[11] He concluded that "thirty years of freedom in this country . . . have failed to accomplish the original purpose of the abolition of slavery, that is, the elevation of the colored race to the moral, mental and economic level of the white race."[12] Hoffman regarded his work as a "severe condemnation of modern attempts of superior races to lift inferior races to their own elevated position."[13] He hammered away at his conclusions, asserting that blacks lacked self-reliance and chastity, the two "essential virtues of modern progress." "Easy conditions of life" and "liberal charity" were useless in the struggle for racial existence.[14] One practical effect of Hoffman's book was to help convince white insurance companies to deny coverage to blacks on the grounds that they represented an unacceptable actuarial risk by simply being a member of the "Negro race."[15]

With remarkable restraint, Du Bois gently chided Hoffman's work and called for a Department of Negro Statistics and a "careful monographic study of the Negro in limited localities and from particular points of view" to prevent the kind of statistical errors that Hoffman made.[16] Hoffman's book represented for Du Bois the chief obstacle to an intelligent and scientific approach to the study of African American life. It was not based on sound analyses of particular black communities, it lacked a way of accurately comparing similar communities in other parts of the country and in other parts of the world to determine how blacks stood not just in relation to whites in the South, but to similar peasant communities in the industrial world, and it operated on prejudicial assumptions about the supposed innate racial traits of black people. Du Bois accused Hoffman of being unscientific in his analysis and upbraided him for making sweeping conclusions about "the race" rather than the various classes of African Americans.

Du Bois's assertion that Hoffman's work was unscientific was a strong claim because Hoffman wrote that his book was a piece of statistical research in which "sentiment, prejudice, or the influence of pre-conceived ideas" had no place. Hoffman argued that the data he brought together spoke for itself. He hoped that his work would lead to "more scientific attention to the relations between superior and inferior races, as contrasted with the present dangerous method of guess work."[17] Although critical of Hoffman's book, Du Bois did welcome it as one of the "first fruits" of a new "unprejudiced, scientific interest" in the "Negro Question."[18] Much rested on the meaning of the term *scientific*. Du Bois wrote as though a scientific approach guaranteed a nonprejudicial, accurate, and "objective" interpretation of African American prospects in America, but Hoffman's own statements indicate that his understanding of what constituted a scientific approach to social problems implicitly and explicitly incorporated notions of superior and inferior races (with an emphatic assertion of black inferiority). Modern historians and scholars cannot so easily regard Hoffman's work as "pseudo-scientific" or "unscientific." Hoffman was a member of the American Academy of Medicine, the American Statistical Association, and the Royal Statistical Society of London. His monograph reflected a summation of the century's medical and anthropological findings on race relations in America.[19] The American Economic Association published his work in three consecutive issues of its journal, thereby lending its authority to his findings.[20] Hoffman's work was also reviewed in professional journals such as *Annals of the American Academy of Political and Social Science* and *Political Science Quarterly*. So Du Bois's conception of what constituted science put him at odds with his white contemporaries (certainly on racial issues).

Dan Green and Edwin Driver argue that Du Bois was deeply influenced by the methodological approach of Gustav Schmoller, professor of political economy at Berlin.[21] Schmoller had encouraged Du Bois to prepare a seminar thesis on "*Der Gross- und Klein Betrieb des Askerbaus, in der Südstaaten der Vereinigten Staaten, 1840–1890.*"[22] Schmoller's methodological approach favored the use of induction to accumulate historical and descriptive material. He saw the goal of social science as the systematic, causal explanation of social phenomena and believed that social scientific facts so acquired could be the basis for social policy. Like Schmoller, Du Bois's early sociological studies, until around 1910, manifested an emphasis on empirical data collection and the use of the inductive method, the collection of facts as a basis for formulating public policy, an underlying interest in social justice, and an emphasis on a historical approach to social development.[23] Du Bois wrote in his autobiography: "I was going to study the facts, any and all facts, concerning the American Negro and his plight, and by measurement and comparison and research, work up to any valid generalizations which I could."[24] Knowledge based on scientific investigation would then cure the ignorance that lay at the basis of faulty thinking about race and the Negro problem.

Du Bois elaborated more explicitly on his methodology in several of his early works. In a public speech delivered before the forty-fourth session of the American Academy of Political and Social Science on November 19, 1897, in Philadelphia, he talked about the study of Negro "problems," placing the emphasis on a variety of issues rather than a singular Negro problem. He called for an acknowledgment of the array of social forces and customs that stood in the path of a systematic study of black life. Du Bois urged those present to stop allowing whims, hasty conjectures, and impulses to take the place of conscious and intelligent action. Society, he asserted, ought to settle its Negro problems in light of its highest aims and study them using the best scientific research available. Du Bois proposed a plan of study that included historical analysis, statistical investigation, anthropological measurement, and sociological interpretation. He regarded his emphasis on sociological interpretation as an attempt to study "the finer manifestations of social life which history can but mention and which statistics can not count, such as the expression of Negro life found in their hundred newspapers, their considerable literature, their music and folklore and their germ of esthetic life."[25]

Du Bois was acutely aware of the deep-seated bias against blacks, manifested in the writings of those concerned with the contemporary problems of black and white relations in the nation. His antidote to prejudices was the necessity of all interpreters receiving technical training, acquiring "breadth of view," and coming to a deeper sense of the "sanctity of scientific truth."[26] Yet for all his emphasis on the necessity of certain traits, training, and qualifications, Du Bois did not make clear what it was about these qualities that would mitigate the power of racial prejudice. Nor did he, as Savage notes, give much attention to black religion or the churches as he laid out his research agenda in this speech.[27] Du Bois did emphasize the need to study blacks historically, especially "the rise of such peculiar expressions of Negro social history, as the Negro church."[28] He made brief reference to paying attention to the social evolution of black life, particularly the "remaining traces of African tribal life" and their "conversion to Christianity."[29] This was another instance of his emphasis on the particular coming to the fore, when he regarded black churches as one of many social institutions among blacks and therefore their relative importance could be ascertained only by attention to different communities over a period of time. All of these assertions were consistent with his call for a more historically grounded and nuanced study of the development of African American cultures in the United States.

We may sum up several basic arguments that stand out in Du Bois's speech: the importance and necessity of science as a method to discover "the simple truth," the crucial nature of local studies that eschewed generalizations, and the humanity of one's subjects. Du Bois asserted that social reform was the mediate, not the immediate object of scientific analysis. He castigated those who aligned their research projects with politicians, philanthropies, and specific schemes of reform. This was consistent with his high faith in the disinterested nature of scientific research. Du Bois also noted that "what is true of the Negro in Massachusetts is not necessarily true of the Negro in Louisiana."[30] This supported his insistence on attention to the varied nature of black life in America and the need to avoid vast generalities about "the race." Astonishingly, Du Bois had to make explicit that his methodology assumed that African Americans were members of the human race and were capable of improvement and "culture." All of these basic assumptions informed his work. The latter two assumptions set him apart from many of his white contemporary interpreters of black culture.

The Problem of the Negro Church

Du Bois later claimed to have abandoned his ideal of a detached social science, especially after 1910, in the face of lynching and the general mistreatment of blacks in the nation. He wrote, "One could not be a calm, cool, and detached scientist while Negroes were lynched, murdered and starved."[31] This was a specific reference to Sam Hose's lynching in Atlanta in 1899. Although Hose killed a white man in self-defense in a dispute over wages, he was lynched and burned to death. A mob of 2,000 white men, women, and children fought over pieces of his flesh for souvenirs. On his way to downtown Atlanta to investigate the situation, Du Bois was unaware that Hose's body had been burned and that his blackened knuckles were on display in a white store owner's window.[32]

This incident shook him to the core and no doubt played a significant role in undermining his faith in scientific objectivity. However, since his entire career took place during the worst years of lynching in American history, it is perhaps more fitting to regard his ideas about the scientific nature of his work as having been in a state of flux from the very beginning of his career. A close look at a public speech that he delivered in July 1897 reveals the nature of this ambivalence in his approach to the study of black culture. Titled "The Problem of Amusement," Du Bois's speech was his first and clearest statement of his understanding of African American religion. The speech could just as easily have been titled "The Problem of the Negro Church" because Du Bois devoted much attention to black religion. He had been conducting research among blacks in Philadelphia and in rural Virginia (in areas where many blacks in Philadelphia had come from) and he presented a preliminary analysis of his findings in a paper that he read at the General Conference of Negroes held at Hampton Institute. The speech itself was based on his particular findings on blacks in Prince Edward County, Virginia. In the context of broader discussions of African American culture, this speech reflected Du Bois's desire that such local detailed studies could be built up in the hope of making firmer generalizations about black life in various other parts of the country.

Du Bois began his speech by modestly noting that he wanted to discuss "superficially a phase of development in the organized life of American Negroes which has hitherto received scant notice."[33] Although he acknowledged that how blacks got their entertainment was not the most pressing problem, Du Bois predicted that it would soon become a major problem and that it was essential to know the places, manner, method, and extent of a people's amusements because a "people's recreation is of vast importance to their welfare."[34] Here, then, was Du Bois the social analyst exploring the nature and role of amusements within the social life of black Americans in a particular community at the end of the nineteenth century. He argued that it was not simply economic opportunities but the desire for amusements that was drawing young blacks between the ages of eighteen to thirty to cities such as Norfolk, Richmond, Baltimore, Washington, Philadelphia, and New York. Du Bois noted that he had observed with silent apprehension for quite some time that amusement was being deprecated as the "peculiar property of the devil" and that the effect of this denigration of amusement was the massive outflow of blacks to urban areas to escape the monotony and restrictions of Southern rural areas.[35]

Du Bois argued that these prohibitions against amusement were particularly troublesome for African Americans because of their exclusion from public entertainments in the cities and because the Negro church, though in theory opposed to most modern forms of entertainment, was the "chief purveyor" of amusements for blacks. The quest for diversion and amusement was going on at the same time that black churches were denouncing the pleasures and pursuits of their young people. Du Bois noted that this unusual development had taken place because black churches had assumed multiple roles because of their difficult history under slavery. He believed that the church assumed this role as provider of entertainment because the black family was destroyed during slavery and was replaced by the church, which became the "first distinct organization" of blacks. Because the Negro church came before the home, it "antedated" the development of a separate social life for blacks. Du Bois explained,

> In origin and functions the Negro church is a broader, deeper, and more comprehensive social organism than the churches of white Americans. The Negro church is not simply an organism for the propagation of religion; it is the centre of the social, intellectual, and religious life of an organized group of individuals . . . it is, in fine, the central organ of the organized life of the American Negro for amusement, relaxation, instruction, and religion.[36]

Now the church found itself vying with the theater, the home, and the dance hall as an "amusement-giving agency." For Du Bois, the church had become an anomalous institution in a changed world.

The time had come, Du Bois insisted, for the Negro church to divest itself of such broad responsibilities. It had nobly fulfilled an enormous task and bore its burden well under difficult historical circumstances. Furthermore, the Negro church had demonstrated the ability of "civilized" blacks to govern themselves. It had heroically taken on a multitude of tasks for a poor and oppressed people. For these reasons, Du Bois commended the Negro church and granted it respect. Yet, he argued, the Negro church could no longer continue to be the center of amusements for blacks. Black youth were leaving the church in increasing numbers, he asserted, because they were tired of the "limited and hackneyed amusements the church offers." The Negro church was therefore overstepping its boundaries by trying to provide entertainment for blacks and was thereby diverted from its "true, divine mission of human inspiration."[37] It was unwittingly cheapening religion by its "incessant semi-religious activity." By attempting to impose restrictions on amusements, Du Bois argued, the Negro church had forgotten that its strictures had arisen in an age when churches tried to separate themselves from the world. He put it this way: "In this tongue [of its early days among Methodist and Baptist revivalists in the late eighteenth century] the Negro church first began to lisp; its earliest teaching was that the Christian church stood apart from and utterly opposed to a world filled with pleasures, and that to partake of those pleasures was sin-ful."[38] "When now," he continued, "the church speaks in those same tones and invites healthy and joyous young people from the back seats to renounce the amusements of this world for a diet of fasting and prayer, those same young people in increasing numbers are positively, deliberately, and decisively de-clining to do any such thing."[39] By denying its youth legitimate entertainment and attempting to entertain them in its own way, the Negro church found itself in the awkward position of fostering an environment that led to criminal activity among its youth who rejected its strictures and sought a life free of any restraint outside the churches (as they continued to move to the cities). Du Bois argued that these youth recognized the hypocrisy of the churches' position and therefore refused to adhere to it.

If the Negro church was to save the next generation and prevent black youth from leaving its walls, it would have to rethink its role within the black community. It had to adjust to a new age. Du Bois asserted: "I now insist that the time has come when the activities of the Negro church must become differentiated and when it must surrender to the school and home, and social organizations, those functions which in a day of organic poverty it so heroically sought to bear."[40] The church should restrict its activities to "spiritual" matters and inspiration of the young for "unselfish work." It should adopt a balanced view of the need for legitimate entertainment and confine itself to dissemi-nating a spiritual message.

Du Bois and African American Religious Historiography

This speech was Du Bois's first public analysis of "the Negro church" and his first use of this particular expression (as far as I have been able to determine). His arguments provide us with about as clear a view of his historical and sociological contributions to the study of African American religion that we are going to get, except for his later, more developed arguments about the lingering influence of African religious traditions among black Americans. In my own close reading of all his later works that treat African American religion in some fashion, I do not see any major innovation in his methodology or in his con-clusions (one exception would be his general aesthetic approach to African American culture in *Souls of Black Folk*). In fact, Du Bois's normative judg-ments on religion (not including his polemical essays written after 1910), were more explicit in this speech than in most of his later sociological works. If examine his *Philadelphia Negro* (1899); his "Religion of the American Negro" (1900), which was minimally altered when it was retitled "Of the Faith of the

Fathers," chapter 10 in *Souls of Black Folk* (1903); *The Negro Church* (1903); and *The Morals and Manners of Negro Americans* (1914)—the latter two he edited but was not the sole contributor to their contents—we find many of the same themes, conclusions, and sometimes even the exact words about the Negro church that were articulated in the "Problem of Amusement." Of course there was development in Du Bois's thought on African American culture, but to the extent that he had a fixed methodology, it was rather formed at this stage in his career and was most evident in his study of African American religion from 1897 to 1910 (which coincided with his time as professor of economics and history at Atlanta University).

As a professor of economics and history at Atlanta University, Du Bois returned to some of these themes on black religion in his essay "The Religion of the American Negro" (1900). But here he was more focused on the historical development of black religion in America and its connection to an African past. In accounting for the slaves' acceptance of Christianity, Du Bois apparently conceded the common claim of black natural religiosity. He asserted, "The Negro has already been pointed out many times as a religious animal—a being of that deep emotional nature which turns instinctively toward the supernatural. Endowed with a rich tropical imagination and a keen, delicate appreciation of Nature, the transplanted African lived in a world animate with gods and devils, elves and witches." This attachment to religion helped elucidate the "inner ethical life" of blacks in America. The African past continued to exert itself in the form of a "vague superstition" that still existed among "unlettered" blacks.[41] But only as a historical aside did Du Bois seem to find any usefulness in this assertion of innate religiosity. After all, the bulk of the essay was intended to demonstrate that the old type of Negro was passing away and that a newer breed of cynical blacks, who were hostile to everything white, was arising because of the harsh racial conditions in the nation. These new types of blacks, Du Bois contended, went to the Northern cities, left the churches for the gambling halls and "bawdy" houses, and became criminals and sensualists.[42] Exposed to radical ideas through lectures, discussions and periodicals in the hustle and bustle of city life, he continued, blacks became bitter and angry. Du Bois's unsparing portrayal of the loss of religion among urban and Northern blacks was perhaps more a reflection of his own romantic conception of aspects of rural black religion than an attempt to provide a balanced assessment of black religion in developing urban centers. Clearly his claim of black disaffection with religion in the North was intended to provoke black churches to reevaluate their prohibitions against various forms of amusement.[43]

Du Bois's analysis of the plight of urban blacks, which appeared virtually unchanged in *The Souls of Black Folk*, was in part a political strategy to remind "the best white southern public opinion" that the growth of hatred among and restrictions against Southern blacks drove some blacks to the urban North, where radical ideas flourished. Blacks, a "naturally honest" and "straightforward" people, were being forced into an alien environment and their moral fiber was being tampered with by such a drastic move. Du Bois argued that the New South had passed into the hands of industrialists, "the sons of poor whites fired with a new thirst for wealth and power, thrifty and avaricious Yankees, shrewd and unscrupulous Jews," who had thrust aside the old Southern gentlemen who at least had some attachment to and affection for blacks.[44] By appealing to those whites who longed for the days when, in their view, friendship and affection between blacks and whites were more common, Du Bois hoped to combine his critique of materialism and industrialism with his portrayal of the "deep religious feeling" of blacks. He wrote, "It is not idle regret with which the white South mourns the loss of the old-time Negro—the frank, honest, simple old servant who stood for the earlier religious age of submission and humility."[45] This was his attempt to use the plantation image of the religious and picturesque Southern Negro against the developing image of the irreligious and dangerous urban, Northern Negro.[46] Ultimately, Du Bois charged, the New South's crass materialism was undermining the very basis for the religious Negro, whose passing was lamented by the sons of the former slave masters. Despite the depressing conditions that blacks faced, the "deep religious feeling of the real Negro heart" remained because it was their distinctive virtue.[47]

Though Du Bois reworked and repeated much of the material from his "Religion of the American Negro" essay, no new theoretical advance was made in *The Souls of Black Folk*. His aesthetic conception of religion did emerge more clearly, and he wrote more like the romantic racialist than the sociologist. He presented blacks as the "sole oasis of simple faith and reverence in a dusty desert of dollars and smartness." They stood as the religious saviors of a materialistic and racist society and the true embodiment of the nation's spiritual ideals. Through their spirituals and folk songs, they brought a special beauty and joy to the nation. Spirituals represented for Du Bois the gift of rural blacks fresh out of slavery. In his view, the countryside was the mystical hinterland that produced these songs, the "most beautiful expression of human experience."[48] Many of these arguments had been stated in at least one of his earlier works. As early as 1897, in his speech before the American Negro Academy ("The Conservation of Races"), Du Bois claimed to find "spiritual" and "psychical" differences between "the races." He argued that blacks were the "first fruits of the new nation, the harbinger of that black to-morrow which is yet destined to soften the whiteness of the Teutonic to-day." Blacks, he continued, must conserve their spiritual ideals and intellectual endowments. They ought not slavishly imitate whites, but contribute their full gifts to American culture. These gifts included a subtle sense of song and a touch of "pathos" and "humor" that would temper America's "mad money-getting plutocracy." But Du Bois's romantic racialism was moderated by a stinging criticism of black moral life. He exclaimed, "*Unless we conquer our present vices they will conquer us*; we are diseased, we are developing criminal tendencies, and an alarmingly large percentage of our men and women are sexually impure."[49] The religion of black folk appeared to be very different from what he described under the rubric of the Negro Church or actual black churches.

Du Bois's *The Negro Church* (1903) has been described as the first book-length sociological study of religion ever published in the United States; the first in-depth study of black religious life; and the first historical, sociological, and empirical study of black religious life undertaken by blacks themselves.[50] The study was coedited by Kelly Miller and Mary Church Terrell. At the time Miller was dean of the College of Arts and Sciences at Howard University. Terrell was the first president of the National Association of Colored Women and was active in the women's suffrage movement.[51] The study was the eighth monograph in a series of sociological studies produced at Atlanta University's annual conferences held between 1896 and 1914. Du Bois and his colleagues decided to include the following quotation at the head of this study:

> The Negro Church is the only social institution of the Negroes that started in the African forest and survived slavery; under the leadership of priest or medicine man, afterward of the Christian pastor, the Church preserved in itself the remnants of African tribal life and became after emancipation the center of Negro social life. So that today the Negro population of the United States is virtually divided into church congregations which are the real units of race life.
> *Report of the Third Atlanta Conference, 1898.*[52]

The apparent meaning of this statement was that black churches were rooted in an African past, and this was perhaps a response to assertions of innate religiosity or to those who wondered about the continued relative importance of churches for blacks at a time when science was seen as the pinnacle within a grand schema of sociocultural evolution. This statement served as an apt preface to Du Bois's attempt to make good on his program of studying Negro problems in all their complexity, and that included an analysis of the development of the social evolution and development of their group life and social institutions, and the "remaining traces" of their African tribal life.[53]

After providing a brief description of African Obeah "sorcery" and various African religious and family customs, Du Bois posited that contrary to the assertions of historians and sociologists that "every vestige of internal development disappeared" among the slaves transplanted from Africa, the power of the "Negro priest" on the plantation continued and eventually was transmuted through the new role of the black Christian preacher. He asserted, "From such beginnings arose and spread with marvelous rapidity the Negro Church, the first distinctively American social institution . . . It is this historic fact that the Negro Church of to-day bases itself upon the sole surviving institution of the African fatherland, that accounts for its extraordinary growth and vitality."[54] Though not stated as such, here, then, was the answer to the question about the reasons for the continued importance of religion for blacks. Here was a historical and sociological answer to the nature and function of the black churches.[55] By arguing that the black churches had taken over the "natural" function of the family, which had been destroyed by slavery, Du Bois explained their continuing importance. The resilience of African culture was also affirmed by rooting current black religious practices in a preslavery past. Included in the study was a call for cleansing, purifying, and reviving the Negro Church. It was urged to become more practical and to assist in the uplift of the family and the morals of the Negro community.[56]

Du Bois's methodological contributions to the study of African American religion emerge with foremost attention to the historical context of his thought and his varied public utterances that reflected on his ongoing research. First, he strongly believed in participant observation of local black communities, with an emphasis on their churches and religious practice in the broader context of the community. This attention to particularity and local geography expressed his underlying assumption that generalizations about one black locality do not necessarily extend to another. Second, time and again Du Bois articulated his presumption of the humanity of African Americans, which he felt allowed his studies to anticipate the possibility of development and unexpected eruptions or happenings within these communities rather than hobbling his theories by fixating on what was innately or essentially black. Third, he made a plausible historical argument about the importance or resilience of the African ancestry of American blacks, the transition from African religions to the practice of Christianity, and the development of slave religious life after its gradual break from direct African influences. All of these points require further elaboration by a brief examination of his less well-known writings and his treatment of religion in his two major works, The Philadelphia Negro and Souls of Black Folk.

When he was asked in early spring 1897 by Carroll Wright, the first commissioner of the U.S. Bureau of Labor, about the ways the industrial history of blacks in the United States might be studied, Du Bois was quick to inform Wright that so vast and varied a subject required many local studies of black communities throughout the South carried out over an extended time period. Du Bois was exasperated by the prejudices and fixed notions that prevented a careful analysis of African Americans and urged for the building up of particular community studies that would test overly broad generalizations. Black churches, then, were to be examined within the context of work patterns, educational institutions, and social and political conditions.[57] Similarly, in his speech before the American Academy of Political and Social Science later that year, Du Bois decried an extreme case of a recently published study of blacks in America that was based on an analysis of fifteen black boys in a New York reformatory.[58]

Du Bois had the opportunity to give the academic world an example of what his research proposal looked like in practice with the publication of his pioneering *Philadelphia Negro*. Here I am not concerned with the history of the work as a sociological text but rather the methodology Du Bois employed and how it shaped his treatment of African American religion. Elijah Anderson asks us to "imagine this stiff and proper Victorian gentleman in his suit and starched shirt moving through the hurly-burly of the noisy, congested neighborhood [as he] talked to people, listened to people, mapped the area, made ethnographic observations, and collected descriptive statistics."[59] Du Bois conducted his investigations from August 1, 1896, to December 31, 1896, except for a two-month absence. He went on a house-to-house canvass, ultimately doing research on 9,000 blacks in the seventh ward. He prepared six "schedules" to conduct his interviews. These schedules contained questions about the number, gender, age, and marital conditions of persons in a household. Information about renters, the number of rooms in a household, places of amusement, types of employment, what church one attended, length of residence in the city, and other issues were asked. Official statistics, census data, and historical studies rounded out the study of black life in Philadelphia.

Du Bois was acutely aware of his social location as a scholar who *studied* the lives of blacks. Yet he was open enough to allow his theories to be shaped by his interaction with real human beings. Reflecting on his study in Philadelphia, Du Bois noted two difficulties that he encountered: (1) Whites sneered, "Why study the obvious?" (2) Blacks said, "Are we animals to be dissected and by an unknown Negro at that?" Yet Du Bois persevered, mindful of the potentially intrusive nature of ethnographic study. He was convinced that his *Philadelphia Negro* work was worth his efforts because it "revealed the Negro group as a symptom, not a cause; as a striving, palpitating group, and not an inert, sick body of crime; as a long historical development and not a transient occurrence."[60] While acknowledging his presuppositions, biases, moral convictions, and some potential "unconscious trend of thought due to previous training," Du Bois remained convinced that his close listening to and conversations with blacks would give a better picture of what African American life was like, religious or otherwise. Too much was at stake for the scholar to neglect an attempt at producing accurate and fair-minded knowledge about what all sides regarded as the nation's greatest social problem.[61] Du Bois thought it his moral obligation to study black life rather than leave it to others, particularly whites, who simply did not regard blacks as adequately human. The presupposition of blacks' humanity, especially in his time, and the use of their lived experiences to challenge the abstractions of one's theories were basic contributions of Du Bois to sociological methodology and ethnography.

In his actual analysis of African American religion in *Philadelphia Negro*, he made good on his research proposal's particulars by tracing the social history of black churches in Philadelphia, noting the social classes within black society, and providing his readers with a few statistics on the number of blacks attending various churches. Even so, Du Bois's rather cursory analysis of black religion was principally centered on "the Function of the Negro Church." In this section, he reiterated his claim that the "Negro Church" was the measure of blacks' increasingly intricate social life, that it had a broader function than white churches in America, and that it antedated the black family. But despite the language of a singular Negro Church, Du Bois provided a description of a fairly diverse array of black churches in Philadelphia at the turn of the century.

In 1901, after having spent several years studying different black communities, Du Bois testified before the U.S. Industrial Commission that his knowledge of the South was based on his local studies, not on mere hunches about what blacks were like. He refused to lump each black community together. For example, he indicated that he detected differences among black churches in various parts of Georgia (which then had the largest black population in the country) and deflected questions that carried implicit notions of uniformity among all Southern blacks. In Albany, he explained, the local black church's meeting place was devoted almost exclusively to religious exercises rather than social gatherings. Du Bois told those gathered that this was not necessarily the case for other communities he had studied.[62] The details of his testimony need not concern us, but clearly he was a true pioneer in his emphasis on community studies over generalized constructs or broad narratives. This was a radical departure from the vast philosophical and sociological abstractions of Spencer, whose work exercised a profound influence on American sociological thought at the turn of the century. Du Bois urged that instead we "more and more school ourselves to the minute study of limited fields of human action, where observation and knowledge can be had." He continued, "The careful exhaustive study of the isolated group then is the ideal of the sociologist of the twentieth century—from that may come a real knowledge of natural law as locally manifest—a glimpse and revelation of rhythm beyond this little center and at last careful, cautious generalization and formulation."[63] In other words, attention to the lived experience of specific groups, tested through additional studies over time that presupposed change and development rather than static notions that sought once-and-for-all judgments (as a basis for public policy).

Perhaps it is a strange claim to argue that Du Bois's presumption of blacks' humanity was a methodological contribution. The dehumanization of blacks in American society in the late nineteenth and early twentieth centuries reached its low point in the early twentieth century. Through the various means of lynching, segregation, political disenfranchisement, demeaning literature and plays, and racist social science, black life was regarded as cheap and expendable in American society. In his *Souls of Black Folk*, Du Bois posed a deeply existential question that many blacks probably felt when he wrote, "How does it feel to be a problem?"[64] He implicitly expressed his doubts about the possibility of an objective social science when writing about the "cold statistician" noting the inches of black progress alongside the feet of black regress. Du Bois lamented that sociologists gleefully counted the number of black bastards and prostitutes.[65] He took the existential leap into the muddy waters of identification with the humanity of his subjects, writing about their "spiritual world," their religion, their "human sorrow," and the struggle of their "greater souls." He attempted to take the reader within the veil, thus leaving behind a superficial "scientific" approach that posited a division between the subject and object and made the "object" into a radical other. Drawing on biblical allusions, Du Bois identified himself as "bone of the bone and flesh of the flesh" with his subjects.[66] He was one of them, and he sought to reveal their "souls" rather than a static dehumanizing Negro problem that so haunted the white imagination when it looked at real black Americans. Here we see his growing disenchantment with a strictly scientific or objective analysis of black culture. By employing concepts such as "soul" and "spiritual strivings," he sought to elude the constricting methodological tools of social science. Literary techniques, cultural immersion through vivid re-creation of his own experience among black communities, and evocative and vivid language were the tools Du Bois used to convey the "essence" of black culture.

Du Bois's attempt to formulate a study of blacks that assumed their humanity, without a priori notions about degeneration, African backwardness, and racial extinction was a real accomplishment. When Walter Willcox, professor of economics at Cornell University, claimed to be agnostic about whether the economic conditions of blacks in the South were attributable to their "persistent characteristics" (that is, defective culture or innate racial inferiority) or external economic and social pressures, Du Bois severely castigated him.[67] Du Bois insisted that Willcox was trying to "spin a solution [to] the Negro problem out of the inside" of his office. He argued that only if Willcox would sit "as I have ten years in intimate soul contact with all kinds & conditions" of African Americans he would be cured of his agnosticism. Willcox and others need to "get down here [in the South] & really study at first hand" black conditions in the South, not pronounce judgments from a "car window" analysis or by writing for Associated Press dispatches. Perhaps rather naively, Du Bois urged the white social scientist to get "off the fence" by coming to the South and studying the Negro question with his own eyes, not through the prejudiced lens of others.[68]

Although often intertwined with his many moral judgments about black churches, Du Bois's assertion of African continuity in the Negro church challenged traditional notions of the black church as a "borrowed institution" (which was based on the presupposition that Africans were incapable of organized social life and cultural creativity apart from white influence). One finds this view, for example, in the review of *The Negro Church* by Walter Fleming, a white historian at West Virginia University. Fleming claimed, contra Du Bois, that he and other historians maintained that slavery destroyed African "superstition" and voodoo worship and substituted for them Christianity and that the Negro church was therefore a borrowed institution. He also challenged Du Bois's assertions about a polygamous family structure in African societies. Fleming insisted that there was no such family in Africa and that the "negro family" was forcibly created in slavery. For Fleming and other white scholars, blacks were culture-less and history-less recipients of white American culture.[69] He argued that Du Bois was simply wrong in his claims about the persistence and the resilience of African culture. What is now seen as Du Bois's contributions to African American religious historiography Fleming regarded as a flawed analysis of African American religion.

Creating the Negro Church

Du Bois was a central figure in the genealogy of the discourse of the Negro Church. Terminology, social location, and institutions are important here. On one hand, it is no surprise that Du Bois would focus on and give extended attention to the churches of black Americans because he repeatedly argued for their influence and central role in the lives of most blacks. We may plausibly conjecture that the use of the expression "Negro Church" follows from this basic fact. On the other hand, it is a curious thing that Du Bois's discourse of "the Negro Church" initiated and has left us with a legacy of futile and sterile questions about whether the "black Church" has been an instrument of social reform or accommodation. This is curious because Du Bois placed so much emphasis on local black communities and the differences among them. He commenced his sociological project with the express goal of refuting abstractions and vast generalizations with empirical studies of local communities. Why did he subsume a diverse group of churches under the monolithic moniker "the Negro Church?" Was it his training in Germany? At Harvard? Was it a logical consequence of his argument that "the Church" replaced the black family during slavery and thus functioned as a "natural" organism or institution?

Du Bois was one of the first social scientists to use the singular Negro Church appellation (1897 seems to be the earliest date). Terminological changes became more noticeable in the late 1890s. As a leading interpreter of black culture in the South (see chapter 2), Booker T. Washington often spoke of "the religion of blacks," "negro churches," and the "Christianity of Southern negroes" throughout the 1890s. Yet by July 1905, even he began using the phrase "Negro Church."[70] These changes in nomenclature signified deeper transformations in interpretations and expectations of African American religion. Few scholars doubted that *the church* as a social institution had been at the center of the black community in the South, but there is no language of the "Negro Church" as such prior to Du Bois's work. I suggest that the concomitant rise of the disciplines and their attempts to carve out their specific niche in the real world (by defining a discrete area of inquiry) were central disciplinary mechanisms in the developing language of the singular Negro Church. David Lewis has rightly noted Du Bois's reliance on German social thought that posited that each people possessed a unique folk spirit, and clearly Du Bois saw black religion as the central expression of the black "soul."[71] It is a reasonable conjecture that his racial theories played a part in his creation of the Negro Church. He remained wedded, in some form, to this notion of separate but equal contributions of races throughout his life. In his most explicitly racialist work ("The Conservation of Races," 1897), Du Bois posited distinct racial gifts for various "races" that he called for black Americans to conserve their "physical powers," "intellectual endowments," and "spiritual ideals." He urged them to build race organizations and strive for racial unity and solidarity.[72] The dire conditions of black life prompted a concern with the political function of the Negro Church and how it could become an instrument in pooling the resources of a poor and downtrodden people. Not surprisingly, in 1908, a young graduate student at the University of Chicago, Carter G. Woodson, wrote to Du Bois, asking him for information and bibliographical data on black churches. Woodson concluded his letter with the notice that he wanted "all such facts as will show what the Church has contributed to the *progress* or *regress* of the race."[73] Thus begins the task of charting the nature and progress of an entity called the Negro Church as a means to various social, political, and economic ends.

Most historians and Du Bois scholars have noted that his academic training at the University of Berlin and Harvard University had a profound and lasting influence on his social thought and theories of race.[74] Joel Williamson attributes Du Bois's emphasis on racial gifts and the group consciousness of blacks to his indebtedness to "significant portions" of the social philosophy of nineteenth-century German philosopher Georg F. W. Hegel. Williamson particularly regards Hegel's view of distinct peoples in history achieving consciousness of their spirit, soul, or genius as a seedbed for Du Bois's reflections on race and African American group life. Williamson argues, "Hegelian *Freiheit*, true freedom, consists in knowing one's self through one's people, of sharing the common vision of reality, and, hence, of governing one's self in accordance with the folk spirit."[75] Certainly we find in Du Bois's "Conservation of Races" (1897) speech the following statement: "For the development of Negro genius, of Negro literature and art, of Negro spirit, only Negroes bound and welded together, Negroes inspired by one vast ideal, can work out in its fullness the great message we have for humanity."[76] This emphasis on a group or race spirit is also present in his *Souls of Black Folk*. This way of describing a spiritual message or folk spirit of the "Negro race" allowed Du Bois to make the startling claim that there was a "Negro church" before blacks became Christians.[77] I take this to mean that he made a distinction between the "Negro Church" as a social institution and the Negro church or black religion as a carrier or conduit of blacks' spiritual message or unique folk spirit.

After describing in his *Souls of Black Folk* the history of the development of black churches, Du Bois noted that he would now turn from "the outer physical development of the church to the more important inner ethical life of the people who compose it."[78] Immediately he launched into a discussion of blacks' "deep emotional nature," their sensitivity to nature, and their alleged "rich tropical imagination," all of which he regarded as constitutive of their inner ethical life or what I call their spiritual message to the world. Therefore, when examining blacks' hardships in the South and the changing religious climate of the United States, Du Bois asserted that the black soul was wrenched and torn by double ideals and *double social classes*. Blacks have therefore not been able to reach their true self-consciousness as a group or race. So Du Bois informed his readers that though black churches were differentiating (based on his previous speech, one would think he would have welcomed this, but apparently the wistful language suggests otherwise), underneath all the divisions and social classes lay "the deep religious feeling of the real Negro heart," one not torn asunder by the racial conflict in the nation. He ended this section of *Souls of Black Folk* with the grand peroration that "some day the Awakening will come, when the pent-up vigor of ten million souls shall sweep irresistibly toward the Goal, out of the Valley of the Shadow of Death."[79] There is an unstated assumption that black ideals and goals would be realized as a group and that this would come about as a realization of racial self-consciousness.

There was also a pragmatic element in the notion of the Negro Church as a singular institution. Here Du Bois was not alone in his call for the black church to conserve its resources, to unite in attacking political and social problems, and to address itself to the general issues that blacks faced in a racist society. As Dianne Savage has argued, Du Bois and other African American leaders had to contend with the fact that black churches were very important in the lives of many blacks. For this reason alone, they could not dismiss the churches.[80] Thus they argued for reform from within the churches. However, this would have been a rather tedious and piecemeal process if in doing so they acknowledged that local black churches had varying stances toward social reform and political empowerment. A call for a united Negro Church to confront the common problems of blacks quite simply had more "cash value" in the public arena than a more "scientific" approach that emphasized the bewildering array of churches and religious practices that existed among blacks in different parts of the country. Therefore continuing ideas about racial essentialism and the persistent problems of black life combined to make credible claims about a Negro Church.

A close reading of Du Bois's major writings on the Negro Church from the 1890s to the 1910s reveals that he was struck by the potential and problems of the church assuming social activities. By having so many forms of entertainment and social events centered in it, he assessed that the church could have enormous potential influencing black people, especially in united causes. But he also felt that this opportunity was being squandered because of timidity, poor clerical leadership, and bickering over religious doctrines and denominational issues. After Du Bois left Atlanta in 1910 and took up residence in New York City as a researcher and writer (or a propagandist, as he liked to say) for the newly formed National Association for the Advancement of Colored People (NAACP), he relaxed his former restraint as a careful observer of black culture. In a 1912 article in the *Crisis*, the official paper of the NAACP, he called for "every effort to make the Negro Church a place where colored men and women of education and energy can work for the best things regardless of their belief or disbelief in the unimportant dogmas and outworn creeds."[81] By this time, he had developed a litany of complaints against black churches, and he lashed out against them in the voice of the enlightened modernist. As Du Bois put it: "Today the church is still inveighing against dancing and theatergoing, still blaming people for objecting to silly and empty sermons, boasting and noise, still building churches when people need homes and schools, and persisting in crucifying critics rather than realize the handwriting is on the wall."[82] The "handwriting is on the wall" comment reflected his growing conviction of the dying influence of outmoded religion in the modern world.

Because white interpreters rarely used the singular Negro Church, my conjecture about the seeming political potential of black religion in the hands of black interpreters seems reasonable. Eventually, the connotation and significa-tion of the term represented quite the opposite of what Du Bois's early socio-logical project sought to undertake. The construction of the Negro Church (and its now common appellation, the black Church) has obscured the very real differences among African Americans that Du Bois himself detected, and it has rendered invisible or regressive those black religious groups and practices that do not fit into such categories as progressive or prophetic. Perhaps this is one of the most ironic of his legacies in light of his earlier methodological contributions.

Du Bois's methodological contributions then included his ethnographic approach of participant observation in a time when it was regarded as pollution to live and work among African Americans. His recognition of blacks' hu-manity, his affirmation of the viability and continuing influence of African culture, and his assertion of the partial autonomy and cultural creativity of blacks were crucial achievements for his day. His detailed studies of local black communities were prescient in that they remind us in important ways of con-temporary postmodern suspicions of grand narratives and abstractions. Even though he often indulged in moralizing and promoted the discourse of prim-itivism that so dominated social thought in the early twentieth century, Du Bois deepened social scientific knowledge of African American life and provided rich insights into the process of interpreting religion in relationship to one's own moral and epistemological stance.

The Prospects and Defects of the Negro Church

Formal and academic studies on African American religion by blacks in the sociological tradition initiated by Du Bois continued, but the new discourse of the Negro Church, romantic racialist conceptions, and psychological critiques of black religion came together rather uneasily in the works of several black thinkers. Black leaders were groping for a way to offer an academic and activist view of black life. In 1903, at the Atlanta conference that produced Du Bois's *Negro Church*, Kelly Miller presented a talk titled "Religion as a Solvent of the Race Problem." All of the romantic racialist conceptions of black religion came together in his speech. Miller repeated uncritically the common assertions that blacks possessed a "deeply religious nature" and were widely noted for their "emotional and spiritual susceptibilities." He asserted that blacks had the "passive virtues" of meekness and humility and argued that blacks were "spiritually predisposed" to Christianity, which was "peculiarly adapted" to their "ethnic characteristics."[83] In his description of vices among blacks, Miller sounded remarkably similar to Du Bois. He wrote, "The criminal and moral status of the Negro race is threatening its physical continuance. After we have made all possible allowances for historic causes and plead all possible exculpatory excuses, the plain, unpleasant, unvarnished fact remains: The American Negro must conquer his vices or be destroyed by them."[84]

Miller, like the romantic racialists of the nineteenth century, argued that blacks and whites possessed virtues that the others lacked. From whites, he contended, blacks would acquire a higher standard of "concrete morality" that would enable them to have more "rational modes" of worship and "orderly habits of life." Whites could learn from blacks "valuable lessons" in meekness, humility, and forgiveness. Although blacks must purify themselves of "carnal corruption" and "grossness," whites must rid themselves of a "pharisaical attitude" toward blacks. Miller believed that blacks should place more emphasis on the ten commandments, and whites should learn to practice the Golden Rule. Only together could blacks and whites demonstrate the true power of Christianity and solve the race problem.[85] He had doubts about the degree to which this could be realized. He averred that Christianity had been unable to wean Anglo-Saxons from race prejudice and that for whites ethnic ties were stronger than faith or moral and spiritual kinship. Perhaps in his mysterious providence, Miller conjectured, God would use the Negro to help the Teuton understand that "race idolatry" was a sin and that the Teuton must practice the "concrete brotherhood of man."[86]

The nomenclature in Miller's address was rather fluid. From time to time he spoke of "the Negro Church" and in other instances he talked about the "religion" of the Negro. But in his general formulations about the social functions of black religion, he contributed to the discourse of the Negro Church, which was not merely a descriptive, academic enterprise but from its inception a normative conception of what role religion ought to play in the lives of black

Americans. Though Miller reiterated romantic racialist themes, most black academics sought to promote their analysis of black religion in the social scientific language of the Negro Church, though theories in the new psychology of religion (that is, theories of the mind and internal states) warred in the social thought of some black leaders. In December 1902, the American Negro Academy held a two-day session in which papers were read on the "Religion of the Negro" and later published one of these, "The Defects of the Negro Church," as an occasional paper in 1904. The author of the paper, Orishatukeh Faduma, was born John Davis in British Guiana (Guyana) to parents recently converted to Christianity and had just become a naturalized citizen of the United States the year he delivered his paper. After his graduation from the University of London, Faduma attended Yale Divinity School from 1891 to 1894, and on graduation, a scholarship enabled him to continue graduate work at Yale University, where he studied Semitic languages and philosophy of religion.[87] He was ordained to the Congregational ministry in May 1895. Under assignment from the American Missionary Association (AMA), Faduma agreed "to work in the South among the lowly as a preparation for missionary work in Africa."[88] From 1895 to 1913 he served as superintendent of Peabody Academy and pastor of the Congregational Church at Troy, North Carolina. Troy was a rural area where the AMA had founded a mission in 1881, and the white staff was being replaced by blacks during Faduma's tenure. Troy became a "living laboratory" for Faduma to study the conditions of blacks there and in other parts of the South and prepare him for his future missionary work to Africa.[89]

Although the American Negro Academy was founded to defend blacks against intellectual attacks, Faduma's unsparing accounts of the defects of black churches presented a challenge for the organization, particularly at a sensitive historical moment when criticism of black churches was widespread among white academics. Archibald Grimké, brother of pastor Francis Grimké, was president of the academy when Faduma presented his paper. The executive committee referred the paper to Grimké because there was concern about its hostility to black ministers, including those who were members of the academy. Grimké accepted the paper based on its academic merit.[90] In his talk, Faduma drew on his personal experiences with blacks in the South and the professional knowledge of religion that he had acquired in the university context. He was careful to indicate in his paper that the "defects" of the Negro Church were "not inherent" to blacks, and he only wanted to discuss the "leading defects" (though it is difficult to see how he could have enumerated any more than the many that he discussed). These defects included the following: (1) stress on outwardness; (2) neglect of rural communities; (3) the black ministry in its current form; (4) an unconsecrated laity; and (5) excessive emotionalism.[91]

Faduma argued that Christianity was a religion of inwardness that trans-forms the soul and the heart. True religion was rooted and grounded in the inner life, but the Negro Church, he insisted, was obsessed with outward manifestations, oratory, and "mere jingles of sound." By bringing converts into the faith through such heightened and extraordinary means, Faduma argued, the Negro Church failed to impress members with the divine life and ideal and consequently allowed them to slip away. He asserted, "The mad rush after quantity rather than quality of converts is another indication of the outwardness of religion" in black churches. By neglecting "intensiveness in the culture of souls" and depth in the spiritual life, undue attention was given to expansion and external evidences of growth. Religion then became a "puppet show" and a parade. Faduma asserted that the "Negro is prone to fall into this error because of the many denials his critics make of his ability in self-government." He maintained that blacks emphasized church buildings, dollars collected, and number of followers as a way of showing their capabilities and demonstrating what they could do on their own. But religion's purpose, he declared, was "to deepen the spiritual life and help men to be in harmony with God and nature, not to satisfy critics and detractors." The foundation of the church must be laid before attention can be paid to its superstructure. Only a church that has a deep spiritual life will be able to suppress worldliness.[92]

Faduma was merciless in his criticism of the Negro Church's alleged ne-glect of rural communities. Within small towns, he argued, there was a preva-lence of ignorance and superstition. The "paganization of Christianity" in rural districts was the saddest spectacle to behold among blacks. Because of neglect, rural blacks, Faduma averred, were presented with Christianity in a "crude, uncouth, and distorted form." He insisted that it was a "form of Christianity with Christ left out." "Weird songs" during revivals were followed by the "un-chaste exposure and hysteria of women." Both genders practiced a "species of voodoism imported from the religion of heathen Africa" that led to "violent physical gymnastics" and other forms of improper behavior. Faduma despaired:

> It is deplorable because its effects are demoralizing. The situation is grave and calls for rebuke, because it is deeply entrenched in our country churches and is encouraged by pastors who ought to point a better way. In Africa Christianity is displacing paganism, in rural America paganism is displacing Christianity. Our rural population is confronted with a form of Christianity which does not civilize. Since the corruption of the best thing is the worst thing, it may fairly be stated that Christianity is receiving an unfair treatment in a pro-fessedly Christian country from a professedly Christian people.[93]

These harsh comments about Christianity among blacks indicated that Faduma's views of "paganism" in the rural South were evolving because they were different from his earlier, more sympathetic views of African religious practices. Perhaps, too, his real objection was to any attempt to fuse Christianity with African religious traditions. Whatever the case, Faduma saw the rural black South as a vast wasteland of superstition that was in desperate need of literate and moral pastors and an ethical "true" Christianity.

More attention was given to the "Negro ministry" in Faduma's talk than to any other topic. His conception of the ideal ministry included men of broad culture and wide sympathies, who were in touch with the "varied interests of the people." A college-educated ministry, he argued, was all the more imperative for the Negro Church because of the influence of black ministers (this was also Faduma's version of Du Bois's call for a talented tenth of educated leaders to uplift the race). Because of their "barren minds" and lack of culture, he maintained, black ministers found it easy to descend into immorality. "Immorality" was one of the most common aspersions cast against black ministers, as Faduma noted, and the term could include all kinds of conduct, but he insisted that there is "only one kind of conduct which is so far-reaching in its results because it is fundamentally subversive of and destructive to the best interests of society." That was sexual unchastity. Sexual immorality, Faduma believed, was a blight on the Negro ministry. He was quick to point out that it was not a "constitutional disease" or a "race trait" as others insisted, because the "ancestral life of the African shows without the shadow of doubt that the morality of the heathen as relates to sexes is part of the religion of most African tribes before they were brought into contact with a foreign civilization." This sexual immorality, Faduma asserted, was a product of plantation life and "Anglo-Saxon civilization." He claimed that in the rural South there were environments that encouraged such illicit living. He spoke of the log cabin where "families are crowded together like cattle, and sexual privacy and decorum are impossible."[94] Black leaders must be taken from such environments, trained, and used to do Christian missions in these areas. "Natural ability" and the "gift of speech" were not enough to make one a moral preacher, Faduma insisted, and only gave black ministers more opportunity to demoralize themselves and those with whom they came in contact.[95]

Much less emphasis was placed on the laity because Faduma believed the "salvation of the church and race is due to the faithful few," especially those in the ministry. Nonetheless, he criticized church members for their worldliness, which he defined as confining the Gospel to hearing sermons on Sundays and not allowing its virtues to be evident in one's life on a daily basis. Faduma argued that black church members lacked a missionary spirit and business methods, which often led to debts and debates about church finances. But even his reproach of the laity was in part contingent on his assertion that black ministers fed only the feelings rather than the intellect and the will, which failed to develop a "trained Christian conscience" in most members. Similarly, Faduma's condemnation of literalistic biblical interpretation by black preachers mitigated his claim that the laity's gospel did not "touch the many interests of life." His assertions of worldliness in the ministry were followed by his claims that what was taught in the pulpit trickled down to what happened in the daily lives of members. So the black ministry was the principal object of his criticisms.[96]

Moses Moore argues that Faduma's training at Yale infused him with sympathy and appreciation for the new theology that was emerging in the 1890s in American Congregationalism. The new theology emphasized, among other things, the immanence of God, a historical critical approach to the interpretation of Scripture, and a more "progressive" approach to the relationship between Christianity and the social order. In part, it was a reaction to traditional notions of original sin, a pre-Darwinian view of the relationship between religion and science, and literal interpretations of the Bible.[97] Faduma's criticism of black interpretations of the Bible and the preaching style of black pastors indeed reflected his indebtedness to the new theology. He argued that the Bible had been made into a "fetish" by unlearned preachers and that the black ministry, because of its "uncultured" nature, was wedded to "non-essentials" in its religious beliefs. Faduma contended that for black ministers "heaven and hell are too much in the future." They envisioned life after death but were unable to see any "heaven on earth" (a point made by Booker T. Washington). Their sermons subordinated truth to eloquence and showed no awareness of the influence of "modern thought." Faduma claimed that the black minister "believes in a revelation which is non-progressive and whose distinctive feature is sameness for all times." Pulpit oratory was "too physical" and lacked grace, beauty, decorum, contemplation, and deep spirituality. All such defects of the black ministry were a direct result, Faduma insisted, of a lack of exposure to modern thought and frozen interpretations of Scripture.[98]

Faduma's critique of emotionalism in black religion combined the methodology of the psychology of religion and sociology. There was a rather odd mixture of a normative sociological vision of the Negro Church combined with a psychological and moral argument against manifestations of black religion under the rubric of emotionalism. Hence Faduma argued that in religion, blacks' emotions constituted their greatest strength and weakness and that the defect of the Negro was "not that he is emotional, but that he is excessively so." He maintained that blacks were among those races in their childhood who possessed a "bundle of feelings." Such races, he averred, feel rather than think or will after God. Because blacks were not driven to action by "the law of duty" or the "moral imperative," they were instead controlled by their "nerves," and so it was impossible for many of them to know where they stood on many moral questions. They needed a new "thermometer" to regulate their lives and a compass to show them where they stood morally. They were attracted, Faduma asserted, to "neurotic environments," which were fostered by churches where sermons appealed to the imagination "in weird pictures of the unseen."[99]

Like liberal Protestant analyses of the process of conversion, Faduma provided an examination of how the psychological process of emotionalism unfolded during black religious revivals. He noted that the first stage was characterized by violent physical contortions that led to exhaustion. The second and third stage resulted in a loss of physical and moral control. Loss of moral control involved a "feeling of abandon leading often to unchaste exposure of the person, wild cries as if demented, and all kinds of extravagances." "Mental infection" and emotional panic ensued. Faduma argued that this "pandemonium" was the site at which many "obtained religion" by a process of infection. The final stage was characterized by lowered physical and moral vitality. He indicated that perhaps susceptibility to these stages of emotional loss of control were in part due to the practice of certain kinds of Protestant Christianity.[100] As he laid out a clinical analysis of these stages, Faduma repeatedly insisted that he was not opposed to the use of emotions in religion. He objected to "excessive emotionalism" because it failed to recognize moral and ethical judgment, did not acknowledge the "volitional side," and left unaffected the rational side of human nature. He argued that excessive emotionalism was at variance with the "concrete experience" of life, which included thinking, feeling, and willing. He contended that it was "sickly feminine" and appealed to neurotics.[101]

The claim that emotionalism in black religion was "sickly feminine" was part of Faduma's broader racial theory that blacks belonged to a child or primitive race in the poetical and emotional stage of their development. The infantilization and the feminization of black religion were different ways of constructing black religion as primitive and emotional. In this schema, black religion represented primitive and bodily religion, whereas the religion of "civilized" whites was regarded as rational and spiritual. Faduma claimed that black religion was in its "barbaric stage" and needed to reach a higher stage with a "developed rule of conduct."[102] A religion of manhood, spirit, and rationality was the ideal for which critics like Faduma aimed. He shared with Kelly Miller the belief that "stern moral qualities" were necessary to lift the race to its manhood. Miller, for example, argued that races faded before the "breath of civilization" because they could not last if they came into contact with the vices of the

Aryan race. To avoid the fate of Native Americans, Miller claimed, blacks had to acquire virtue and Christian morality. Backward races would lose their vitality unless they were quickened by a "spiritual motive."[103] A neurotic and sickly emotionalism was of no use in furthering the manhood of the race and restoring its dignity. Though Miller and other black leaders could write about the need for blacks to develop their manhood, they also urged them to bring their "passive virtues" or a softening element to a harsh American culture. Tensions of this kind abound in the thought of many of these black leaders in the early twentieth century.

A Black Social Gospel

The Great Migration, as this watershed event in African American history has come to be called, involved the relocation of nearly a half million black Southerners to the urban North between 1915 to 1918, looking for jobs and fleeing economic and political oppression.[104] This migration, which continued throughout the 1920s, had profound implications for interpretations of African American religion. Milton Sernett argues that it fostered different expectations of the church's mission, engendered a wave of scholarly studies on black life, and spurred the rise of what he calls the instrumentalists. Sernett describes the instrumentalists as black religious and secular leaders, primarily (though not exclusively) located in the North, who attempted to direct a greater proportion of denominational resources and the focus of black church life from internal to external concerns. He argues that the instrumentalists came to dominate the discussion of the mission of black churches, North and South, after World War I. Instrumentalists fought against traditionalists who were fearful of losing the "old-time" religion and who wanted the church to confine its mission chiefly to salvation, spiritual refreshment, and worship. The instrumentalists, Sernett contends, were influenced by the Social Gospel movement and were principally concerned with urban churches, though their attention was redirected to Southern rural churches after it became apparent that many blacks would remain in the South.[105]

The instrumentalists often pejoratively labeled the religion of their opponents "otherworldly." Otherworldliness, in their view, represented an outmoded conception of religion that was not attentive to the real problems that blacks faced in a modern industrialized America. Yet instrumentalist conceptions of the church did not simply emerge during the Great Migration, though they increased as a result of discussions about the issues faced by the newly arrived migrants. Instrumentalism had roots in the broader social critique of religion in American culture that was a part of the Social Gospel movement and was fostered by the challenges of urbanization and industrialization. The Social Gospel movement involved a variety of activities taken by churches and church-affiliated and urban organizations to confront the specific problems that blacks, immigrants, and urban residents faced in a rapidly industrializing country: tenement and housing problems, labor and working conditions, basic sanitation, poverty, social dislocation, disease and squalor, discrimination, and economic oppression.[106]

The political and social aspect of the Social Gospel critique of religion was the Progressive movement that centered on urban reform. Progressives, as Gilbert Osofsky writes, were primarily social workers and urban reformers who attempted to improve the living conditions of the industrial areas and tenement houses of Northern cities.[107] By 1900, 70 percent of African Americans in the North lived in cities. High mortality rates, inferior housing, crime, broken families, and low-wage jobs were among the issues highlighted by the early studies of social reformers.[108] Interpreters of the roles of the black churches did not conduct disinterested studies in the midst of such physical and psychic hardship. They had very particular recommendations for changes within the black churches. The Great Migration, however, forced the encounter of black churches and the city more than ever before.[109]

In 1907, Richard R. Wright Jr., a special fellow in sociology at the University of Pennsylvania, presented a report on the social work of the Negro Church before the American Academy of Political and Social Science. Wright was a member of the African Methodist Episcopal Church (AME) and later obtained his doctorate in sociology in 1911 at the University of Pennsylvania. He had practical experience with churches, having served as assistant pastor of the Institutional Church in Chicago, the first black Institutional Church in America established under the leadership of Reverdy Ransom, a member of the AME and a leading black advocate of the Social Gospel.[110] Institutional churches were the most visible expression of the Social Gospel movement. They provided a broad array of services beyond the traditional church functions of worship and religious education. These included employment services, kindergarten, day care, and a number of other ministries to outcasts.[111] Service at the Institutional Church proved to be a social experiment that allowed Wright an opportunity to learn more about the black population in Chicago. From 1905 to 1907, he resided at a social settlement in Philadelphia, during which time he participated in many social organizations concerned with the conditions of the city's black population.[112]

Wright defined the Negro Church as that "portion of organized Christian teaching which is conducted exclusively by Negroes among the members of their race." He found that only a few black churches were confronting the problems of the city. He contrasted the social work of institutional churches to the emotionalism and "unorganized enthusiasm" of small-town black churches. He lamented that the black masses practiced a form of religion that was more "connected with heaven and hell than with earth and daily life." Wright was convinced that this emphasis on emotion and the accompanying dissatisfaction with "anything in the Church which merely pertains to earthly affairs" were major hurdles for "progressive Negro ministers" in reaching out to the black masses. He urged the black churches to revise their attitudes toward entertainment and not simply reject it, adjust their social work to meet the needs of urban residents, and reorient their ministry toward the everyday problems of blacks. He ultimately put his hope for improvement of the church's social ministry in better social and educational opportunities for black ministers.[113]

Wright's concern about the churches' failures to meet the needs of the growing black urban population and his criticism of their negative stance on amusements were shared by Du Bois. As Du Bois had argued as early as 1897, Wright contended that black churches must not have merely a negative stance on amusements, otherwise they would lose their appeal to urban residents. Du Bois returned to this theme in his later writings. By 1912, he had dropped any semblance of the disinterested social scientific approach in his studies of black religion. He denounced black churches for "inveighing against dancing and theatergoing" and called for programs of education and social uplift. He criticized black ministers for giving "silly and empty sermons" and urged the black churches to elect only bishops and leaders who were men of honesty, probity, and efficiency.[114] This was a shift from Du Bois's earlier position in which he had called on black churches to socially differentiate and give up various functions to the school and home. Now he was demanding that they assume additional tasks on the model of the institutional churches.

The Atlanta University conferences that had begun in 1896 were to be repeated every 10 years on the same problem or issue in the black community for a 100-year period.[115] Such an ambitious project was never completed, but the topic of black religion was revisited in 1913, ten years after the original study on the Negro Church. Du Bois was one of the editors of the published report, "Morals and Manners among Negro Americans."[116] The study indicated that the historical and institutional phase of the Negro Church did not require further investigation since the first report was completed in 1903. It also found that strengthening of home life of blacks had occurred, that cleanliness and thrift were better, and that a "wider conformity to the rules of modern morality" was evident in black churches. The study observed "signs of awakening" in the Negro Church: new duties, broader responsibilities, and new institutional work of social uplift under a few trained men. The report noted that black churches were still primarily "financial institutions catering to a doubtful round of semi-social activities." If black churches hoped to survive, Bois and the editor announced, they would have to adopt new attitudes toward "rational amusement" and "sound moral habits." Du Bois and his colleagues were optimistic because they saw evidence of social uplift and a moral awakening particularly in the work of black women's clubs and institutions. This work of black women was viewed as the reason for the improvement of black home life and the morals of black children.[117]

Two central issues that appeared in the 1913 report became even more prominent in Du Bois's critique of the Negro Church in an essay that he wrote in 1917. First, Du Bois charged that the church no longer was the sole center of Negro activity. The Negro Church was being criticized and forced to justify its programs and its restrictions. Second, the "imported puritanism" of the churches and their "theoretical crying down of amusements" were imposing a terrible burden on black youth. The "older church," Du Bois asserted, was standing in the way of reform and social progress. The "new Negro Church," he argued, must take a consistent stand on amusements and cease its condemnation of dancing, entertainment, and playing of various games if it hoped to retain its youth. Du Bois maintained that if the black churches continued to classify all forms of entertainment as "debauchery and lewdness" they would lose their standing among black youth or they would force young blacks into immoral, furtive, or questionable forms of entertainment.[118] He pointed to the following as reasons for his recommendations: the urbanization of the black population, the rise of a new generation of blacks, and the social differentiation of society that accompanied urbanization and industrialization. The church could no longer speak "ex cathedra" because of these developments, Du Bois had insisted in the 1913 report. There was now, he continued, a distinct "tendency to bring [the church] down to definite present social ends and to criticize it severely if it does not accomplish something along these lines." If black churches desired a following and if they were to have a place in the modern world, they would have to change, he argued. The Negro Church was now one institution among others and it was to be used as an instrument of social reform and racial uplift.

Conclusion

World War I witnessed increasing demands among black leaders that the Negro Church uplift the race and devote more of its resources to economic and political advancement. As blacks flooded into Northern cities, less attention was paid to the internal dynamics of worship and personal salvation, but black churches were often regarded as instruments for other racial and social ends. The Negro Church was then a normative discourse created by black leaders under the pervasive influence of the social sciences, and these leaders were determined to mine these new tools of social science to radically transform the nature of black religious life. Eager to turn their backs on a shameful Southern past, which they saw as a locus of otherworldly and primitive religion, they vehemently sought to influence black church leaders to pool the resources of the churches to help an oppressed and downtrodden people. Yet even as these leaders sought to turn their backs on a haunted past, Northern white artists and dramatists sought to mine the folk wisdom and alleged primitive religiosity of this rural black Southern culture.

5

The Drama of Black Life

In 1917, James Weldon Johnson, field secretary for the National Association for the Advancement of Colored People (NAACP) and editorial writer for the black weekly *New York Age*, called on the Negro Church to become an "instrument for bettering the conditions of the race." The time had come, he wrote, when the power of the black church should be used to "secure for the race a larger fore-taste of better things right here and now." He was insistent that the Negro church harness its resources for the race because it was the only medium through which the masses could be reached. Johnson asserted that black ministers had a much greater obligation than white ministers to help the broader community. He recommended that less attention be paid to "larger collections for handsomer churches" and that more effort be made to raise money to fight for the rights of blacks. The Negro Church, he continued, must be put "into close contact with the practical questions that affect the welfare of the Negro people as citizens." Less attention, he wrote, should be paid to what Saint Paul said and more to what was being said and done by "makers of current history." The race needs union, Johnson proclaimed, to advance and achieve its goals. If the "Negro ministry would come together and solidify the Negro church," he noted, "race-wide" power could be realized and wielded. Such a unified church, working in cooperation with civic organizations, he asserted, "would constitute a force within the race that could not be defeated."[1]

The critique of the Negro Church offered by Johnson can be taken as a symbol of broader developments in interpretations of African American religion that have seldom been linked before now. Johnson, as a creative writer and literary figure, was an agnostic who nonetheless had a deep appreciation for the aesthetic dimension of black religious experience. His many writings on black religion reflect both an instrumentalist conception of religion *and* a valorization of black folk religious experience. These two approaches developed in parallel yet overlapping trajectories in the thought of black and white interpreters of black religion, though white interpreters in this period were primarily responding to dramatic and literary representations of black religion. These two trajectories of appreciation and criticism were especially evident in the writings of black intellectuals like Johnson and W. E. B. Du Bois. Among some whites who expressed an interest in the flourishing of black art and literature in Harlem during the 1920s, there was a tendency toward a romantic racialist conception of black religion, and this image of rural black religion was often invoked as a contrast to the alleged sterility and materialism of white American culture. Some black interpreters, however, experienced a conflict between their appreciation of black religious expression and their desire for an activist and socially progressive religion. Traditional images of blacks in the white media also figured prominently in black evaluations of black folk religion. This problem with images of black religion would become especially acute in black responses to *The Green Pastures* (1930), a Broadway play that appealed to a broad audience even though it was written about rural Southern blacks from the perspective of a white agnostic, Marc Connelly.

Interpreters of black culture like Harlemites Langston Hughes, poet and writer, and Zora Neale Hurston, anthropologist and folklorist, tried to break away from "race problems" or "race relations" in their writings and dramatic productions. Hughes and Hurston hoped to write about the laughter, triumphs, and sorrows of blacks apart from how these features helped or hindered blacks in confronting the problem of race in America. But writing about black culture "on its own terms" was complicated by the fears of other black leaders that a focus on the folkways and religious practices of rural and urban black culture would reinforce stereotypical images. Potential black integration into the American mainstream was jeopardized, some believed, if literary and artistic depictions provided evidence of a distinctive black culture.[2] This problem of the distinctive nature of black culture was taken up in the 1930s and later by sociologists, but in the hands of novelists, literary critics, and interpreters of African American religion in the 1920s, it partially resolved itself into an uneasy combination of criticism of the actual religious institutions and beliefs of African Americans *and* praise for what were seen as blacks' gifts and the distinctiveness of their folk religious tradition.

Instrumentalism and the Critique of Otherworldliness

Criticism of black churches by black Northern leaders was exacerbated by World War I and the continued migration of blacks to the urban North. In one of the most detailed studies of black churches published after the war, *The History of the Negro Church* (1921), Carter G. Woodson gathered up nearly all the ideas of the instrumentalists and propounded what would become the most salient critiques of black religion by socially progressive black leaders. Woodson was the first American of slave parentage to earn a doctorate in history and the second black (after Du Bois) to receive a doctorate from Harvard in 1912. He settled in Washington, D.C., one year after finishing his dissertation, to begin his life's work of making more readily available the history and achievements of African Americans. Woodson founded the Association for the Study of Negro Life and History in 1915 and the *Journal of Negro History* in 1916.[3] His book *A Century of Negro Migration* (1918) was one of the early monographs that detailed the effects of the Great Migration on African American life. Woodson's study of the Negro Church was the most comprehensive survey of black religious history of his time and was the major work on black religion prior to the publication of Benjamin Mays and Joseph Nicholson's *The Negro's Church* (1933).[4]

Woodson's telling of the story of black religion was centrally about the institutional life of black Methodists and Baptists and the contributions of its male leaders. He argued that his work was "an effort to study the achievements of all of these groups [black denominations] as parts of the same institution and to show the evolution of it from the earliest period to the present time."[5] The central issue, he contended, was about the Negro Church "finding itself" or determining what its functions and ideals should be. In a chapter titled "The Conservative and the Progressive," he presented his analysis of a division within the Negro Church between those who wanted progressive and enlightened change and those who held fast to the old-time religion. Woodson located the origin of this split in the Reconstruction years, when white and black Northern missionaries taught young blacks a "new point of view." What began as a division based on age between "enlightened" young blacks and their elders who were "embalmed in ignorance" became a division based on different understandings of the meaning and purpose of religion.

Woodson argued that there were four major issues on which the progressives and the conservatives disagreed: (1) interpretation of religion, (2) the relative importance of the church in the community, (3) the relations of the church to the individual, and (4) standards of public conduct. The progressives, Woodson maintained, rejected "crude notions" of biblical interpretation and the "grotesque vision of the hereafter as portrayed by the illiterate ministers of the church." For the progressives, religion meant Christian experience instead of "wild notions of revelation, which among some of the uninformed bordered on superstition and voodooism of the middle age [sic], after the restraint of slavery had been removed and the Negroes as a group exercising freedom could indulge their fancy at will."[6] In Woodson's view, religion was no longer seen by progressives as a "panacea for the ills of the race." Progressives insisted on education because no revelation from God was to be had if those with "arrested mental development" received it. From the perspective of the progressives, Woodson went on, there was simply no virtue in "unrestrained emotion," which resulted from a lack of understanding and an "unwillingness to search the Scriptures for the real revelation of God."[7] The Bible, education, and literacy on the side of the progressives were pitted against the bombast and emotionalism of the conservatives.

Conservatives, Woodson argued, dubbed the progressives the "educated" Negroes and decried their ideas as a growing menace to the church. Conservatives were particularly disturbed by the progressives' different conception of the relation of the church to the individual. Woodson contended that conservatives believed that the individual should sacrifice all for the church, but progressives asserted that the church existed for the good of the individual. For the progressives, the church was "the means for making the bad good, and if the institution were defective it might be so reshaped and reorganized as to serve the useful purposes of men."[8]

Woodson noted that progressives insisted that religion was a social virtue, not an "individual boon." Christian doctrine for them had to be reshaped to include a newer understanding of humanity's relationship to itself and to God. Virtuous behavior, the progressives demanded, was not simply an individual matter but involved social progress and practices "in keeping with the ethics of the most enlightened of the land." Therefore progressives were angered by prohibitions against such harmless amusements as dancing and card playing. In Woodson's view, these heroic figures simply wanted a church that was well managed, confronted an unjust social order, and kept its members abreast of the political and social issues of their day.[9] All of this extended narrative was relevant to the pressing problems that blacks faced in the urban North when Woodson was writing, and it took little imagination to figure out what he was urging black churches to do. This was his first major criticism of black churches and their "otherworldliness" and "outdated" theological ideas. He returned to these issues with even greater stridency in the 1930s. Other instrumentalists joined him in these attempts to reorient and reshape the Negro Church for the challenges of an urban environment.

An efficient minister who actively participated in the uplift of the race was what blacks needed, Woodson argued. Among the progressive church leaders he listed was Adam Clayton Powell Sr., pastor of Abyssinian Baptist Church in Harlem, where he served from 1908 to 1937. With more than 10,000 members, Abyssinian became one of the largest Baptist churches in America. Powell had battled with church members to move the historic church into the heart of Harlem in the early 1920s and used the new church building to open a soup kitchen for hungry migrants and to recruit new members. By 1920, the "mid-belly" of Harlem was predominantly black and was the product of the deluge of black migration from the South to New York City. Between 1910 and 1920, the black population of the city increased 66 percent (91,709 to 152,467) and from 1920 to 1930 it expanded 115 percent (152,467 to 327,706). High rents, poor salaries, unsanitary conditions, and congestion were some of the problems blacks faced in Harlem.[10]

Working in these surroundings, Powell urged members of his church to invest in black businesses and develop economic power.[11] He preached a Social Gospel in which the church "must go into the highways and hedges during the week caring for the sick, the wounded, the distressed and all that are needy." Powell criticized black churches for failing to provide an alternative to disreputable places where many urban blacks were choosing to go for fellowship, like pool halls and gambling dens. He charged that the church must carry out a broad program of "applied Christianity" that was "more spiritual than the one which deals simply in emotional religion."[12] As a pastor who had graduated from Wayland College and Seminary (Washington, D.C.) and Yale Divinity School and who preached to pimps and prostitutes in the worst parts of the city, Powell represented the model Negro preacher for men like Woodson, who were critical of black churches. The notion of a powerful manager of a vast black empire that made its influence felt and one who sought to unite blacks to confront their common problems had great appeal to Woodson, who desired unity in what he called the "Negro Church."

Commendations of the institutional church were made alongside criticisms of the growth of storefront churches. By renting a vacant store in urban centers, the time-consuming and costly process of erecting a church building was eliminated. In the mid-1920s storefronts comprised 39 percent of black churches in New York City.[13] In 1924, George Haynes, the first black to hold the position of executive director of the Federal Council of Churches' Commission on Race Relations, observed that there was an explosion of storefront churches in the North, which he regarded as a "hindrance to progress." He contrasted their lack of trained leadership to that of the institutional churches and the growing work of professional social workers. Haynes urged social workers to be more patient with the Negro Church's lack of "technical efficiency" because it was still "by far the most substantial institution we have for reaching the Negro rank and file with our social programs." To sell social programs to the masses, Haynes insisted, social workers had to figure out how to work through the black churches. "If we get our plans accepted in the programs of those churches," he noted, "much of our efforts would not need to go into building social service programs and trying to force Negroes into them." While acknowledging that there were "baffling difficulties" and "restricted" vision in black churches, Haynes was still confident that they were willing to serve the community. The challenge was to find a way to link church efforts with the "scientific" techniques and skills of social workers. Haynes pointed to the work of organizations like the Urban League as examples of what could be done through cooperation with the churches.[14] The Urban League and other groups had been founded to deal with the special problems of black migrants in the North, and they employed social workers and skilled secular professionals who found themselves vying with the traditions of the black churches. Haynes held out hope for compromise and cooperation between such agencies and the black churches.

In 1925, Mark Fisher, a Baptist minister who taught at Virginia Union University, in his study of developments in the black churches during World War I, found that prior to the war the "negro preacher was expounding otherworldly topics in addition to an occasional sensational or practical sermon" and had "little interest in the everyday problems of members." Though Fisher's comments about black ministers reflected the bias of an instrumentalist, he was surely right when he argued that one effect of the war was more denominational cooperation and the acquisition of skills as a result of major building projects to deal with the needs of such a massive shift in the black population. "Race consciousness" was another effect of the war, Fisher asserted. The presence of so many people from different backgrounds and who suffered from similar forms of oppression led to a sense of common purpose and goals. But along with these gains, he believed, came such losses as diversions in the city, capitulation to worldliness in the form of jazz and dancing, and the loss of faith among some black Christians. This worried preacher documented instances of sexual immorality, schisms, and conflict in the black churches.[15] For Fisher the war and new opportunities and temptations in the North had forever changed the black churches. Blacks had entered the modern world.

The war and race riots that occurred in twenty-five cities during and after the summer of 1919 fostered a growing sense of disillusionment among disaffected blacks in the North. Two black socialists, A. Philip Randolph and Chandler Owen, founded the radical socialist monthly *The Messenger* in Harlem in 1917 and pushed the socialist program among black workers. The Socialist Party was the foremost advocate of a radical reorganization of America's economic structure in the postwar period. Its emphasis on working-class unity and economic exploitation among workers in America's capitalistic system garnered some support among blacks in cities like Chicago and New York.[16] In the early 1920s, black socialists were fierce critics of "too much talk of heaven" in the black churches. They promulgated a Marxist critique that religion was an anodyne for the economic and political hardships of the masses. Walter Hawkins, a poet for the *Messenger*, wrote caustically that there was "too much talk about riches / You expect to get 'up there'. / When one will not do his duty as a decent Christian here."[17] Although these criticisms of black religion were not new, their frequency and openness indicated a heightened hostility to traditional black religion. Though some earlier critics had urged blacks to live up to the creed of Jesus as the lowly Nazarene, some of the socialist critics (and later black communists) argued that the actual practice of Christianity in the real world was wholly impractical and that to the extent that blacks lived up to the ideals of Christianity, their economic and political condition would worsen.

In 1928, Eugene Gordon, an African American Marxist and journalist who was assistant feature editor of the *Boston Post*, argued that so long as blacks were Christians, they would remain slaves psychologically. He lamented that although blacks of his generation were trying to "exchange some of Jesus for a bit of the world," they were still "rich in Jesus even if poor in the world." He contended that it was precisely because blacks approached the Christian ideal more than any other group in America that they wallowed in poverty. Gordon sadly noted, "Christianity is not a virile man's religion, and that is why virile men are seldom if ever *true* Christians." Yet the "black American," he continued, "because of his innate guilelessness and his genuine naiveté, approaches nearer the Christian ideal" and therefore cannot acquire wealth and power. He argued that the Negro Church, "through its greedy exactions of time and money, has held the Aframerican in moral, intellectual, spiritual, and economic thrall."[18] By sticking with the Christianity of those who held their ancestors in bondage, he asserted, blacks not only continued to hold themselves in mental slavery but hindered their ability to advance economically. Blacks needed a new religion that would enable them to live in the *here* and *now*, Gordon exclaimed.[19]

For many black activists and leaders of the labor movement, the struggle against otherworldliness was an attempt to free themselves from a shameful past. This struggle evinced a heightened awareness of the economic plight of blacks that existed alongside their fervent religiosity, especially in the South. In 1930, George Schuyler, a journalist in Harlem, contended that there was "no greater racket preying upon the Aframerican than religion." Schuyler argued that religion was the "black man's burden" precisely because it stole his economic resources and inhibited "group progress."[20] He believed that this burden held blacks in "ignorance, poverty and degradation, and [that] although rationalism is growing in Afroamerica, it has a hard row to hoe."[21] Religion then, particularly in its otherworldly rural expression, was seen as the chief obstacle to blacks' economic and political advancement. As Benjamin Mays, the African American religious leader most vocal in the critique of otherworldliness in the 1930s, put it:

> Revolt against other-worldly religion is really a protest against those
> who seek to achieve the complete needs of the groups in a far off,
> future heaven rather than put forth an active effort to get them there.
> The revolt against the white man's religion is due to the conviction
> shared by some Negroes that it serves as an opiate for the Negro,
> makes him satisfied with occupying an inferior social status and with
> occupying an economic position that is unstable.[22]

These black leaders believed that traditional black religion had to be either abandoned or radically reformed if economic and political power were to be gained by blacks as a group.

Even as these black leaders and interpreters of African American religion were advocating a socially progressive church that repudiated its otherworldly past, attempts to find the creativity and value of black folk culture were proceeding apace. At the time when a repudiation of otherworldly religion came to mean a rejection of the dominant religious expression of black Southern rural religion, reevaluations of black folklore and "superstitions" were under way. Whites were particularly interested in these images of blacks at the same time that black leaders were growing more wary of them. Among blacks, especially Harlem literary critics and novelists, the desire to find the "good" or the "interesting" aspects of black culture was never so simple that it led to outright rejection or acceptance of prevailing white depictions of blacks. This struggle to adopt a balanced view of black folk culture was made all the more difficult when a select white audience of literary and drama critics (centered mostly in Manhattan), who were distressed with the ugliness and materialism of modern bourgeois society, found something appealing in depictions of black folk religious expression.

Reiterations of Romantic Racialism

Some assessments of African American culture in the early twentieth century by religious persons and scholars were reminiscent of the older forms of romantic racialism. One long-standing belief in black innate religiosity in the scholarly and religious literature proved quite enduring. This invocation of blacks as naturally religious had a scientific and religious significance. Scholars who made this claim asserted that innate religiosity was a product of a peculiar racial temperament. The alleged emotional disposition and nonintellectual temperament of African Americans was said to be responsible for the widespread influence of religion in black communities. From its earliest advocates, romantic racialism was also invoked by missionaries to inspire other missionaries to continue their work among blacks despite any hindrances. Such "naturally religious" people, the argument went, were receptive to the Gospel, and this was evidence that God was preparing them for a great work of conversion. Assertions of black natural religiosity could be put to many different uses. George Mundelein, Catholic archbishop of Chicago, wrote in a letter dated October 26, 1917, that missionary work must proceed among transplanted rural Southern blacks pouring into Chicago, even though many obstacles were in the way. The "strong religious spirit" of blacks was proof for him that the mission would not fail and that blacks' receptive spirit made them ready for the true Catholic faith. He wrote that he had "never yet met a colored man who was professedly atheistic or blasphemous. The Creator seems to have given them a spirit of reverence and religion that is often lacking in other races."[23] These long-standing and recurring religious images of blacks had their academic version in the works of prominent white social scientists.

Robert E. Park, who came to be recognized as the foremost sociologist of race relations between the two world wars, expressed the ambivalence of white writers on black culture in the postwar period. A few years after completing his doctoral work at Heidelberg University and his doctoral thesis at Harvard University in 1903, Park was offered a position at Tuskegee Institute, where he became Booker T. Washington's trusted aide and ghostwriter. He spent about seven years roaming the South and becoming acquainted with the life, culture, and problems of blacks. After an invitation to teach at the University of Chicago in the summer of 1913, Park stayed on for the rest of his career as professor of sociology.[24] At what became known as the Chicago school of sociology, Park was the most prominent white theorist of race and race relations. He trained generations of students and emphasized a rather dour view of black prospects in the city.[25] Perhaps his experiences in the rural South colored his under-standing of city life, but it is certain that his ideas on the negative impact of urbanization on black life affected his views of black religion in the modern world.

Park's analysis of black religion and culture demonstrates the complex ways that debates about intelligence, religious capacity, and racial tempera-ment evolved and intersected, especially as they entered a new phase in the postwar context. Given the importance of psychological tests during World War I and immediately after in supporting belief in the intellectual inferiority of blacks, Park was noteworthy for acknowledging in 1919 that anthropologists admitted that "the average native intelligence in the races is about the same." But he was also convinced that blacks and whites possessed a different tem-perament, which he defined as "certain special traits and tendencies which rest on biological rather than cultural differences."[26] These differences in tem-peraments and "racial aptitudes" were innate and manifested themselves in "objects of attention, in tastes and in talents."[27] By *temperament* Park meant a few basic but distinctive characteristics "determined by physical organization and transmitted biologically."[28] These qualities included for blacks a "genial, sunny and social disposition"; an attachment to external, physical things rather than to subjective states and objects of introspection; and an inclination for expression rather than enterprise and action. In an often quoted statement, he wrote:

> Everywhere and always the Negro has been interested rather in ex-pression than in action; interested in life itself than in its recon-struction or reformation. The Negro is, by natural disposition, neither an intellectual nor an idealist like the Jew, nor a brooding intro-spective like the East Indian, nor a pioneer and frontiersman like the Anglo-Saxon. He is primarily an artist, loving life for its own sake. His metier is expression rather than action. The Negro is, so to speak, the lady among the races.[29]

Park reiterated in the language of social science deeply gendered notions of black life that Harriet Beecher Stowe and Robert Dale Owens had articulated in the discourse of romantic racialism in the mid-nineteenth century. He seemed to agree that "the Negro, because of his natural attachment to known, familiar objects, places and persons, is preadapted to conservatism and to local and personal loyalties."[30] Owen and Stowe had prophesied that blacks in America would not be naturally daring, enterprising, or intellectual. Had they (partic-ularly Stowe) not also emphasized that blacks would be home-loving and locally attached and therefore not a race that would make a "material improvement" in the world (as Owen put it)?[31] This discussion of blacks was not mere speculation because, as Park put it, "if these things are true, we shall eventually have to take account of them practically."[32] He had in mind contemporary discussions about the assimilation of blacks and immigrant groups and practical programs based on the "natural" and cultural traits of these various groups.

Park asserted that it was "difficult to find in the South today anything that can be traced directly to Africa." Yet he also argued that African slaves brought with them to America a "tropical temperament."[33] Park contended that blacks had an African temperament but an American tradition. He found evidence for a durable African or Negro temperament existing under changing and external cultural forms.[34] In particular, he posited that a distinctive African temperament made itself felt in black churches, not an African tradition as in particular premodern African religious practices.[35] Also, in American Negro folk songs and spirituals, he detected something that was "thrown up from the depths of the Negroes' consciousness" and that expressed "the profounder and more permanent moods and sentiments" of blacks.[36]

The otherworldliness of Negro spirituals during slavery was their most striking and enduring feature, Park wrote. This longing for a heavenly home represented "reflections of the imagination and the temperament of Africa and the African" in conjunction with the Negro's experience in slavery. Park asserted that though otherworldliness was not peculiar to the religion of the slaves, it acquired a special emphasis under the harsh conditions of slavery. "I assume, therefore," he wrote, "that the reason the Negro so readily and eagerly took over from the white man his heaven and apocalyptic visions was because these materials met the demands of his peculiar racial temperament and furnished relief to emotional strains that were provoked in him by the conditions of slavery."[37] He was careful to say that his thesis was "merely" a hypothesis; he showed, too, that temperaments could change slowly over time. But Park was firmly convinced that schemes for Americanization, Christianization, and assimilation should take his ideas about a racial temperament into account.[38] His ideas lent social scientific authority to the notion of a racial temperament, and he explicitly noted that his academic theories should be relevant to the education of blacks in America and the work of foreign missionaries.[39]

Park's argument that "racial aptitudes" manifested themselves in tastes, talents, and objects of attention was confirmed in an essay by Albert Barnes, a white philanthropist and art collector. Barnes was a student and friend of John Dewey, noted pragmatist philosopher and educator at Columbia University. Barnes was one of the few white contributors to the *New Negro* (1925), an anthology of writings about black culture, arts, and literature edited by

Howard University professor Alain Locke. Although raised in poverty, Barnes helped invent a chemical to treat urogenital diseases, became a multimillionaire, and located a factory in a poor black Philadelphia neighborhood where he employed an interracial workforce. His wealth allowed him to become a voracious buyer of modernist art. After founding the Barnes Foundation in 1922, he began speaking regularly on African and African American art.[40]

George Hutchinson argues that Barnes set himself against notions of Africans as primitives and exotics who were endowed with "mythical virtues" by "over-civilized" and "jaded imaginations." Hutchinson contends that Boasian anthropology, pragmatism, literary realism, and historicism exerted a powerful counterpressure to the exploitation of primitive and exotic depictions of the "white racial psyche." Hutchinson's painstaking analysis and revisionist critique of key aspects of interracial literary and cultural work in the 1920s are convincing in many instances, but it is difficult to find in the essay that Barnes contributed to the *New Negro* any evidence of a challenge to the notion of the black primitive as an antidote to the sterility of civilization.[41] It is true that Barnes did not indulge in any of the reiterations of black primitive sexuality, but his statements about blacks' "natural" talents do contain hints of his belief in a fundamental racial difference between blacks and whites.

Barnes's reflections on the aesthetic or cultural elements of black life demonstrate how remarkable was the cultural shift from a Victorian fear of the primitive and emotional to a modern valorization of these qualities as the antidote to the aridities of bourgeois society. A romantic racialist conception of blacks appeared in a transmuted form in his essay. Whereas "emotional endowments" once evoked fear and supposedly threatened civilization (at the turn of the century), as evidenced in the writings of G. Stanley Hall and Frederick Morgan Davenport, by the 1920s emotionalism and spontaneity were viewed as authentic expressions of primal human urges or as healthy complements or the superior alternative to the alleged sterility and materialism of white urban American culture. Every one of the "natural gifts" that Hall saw as unique to blacks was repeated in nearly identical fashion in Barnes's essay: large emotional endowment, sensitivity to nature, oratory, music, spontaneity, patience, humor, and a "peculiar depth of religious life." For Hall, however, emotionalism was the physiological basis for blacks' putative unrestrained sexual activity, violence, and fanciful religious imaginings and superstitions. Barnes transformed the black primitive from a threat to civilization to its antidote.[42]

During the first three decades of the twentieth century, the modernist movement reconfigured the meaning of the primitive. Modernism, especially as it related to interest in the arts and views of black culture, referred to a "constellation of related ideas, beliefs, values, and modes of perception" that came into existence in the late nineteenth century and had a profound impact on the arts and intellectual and social thought on both sides of the Atlantic after the turn of the century. Modernism also entailed radical movements of renewal within the arts, which challenged received canons of artistic form and representation.[43] Identification with the primitive now meant "dis-identification" with white bourgeois society. The primitive became that which was basic, creative, and free.[44] The "animal vitality" and emotionalism of the so-called lower races were reassigned their romantic role as an object of value to be retrieved for the benefit of a degenerate and vulgarized European or American civilization. But as John Jervis argues, this identification with the primitive was often "little more than an artistic version of the tourist spectacle of otherness already present in Western culture."[45] It was difficult for whites interested in black culture to avoid using the image of the black primitive and investing it with those qualities that were thought to be lacking in a white overcivilized world.

When Barnes wrote "Negro Art and America," he was attempting to describe a broad range of activities, for by *art* he meant aesthetic activities "from the creation of spirituals to the managing of baseball teams."[46] He argued that Negro art was representative because it came from the hearts of the black masses. Black art was sound, he wrote, because it was "from a primitive nature upon which a white man's education has never been harnessed."[47] It had its basis in the "psychological complexion" of blacks, which was inherited from their African ancestors and was manifested in contemporary black life. The outstanding characteristics of blacks, Barnes asserted, were the following: a "tremendous emotional endowment," a luxuriant and free imagination, and a "truly great power of individual expression." The fire and light within blacks impelled them to give expression to what was deep within them.[48] This psychological complexion gave shape to the entire cultural life of blacks, he claimed.[49]

Barnes argued that blacks were poets "by birth." For the black masses, he maintained, poetry expressed itself in religion, which involved a "surrender to emotion," ecstasy, "automatisms," and simple and picturesque rituals. Worship services were joyful and fervid affairs punctuated with outbursts by average blacks who possessed a "normal endowment of eloquent and vivid imagery." This poetry, Barnes believed, was the "essence of the Negro soul." Everywhere that blacks went, into the factories, fields, and shops, they carried with them, he observed, this poetry, this deep religious expression of the inner Negro being.[50]

The white masses, Barnes maintained, simply could not "compete with the Negro in spiritual endowment." After "many centuries of civilization," the white American "had attenuated his original gifts and made his mind dominate his spirit." "He has wandered too far," Barnes wrote, "from the elementary human needs and their easy means of natural satisfaction. The deep and satisfying harmony which the soul requires no longer arises from the incidents of daily life." He proclaimed that "the requirements for practical efficiency in a world alien to his spirit have worn thin his religion and devitalized his art." In his view, the primitive was therefore superior to modern humans. Unlike "primitive man," for whom life and art were united, modern white Americans regarded art as something "exotic," an "indulgence," or "something to be possessed." This left modern humans in a situation that "forced art into being a mere adherent upon the practical affairs of life which offer it no sustenance." Barnes detected a confusion of values resulting from this unnatural divorce of art and life, but he found among blacks "the ideal of man's harmony with nature" and regarded this as a "blessing" that made blacks vagrants "in our arid, practical American life."[51]

Barnes provided a summary of black achievements since Emancipation. He dated the beginning of the "Negro renascence" at 1895, when Booker T. Washington gave his noted address in Atlanta and Paul Laurence Dunbar, a black poet, became recognized by large white audiences. The structure of Barnes's essay, however, gave prominence to the suffering of blacks and the qualities and cultural products he believed were produced by suffering, which included patience, spirituals, and resignation. The sterling qualities born of suffering were contrasted with the easy accomplishments and material things of an overcivilized society. "Civilization" became the enemy against which whites and blacks must fight. Whites must do so because it has destroyed their souls and rendered them cold and unfeeling and blacks because civilization "has done practically nothing to help the Negro create his art." To be sure, Barnes argued that blacks could and should work with whites to create a "richer American civilization" and encouraged education, greater economic power, and social equality for blacks. Yet his argument that "unjust oppression" had been powerless to prevent blacks from expressing their rare gifts and that blacks in their oppressed condition had developed those very qualities that the "prosaic civilization" of white Americans lacked seemed to be an argument for the superior qualities of the average, uneducated black person.[52] Suffering and oppression in his rendering were necessary to produce the qualities that he lauded. There was a fine line between extolling the virtues that blacks had developed through their suffering and valorizing the suffering itself as good for them.

Black leaders did not uncritically accept these cultural images. Alain Locke, professor of philosophy at Howard University and editor of the *New Negro,* argued that the "emotional temper" of black Americans, contra Barnes's claims, was "neither characteristically African nor to be explained as an ancestral heritage." Locke asserted that blacks' emotional temper was a product of their "peculiar experience in America" and the result of "environmental forces rather than the outcropping of a race psychology."[53] He interpreted Barnes's comments as having granted race an unnecessary explanatory power. Similarly, Horace Bond, a young African American student studying education and psychology at the University of Chicago, rejected the claims of psychologists in the 1920s who posited that blacks and other "racial" groups possessed a distinct temperament. Positing that blacks possessed a special temperament followed on the heels of psychological theories that held that they were intellectually inferior to whites.[54] Because of the varying interpretations about the "inherent traits" of blacks, Bond concluded that "temperamental differences are no more to be relied upon as separating races than anatomical or intellectual differences."[55] Bond's voice was a minority when he implied that intellectual differences were not reliable ways of distinguishing between racial capacities. Psychological tests since the end of World War I were being used to prove precisely this point.

Bond clearly differed from Park and Barnes, noting that "manners of acting and the expressions of emotions are controlled more by social pressure than by instinctive promptings."[56] He observed the "anomalous variety of adjectives" used by different commentators on the Negro temperament. Some claimed that blacks were cowardly, docile, loyal, submissive, and truthful. Others argued that they were ferocious, treacherous, deceptive, recalcitrant, and individualistic. An "astonishing amount of literature" lauded the loyalty and faithfulness of blacks, and "an equally astonishing amount of literature" explained in copious details that blacks were thieves, rapists, and treacherous scoundrels. All of these varied descriptions of "one racial type" existed, Bond wryly noted.[57] None of these wildly contrary images could be taken as conclusive evidence of a racial temperament, he proclaimed.

Bond conceded, however, that "there is almost general agreement in regarding the Negro as possessing a high degree of emotional tonicity." Docility, emotionalism, and submissiveness were regarded as native traits of blacks. Bond argued that one of the chief pieces of evidence "most usually relied upon in demonstrating the inferior control which the Negro—inherently—possesses over his emotions is his religious activities." He admitted that the "typical Negro religious gathering is replete with all sorts of emotional scenes" and that "ejaculations" (that is, verbal outbursts and shouting), physical contortions, and other phenomena were common in this religious atmosphere "surcharged with impulsion." He attributed such religious expressions to "custom" and "exhibition."[58] Black worshipers expected expressive services, and it was their convention to be demonstrative in worship. Bond pointed to certain black churches that forbade such outbursts to prove his point that this could not be an expression of a racial temperament.[59]

Although he did not cite his name, Bond disagreed with "one prominent thinker" who claimed that a "distinct religious fervor as part of the Negro's temperament" was "the hope of the Negro's contribution to civilization." This individual, he continued, argued that the "white man" has developed a "highly mechanized form of society which is the child of Mammon, but sadly neglectful of the glories of theistic devotion." Continuing his summary of this person's ideas, he wrote, "The Negro was divinely introduced into America in order to offer salvation to this mercenary people in the form of a fervid devotion to religion. The Negro faith is to be the leaven of American unrighteousness."[60] Bond rejected this reasoning, arguing that it was "forgetful of all of the facts of Negro life" and that it was "careless of the facts of social psychology." He contended that if blacks were to make a distinct contribution to American religion, or to any other field, it would come as a result of their "unique experience involving group pressure," not because of a "peculiarly constructed racial complex or psychosis."[61] Bond did not mention Barnes, but ideas like Barnes's (and to some extent, Park's) are the kind that he had in mind. Attuned to the social and political implications of particular images of blacks, Bond argued that positing a distinct temperament for blacks justified different treatment for blacks and whites. He wrote, "If the white is temperamentally individualistic, independent and aggressive, democracy may be said to constitute his ideal of government; while for a people who are highly emotional, dependent and submissive by nature, domination by another group is the most logical treatment."[62] For Bond, then, speculations about a racial temperament were not idle exercises but attempts to construct particular group traits to justify systems of domination and power over others so constructed.

As a beginning doctoral student at the University of Chicago in the fall of 1927, E. Franklin Frazier must have had his mentor in mind, professor of sociology Robert E. Park, when he wrote that some "pointed out that the facility with which the evangelical denominations spread among Negroes as well as the spirituals, and the seeming lack of strong economic motives" were "indications of the peculiar racial temperament of the Negro."[63] Frazier rejected this claim of a "temperamental endowment" for blacks, arguing instead that cultural and historical factors explained why most blacks were Methodists and Baptists.[64] For Frazier, Bond, and other black leaders, it was superfluous and harmful to invoke a racial temperament to explain blacks' cultural expressions and distinctive social forms. Yet the invocation of a racial temperament by whites was, in their view, praise for blacks' authenticity and a call for blacks to embrace their true selves rather than conform to a barren white American culture, as Barnes noted. Ironically, however, Barnes's laudation of the virtues that blacks allegedly developed during their long night of oppression and white critics' claims that blacks should embrace their distinct emotional disposition were occurring precisely at the time when black critics of the churches were arguing for an exchange of the virtues of the lowly Jesus for the goods of this life. These developments were complicated by the fact that black leaders and intellectuals were also looking to the arts to provide the way out of stale "race relations" discussions. Romantic racialist conceptions of blacks persisted, even though they were transformed and given more secular meanings by some writers. As Wilson Jeremiah Moses argues, the myths that had once served to demonstrate black inferiority were reinterpreted to signify cultural and mental health.[65] Black leaders insisted, however, that they would play the role of shapers and creators of their own images and help make the terms of their cultural contributions to the nation.

So Much Drama

African American intellectuals like James Weldon Johnson and Du Bois had turned to the arts and literature as strategic paths toward racial advancement and the improvement of race relations. The increasing popularity of blacks on stage, in motion pictures, and in literature heightened hopes that African Americans would develop a more positive image of themselves. Johnson, a poet, novelist, and playwright (among other things), wrote in 1928 that black artists (in the broad sense of this term) would be the major force in helping alleviate racial prejudice against blacks, which they could do by producing plays, creating literature, and spreading the music of black Americans. Johnson saw these efforts as vital to changing national attitudes toward blacks.[66]

There has been much debate among historians and literary scholars about the extent of white fascination with and interest in the "exotic primitivism" of blacks during the New Negro movement of the 1920s. The phrases "Harlem Renaissance" and "New Negro movement" are sometimes used interchangeably in the literature. David Levering Lewis describes the Harlem Renaissance as a "cultural nationalism of the parlor" that was centered in Harlem between 1917 and 1938. In Lewis's view, it was a flowering of black literature, arts, music, and drama that was "institutionally encouraged and directed by leaders of the national civil rights establishment for the paramount purpose of improving race relations in a time of extreme national backlash, caused in large part by economic gains won by Afro-Americans during the Great War."[67]

Gerald Early argues that the Harlem Renaissance was a phase of the New Negro movement. He dates the New Negro movement from 1908 to 1938 and contends that it was influenced by several historical events: (1) the movement of black people away from a rural to an urban way of life; (2) experience of war (the Spanish-American war and World War I); (3) increasing popularity of black nationalism and a sense of connection with peoples of African descent and the African continent; (4) intense focus on black history and the achievements of black Americans; and (5) the development of jazz and blues music as a significant element of American popular music. Early writes that this movement represented a new independent spirit, a politicized sense of selfhood, and "some notion of self-determination." A new racial consciousness led to a new understanding of African American history and culture.[68]

Nathan Huggins places great emphasis on primitivism and exoticism in his interpretation of the relationship of whites to blacks in the New Negro movement and argues that whites persisted in perpetuating stereotypical images of blacks that met whites' emotional needs.[69] George Hutchinson, however, argues for genuine interracial cooperation between blacks and whites in the production of literature and newer images of blacks. Hutchinson contends that white perceptions of blacks as exotic primitives that released them from the constraints of an overcivilized Victorianism were only one side of a much more complicated story.[70] Hutchinson's work should lead to a more thorough reexamination of aspects of this crucial period of interracial relations, but Huggins's views about whites' fascination with black religious primitivism are borne out in my study. Perhaps even more succinct and on the mark in his analysis of the motives of the white literary critics and urban reformers who took an interest in black life throughout the 1920s, Lewis writes that their motives "were an amalgam of inherited abolitionism, Christian charity and guilt, social manipulation, political eccentricity, and a certain amount of persiflage."[71] Just as modern scholars disagree about the extent of white fascination with blacks as primitives, so did blacks who followed or participated in the New Negro movement.

Henry Louis Gates Jr. writes that of all the African American arts, "great expectations were held for none more than for black theatre."[72] Black theater represented a quest for authenticity, and among playwrights, it was a matter of who could best represent blacks to the larger public. Black leaders in the New Negro movement desired a national theater where blacks themselves would be responsible for images of blacks. Montgomery Gregory, who had been involved in organizing dramas at Howard University and served there as professor of English from 1911 to 1927, expressed these aspirations in this way:

Our ideal is a national Negro Theater where the Negro playwright, musician, actor, dancer, and artist in concert shall fashion a drama that will merit the respect and admiration of America. Such an institution must come from the Negro himself, as he alone can truly express the soul of his people. The race must surrender that childish self-consciousness that refuses to face the facts of its own life in the arts but prefers the blandishments of flatterers, who render all efforts at true artistic expression a laughing-stock by adorning their characters with the gaudy gowns of cheap romance. However disagreeable the fact may be in some quarters, the only avenue of genuine achievement in American drama for the Negro lies in the development of the rich veins of folk-tradition of the past and in the portrayal of the authentic life of the Negro masses to-day.[73]

Black leaders had grown weary of polemical and apologetic literature that refused to see the good *and* bad in the lives of everyday black people. But this new theatrical and literary vision entailed obstacles. There was the shame of blacks' past and the deep-seated apprehension of "airing the race's dirty laundry" before an amused and unsympathetic white audience. The "superstitions" of the masses and their "uncouth" and "unseemly" behavior, some believed, would bring disgrace to more educated blacks who wanted to prove to whites their fitness and capacity for civilized behavior. Paul Robeson, who appeared in playwright Eugene O'Neill's play *All God's Chillun Got Wings* (1924), was one of the leading black actors on stage in the early 1920s. In *All God's Chillun*, Robeson starred as Jim Harris, a young black law student who was filled with "protective ardor" for a white girl, Ella Downey, who had gone bad after she was seduced by and forced to marry her gangster lover. Out of a sense of duty, Jim promised to take care of Ella. Black critic and poet Sterling Brown argued that Jim resembled Uncle Tom and was too "selfless for belief."[74] Both the slightest implication of miscegenation and Robeson's role as a selfless figure who helped a white girl in distress angered white and black audiences. In December 1924, Robeson wrote that blacks said to him after he appeared in the play, "I trust that now you will get a truly heroic and noble role, one portraying the finest type of Negro." He chided blacks for being "too self-conscious, too afraid of showing all phases of our life." Robeson argued that this heightened concern about how they looked in the presence of white audiences was one of the greatest obstacles to the "development of a true Negro art."[75]

Then there was the long tradition of white authors holding blacks up to ridicule in their writings. James Weldon Johnson complained of two dominant images of blacks in the imagination of white Americans: the simple, indolent, docile, improvident, and picturesque black who smiled and bowed before his lordly white superiors, and the impulsive, irrational, passionate savage who hated the white man and threatened the very civilization of whites. Black authors and those who attempted to represent artistically the black masses, Johnson insisted, had to break out of these "hard-set stereotypes."[76] They had to figure out a way to appeal to both whites and blacks while maintaining the "sincerity" and "soundness" of their work. Black authors should fashion something that rose above race, Johnson argued, and reached out to the universal in truth and beauty. It was a difficult task, he acknowledged, but one worthy of mastering.[77]

Other black writers and authors, among them Langston Hughes (in his early works) and Claude McKay, a Jamaican-born poet residing in Harlem, took this one step further. Not only did they write about the black masses, the life that they personally knew, but they portrayed blacks as expressive, uninhibited, and spontaneous persons trapped by a white world of work, urban asphalt, and sterility. In his famous essay in 1926 in the Nation calling on black writers and artists to express their "racial individuality," Hughes contrasted the "weariness in a white world, a world of subway trains and work" to the "eternal tom-tom beating in the Negro soul." The joy, laughter, and spontaneity of black life were seen as the antidote or the superior alternative to the sterility of white life (and its "Nordicized Negro" imitations).[78] These black leaders intended to present what they saw as an honest, unrestricted representation of black life (preferably by blacks themselves).

Hughes insisted that he was among the "younger Negro artists" who would create literature that expressed their "individual dark-skinned selves" without fear or shame. They would write about racial themes and issues that derived from the life they knew. No longer ashamed of those aspects of their culture that made them different from whites or that was viewed as unique, they would present to whoever cared, Hughes continued, the ugliness and the beauty of black life. This variety and distinctiveness of black life, he argued, was to be found among the "low-down folks," the black majority whose behavior was seen as scandalous by blacks concerned about what whites thought of them. Hughes wanted to write about those who did not "care whether they are like white folks or anybody else." Spirituals, jazz, dancing, cabarets, "shouting" churches in the urban North, and all facets of black life would be material for the artist, Hughes proclaimed.[79]

Several developments exacerbated these debates, and probably one of the most important was a growing white interest in black life. Literary, drama, and art critics began noticing a gradual increase in novels and dramatic productions on black life in the 1920s. David Levering Lewis writes that the moment of fusion between two bohemias, Harlem and Greenwich Village, occurred in the fall of 1917 when playwright Ridgely Torrence's three one-act plays with all-black casts were staged. Three years later, Eugene O'Neill's *Emperor Jones* appeared, with African American actor Charles Gilpin starring. Lewis dates these events as the beginning of the "vogue of the Negro in cosmopolitan white America." White village bohemians came in droves to Harlem's nightspots and rent parties in the 1920s.[80]

This interest was especially prompted by Carl Van Vechten, novelist, photographer, and drama critic. Van Vechten was a member of Mabel Dodge Luhan's famous salon at 23 Fifth Avenue in Greenwich Village. Luhan's salon members had begun meeting in 1912, and their gathering developed into a literary and cultural movement that included such noted writers and artists as Walter Lippmann, Ridgely Torrence, DuBose Heyward, Sinclair Lewis, and H. L. Mencken. Van Vechten was the most important figure in Luhan's salon to establish a link between the Harlem and Greenwich artistic movements.[81] In 1924, through his connections with publisher Alfred Knopf, Van Vechten met Walter White, assistant secretary of the NAACP, whose *Fire in the Flint* had just been published, and White later arranged a meeting between Van Vechten and James Weldon Johnson. By the end of 1924, Van Vechten claimed to know almost every important black person in Harlem and many who were not so famous. From this time forward, he began a regular habit of inviting blacks to his home and to parties for which he became famous. Van Vechten was fascinated by Harlem's night clubs and threw himself into every facet of Harlem's night life. He introduced a number of blacks to publishers and broadened the awareness of black arts and literature to the white public.[82]

After returning to Harlem from his medical residency at Howard University, African American novelist and physician Rudolf Fisher wrote in 1927 that Harlem, especially its night clubs, was being "stormed" by whites.[83] Huggins characterizes the 1920s as a time that "witnessed a wave of white literary efforts to take up the Negro as artistic subject."[84] This newfound white interest in black life presented problems and possibilities for blacks. Lewis notes that black leaders were determined to exploit white fascination with black Americans to launch their effort at a racial breakthrough.[85] Johnson, with evident exasperation, enumerated the various approaches that had been tried to solve the American race problem: religious, educational, political, industrial, ethical, economic, and sociological. He admitted that "considerable progress" had been made in these areas, but he still believed that a newer approach was now warranted. This newer approach would entail a minimum of pleas, propaganda, and philanthropy. It would depend more, Johnson proclaimed, on what blacks did for themselves. He labeled it the "art approach to the Negro problem."[86]

Given the new white interest in black life and blacks' discovery or recovery of their own heritage, the turn to literature and the arts seemed to be the best route to affirm their unique contributions to American society *and* to enhance their struggle for economic power and social justice. Despite aspirations for racial individuality and racial self-expression, black leaders found themselves dependent on the beneficence and cultural legitimacy of whites, in part because of the experience and expense required for dramatic productions. In 1928 Johnson conceded, for example, that this new method of intellectual and artistic achievements had as its desired effects the amelioration of white attitudes toward blacks and whites' recognition of blacks as a "great people" because only the production of literature and art determined a people's greatness. As he noted in an earlier work, "No people that has produced great literature and art has ever been looked upon by the world as distinctly inferior."[87] Johnson was convinced that the folk-art creations of African Americans had done much to change national attitudes toward them. In his view, the production of great literature and art demonstrated the "intellectual parity" of blacks and whites and would raise the status of blacks while changing the "mental attitudes" of whites. When blacks drew on their "natural endowments" and gave to America from the store of their "racial genius" such qualities as warmth, color, movement, rhythm, abandon, "depth and swiftness of emotion," and the "beauty of sensuousness," Johnson proclaimed, they would smash the stereotype that they were beggars "at the gate of the nation, waiting to be thrown the crumbs of civilization." He insisted that through their artistic achievements African Americans would destroy the common notion that they were to be filled with education, religion, culture, and morality. Instead, he maintained, blacks were helping shape an entirely new national conception of themselves and were challenging the very core of the "Nordic superiority complex" that supported prejudice against them. The new black artists were heralding a new age of race relations, Johnson optimistically asserted.[88]

In 1928, just as Johnson was offering his more hopeful view of arts and race relations, Allison Davis, an African American instructor of English at Hampton Institute, complained that for nearly ten years "our Negro writers have been 'confessing' the distinctive sordidness and triviality of Negro life, and making an exhibition of their own unhealthy imagination, in the name of frankness and sincerity." Davis had little hope that the black creative artistic movement was ushering in a new age. He thought it was mostly detrimental in its "realistic" depictions of blacks. He condemned the "modern novel's" preoccupation with sex and contended that even a dog or savage could be "sincere" about his "bestialities," but that would not raise him above them. He argued that if "sincerity is to justify one in exploiting the lowest traits of human nature" while ignoring that part of humans that distinguished them from the animals (a "sense for what is decent"), then it was no more than a "pander to torpid animalism." Davis criticized the "exhibitionism" of Eugene Gordon and George Schuyler and proclaimed that their "coarse frivolousness and scandalmongering falsely represent that the Negro has no respect." (Gordon and Schuyler, as noted earlier, were African American journalists who frequently criticized black churches.) He insisted that a "bawling" confession was no more a substitute for honest and discriminating self-examination in "race criticism" than it was in religion.[89]

Davis divided black writers into two camps: the sensationalists or Van Vechtenites and the exhibitionists or the Menckenites. He characterized the writings of Gordon and Schuyler among the Menckenites. Gordon and Schuyler had been influenced by Baltimore journalist H. L. Mencken's ideas and wrote in his acerbic and mordant style.[90] They lampooned black religion in their writings and held up to ridicule anything in black life that that did not meet with their approval. Davis argued that Gordon and Schuyler were "inspired by their master's attack upon Negro preachers and 'misleaders', and his heralding of the self-critical Negro." Davis believed that blacks or any other group needed criticism, but he reprimanded Gordon and Schuyler for what he regarded as their unseemly display of their own and the "race's eccentricities" as substitutes for the virtues that true criticism required. He complained that they were only interested in "expressing themselves, their cleverness without taste, their radicalism without intelligence, their contempt for Negro leaders and our upper class, uninformed by serious principles."[91] Davis feared that Gordon and Schuyler were forerunners of a "line of young critics" who would pose as the thoughtful and emancipated Negro who pretended to "represent a positivistic and experimental attitude toward the Negro's situation, to replace the religious fatalism and inferiority complex of our older leaders." This "specious liberalism of our little Menckenites," he sneered, made them dangerous precisely because blacks were at a "critical and strategic point of transition, where the cry of intellectual emancipation" could lead them after "false lights," unless blacks were willing to be "thoroughly critical." Davis insisted that blacks must not adopt one extreme in exchange for another. Smartness and "superficial criticism" were no substitute, he argued, for reflection and vision, and complete trust of what paraded as intelligence and hypercriticalness were not the cure for an "inferiority complex."[92]

Davis was just as critical of the Van Vechtenites. As representative of these, he chose Rudolf Fisher's *High Yaller* (1925) and Langston Hughes's *Fine*

Clothes to the Jew (1927). Davis was one of many black critics of Hughes's book of poems. These critics decried Hughes's "obsession for the more degenerate elements" of black life and called his poems a "study in the perversions of the Negro." They were especially worried about the depiction of "unprintable sexual mores" in the book.[93] In Davis's view, Hughes was one of the many black writers who pandered to the sensational and primitive.[94] He took offense at these writers who he believed had exploited the Harlem cabaret and the "African jungles" to such an extent that they made it appear that "Negro life is distinctive for its flaming 'color', [and] its crude and primitive emotion." He lamented that the Harlem cabaret had become such an "unhealthy obsession" with young black writers "who in their relative naiveté imagine that there is something profoundly stirring about the degradation of its habitués."[95]

This "mad rush to make the Negro exhibit his sensational and primitivistic qualities," Davis observed, was fueled by white support and was part of the broader current of American literature that reveled in "popularizing the jazz complex."[96] He regarded Van Vechten's *Nigger Heaven* (1926) as the "telos, the perfect flowering of the 'cabaret school.'" Blurring distinctions between social classes in this literature troubled Davis, who complained that what was "most pernicious in *Nigger Heaven* was the representation that the Negro upper class is identical with the pleasure-seekers and cabaret-rounders." By his portrayal of blacks in his novel, Van Vechten had "warped Negro life into a fantastic barbarism."[97] Davis chided blacks for supporting the novel and defending Van Vechten on the grounds that he was exercising his "artistic sincerity," particularly because of his social mixing with blacks. He argued that here again "the pretense of sincerity justified the most unalleviated sensationalism" and concluded that the cabaret theme in black literature was completely harmful because it regarded blacks as "sincerely bestial." By adopting the "white man's facile point of view" of blacks as "yearning for savage Africa," which signified "tom-toms," "love dances," and strange passions and urges, black writers had allowed themselves to appear "as the white man would have them."[98]

Davis argued that black writers and "race critics" had capitalized on the sensational aspects of black life at the expense of "general truth" and "sound judgment." "Primitivism" carried their imaginations into the "unhealthy" and the "abnormal." For the Van Vechtenites, Davis asked, "Are there any traits peculiar to Negro character, and if so, are those traits especially crude emotions?" The Van Vechtenites, in his view, needed to settle whether black culture was to be interpreted in relation to the human race or "the Negro race." In response to his own question about traits peculiar to blacks, Davis argued that the qualities of fortitude, irony, and a relative lack of self-pity were the most important qualities in the lives of blacks and that these qualities were the "secret strength of that part of us which is one with a universal human nature." Because black writers had failed to interpret this broader humanity of blacks, in part because of their obsession with primitivism, he averred, they found it "relatively easy to disguise their lack of a higher imagination by concentrating upon immediate and crude emotions."[99] Davis seemed to suggest that black writers overworked black distinctiveness to such an extent that they failed to see blacks' "universal" qualities. It is clear that he did not think that black writers were representing "real" blacks.

Davis also chastised the Menckenites for their preoccupation with sordid and "trivial aspects" of black life. He acknowledged that "on the whole" the facts of black life in America were sordid because of slavery and various discriminatory restrictions. Yet Davis proclaimed, "*We are going on our grit*, and it is these higher secret powers which I have indicated, (call them spiritual or chemical, as you like) which we must preserve and apply intelligently to our future development."[100] He argued that self-respect was essential for blacks to go forward and to retain their courage and that the "race critics" lacked true self-respect.[101] How else, Davis wondered, could one explain their lampooning and trivializing of black life? The "true critic," from his perspective, held fast to "his perception of what is excellent and real, in the midst of appearance" and applied "his standards with discrimination to the flux of actual life." The genuine critic, he insisted, must fix his attention on the "inner strength of Negro character" that had persisted over the past 300 years and, "discounting the trivial and irrelevant," interpret the "persistent characteristics for the new Negro to whom he will be as an eye." It was the critic's responsibility to hold before blacks a mirror of themselves and show them the permanent amidst the transitory. Pointing to this seed would help them determine how it could be made fruitful and useful for betterment and human flourishing in varying circumstances.[102]

Conclusion

Davis's arguments obviously did not end this debate about black artistic contributions and attempts to re-create images of blacks. In a letter to *Crisis* magazine (where Davis's essay was published), Hughes criticized Davis, insisting that he wrote about what he knew and that Davis was simply wrong by implying that Van Vechten or any other white writers controlled or determined the final content of his work.[103] By 1929 Johnson observed that even the "younger Negro writers" were complaining that white publishers were not interested in their work unless they wrote books about the "so-called lower-type of Negroes and lower phases of Negro life." Johnson doubted that this was true and took offense at statements about "lower" classes of blacks, noting that it was better dramatic and artistic potential to write of lower groups because it took "nothing less than supreme genius to make middle-class society, black or white, interesting—to say nothing of making it dramatic."[104]

As these writers suggested, debates among blacks over depictions of themselves in drama and literature were increasing and becoming more divisive. Certainly the fear of whites exploiting traditional images of blacks remained. Black religion in particular, as I have repeatedly noted, had been a long-standing object of white attention. When Du Bois wrote in 1924 that blacks had injected a "peculiar spiritual quality" into American culture and that religion was their most distinctive gift to America, it seemed that many whites would have agreed based on their responses to Marc Connelly's *Green Pastures*. Du Bois probably did not imagine that his claim that "every day belief in an anthropomorphic God owes it origins" in no small way to black Americans would find dramatic confirmation on stage in a few years after he wrote it.[105] *The Green Pastures* gave support to Du Bois's musings that religion or spirituality was a distinctive "gift of black folk," but the nature and the depictions of this gift were again the subject of great controversy.

6

The Religious and Cultural Meaning of *The Green Pastures*

In their *American Drama between the Wars,* Jordan Miller and Winifred Frazer describe *The Green Pastures* as a "delightful comedy" and a "serious drama."[1] Miller and Frazer lament that the play has been criticized for having a "condescending view of ignorant folk who visualize a fish fry with God as the height of happiness or who see whorish Babylon in a Negro nightclub."[2] They believe that this criticism overlooks the "sincerely religious atmosphere" of the drama. Miller and Frazer contend that the play's acceptance by white and black audiences is proof of "its inoffensive and positive nature." In their view, Richard B. Harrison's role as God marks "one of the most outstanding performances in American theater history." Miller and Frazer regret that a "changing and more enlightened view of American blacks" has made the play less acceptable to a broader public. In their assessment, the play is about "all mankind," and thus it "still retains its universal value." As the authors write, "When the black God is driven to renounce his people, he speaks directly and equally against all of whatever race."[3]

Reflecting on both the play (which ran from 1930 to 1935 and was briefly revived in 1951) and the movie (produced in 1935), Thomas Cripps has recently offered a very different view of *The Green Pastures* than that of Miller and Frazer. Cripps calls the drama a "monument to lost innocence" and situates the play within the context of the migration of Southern blacks to Northern cities. He argues that it was part of a trend in Hollywood to pay sentimental tribute to the "good

Negroes" whose virtues were allegedly expressed in the midst of tough times.[4] Cripps notes that "romance has often been the vehicle for conveying a sense of lost innocence" and that *The Green Pastures* was a "fable of black folk religion [which] appeared at the end of the first decade in which blacks and whites self-consciously confronted each other across the boundaries of their urban neighborhoods." This "sense of lost innocence and of a disappearing rural, primitive folklore that would soon be no more informed and colored Connelly's scenes." Cripps maintains that "Connelly's fable romanticized and memorialized the history of the rural black South that had been decimated by the northern black diaspora and, in disarming style, brought it to a broad national white audience for whom black life had been exotic."[5]

These two very different reactions to *The Green Pastures* demonstrate its power to evoke opposing views of its political and social implications. The play, especially in its original production, was caught up in debates about the place of blacks in the nation and the "true nature" of black religion and culture. The forces of migration, economic distress, and different expectations about the role of religion in the lives of black Americans helped shaped the precise nature that these analyses took. Rural religion figured prominently in the interpretations and imaginations of whites and blacks concerned with African American religion, and these surfaced in the range of reactions to the play. Blacks had neither the power nor the cultural authority to shape images of themselves as did their white counterparts. But black interpreters of African American religion were keenly aware of the ability of diverse media (movies, plays, and radio) to construct particular representations of black religion, and they responded to white images of black culture and formulated their own conceptions of a progressive, socially active faith.

Though some black leaders expressed approval for the play, especially because it employed an all-black cast, others were concerned about its image of blacks and its social and political implications. There was particular concern among black commentators about the seeming portrayal of the rural South as the "natural environment" of blacks unburdened by the problems of an urban, industrial society. In her recent work on African American urban experiences in film, Paula Massood argues that in "its dichotomy between heaven and earth, *The Green Pastures* suggests that rural southern space is a paradise in comparison to the city."[6]

Coming on the heels of the upsurge in black literature, arts, and drama in the 1920s, it is fitting to look at this cultural product as a site of race debates and changing images of blacks in the public arena. *The Green Pastures* can also be used as a cultural text through which we can read its script as a way of ascertaining how its interpretation of African American religious life in a certain section of the rural South was caught up in broader discussions about black migration and the nature of what kind of religion was good for the black masses. The play reflected a longing by white admirers for a simple rural past that was being lost. I argue that through the image of naive religious blacks, it spoke to the needs of those who, in the words of journalist Walter Lippmann, were haunted with the need to believe, to those who wanted to kneel and be comforted at the "shrine of some new god."[7] Mary Austin, a lecturer in folk drama at Yale University, noted that it "now begins to look as though we [whites] might have to thank the Negro for mediating our spiritual experience for our own use."[8] Images of black religion continued to prove a compelling and enduring solace for white Americans in moments of cultural stress. *The Green Pastures* provides evidence for this claim.

The long-running drama requires explanation. Why was it so popular, becoming one of the longest-running plays on Broadway (particularly with an-all black cast)? How did this explicitly religious play appear to blacks and whites? Paul Nolan, a biographer of Marc Connelly, argues that the play is distinguished by its scope in that it deals with "the central religious-philo-sophical myth of Western civilization, the Hebraic-Christian accounts in the Bible" and explores these through Connelly's understanding of black folk culture in the rural South.[9] The significance of the play can perhaps be seen from a different angle (than previous interpreters have observed) when placed in the historical context of broader interpretations of black religion and black critiques of Southern black rural religion in the 1920s and 1930s. In his book on the Harlem Renaissance, Nathan Huggins briefly discusses *The Green Pastures* at the end of his analysis of minstrelsy and the struggle of blacks to find a niche as legitimate actors in the theater. He argues that *The Green Pastures* "for a moment" was able to make "faith possible and vicariously experienced." Huggins notes that doubt "seemed impossible in the black child's fantasy" and that the play allowed whites to come to terms with their own guilt over the loss of belief in the decade after the First World War. The character of De Lawd, in his view, was a "transmuted Uncle Tom." Comparisons with Harriet Beecher Stowe's *Uncle Tom's Cabin* readily come to some critics' minds. In a discussion of the popularity of *The Green Pastures* a 1931 issue of the *New York Times* noted the "Last Days for 'Uncle Tom'" as a play, which was supposedly giving way to modernity (which meant that motion pictures were making dramas obsolete).[10] *The Green Pastures*'s immense popularity as a drama suggested otherwise, at least for a while.

Black critics of the play were quick to point out that the idealized image of the South and black rural life was hardly consistent with actual life in the South. Less than a month before the play opened to wide acclaim, black newspapers found themselves busily reporting on a different version of reality in the rural South. On February 1, 1930, in the small town of Ocilla in south Georgia, news wires provided graphic accounts of the lynching of James Irwin, a black man charged with the rape and murder of a white woman. Irwin was seized from the sheriff's custody and tortured by a mob that cut off his fingers and toes and rammed a red-hot poker into his throat before finally burning him to death.[11] Eleven recorded lynchings had occurred in the South in 1929, causing some to have hope that things were getting better because lynching deaths had been on the decrease throughout the 1920s. But that number doubled to twenty-two in just the first eight months of 1930. The Depression, hard on all Americans, was particularly devastating in the rural South. Remote agricultural areas felt the brunt of economic disaster.[12] Though not by any means limited to such regions, lynchings occurred more frequently in the back roads and open country of small towns of the rural South. In some ways, the modernization of the South was a contributing factor to the decline of lynching.[13] Cultural isolation decreased because of increased use of the radio, the automobile, and improved highways. Rising standards of living and improved education gradually replaced the illiteracy, poverty, and cultural stagnation that were viewed as the root causes of mob violence.[14] It appears that the nostalgia for this imagined "natural environment" for blacks was heightened precisely because "rural worlds" were being lost as blacks and whites continued to leave the South.[15]

Mediating the Spiritual Experience of Whites

White admirers tended to laud what they saw as the peculiar qualities of blacks exhibited in *The Green Pastures*—lack of vindictiveness, resignation under suffering, a joyful carefree spirit, and a simple, innate religiosity—even as leading African Americans insisted that such qualities (whether real or depicted in fiction) had to be changed if blacks were to advance politically and economically. The popularity of *The Green Pastures* during the hardships of the Great Depression years spoke to a deep need in white audiences. Comments about the simplicity of Southern black religion, the ability of this dramatic presentation to make belief possible again (at least vicariously), and the friendliness and forgiving nature of the anthropomorphic black God, "De Lawd," all demonstrate that the longing for what this image of blacks offered to whites (psychologically, spiritually, and emotionally) was a key component in continued fascination with blacks as naturally religious and exotic. The acclaim of the play perhaps also expressed a preference for "safe" rural blacks who were not coming to cities of the North and competing for jobs and neighborhood space.

Connelly, a white agnostic, wrote and directed a play that claimed to represent the authentic religious beliefs and practices of blacks in the rural South.[16] The play was the most popular image of black religion in the white mind during the early 1930s. Marc Connelly was born in 1890 in McKeesport, Pennsylvania. By age twenty, he had drifted to Pittsburgh and worked for a while as a reporter for the *Pittsburgh Sun*. In 1915, Connelly came to New York and developed an interest in theater. Between 1916 and 1920, he supported himself by writing lyrics for an ultimately unsuccessful musical and composing verse for a popular comic weekly.[17] Sometime in 1928, Connelly was encouraged by a friend to read Roark Bradford's *Ol' Man Adam and His Chillun* (1928), a retelling of some of the stories of the Old Testament in black Southern dialect. Bradford was a white journalist living in New Orleans. After reading Bradford's book, Connelly made two separate trips to New Orleans to study Negro spirituals and religious services. Bradford accompanied him to many of the black churches that he visited. Late in 1928, Connelly signed a publishing contract with Harper and Brothers, which assigned him the right to make a play from Bradford's book in return for which Bradford would receive 30 percent of the royalties.[18]

Connelly's play opened at the Mansfield Theater, New York, on February 26, 1930. It ran for a record 640 performances in New York and won Connelly the Pulitzer Prize for the 1929–1930 theatrical season. The play was quickly rated a box office success. On March 15, 1935, the musical drama returned to New York after having traveled the country. By that date, it had made its 1,652nd appearance in Baltimore, Maryland. *The Green Pastures* company had traveled 40,000 miles, played in 203 towns, and appeared in all but 8 states. Harrison had become an iconic figure by the time of his death (March 14, 1935). The play was made into a motion picture in 1935.[19]

The Green Pastures contained a number of spirituals at various interludes, which enhanced its appeal in the eyes of reviewers and audiences. The play contained two parts dealing with events from the Creation to the Flood and the story of Moses to the Crucifixion, in the language and idioms of blacks in rural Louisiana (outside of New Orleans). This is how Connelly described the play:

> *The Green Pastures* is an attempt to present certain aspects of a living religion in terms of its believers. The religion is that of thousands of Negroes in the deep South. With terrific spiritual hunger and the greatest humility these untutored black Christians—many of whom cannot even read the book which is the treasure house of their faith— have adapted the contents of the Bible to the consciences of their everyday lives. Unburdened by the differences of more educated

theologians they accept the Old Testament as a chronicle of wonders which to people like themselves in vague but actual places, and of rules of conduct, true acceptance of which will lead them to a tangible, three-dimensional Heaven.[20]

Connelly said that he made special efforts "against the imposition of any humorous concept not racially proper."[21] His stated intention was to make a comedy of sorts in line with Bradford's depiction of Southern blacks but to include nothing that was funny just for "fun's sake" or that denigrated blacks. "Any creed that has lasted more than five hundred years," Connelly said about black Christianity, "has merit in it somewhere."[22] He wrote that he was eager to respect the faith of black fundamentalists at all times, even if as an agnostic he could not accept the "insistences by sectarian hierarchies or sectarian policing." Writing the play was his way of interpreting the "search of God for man, and man's search for God."[23] Within that skeletal outline, the play could proceed without denigrating the beliefs of religious persons in general or black Christians in particular. Connelly used the distinctive experiences of one group to speak to a more general audience.

Connelly adapted the story of the ancient Israelites to the experience of blacks in the rural South. His audiences encountered "mammy angels," God and cherubim smoking cigars, a grand fish fry, Southern juke joints and dance halls, and all the varied colloquialisms of the rural South. Viewers saw God "walking' de earth in de shape of a natchel man." Anthropomorphic and humorous, God stumbled into situations, experienced surprises, and broadened his view of humanity by the end of the play. God's frustration with humanity culminated in his destroying the Earth by a great flood. After restoring the Earth, God decided to bless the patriarchs and their descendants (Connelly stuck closely to the biblical story). God learned from humans as the drama proceeded; toward the end of the play, God declared that only through suffering is mercy known, and he exclaimed to Noah, "No, suh, mankind's jest right for my earth, if he wasn't so doggone sinful." Through his experience with humans, God was transformed from a god of wrath to a god of mercy and long suffering.

White responses to the play were overwhelmingly positive. They were thrilled by this vivid portrayal of the simplicity and sincerity of the Negro's faith and the attractive character of God (De Lawd). J. Brooks Atkinson, writing for the New York Times, called it a play of "surpassing" and "sublime" beauty. Its "great emotional depth" complemented the "utter simplicity in religious conception" of the "ignorant religious negroes of the South." De Lawd allowed one to believe in him implicitly. The play itself, Atkinson proclaimed, was "belief incarnated."[24] Louis Azrael, of the *New York Telegram,* felt that the drama "teaches that man's suffering is not God's punishment for man's evil," a powerful and appealing message amid the economic and social distress of the early 1930s.[25]

White critics were also prompted by their reactions to reflect on the state of religion in the modern world. William Bolitho of the New York *World* journal believed that the simple religious faith of the Negro depicted in *The Green Pastures* could redeem the Bible from "all the subtly limited rationalisms which all the Protestantisms have put into it." Blacks possessed the "purest form of Fundamentalism." Connelly's expression of Christian fundamentalism in Negro form was far more appealing than the likes of William Jennings Bryan to Bolitho's way of thinking. Bryan could never convey "the touching poetry, the ingenuous conjuring away of logical difficulties, [and] the secret charm" of the "Fundamentalist vision of the universe" in the way that Connelly had done so masterfully. Bolitho wrote that in the end, religion in the play was shown to be more than rational argument and disputations:

> Men may fight for their religion with arguments on their lips, but in their hearts the hidden motive is always tinseled candles they saw on the altar when they were children, the light stained glass throws on Sunday mornings, the frock coat and white tie and the old benevolent face once attributed to God. So Mr. Connelly—what is art but supernatural?—has here explained not only the Negro heart but the kernel of the Fundamentalist position, their vision of the universe. This, O [H. L.] Mencken, is what the Bible belt is trying to say: however unpleasantly they fight, they are defending a Christmas tree.[26]

Bolitho was critical of Marxists who argued that religion diverted attention from the problems of this world to focus on the next world. He wondered, "What would this poor people [American Negroes], the victim of the strangest and most terrifying fate that has ever, perhaps, befallen a race, what would they have done without the consolation of the Christian religion?" Religion is a "wine," not an opiate, Bolitho contended, useful and necessary for the masses. It was fine for people to have the comforts of religion and the modern state should regulate organized religion in such a way that it does not become too powerful in the realm of politics. But it was cruel, tyrannical, and "probably impossible," he proclaimed, to deprive poor people of their religion as the Russian Marxists were attempting to do. Of all people, the poor needed the "irrational comfort" provided by religion and it was silly to think that they would behave like "little philosophers." Perhaps, Bolitho wondered, Marxists were wrong if Connelly's

play was right when it dramatized that religion had indeed sustained an oppressed people like black Americans.[27]

Heywood Broun, a white columnist, socialist, and friend of James Weldon
Johnson, used the occasion of his review of the play to reflect on the meaning
of Christianity among oppressed groups. He argued that blacks redeemed
Christianity and restored to it those qualities that were lacking. Black folk
exemplified a kind of Christian faith that was not evident among whites. To
those who maintained that Christianity was a slave religion, Broun acknowledged that although this was so, if he were a Negro preacher, he would "accept
this reproach and wear it as a plume." After all, "who among us has broken
every fetter of mortality?" The drama reminded its audience that Christianity
had in it, he averred, a "ferment of immediacy" and that eager anticipation for
another world was a central part of its ethos. Untutored blacks in the South also
longed for deliverance from present bondage, as expressed in their conceptions
of heaven. For Broun the play dramatized the most fundamental conflict of the
human soul; it told of the ultimate triumph of mercy over hatred. The Negro
alone of all oppressed peoples did not allow bitterness to take root in his soul.
Thus the Negro "has played a vital part in bringing back to current Christianity
its kindliness."[28]

The Green Pastures seemed to make religious belief briefly possible again
for some white skeptics. Literary critic Joseph Wood Krutch's response to the
drama illustrates this point. William Hutchison argues that Krutch and journalist Walter Lippmann were among the principal critics of religious liberalism in the late 1920s.[29] Krutch's *Modern Temper* (1929) and Lippmann's
Preface to Morals (1929) were two signal texts that somberly pronounced the
death of traditional religious beliefs and the depth of skepticism that had
entered the souls of modern intellectuals. Krutch felt that human illusions
had been "lost one by one" in the decade after World War I. "God, instead of
disappearing in an instant," he claimed, "has retreated step by step and sur-
rendered gradually his control of the universe."[30] A yearning for a lost anthropomorphic God who was created in humanity's image and so who understood
human desires haunted Krutch's work. He gloomily noted that the world of
religion, myth, and poetry, which represented the world "as man would like
to have it," was in conflict with science. Modern man gave up his belief in the
notion of a "cozy bowl of the sky arched in a protecting curve above him" in
exchange for "the cold immensities of space." Krutch continued, "God he
loved *because* God was anthropomorphic, because He was made in man's
image, with purposes and desires which were human and hence understandable."[31] But now, like adults rudely awakened from childish dreams,
modern humans had to confront the cold fact that nature had no purposes and

life had no intrinsic meaning. The myth and poetry of the child's world were lost to modern man.[32] Though the intellect could rejoice at the findings of modern science, the emotions could not comprehend this world and the spirit, "frightened and cold, longs to have once more above its head the inverted bowl beyond which may lie whatever paradise its desires may create."[33]

Not surprisingly then, Krutch confessed that he found his emotions deeply stirred by De Lawd's character in *The Green Pastures*, which moved him at a level he found hard to explain. The Negro's "version of mythology is the only one now living enough to touch us," he maintained. Unlike "sophisticated religions" (by which he meant religious modernity), this Negro drama dealt intimately with what it professed to believe. Modern religion was "merely the result of skepticism unwilling to confess that it is forced to doubt anything which it allows itself definitely to conceive." But this remarkable drama was true art because it had faith enough to embody itself in concrete images. It aroused "enthusiasm" and enabled modern audiences to feel the "religious emotions." Indeed, Krutch implied, Negro mythology was the last thing left that would call forth the religious emotions because there was certainly no way moderns were capable of generating them for themselves.[34]

Did white reactions to the play reflect unconscious racist desires to keep Southern blacks in their place? Perhaps, but the responses of those whites who were seriously interested in urban work among blacks should caution us about being too sure on this point. Mary Ovington, for example, had proven her devotion to black causes as one of the founding members of the National Association for the Advancement of Colored People (NAACP) by helping with the work of the National Urban League and by befriending Du Bois and a number of other black leaders concerned with urban and racial reform. Ovington was asked to explain in the early 1930s why she became interested in "taking up the Negro's cause," and the result was a series of articles that she wrote for the black newspaper the Baltimore *Afro-American* in 1932 and 1933. Ovington was a socialist, so her remarks on this explicitly religious play are particularly revealing. She felt that the play had more "converts than any evangelist who has been preaching since the play began." Though there was "much controversy" concerning the play among blacks, she noted, there was "none among whites." Ovington confessed that every time she talked with blacks about the play the discussion became so heated that she was forced to drop the subject. So she presented her reminiscences as the final word in her ongoing attempts to commend the play to blacks.[35]

Ovington was puzzled by constant complaints among blacks about the play's folk character, especially its image of heavenly picnics and fish fries. Blacks could not appreciate the audience's laughter at such apparently funny scenes, she fretted, because they feared that surely these admiring whites were laughing at blacks doing silly things. Blacks always asked, "Why do they always show the ignorant Negro? Why can't they show us at our best?" But Ovington was convinced that the play was successful precisely because it depicted blacks, who, humble enough, belonged to a social sphere that was "deep-rooted," whereas the "educated Negro of today has been uprooted and has rarely achieved a culture comparable artistically to the old." By "heroically trying to keep up with the procession" of modern life in the city, blacks were simply not impressive figures. She elaborated:

> The son of a Maine fisherman comes to New, buys a Hart, Scaffner, and Marx suit of clothes, gets a job in a shop, and feels that these city folk ought to know how he had advanced over his forebears. But do they notice? Not at all, unless it be to make fun of him. Instead, he goes down to Maine, finds the father, who, in his oilskins, has come back from a morning's catch, hears salty talk and stories of adventure and hardships as old as sea itself. Here is reality, a culture that is secure.[36]

Black city folk, Ovington wrote, simply did not possess a secure culture as the blacks depicted in *The Green Pastures* from whom Connelly gave audiences "something secure, deep-rooted, imaginative as the heart of a child."[37] So for Ovington and other white critics who lauded the play, something deeply rooted in black culture was revealed, and it contained an evangelistic message for white Americans. Many of these white fans were Northerners who were interested in literature and dramatic productions. Their comments on *The Green Pastures* should not be viewed, however, in isolation from the broader critique of modern bourgeois culture's scientific rationality and its alleged aridity.

The *New York Times* reported in 1934 that *The Green Pastures* had toured every Southern state, except Mississippi because of its lack of a "suitable theater."[38] An editorial writer for South Carolina's *Columbia Record* wrote that the play proved that there were "normal" people in New York City. He hoped that the play would produce "as many real conversions to Christianity" as religious revivals did.[39] A writer for the *August Herald* raved that it was an "altogether delightful play."[40] Some white Southern critics, however, expressed concern about the lines attributed to God in the play. They considered it a sacrilege to have God walking around on Earth, smoking and handing out ten-cent cigars, and complaining because he did not have enough ferment in his custard. These commentators also disliked the portrayal of God speaking in Southern black dialect and succumbing to frequent "grammatical lapses." Others were concerned about the "further negrification of the nation along lines intellectual, psychological, and artistic," a reference to the cultural rejection of Victorianism in the 1920s. William M. Groom, pastor of Ross Avenue Baptist in Dallas, Texas, said *The Green Pastures* was "one of the most blasphemous and sacrilegious things ever placed before the public and shamefully caricatures the Lord Almighty, the angels, and the patriarchs." Groom called on his congregation and the public to demand that this "outrageous" insult against the revealed word of God "be immediately discontinued."[41] But overall it appears that most white Southerners who watched the play enjoyed it and strongly warmed to its religious message. Remarks about Southerners' unique understanding of the "antebellum Negro's conception of God" indicated that white Southerners still held deep attachments to the plantation depictions of happy and contented blacks.

Clowning the Black Man's Spiritual Pose

Black critics debated the play's artistic merits and its impact on broader depictions and images of African Americans, though many were happy to see an all black cast employed. Differences emerged particularly about the nature of the play, whether it was a sacrilegious portrayal of God or a caricature of heaven, and about how blacks were depicted religiously. Du Bois labeled *The Green Pastures* an "extraordinarily appealing and beautiful play based on the folk religion of Negroes," but he predicted that blacks would not like the play because of its representation of God in a frock coat and its depiction of heaven as a fish fry.[42] Mary Burrill, an "educated woman of Negro birth," in a letter to the *Nation* asserted that the play was not a Negro version of Christian mythology. Blacks did not think of God as black, she maintained (a point also made by some Southern critics), but as "an anemic WHITE gentleman with a golden beard, wearing a long nightshirt with bishop-sleeves."[43] Burrill wrote that the situation of blacks in the South prevented them from conceiving of God as black. In her words, the "reason for such a conception on the part of the Negro is simple enough. Has he not spent his life in a country where to be black is despised? Is it therefore likely that he will want to take such a handicap with him to heaven?" Blacks did not interpret the afterlife in terms of their present experience, she wrote. She called on critics of the drama to appraise it as "a white man's conception of the Negro's conception of religion and heaven."[44]

No black critics could avoid the question of the play's relation to blacks' place in contemporary American society, even if they attempted to eschew this approach by judging the play on its artistic merit. An Oklahoma *Black Dispatch* editorial opened with the simple question reportedly asked by a "young white girl" at a public talk (given by the editor) at Pilgrim Congregational Church: "Is *Green Pastures* really a genuine expression of the Negro's religion?" "No," the author replied, "*Green Pastures* does not reflect properly the black man's religion. *Green Pastures* was written by perverse white people who sought to clown the black man's spiritual pose." The editor related the young girl's relief at this response and how she indicated that "*Green Pastures* distressed me, and I was loath to believe that any people, and especially colored people, could have any such twisted, distorted outlook at the universe and God." This young lady, the author assured his readers, provided "ample justification for the assault that we have continuously made against" the play's presentation. He went on, "Here we find a liberal-minded white girl hoping against hope that black people are not like she had seen them falsely presented to her on the American stage." The author could scarcely conceal his rage when he uttered, "No more cruel stab has ever been thrust at the black man in America than is exposed in the derisive, contemptuous and ridiculous complex attributed to him in this ignoble, defaming play."[45]

The author was puzzled that the "Negro intelligentsia" could not see the harm done by the play. He was deeply disappointed that in his native Oklahoma City 1,100 blacks "hurried from all over Oklahoma" paying high prices for seats "to look at a drama which in its fundamentals cuts the heart and humanity out of black folk." He conjectured that perhaps they had been duped by the "sugar-coating" of fine music and beautiful scenery, which made the play all the more dangerous in his view. Because so few black leaders could see the play's perniciousness, the author vowed he would renew his efforts to reveal its true nature. He argued that just as he had fought against *The Birth of a Nation* (1915), a hugely popular silent movie that lauded the Ku Klux Klan's actions during the Reconstruction years (among other things), he would fight against *The Green Pastures*. The editor believed *The Green Pastures* was more dangerous because, unlike *The Birth of a Nation*, which "did damage to white people" because of its explicitly racist images, it struck at the "probity, integrity, mental poise, and morality of black folk." "When you remove such attitudes from a man," the author concluded, "you have destroyed the man."[46] The author still believed at this late date in the play's run (1934) that it remained a threat to blacks and that he could do something to counter its images. His comments did indicate, however, the enormous issues that were at stake from the perspective of black leaders like himself.

Black journalist and satirist George Schuyler was also a vocal critic of the play, offering his views even before he saw it. Schuyler believed that *The Green Pastures* reinforced white stereotypes of the Negro "as a child of nature unfortunately stranded in the midst of white civilization." He dismissed black critics who thought the play was superior; he claimed that they unthinkingly applauded anything that white intellectuals and critics praised. Schuyler was also skeptical of whites who lauded the play. He was persuaded that if whites had been the central characters, the play would hardly have been so lavishly praised. He asserted that the play comforted and flattered whites precisely because it appealed to their stereotypical notions of blacks. Denying that the play accurately represented the Southern rural Negro's conception of heaven, Schuyler appealed to the authority of Zora Neale Hurston, a black anthropologist and folklorist, who had collected black folk tales in the South from 1927 to 1930. He quoted Hurston as saying that the play was the "white man's idea of heaven palmed off to perpetuate the belief that the Negro's status, even in eternity, will be that of a menial." For this reason, Schuyler concluded that he could not agree with those who believed that plays like *The Green Pastures* did blacks a lot of good. He intimated that such productions hindered blacks from demanding their rights and reinforced the harmful images of blacks already prevalent among whites.[47]

Hurston's most recent biographer, Valerie Boyd, argues that Hurston was prompted by the success of *The Green Pastures* to sense possibilities for herself as a playwright. The play rekindled her long-standing interest in the theater. Hurston never published a formal response to the play, but she wrote an unpublished article in 1934 in which she praised Harrison as a "great actor" and commended Connelly for his skills as a dramatist. She argued that the play reflected very little about black religion or folk life. "The Negro's idea of heaven," Hurston wrote, "is certainly not dusting out a plantation boss's office with aprons on their wings. Nothing like work and bossy white folks in our heavenly concept."[48] She had often complained that white authors of black dramas "squeezed all Negro-ness out of everything."[49]

The central concern for Hurston and other black leaders was who could more accurately or authentically represent blacks. Representations of black life on stage and elsewhere were inextricably tied up with the problems of racism and traditional stereotypical images of blacks, as we have seen. Carl Van Vechten, for example, wrote to Langston Hughes, urging him to collaborate with Hurston in the production of a play (later called *Mule Bone*) that would present a realistic picture of black life in the South. Van Vechten had hopes that the play would "duplicate the success" of *The Green Pastures*, but it was never produced in the lifetime of Hurston and Hughes because of personal conflicts.[50] Here again was the scenario of blacks struggling to control the discourse of race and representation after whites had already made success in the same arena.

Black Interpreters of Southern Black Rural Religion

The Green Pastures was one production among others in a changing social environment that prompted greater attention to rural religion among blacks in the South. The emphasis on rural religion among black leaders in the late 1920s and the early 1930s evolved in several ways. The continued migration of blacks to the urban North sparked concerns about how best to address the needs of the migrants, and this led in turn to closer contact between uprooted Southerners and Northern black Christians. The harsh conditions of life in the South incited black social scientists and colleges to send out students and researchers to collect data on the lives of blacks in isolated pockets of the rural South. For black leaders like Carter Woodson and Benjamin Mays, for example, who conducted many of these early studies, rural religion connoted an orientation or a mindset that was seen as out of touch in the real world. So they sought ways to address the problem of rural black religion.

The migration of rural Southern blacks to the urban South and North in the first three decades of the twentieth century was crucial to contemporary discussions about black religion. Woodson and Mays and his coauthor, Joseph Nicholson, deserve special mention because their detailed studies of blacks in the rural South contrasted sharply with the representation of religion in *The Green Pastures*. Mays and Nicholson and Woodson had spent far more time, expended more effort, and used more professional methods to study the religious beliefs and practices of rural black Southerners than did Connelly.[51] Yet it is doubtful that either of their works had the widespread influence (among white audiences) of Connelly's play. Woodson, a major figure in the development of "black history," commenced his study of rural Southern black communities in 1926 and completed the project in 1929. His study was published in April 1930 as *The Rural Negro*. Hurston was among those who helped collect data for this endeavor. Mays and Nicholson based their study on a firsthand analysis of 609 urban and 185 rural black churches, distributed over twelve cities and four counties (in the North and South). It took about fourteen months to complete the fieldwork and collect data and ten months to prepare the material for publication. *The Negro's Church* was published in 1933 under the auspices of the Institute of Social and Religious Research in New York. Mays also published *The Negro's God* in 1938, which dealt more extensively with black conceptions of God and was in part a response to works like *The Green Pastures*.[52]

The problem of otherworldliness and the way forward to a more socially active church were crucial to the works of Mays and Nicholson and Woodson. What troubled these critics was "otherworldliness," which represented to them a preindustrial, premodern worldview that adhered to a literal interpretation of the Bible and manifested scant concern for economic and social reform (at least as these critics envisioned it). Overchurching (which meant for critics that there were too many black churches in one area), an untrained and often absentee leadership in the ministry, emotional worship, lack of a program for rural education, failure to focus on the specific needs of youth, and insufficient attention to economic and social problems because of an outdated, other-worldly approach to religion were the most commonly cited weaknesses of the rural black churches. Invariably contrasting the rural churches to urban ones, Woodson argued that though the "urban church has become a sort of uplift agency; the rural church has become a mystic shrine. While the urban church is often trying to make this a better world in which to live, the rural church is engaged in immediate preparation for the 'beautiful land of by and by.'" Church members in rural churches exhibited "paroxysms which could hardly be expected outside of an insane asylum," he complained. With pictures of blacks being lynched and burned alive scattered through his book, he had little sympathy for a romantic notion of the rural South filled with "green pastures." Woodson placed his hope in outside help for the rural Southern churches and in the work of those in urban areas of the South and North.[53]

Mays was an ordained Baptist minister and had served as the national student secretary of the Young Men's Christian Association (YMCA) from 1928 to 1930. At the time of the publication of *Negro's Church*, Mays was working on his doctorate at the University of Chicago. The coauthor of this work, Nicholson, had received his doctorate in religion from Northwestern University in 1932. Nicholson was also the pastor of Jubilee Temple, a Colored Methodist Episcopal (CME) church in Chicago, until 1936. W. Clark Gilpin argues that Mays's theology was a significant variation of the liberal Protestant contrast between traditional religion and modernist "social spirituality." This social spirituality, Gilpin contends, was viewed as a necessary organization of "Christian forces into effectiveness" because Christianity had passed from a dogmatic to a sociological conception of the content of religion in the modernists' assessments. The otherworldly "compensatory" religion represented for black leaders like Mays what fundamentalism represented for white modernists. The church now had to become more efficient and practically engaged in concrete issues.[54]

Mays had studied with Shailer Mathews at the University of Chicago, and he was deeply influenced by the Social Gospel emphasis on the social nature of religion.[55] Mays's challenge, and that of other black church leaders informed by the Social Gospel movement, was to make Christian ideas efficient tools of social reform. Gilpin and Milton Sernett note that these ideas developed from an instrumentalist conception of the church, which regarded the church as an instrument for bringing about social and political changes in broader society.[56] Although Mays and Nicholson listed the standard litany of rural church problems, Mays was particularly troubled by the problem of black "innate religiosity" and otherworldliness (manifested especially in his *Negro's God*). Mays was concerned about depictions of black religion as conveyed in *The Green Pastures*. He felt that the play perpetuated the notion of the "super-religious" Negro. He sought to demonstrate that the "Negro's ideas of God grow out of the social situation in which he finds himself" and not from a primitive or innate religiosity.[57]

Mays and Nicholson defined an otherworldly sermon as "one that is concerned so predominantly with the hereafter that the practical aspects of life on earth are secondary or submerged, or one in which fear or reward, not in this life but in the world to come, is the dominant note." Such sermons placed their primary emphasis on the magical and mysterious and on heaven more than on daily living and familiar things. Of the 100 sermons that they studied, Mays and Nicholson found that only 26 touched on concrete life situations. Fifty-four were predominantly otherworldly.[58] In *Negro's God*, Mays contended that the compensatory, otherworldly view was not unique to blacks but was common among poor and oppressed groups in general. He detected that migration and improving economic circumstances had brought about a reorientation away from otherworldliness among blacks in the cities. This was cited as evidence for Mays that blacks' ideas of God grew out of social situations, not from a racial temperament or innate religiosity. He believed that the racial caste system in the South was to blame for the unfulfilled yearnings of blacks, which were projected into another world. Mays recommended an improvement in the economic status of blacks and an enhancement of their opportunities for education, especially for ministers.[59]

Though Woodson and Mays (among others) had their doubts about the image of God depicted in *The Green Pastures*, they repeatedly criticized rural black believers for their focus on the "by and by." Was this indirect confirmation of the commonly held claim that blacks were naturally religious and more concerned about an afterworld than this world? Surely there is irony in the effort to reconstruct the image of blacks as not being, in Mays's view, overly emotional and super-religious, when he and Nicholson spent so much time criticizing them precisely because they believed they were practicing an "otherworldly" and "emotional" religion. The alleged qualities of blacks that were deemed so attractive and natural to those who appreciated *The Green Pastures* were precisely those that vexed black critics: a rural, small-town worldview, a fundamentalist, literal conception of the spiritual life and the world hereafter, an anthropomorphic conception of God, and a reportedly carefree spirit about the hardships of this life.

Although Mays indicated that he intended to show that black religious ideas grew out of their social situation and to refute indirectly the "Negro's idea of God" depicted in *The Green Pastures*, it is not clear how and if he accomplished his goal because Connelly's work was about more than "ideas." It was about fantasy, imagination, and unconscious longings (especially among whites). Mays did show that blacks were facing extraordinary economic and social hardships and that there was no biological or racial basis to black religious practice. He demonstrated that there was a small number of highly literate African Americans who forsook religious belief entirely. Yet his central claim that the bulk of blacks in the rural South adhered to an otherworldly religion seemed to confirm the inferences that many blacks thought whites would draw from such plays as *The Green Pastures*. It is true that Mays pointed to economic deprivation of the black masses and their turn to religion as a compensatory mechanism to seek the symbolic and spiritual goods that another world offered as a substitute for the material and psychological goods that they lacked in this life.[60] Though the reason or motive for belief among the masses was given a new spin in social and economic terms rather than basing it on racial or biological foundations, the fact of widespread religious belief and practice was still assumed. Though innate religiosity was denied by this new interpretation, Mays may have inadvertently documented what he set out to disprove, namely, that the kind of religious images conveyed by *Green Pastures* was similar to what he found in the South, as he himself testified to in his constant criticisms of the otherworldliness and emotionalism of black rural religion.

The Meaning of *The Green Pastures*

In 1936, B. R. Crisler, writing for the *New York Times*, made one final comment on the short-lived movie version of *The Green Pastures*. He wrote, "It is, indeed, hard not to like the simple and gratifying theology of *The Green Pastures* as much as anything about it. It has concreteness and gives one a nostalgic feeling that it ought to be true and that if it isn't we are all, somehow, obscurely the worse for it."[61] The Hebrew narrative had acquired a new life on stage in the words and actions (from Connelly's perspective) of simple religious black folk from the rural South. White admirers of the play were able to relive a faith that they had either forgotten or put aside in their move away from the traditions and location of their parents. This segment of white Americans who were a part of a recently urbanized America felt a nostalgic longing for what was apparently lost.[62] The stage became a way of working through their spiritual and psychological issues. Black images have long functioned in this manner. A cursory comparison with Harriet Beecher Stowe's *Uncle Tom's Cabin* indicates how strongly the image of the deeply religious black has appealed to those who groped for a way to criticize the materialism and harshness of modern American life. This analogy with Stowe's created character was invoked again and again by critics of Connelly's play because for them "Uncle Tom" had become a negative reference, not a heroic figure. It was not the first time that whites had reproduced a comforting image of blacks to suit their own needs.

When Connelly's black God looks out pensively at the crowd and another figure exclaims, "O dat's a terrible burden for one man to carry," we are left wondering if it is Jesus or God who has to suffer this burden alone. Could it be that the question that ought to have been asked was: Must blacks suffer this constant burden of representation, despite their oppression, to teach whites a lesson about God or striving in the midst of suffering and hardship? Could whites not work out their own salvation without projecting their own fears and desires into black images? The image of black religion in particular has been crucial to white attempts to recover a lost or innocent past. As Nathan Huggins argues, black identity has often been the projection of white vision and white needs.[63] Whites reproduced a comforting image of blacks to the extent that it fit their own needs. In reacting to the white images of blacks, black critics have often pointed to the social and economic conditions that produced a certain religious expression. They believed it was their task to prove that black religion was not an innate or immutable quality but a feature of black life that could be transformed and enlisted in the nation's racial struggle.

Conclusion

George Fredrickson argues that romantic racialism, in its traditional and re-cently "jazzed-up versions" during the 1920s, lost much of its credibility among the "white liberal intelligentsia" by the 1930s. Fredrickson attributes this development to the repudiation of the validity of psychological tests that had been used extensively in the 1920s and that gave support to popular claims of the intellectual inferiority of blacks and the notion of an inherited racial temperament (which, in my view, places too much weight on ideas and intellectual developments). He points to the increasing popularity of liberal environmentalism, which came to dominate the fields of sociology and an-thropology by World War II. Another important development was the rise of the militant stance of black intellectuals who rejected notions of a racial temperament and who turned increasingly to social and economic factors as the causal forces underlying the unique situation of blacks in the nation.[64] This major assault on black innate religiosity and a racial temperament culminated in the social scientific works of the 1940s.

7

Urbanization and the End of Black Religion in the Modern World

On the eve of World War II, Gunnar Myrdal and his colleagues had amassed the most comprehensive collection of data on black life than any previous study. Myrdal, a Swedish economist, had come to the United States in 1938 at the invitation of the Carnegie Corporation of New York, a private philanthropic foundation. The foundation wanted someone from a country with "no background or traditions of imperialism" to study the "Negro problem." Myrdal's *An American Dilemma* (1944) was a massive work of over 1,400 pages, supported by many unpublished works, many of which were authored by black social scientists. The Myrdal-Carnegie study represented the latest and best thinking of social science on the problem of race and culture and provided a detailed analysis of the most salient and pressing aspects of the nation's long-standing Negro problem. Myrdal and some of his co-workers expressed great faith in the power of social science and social engineering to address the persistent problem of racism and caste oppression.[1]

African American religion, though treated tangentially and briefly in Myrdal's text, received some attention in several texts that informed and supported his book. Discussions of African American religion were at the center of the still unsettled national debate about the nature of black culture and its relationship to African cultural practices. Did blacks have a distinct culture of their own, with roots in Africa or was it distinctive to the New World? Were the cultural products of blacks merely a variant, at times pathological, of "white"

Christian culture in America? These ways of framing the matter touched on a host of other issues: Had blacks produced a unique contribution to American culture? Did "black culture" have an autonomy of its own that testified to the resilience of black life under oppression? To what extent did black society represent a subculture in the broader American world, and how should blacks relate to white American culture should the nation ever repeal its laws of segregation?

Social scientists, white and black, and African American leaders had argued for half a century that black churches were central social institutions that had long been compelled to take up more responsibilities and a broader range of roles than white churches. But there was another, equally if not more important reason these churches were deemed central to black life and culture. The claim that blacks were peculiarly religious or that they possessed a racial temperament, as sociologist Robert Park argued, still persisted. The argument of black innate religiosity had gone through profound permutations from the antebellum period up to the 1940s. White social scientists of the early twentieth century had argued that blacks were in the emotional stage of sociocultural evolution and religion was natural to them because it was an expression of their more basic sensual and emotional psychological makeup, ideas that lingered up to the 1930s. The social scientists who contributed to the Myrdal-Carnegie project set out to bury such residual notions of natural religiosity, which assumed a racial temperament that inhibited the ultimate assimilation of blacks into the broader society.

The denial of a racial temperament or a *racially distinct religious culture* had intended and unintended effects. Social scientists of both races involved with the Myrdal project made it clear that blacks should eventually relinquish peculiarities in their culture that were deemed unassimilable or undesirable by whites. But the unintended consequence of such depictions of black culture was a perception that blacks did not really possess a culture or history of their own. Increasingly, as blacks moved to the urban North in greater numbers, there was a tendency on the part of social scientists to view their culture as if it had merely sprung from an oppressive past or, in the case of the rural South, as a gradually accreted pastiche of maladjusted practices that hindered their ability to make it outside the segregated black world. Hence, Myrdal's *American Dilemma* declared that black culture was "a distorted development, or a pathological condition, of the general American culture."[2]

The rejection of innate religiosity was not easily replaced with an alternative explanation of African American religion. Denial of a distinctly racial temperament or an innate racial character could at times appear to be tantamount to the claim that blacks could not create a distinctive and viable culture in the face of oppression and racial discrimination. Commonly, the assertion that black culture was a dysfunctional imitation or debased variation of white culture denied the agency and creativity of blacks. By the late 1960s, the affirmation of black "soul" and the hesitance and in some cases the rejection of the need or value of black integration into the broader culture provoked a serious rethinking of black culture. Within this context a major reconsideration of the culture and the meaning of religion for oppressed peoples led to the production in the late 1960s and early 1970s of the most fruitful outpouring of works on virtually every aspect of the black experience, especially black religion.

The End of Naturally Religious Blacks

In 1940, in an essay prepared for the Carnegie-Myrdal project, Margaret Brenman, a psychologist at Columbia University, observed, "Long observations and conscientious study of the Negro group have made it impossible for us to feel any fundamental validity in the stereotyped 'white defensive belief' . . . in the inherent religiosity or primitive emotionality of the Negro."[3] Brenman's essay dealt with questions about whether race differences were real and the basis of variant cultural expression in black and white communities. She was particularly struck by what she saw as the "greater role of religious feeling in the individual personality of the middle-class Negro girl than in a comparable White girl." She noted that religious feeling was important to black females even separate from church activity. She observed that the only comparable instance of such deep religiosity was that of white Catholics. Ultimately, after delicately offering her conclusions "at the risk of being misunderstood," Brenman tentatively arrived at the position that a "defensive adaptation in an insecure minority group" of middle-class black females was responsible for the religious differences that she observed in her two control groups (fifty black and white women of a similar socioeconomic status). Black women exhibited symptoms of "greater psychological insecurity," and thus their need for religion was stronger because they had to cope with the stresses and hardships of an oppressed minority group.[4]

Two important issues stand out in Brenman's study as significant for the approach of social scientists to African American religion in the 1940s to the 1960s. First, she and others felt that "the Negro church" would decline in importance as the economic, social, and psychical "handicaps" of blacks were gradually removed. This notion of the disappearance of the "psychic function" of black religion was a local variant of a theory of secularization: As blacks climbed the socioeconomic ladder, religion would no longer be necessary.

Religion was seen as secondary to or derivative of more fundamental issues, such as economic hardships, social deprivation, and psychological maladjustment. Second, a corollary to the claim about the putative future disappearance of black religion was the belief that African American culture, in part because of racial discrimination and segregation, was a pathological subculture that would or should be radically altered to promote rapid assimilation into the mainstream white culture. Religion was generally viewed as a psychological device or mechanism that enabled blacks to deal with their painful condition of subordination. In this regard, it was rarely seen as a healthy orientation to living or a fundamental aspect of their culture. Innate religiosity as a biological and therefore abiding expression of the African temperament had given way to the "Negro Church," a temporary institutional response that mostly impeded the progress of the race, but one that at least allowed a degree of psychic sustenance until better economic and social conditions prevailed.[5]

Although by the 1940s most black and white social scientists rejected the notion of a racial temperament and the argument that blacks possessed special or innate religious qualities, there was at least one influential, dissenting voice. As Walter Jackson notes, Melville Herskovits's views in his *Myth of the Negro Past* (1941) ran counter to the prevailing consensus in American social science of the 1930s to the 1960s. Herskovits studied anthropology at Columbia University, focusing on East African pastoralism. By the time his book was written, from his post at Northwestern University, he was seeking to develop Afro-American studies nationally as an interdisciplinary field. As a highly qualified anthropologist who had done fieldwork in Africa and was trained as a specialist in African studies, his views could not be easily ignored.[6]

Herskovits was not convinced by the common assertion, reaching back at least to the 1930s, most prominently in the work of Benjamin Mays, that the religious practices of black Americans had developed as "compensatory devices to meet the social and economic frustration experienced by Negroes during slavery and after emancipation."[7] He argued that these were at best only partial explanations that illuminated "various phases of Negro secular life." It is necessary to quote him at length to give a clear sense of his thesis.

> For underlying the life of the American Negro is a deep religious bent that is but the manifestation here of the similar drive that, everywhere in Negro societies, makes the supernatural a major focus of interest. The tenability of this position is apparent when it is considered how, in an age marked by skepticism, the Negro has held fast to belief. Religion is vital, meaningful, and understandable to the Negroes of this country because, as in the West Indies and West

Africa, it is not removed from life, but has been deeply integrated into the daily round. It is because of this, indeed, that everywhere compensation in terms of the supernatural is so immediately acceptable to this underprivileged folk—and causes them, in contrast to other underprivileged groups elsewhere in the world, to turn to religion rather than political action or outlets for their frustration.[8]

Several important points are to be noted here. First, in the end, Herskovits seemed to agree that religion was a compensation for economic deprivation, but he refused to understand religion as *simply* an epiphenomenon of broader social and economic forces. Rather, he located most elements of African American religion in an African past. Second, his claims were extremely broad. The use of such phrases as "everywhere in Negro societies" and "Negroes of this country" in addition to those of the West Indies and West Africa assumed a uniformity that was rooted in a racial or African lineage, which was what drew the greatest criticism from other social scientists. Such sweeping assertions invited critical scrutiny and controversy, even if Herskovits later tried to give a more nuanced rendering of his central claims.[9] Finally, Herskovits mixed terms such as a "bent" toward certain actions (implying a biological predisposition) and "turning to" various religious practices (as a semi-conscious choice in the face of options) without any clear delineation in this case of precisely how he differentiated race and culture.

At first glance, Herskovits's claim that African Americans possessed a religious bent seemed very similar to the arguments that had been used by many other whites who had long claimed that blacks were naturally religious or that the African lived in an imaginative world of spirits, gods, and demons. Myrdal, a chief critic of Herskovits's postulation of African cultural retentions among American blacks, raised this very point. Myrdal was astutely aware of the protean nature of assertions of an African heritage in black culture in the United States. He argued that a "long line of writers" had regarded African heritage as a sign of blacks' lack of capacity for higher civilization. These writers and social scientists usually pointed to alleged amorality, criminality, lack of ability for organized social life, and little talent for inventiveness as a product of their Africanness. As Myrdal wrote, "It was a basic means of satisfying white men's needs to justify slavery and white superiority that the 'dark continent' be regarded as a place of cultureless savagery."[10] So why should anyone want to link contemporary American blacks to a shameful legacy? Because Herskovits and others were among the "modern school of anthropologists and historians," Myrdal noted, who tried to demonstrate that "peculiarities" in black music, art, religion, dance, and family structure were products of highly developed African societies with a rich and varied history. They extolled the contributions of blacks, thus reversing the association of an African heritage with cultural degradation and primitivism.[11]

African American anthropologist and folklorist Arthur Huff Fauset was one of the first social scientists to make the connection between Herskovits's claims about an African heritage and the long history of arguments about the innate religiosity of blacks. Fauset had spent years collecting black folklore in the South. In 1939, he began a research project on urban black religious movements in Philadelphia, later published as his *Black Gods of the Metropolis*. He observed: "The religiosity of the Negro is often taken for granted. Not only is this a popular opinion, but important social scientists intimate and even emphasize this fact."[12] Fauset was particularly concerned about the implications of Robert E. Park's and Herskovits's respective writings about a "racial temperament" and a "religious bent," namely, that the "inference to be drawn from such opinions is that there is something in the Negro amounting almost to an inner compulsion which drives him into religious channels."[13] He felt compelled to note that "to the extent that Parks' [sic] suggestion of 'temperament' and Herskovits' analogous use of the term 'bent' imply an almost instinctive participation by American Negroes in religious pursuits, these options need to be received with considerable caution."[14] Fauset was determined to challenge this notion of black innate religiosity.

Fauset cited Benjamin Mays and Joseph Nicholson's *The Negro's Church* (1933) to support his claim that there was nothing inherently religious about blacks. It bears repeating that Mays and Nicholson pointed to economic deprivation of the black masses and their turn to religion as a compensatory mechanism to seek the symbolic and spiritual goods that another world offered as a substitute for the material and psychological goods that they lacked in this life. They sought to demonstrate that blacks' religious ideas grew out of their social and economic situation and were not rooted in primitive or innate religiosity. *The Negro's Church* became a standard point of reference in ensuing debates about African American religion. This line of argument brought Fauset back to an affirmation of what Herskovits denied: that compensation could be taken as a sufficient explanation of blacks' turn to religion. He noted that the proportion of white men attending church was higher than that of black men, additional evidence that blacks were not naturally religious, for which again he cited Mays and Nicholson's text.[15] Fauset expressed exasperation that in spite of statistics that indicated higher white male church membership, "the opinion of the universality of religious attitudes among Negroes, as contrasted to whites, persists."[16] Of course, he realized that church membership was not the only measure of religiosity. Although some blacks who left "orthodox evangelical churches" joined the religious cults of the North, thus exchanging one form of religious practice for another, he conjectured that there were some who left the churches *and* dropped their beliefs altogether. In the end, Fauset maintained that we cannot expect all blacks to give up religion because few people of any culture become atheists.[17]

Fauset was left with the task of explaining why churches and religion were important to so many blacks because he argued that "there can be no doubt, of course, that the church, and consequently to a degree religion, have played conspicuous roles in the lives of a vast majority of American Negroes, today and in the past."[18] He argued that black religion did not develop because of some inexorable law peculiar to the nature of blacks or because of an inner drive that constrained them, as Herskovits argued, "to turn to religion rather than to political action or other outlets" for their frustration. Fauset turned to his own work among black sects in the urban North to prove that such "nationalist cults" as the black Jews and the Moorish Science Temple of America were not strictly religious alternatives to political action. Such "nationalist cults" were demonstrable proof for him that for a group to aspire for political action, the requisite concepts must be in place. "Stated in political terms," Fauset explained, "in order for a people to act politically there must be political concepts, and these concepts must be made concrete by means of a political organ or organism, such as a political organization (party) or a political identity (nation)."[19] In the struggle for a national identity, a national homeland, or national unity, as understood by nationalist groups he studied, he found evidence that at least some blacks were not choosing religion as an *alternative* to political and other outlets.[20]

Fauset acknowledged that these black nationalist groups were religious, but he contended that they were "compelled by the logic of their thinking to emphasize the political aspect of their life in America, even though essentially they are a religious group."[21] Because of historical factors, such as the "transfer of the Negro people from Africa to America, and possibly because of the infiltration of blood from practically all the other groups in America into the veins" of black Americans, blacks had developed a "corresponding confusion of national emphases" and only recently were developing a consciousness of "national roots" as other groups in America had like the Germans, Poles, and Irish. The black masses, Fauset continued, historically lacked strong political convictions because they had no sense of a homeland, having been spiritually and physically uprooted from Africa and therefore unable to identify it as their "national homeland," and feeling no conviction that racially oppressive America was their home. But with the growth of the National Association for the Advancement of Colored People (NAACP), the National Negro Congress,

Marcus Garvey's movement, and other such organizations for the uplift and common interests of blacks, he argued, blacks were slowly developing a "national consciousness" and claiming America as their homeland.[22]

Because of this growing national consciousness, Fauset observed, blacks were becoming more politically active, and a sense of national pride was emerging. He noted that Mays and Nicholson found in *The Negro's Church* that as the proportion of "orthodox" black churchgoers declined, there was an increase in the proportion of blacks entering trade unions and organizing consumer cooperatives, economic boycotts, and protest organizations. Fauset insisted, "This latter trend is no more the result of 'temperament' or 'bent' than is the association with religious attitudes which scholars often ascribe to the Negro. Clearly it signifies that because of the exigencies of the times, affecting not only the Negro but the entire nation, the need for wholesale political action is being felt and understood among the masses."[23] He believed that a mechanism of action would logically follow this development. For this reason, he argued that it was only "natural for such a mechanism to utilize the religious organization as one means of bringing about the desired end." This was an adaptation of a religious institution, the church, for various nonreligious needs because of the particular historical role that the church had been required to play in blacks' lives, Fauset asserted. Historical exigency and broader cultural, political, and economic trends, he concluded, more adequately explained the place of religion and the church in the lives of African Americans than Park's claim of a religious or racial temperament or Herskovits's positing of a religious bent.[24]

Furthermore, Fauset noted that urbanization was the crucible that led to the most important transformation of black religion. "With the migration of the Negroes from the rural South to urban centers," he wrote,

> a transformation in the basic religious life and attitudes also is observable. The church, once a *sine qua non* of institutional life among American Negroes, does not escape the critical inquiry of the newer generations, who implicitly and sometimes very explicitly are requiring pragmatic sanctions if they are to be included among churchgoers, or if indeed they are to give any consideration at all to religious practices and beliefs.[25]

Thus for Fauset and many other social scientists, social scientific assertions of innate religiosity could not be sustained based on the evidence from black urbanization. It was now through the lens of urbanization that the Negro Church would acquire its salience even as its presence and influence were thought to be diminishing.

Throughout the 1940s, as the emphasis of social scientific studies moved from a rejection of black innate religiosity to the nature and role of the Negro Church, increasing attention was paid to the effects of urbanization. Though a number of studies had explored the dynamics of urbanization in black life during the Great Migration after 1914, a new spate of studies in the 1940s was preoccupied with whether urbanization would lead to the secularization of black America. Indeed, social scientists increasingly welcomed secularization to the extent that it meant a repudiation of notions of black primitivism, blacks' alleged inability to make it in a modern industrial world, and an affirmation of black assimilation into American culture. Secularization, though ambiguously and variously defined by these social scientists, signified modernity and thus blacks' ultimate arrival and assimilation into the heart of America's main-stream white culture. In 1944, Thelma Ackiss at Houston College for Negroes, wrote, "No other conclusion about the Negro in America has been so taken for granted as that concerning the innately religious character of his tempera-ment." She continued, "Great credence has been given to the belief that Ne-groes are 'naturally' inclined toward religion; and frequently the cultural possibilities of the race have been evaluated from premises based on this pre-cise belief."[26] Here was the political and cultural force of claims of innate religiosity. These claims were inextricably linked to the place of blacks in the nation, as Ackiss contended, and the putative inability of blacks and whites to live as equals in America. She observed, "The idea has developed that there is some mystical and 'different' quality about the religion of the Negro, due in part to his inherent emotionalism and otherwise to the fact that he is of a childlike, credulous disposition. Ergo, the Negro is unsuitable for complete integration into the general society."[27] Ackiss offered an alternative explanation to this understanding of black religion.

With the rejection of the notion of blacks as naturally religious, two im-portant questions demanded an answer. First, compared to whites, why did religion generally, or the Negro Church in particular, play such a prominent role in the lives of blacks? Second, how could black religion or the Negro Church be used to improve the social, economic, and political condition of blacks? Though Ackiss left it to others to deal with the second question, she provided three responses to the first: (1) Religion was an "outstanding social value" of the total cultural pattern of blacks in America; (2) religion was a compensation for the dearth of black opportunities in other phases of the broader society; (3) the emotional release offered by the black churches averted aggression against white supremacy into relatively "safer" channels. Black re-ligion then, for Ackiss, was a "striking element in the acculturation process of the Negro and has played no minor role in his accommodation to the biracial societal structure."[28] Historical exigencies and social function were then adequate explanations for the role of religion in black culture.

Ackiss was interested in the changing patterns of church attendance and opinions about religion and church membership among blacks in Houston, Texas. In her analysis of 100 black students between ages seventeen and forty at Houston College for Negroes, she found that "religion" was minimized in favor of the "church" as a social institution.[29] "Religion," in her view, meant beliefs about black Christianity and religious practices as a "panacea" for present problems and trials. Religion was associated with older blacks for whom it involved something "personal" and "intimate" in their understanding of God and conversion.[30] Especially for black women, however, Ackiss argued, "church" was now a "badge" of respectability and conventionality, which she regarded as "supported and motivated by the national climate of opinion on the 'respectability' of 'belonging to church.' "[31] Because of the "matriarchal quality" of the black family, she wrote, black mothers found social contact and respect in the churches. However, church affiliation for blacks in general signified, Ackiss averred, a means of improving one's social or community status. "Respectability" or "belonging to the church" was therefore acquiring greater salience in these black communities because of the churches' traditional association with education, interracial goodwill, and "Negro uplift."[32] Hence, for Ackiss, black churches were functional institutions that changed over time and varied in regard to the specific niche they filled in the black community.

Although Ackiss gave little attention to the emotional release that she claimed was offered by black churches, this function of theirs had a long history of explanations by critics of black churches and in the social scientific literature. In 1928, George Gordon, a black journalist from Boston, chastised blacks for their alleged meekness and religiosity. He was particularly critical of Christianity because it "made the Negro meek when he should be proud." Gordon could not countenance a religion for blacks that "lays emphasis upon [a] future life to the neglect and detriment of [this] present life in a hard-fisted, uncompromising, cunning, and militant world." He proposed that a commission be convened to study world religions for the purpose of culling principles from each of them that would suit the situation of blacks in America. So he hoped that from Islam blacks would "take a spirit of militancy"; in Confucianism he found material for "the abolishment of fear of the hereafter and renunciation of the idea of heaven"; in Judaism, he discerned "the righteousness of retaliation" that blacks desperately needed.[33] For Gordon, blacks represented all of the stereotypes that were invested in the suffering Uncle Tom. For him, this was the ultimate tragedy.

The criticism of black religion and black churches by Marxists, socialists, and other disaffected black leaders was rather standard fare by the late 1920s (as noted in chapter 5). But the specific argument that blacks possessed a docile, nonaggressive temperament, and that this temperament figured into their adherence to Christianity, was a particularly troublesome claim because it suggested that blacks were complicit in their own enslavement. By accepting Christianity and having a forgiving spirit toward whites, they had in some sense, or so it was feared, granted legitimacy to their condition of oppression in America. Their acceptance of Christianity, for critics like Gordon, was as genuine as it could be and was the major impediment to their liberation from white oppression.

The attention paid to black aggression or docility was not limited to critics of black Christianity. When social scientists in the 1930s began to pay close attention to the effects of segregation on blacks' personality, they were drawn to the problem of aggression within black communities. It had been a well-known fact that white Southern authorities rarely punished blacks for crimes against each other. Many social scientists felt that this double standard of swift and vicious punishment of blacks for any alleged crime against whites, while turning a blind eye to crime within the black community, encouraged black-on-black crime. The turn to studies of black aggression sought to understand how various social structures and institutions helped blacks to deal with their displaced anger, which meant that the anger blacks had toward one another was really sublimated anger whose original object was whites.[34]

In this evolving context, social scientists saw the black churches as a medium of catharsis, providing space where their aggression could be released in the emotional worship of their churches. These studies seemed to confirm what critics had suggested: that black churches focused on another world instead of this world, thus taking their attention away from the very real problems of their day-to-day lives. Such studies also indicated that churches helped blacks defuse their anger or displace it rather than direct it toward whites and their oppressed condition (as the critics thought they should). The churches became mechanisms of internal constraint, enabling blacks to channel their anger inward, hiding it safely from the white world (at least for most of the time). In 1931, R. A. Billings, professor of psychiatry at Howard University, claimed that among lower-class blacks in a "House of Prayer" church in Washington, D.C., insistent professions of love "for everybody in the world" testified to "the hate in their unconscious minds."[35] This hatred was so "strong as to be pushing or bubbling over into the consciousness" of blacks, he contended, "and the forces of repression" were so great that blacks were being compelled to declare their love for everyone, even though inwardly they envied and feared those who mistreated them.[36] He interpreted such calls for church members to love others as an attempt to mask the "devastating waves of hatred [which] are escaped by compensatory mechanisms of great love."[37] There seemed to be no limits to the power of psychoanalysis to provide such clear and unambiguous insights into the human psyche. (One wonders if Billings, based on the premises of his analysis of black religion, would have labeled an act of violence a form of love for the one injured!)

Similarly, white anthropologist Hortense Powdermaker in her *After Freedom* (1939), which was a study of black life in Indianola, Mississippi, noticed a great emphasis on the Christian virtue of brotherly love in black churches. Powdermaker heard from the black pulpit frequent admonitions to church members to love others. She interpreted this emphasis on love as a valiant attempt "to vanquish bitterness in their hearts."[38] White social psychologist John Dollard's study of blacks in Indianola in 1937 anticipated Powdermaker's observations. He argued that because open resistance to the South's racial mores was futile, blacks had to engage in various forms of accommodation to their subordinate status and went beyond or outside the churches in their attempts to deal with the harsh conditions imposed on them. Dollard believed that blacks resorted to magic to help them accept the status quo. He defined magical practices as lagging cultural practices or "forms of action in reference to current social life." Magic, he asserted, accepted the status quo and took the place of political action, agitation, solidarity, organization, or any "real moves to change" blacks' status. Though magic was harmless from the standpoint of the caste system, it held great private value for its practitioners and granted them psychological satisfaction. Magical practices, Dollard averred, absorbed some of the discontent that would otherwise have been directed at the racial caste system in the South.[39] Through fetishes, amulets, and practices associated with lucky and unlucky days, some blacks hoped to gratify a wish for love, revenge, or power. Psychic health was, in Dollard's view, gained even as the means to achieve it supported accommodation to an overbearing and oppressive system of white supremacy.[40]

By World War II, social scientists had begun to argue that the newly evident anger and impatience of blacks testified to a decline in the emotionalism of the older forms of worship. The decline of the influence of the church was thought to be linked to increasing dissatisfaction with the status quo and a greater likelihood of protesting against segregation and political oppression. Myrdal theorized that "emotionalism in religion" was "well suited" to deflect blacks' attention away from their degradation and frustration. He conjectured that the "growing resentment and caustic bitterness" of blacks in the early 1940s were probably linked to a "decline in emotionalism in religion."[41]

In a widely cited article written in 1943, Powdermaker offered an intriguing theory about the growing trend of black aggressive behavior. She argued that Christianity was central to the production of feelings of guilt about black hostility and aggression toward whites during and after slavery. Christianity had served as a force in sublimating black aggression, and was a major factor underlying the behavior of the docile and meek Negro. She wrote:

> Our hypothesis is that the meek, unaggressive Negro, who persists today as a type and whom we have opportunity to study, feels guilty about his conscious and unconscious feelings of hostility and aggression toward white people. These Negroes are believing Christians who have taken very literally the Christian doctrine that it is sinful to hate. Yet on every hand they are faced with situations which must inevitably produce hatred in any normal human being. These situations run the scale from seeing an innocent person lynched to having to accept the inferior accommodations on a Jim Crow train. The feeling of sin and guilt is frequently and openly expressed. In a Sunday-school class in a Southern rural colored church a teacher tells the tale of a sharecropper who had worked all season for a white planter, only to be cheated out of half his earnings. The teacher's lesson is that it is wrong to hate this planter, because Christ told us to love our enemies. The members of the class say how hard it is not to hate but that since it is sin they will change their hate to love. They regard this as possible, though difficult.[42]

Powdermaker found that this masochistic "good nigger" type (her words) who was able privately to entertain fantasies of moral superiority over whites was declining in number. A decline in religious faith among black youth led them "to refuse to assume the unaggressive role." No longer possessed with a vivid sense of the future life as their parents, they were more easily hurt by slights and insults from whites ("because they do not [any longer] put their faith in the promise of heavenly victory").[43] With a rise in educational levels, urbanization in the South and the North, and a lessening of "emphasis on the rewards of heaven," blacks were gradually attaining their goals "through the competition and aggressive struggle so characteristic of our culture rather than through meekness and subservience."[44] A broad "social insecurity" among blacks and whites made room for greater dissatisfaction among blacks with the old way of reacting to their plight. As Powdermaker noted, "When the cultural process takes away rewards for a certain type of behavior, dissatisfaction with that behavior appears and there is a gradual change to another form which is more likely to bring new compensations."[45]

So for Powdermaker, Ackiss, and other social scientists, the importance of black churches as outlets for black aggression was declining and other institutions were taking the place that churches formerly occupied. Escape, compensation, repression, and various other explanations of the role and significance of religion in black life were gradually making the older framework of innate religiosity obsolete. Yet as religion was increasingly seen as adaptable and subject to historical exigencies and vicissitudes rather than an innate quality or expression of black life, attempts to address the question of how to use the Negro Church to improve blacks' conditions proliferated. Especially for black social scientists, there was an attempt to clear away any obstacles that would hinder black integration into the broader society, so traditional images of innate religiosity had to be supplanted. It was hoped that the Negro Church could be shaped and reformed to improve the conditions of black life because it still held the allegiance of the masses of blacks. Until it passed away, it would have to be harnessed for social, economic, and political purposes.

Debating the Nature and Role of the Negro Church

Even as claims about the natural religiosity of blacks had become increasingly unpopular among social scientists during the 1930s, the debate about the nature and role of "the Negro Church" assumed greater prominence. This discussion was occurring even as sociologists and anthropologists continued to assert that black churches would relinquish their centrality within the black community as more opportunities became available to more blacks as a result of the attack on segregation and racial discrimination. The pressing demands for assimilation, economic empowerment, and the renunciation of "peculiar" black cultural practices placed added scrutiny on the Negro Church. By the late 1920s and into the 1930s, newspaper articles appeared throughout the black community, North and South, on varied topics such as overchurching and the loss of religion among blacks. In February 1930 the *Baltimore Afro-American*'s headline asked, "Are there too many churches?" The article reported that there was an average of 122 black members for every church building compared to 261 white members. The writer declared that the economic drain of black churches was just too much to bear.[46]

Just two years later, irascible black journalist George Schuyler provoked a furor when he wrote his inflammatory article, "Black America Begins to Doubt," in H. L. Mencken's *American Mercury* magazine. Schuyler argued that blacks were doubting religion because of the heavy financial burden of maintaining the churches; the ignorance of black ministers and the growing intelligence of lay members; the immorality of ministers, their lust for wealth and power, and their lack of interest in business and politics; and the growing consciousness of lay members of the un-Christian attitude of whites, who still demanded a separate white and black church. Although critics may have disagreed with Schuyler's findings, in their attempts to refute his assertions they confirmed his claims that blacks were drifting away from the churches and falling prey to the vices of the cities. Reverend B. B. Evans, pastor of the First United Presbyterian Church in Norfolk, Virginia, denied that the church was to blame entirely for the "increased illegitimacy found in the race today," but he conceded that the "trend of the age, with its questionable and often immorally suggestive movies, its pornographic literature, the automobile, the shifting of large numbers of green country girls into the segregated sections of our cities, with their poorly lighted streets, their bad and overcrowded houses, and with everything conducive of filth" was posing a massive challenge to the church's position in the black community.[47] These pressing problems, all agreed, required drastic solutions.

Recall Milton Sernett's argument that the Great Migration instigated a greater preoccupation with churches as means to ends other than those of "offering members spiritual refreshment and a place to worship." The instrumentalists, as Sernett calls these black leaders, based primarily in the North, were interested in urban churches, and some of these thinkers were deeply influenced by the Social Gospel movement.[48] The rise of social scientists, particularly black ones, as the principal interpreters of African American religion in the 1930s also had profound consequences for conceptualizations of the Negro Church and discussions about the role of religion in the lives of blacks. Within the context of the suffering and economic hardship of the Great Depression, the social science race relations experts, black and white, became the principal "voices" of black Americans. They conducted detailed studies of every aspect of the Negro problem. Black family life, churches, economics, and a host of other issues were examined in an attempt to get to the roots of the pressing problems within the black community. Increasing pressure on the black churches to "perform" and do something about the economic and social plight of blacks was one primary result of these developments.

Although the Great Migration propelled instrumentalist conceptions of churches to the fore in the 1920s, it was not until the 1930s and 1940s that the major sociological and anthropological studies (by blacks and whites) of black culture and life appeared. Owing in part to the federal government's Works Progress Administration and other projects that provided jobs for black writers and artists and gave detailed studies of black life, interpretations of black religion became more nuanced *and* more focused on using churches to address social and political issues. Precisely how to harness the energy of this institution called the Negro Church, which held the allegiance and attention of more black people than any comparable institution, for economic and political purposes became the pressing question for those who wrote about black religion.

Carter G. Woodson, a leading black historian based in Washington, D.C., appealed to black churches to change their old ways in ever more strident terms. In a series of communiqués to the Associated Negro Press in 1931, he lambasted the churches for their failings. In the first of a series of articles for the black weekly *New York Age*, he called for a "United Negro Church." The historical background to Woodson's screed against the churches was particularly relevant because the cry against overchurching was related to the desire for a strong unifying economic and political center for blacks. As Barbara Savage notes, the idea of a unified body of black churches across denominations had been advanced in the 1920s by Richard R. Wright Jr. of the African Methodist Episcopal Church and editor of the journal *Christian Recorder*.[49] In November 1925, Kelly Miller, a sociologist at Howard University and a popular essayist, looked longingly forward to a conference that would be held in Washington, D.C., in December of the same year. This conference led to the formation of the Federated Colored Catholics (FCC) under the leadership of Miller's former colleague Thomas Wyatt Turner, who taught at Hampton Institute. The FCC's avowed purpose was to "weld all others [black Catholics] into a solid unit for race betterment."[50] Although Catholics were making slow progress bringing blacks into the church, Miller held out hopes that more blacks would consider the Catholic Church. He argued that the "Negro in America represents an inherently weak group which needs to attach itself to some great body which has the power and disposition to protect and defend him."[51] Conjuring romantic visions of the Catholic Church's "excellent" record on race relations and its alleged unity over against Protestants' mistreatment of "lower races" and their constant divisions, Miller wrote that perhaps Catholicism would do a better job of uniting and advancing blacks than Protestants had done.[52]

Woodson was deeply disappointed at what he saw as the black churches' failure to unite and pool their resources. Woodson was not an ecumenist interested in discussions about unity in the "body of Christ"; he was a hard-nosed churchgoing "outsider" who was disgusted at pointless doctrinal differences, meaningless denominational feuds, and the "spectacle" of black churches taking up the "religious disputes of the whites." He angrily wrote that because most blacks were Protestants, they should put aside their minor theological differences and unite for the sake of the greater good of the larger black community. "These two large groups [Methodists and Baptists] are very much alike," Woodson proclaimed, "and they should forget the mischievous doctrinal differences taught them by ignorant white men and come together with one Lord, one faith, and say nothing about baptism." He was puzzled at what appeared to him a conundrum: the relative lack of attention to doctrine among black preachers and leaders and the constant divisions in their churches apparently based on doctrines and denominational distinctions. Although he acknowledged that there were problems of class and geography that partially accounted for divisions among black churches, Woodson did not pay much attention to these factors. His desire for a "United Negro Church" was so fervent and his dislike of disunion within "an already weak people" so fierce that he offered his proposals with overpowering urgency.[53]

Woodson noted that a friend attempted to discredit him because he was not a theologian. Woodson argued that it was a "high compliment" not to be labeled a theologian. He blamed theology for confusing people with useless disputes, stimulating divisions, and diverting the church's attention away from its function "as a Christian agency for the uplift of all men." He proclaimed that the "world would be wonderfully blessed if the theologians were silenced and schools of theology were closed." Instead, the black churches needed "schools of Christian ethics conducted by teachers of the Golden Rule," not "medieval dogma" that had little relevance to the real world. His ire against the theologians included the "brawling pulpit orator" and the "preacher who is riding around in a Cadillac car to visit the sisters when their husbands are at work." With this broad definition of "theologian," Woodson could denounce whatever he thought detracted from his vision of an ethical, socially progressive Negro Church.[54]

Woodson was just one of many other black leaders who wished to "use" the Negro churches as means to various ends. As professor of creative literature at Fisk University, James Weldon Johnson wrote a pamphlet, *Negro Americans, What Now?* (1934), that listed "the Negro Church" as one of the "forces and resources" of African Americans. He asserted that it could become "the most effective medium we possess," if it underwent "some special reforms," including stamping out "bootleggers of religion" (that is, immoral pastors), abolishing "hypnotic religion" that ignored the problems of this life and preached "obsolete doctrine," putting an end to raising money for "fine edifices," and ceasing the "needless multiplication of congregations."[55] Johnson was particularly frustrated with the multiplication of churches. "One church might be made into an agency that would improve their industrial, social, and civic status, as well as their spiritual state," he counseled. "Five churches [as he observed in a Northern city] do not multiply, they nullify whatever strength and effectiveness the one church might have."[56]

In his *Black Manhattan* (1930), Johnson had enumerated common complaints against black churches: Churches and their operation cost blacks too much, blacks had too many churches, and church buildings were too ostentatious and too expensive. Johnson complained that in 1930 Harlem had 160 black churches and that of these 100 should be closed, leaving only a "sufficient number to supply the religious needs of blacks." He agreed with the claim that the multiplicity of churches in Harlem and other black communities was "accounted for by the innate and deep religious emotion of the race," but he added that because churches provided entertainment and met social needs, blacks flocked to them.[57] By 1934, however, Johnson was not interested in this argument about innate religious emotions but was dismayed at how "over-churching" had produced an inefficient misuse of the black community's limited resources. He proposed that black churches adopt the ecclesiastical model of the Catholic Church as a "grand example of the conservation of power" to carry out a process of consolidation and abolishment of unnecessary churches.[58] It was imperative that the Negro Church conserve the finite resources of an impoverished people. Because the Negro Church remained the most powerful agency that blacks commanded "for moving forward the race as a mass," Johnson wrote, then it was "not too much to call upon the church to meet the exigency as it met the situation confronting it in slavery days and in the post–Civil War period."[59] The Negro Church was to be a product of social engineering just as any other institution and perhaps more so because of the number of black members who could be reached through it.

Johnson asserted that "outside" criticism of the Negro Church would not go very far in changing it. He hoped that reform would come from within and that there would "rise up out of the element of the colored clergy which realizes the potentialities of a modern Negro Church a man with sufficient wisdom and power to bring about a new Reformation."[60] In the meantime, he counseled the Negro Church to live up to more fully the "responsibilities and opportunities which it has over and above those of the churches of other groups," to get rid of its "moss-back theology" and "obsolete dogmatics," and to provide a larger return for the "millions of dollars the Negro masses pour into its coffers."[61] The Negro Church must cease its "terrific fulminations against dancing, theater-going, and card-playing" and instead focus its attention on educating the black masses about the "economic factors involved in the condition of the race."[62] Black church members, Johnson proclaimed, had every right to demand changes in the church to ensure that it was using their resources wisely.

As the Depression deepened and the condition of blacks grew worse, more specific programs for reforming churches were advanced by leaders. After a breakfast meeting following an address to a conference at Howard University in late April 1935, W. E. B. Du Bois had agreed to become the contributor to the Bronze Booklets, a series of small volumes to be edited by Alain Locke, then professor of philosophy at Howard. The Bronze Booklets were published by the Associates in Negro Folk Education (ANFE), a new organization that was supposed to take a fresh look at race relations in America. The ANFE was created by the American Association for Adult Education (AAAE), a ten-year-old organization that was founded by the Carnegie Corporation.[63] Locke assured Du Bois that the booklets would be a platform for "bold ideas." After receiving it, Locke was troubled by Du Bois's booklet "The Negro and Social Reconstruction," rightly fearing that it was not what the AAAE wanted. Locke hesitated to make his feelings known until Du Bois had sailed to Europe and Asia in the spring of 1936.[64] In November 1936, Locke sent Du Bois notice that the board of the ANFE had voted to decline the manuscript "largely because of its frequent references to specific situations of public program and policy."[65] Du Bois's ideas about economic justice and workers' control of the means of production were too radical. He later wrote that he wanted to put "into permanent form that economic program of the Negro which I believed should succeed, and implement the long fight for political and civil rights and social equality which it was my privilege for a quarter of a century to champion."[66] "The Negro and Social Reconstruction," Du Bois asserted, was a preliminary step toward accomplishing these goals.

Du Bois's views on the Negro Church reflected the almost desperate search for solutions to the plight of blacks during the throes of the Depression years. He had come to the conclusion that blacks had to rely on themselves because white prejudice was more intransigent than he had once believed. He proposed that blacks along "economic lines, just as in literature and religion" carefully plan and organize the nature of their segregation because it "would remain for many years."[67] In the midst of his analysis of how various black organizations could deal with the problem of labor, Du Bois criticized black churches for their expensive buildings and outdated theology and creeds. The "Negro church needs something to do and someone to do it," he asserted. He had come a long way from his criticisms of the late nineteenth century, when he had asserted that the Negro Church should surrender its many functions to the home, schools, and other social organizations. In the context of the Depression, Du Bois wondered why it would not be "possible for the Negro church to add to its organization a business manager: a man trained in business methods, particularly in a knowledge of non-profit business methods, who had studied the work of consumers' cooperation throughout Europe and in the United States?" After all, he argued, "If the church today furnishes recreation and information to its members, there is no reason why tomorrow it should not furnish coal, food, houses, and clothes."[68]

Under Du Bois's program of social reconstruction for the Negro Church, a black pastor would become like a Reformed Jewish rabbi who was an ethical leader and "source of intellectual information for his people." A new training process for ministers would be required to produce young men of character and intelligence. Theological study would have to be radically altered. Instead of "a stressing of liturgics, homiletics, exegesis, and Hebrew," Du Bois insisted, there would be an emphasis on "economics, sociology, history, modern languages, music and art." Elimination of supernaturalism and theology from the churches would be necessary for this program to succeed, he proclaimed.[69] Miracles would be relegated to the "lore of fairy tales" and prayer would become "earnest and purposeful action." Black and white churches had to make such radical changes, otherwise they would lose their meaning in the modern world. In Du Bois's words, "The Negro church and even the white church, faces grim alternatives: either it becomes a great social organ with ethical ideals based on a reorganized economics, or it becomes a futile and mouthy excrescence on society which will always be a refuge for reaction and superstition."[70] All of this was part of his proposal for a segregated but internally vibrant black community that would engage in cooperative industrial development. Though it would be an exaggeration to say that the black churches were central to his program, they did play an important role simply because they had so many members and because any program of social reconstruction for blacks needed to take them into account. Strong dislike of theology and churches notwithstanding, Du Bois had to reckon with their continuing importance in the lives of many black Americans.[71]

The New Sociological Framework

Unlike the writings that presented and critiqued black churches in instrumentalist terms, the materials on the Negro Church in the Myrdal-Carnegie study were of a different sort. Little of the activism and programmatic statements appeared in them, though their negative assessment of what they regarded as the "accommodationist" role of black churches was readily discernible. Perhaps activist language was muted in their studies because of their desire for an objective social science and partly because of the original demands of the study. Myrdal, in the preface of the *American Dilemma*, noted how Frederick Keppel, president of Carnegie Corporation, invited him in 1937 to become director of a "comprehensive study of the Negro in the United States, to be undertaken in a wholly objective and dispassionate way as a social phenomenon."[72] The Carnegie Corporation was founded in 1911; under the leadership of Andrew Carnegie, who had made a fortune from the steel industry, the group had donated funds to black colleges and universities in the South through the network of Booker T. Washington's Tuskegee Institute. During the 1920s, under Keppel's leadership, the Carnegie Corporation realized that a new approach to the race problem was necessary to deal with the poverty, prejudice, and violence that blacks faced in the Northern cities. The corporation began seeking new ideas and new data on which to base a program of racial betterment and expressed a desire to go beyond simply handing out money annually to select black educational institutions.[73]

In 1935, Newton D. Baker, a trustee of the corporation, suggested a comprehensive, foundation-sponsored study of blacks in America. Barker argued that the corporation needed to know more about racism in America before it could spend its money with confidence that it was doing the most for blacks. After Baker's death in 1935, Keppel took a greater interest in the "Negro problem" and set out to look for an expert and well-traveled man to conduct the study. According to Walter Jackson, it was the Carnegie tradition, influenced by its founder, to seek the "exceptional man" to address pressing issues, and this tradition had some influence on the initial search for the person to direct the study. Only after receiving advice from experts and friends did Keppel decide to make this a social science research project. He concluded that black and white American social scientists had too many prejudices to write an objective study and began focusing on European countries that had no history of "imperialistic interests." After narrowing his search, Keppel chose Myrdal, a young Swedish economist, to direct the study. Myrdal's name had come up in several board meetings and through references from other foundations, such as the Rockefeller Foundation, which had funded Myrdal's visit to America in 1929–1930.[74]

After arriving in the United States in 1938, Myrdal began a two-month exploratory journey of the Southern states. After his Southern tour, he immersed himself in the writings of American social scientists on black-white relations. In 1939, he presented a memorandum to the Carnegie Corporation, indicating the plan of his research project. Myrdal took care to have a wide range of collaborators, including black scholars. Most prominent among them was a circle of young black social scientists at Howard University, notably Ralph Bunche, political scientist, and E. Franklin Frazier, sociologist. The two black authors chosen to write on black religion were Allison Davis and St. Clair Drake.[75]

Davis's "The Negro Church and Associations in the Lower South" (1940) and Drake's "The Negro Church and Associations in Chicago" (1940) were just two studies among many others conducted by social scientists that served as the raw data on which Myrdal's study was based.[76] Both Davis and Drake provided detailed analyses of black religious life and based their studies on extensive survey reports, ethnographic data, and personal conversations with religious persons. Davis and Drake were sociologists who had been influenced by W. Lloyd Warner's caste and class approach to race relations. Warner, a social anthropologist at the University of Chicago, argued that blacks and whites formed separate castes in the South and that the caste system prohibited movement between the two groups.[77]

As John Dollard, whose *Caste and Class in a Southern Town* (1937) was the most celebrated work of the caste and class school, explained, caste and class were ways of dividing people according to the behavior expected of them in a society. Caste, he argued, replaced slavery as a means of maintaining the essence of the old status quo in the South. Caste functioned to keep racial animosity at a minimum and was seen as a barrier to most forms of social contact. Caste defined, Dollard continued, a superior and inferior group and regulated the behavior of members of each group. Caste stood as an absolute barrier between consensual sexual relations between blacks and whites and rendered offspring from such encounters as "illegitimate." Caste relations in the United States, he maintained, defined blacks as "categorically inferior" and demanded special privileges for whites. Though blacks and whites could not transgress caste barriers, social classes were permeable within each group (that is, within the separate castes). Yet even the lowest class of whites derived benefits from this system of caste distinctions, and whites of all classes identified themselves over against an "inferior" caste of blacks, even if blacks had a higher economic and social standing than whites.[78]

To the extent that religion was treated in the writings of Dollard, Warner's students, and those influenced by these ideas, its role in the social system was the object of analysis. Davis and Drake, for example, were primarily interested in the "accommodating role" of black churches in the South and urban North. Economic stratification, differences among social classes within the black community, and the relationship of black churches to political, economic, and social structure were examined. On one hand, the churches provided an opportunity to study the most segregated institution of black life and were places where researchers could ascertain the values, meanings, and aspirations of blacks separate from the white world. On the other hand, these studies demonstrated the enormous diversity within black churches, especially along socioeconomic lines. Though the churches were studied as ways of getting at what blacks practiced and thought, researchers noted that one could not study any black institution without at the same time analyzing how it helped blacks come to terms with their place in a racially segregated and class-structured society.

Davis, first discussed in chapter 5, was now head of the Division of Social Studies at Dillard University in New Orleans, Louisiana, and did field work in New Orleans, Natchez, Mississippi, and smaller communities surrounding each area.[79] Other researchers gathered information from the various communities over a period ranging from eighteen months to three years. Davis had also collected information on 123 black children and adolescents in New Orleans and Natchez (which was the basis of his study *Children of Bondage* [1940], coauthored with John Dollard). What he found were ongoing efforts by black church leaders to secure the patronage of whites at concerts, church rallies, programs, and the financing of church buildings, leading him to conclude that patronage was a central part of the subordination of blacks to whites in the racial caste system of the South.[80] Davis contended that whites used this power as leverage to force blacks to comply with the segregated restrictions of the South, or "to penalize aggression against caste controls."[81]

The dogma of the childishness of the Negro, Davis asserted, was supported by the *religious dogma* of the "inherent humility, child-like faith, and other-worldiness of the Negro." This religious ideology, he noted, was the "most powerful dogma underlying the subordination of Negroes to whites." [82] White Southerners could appeal to their own religious doctrines and what they regarded as the religiously racial traits of black religion to defend the social arrangement of the South. For example, Davis noted the recent hanging of two "Negro murderers" in one of the cities he studied. All of the whites he interviewed, including the sheriff, the judge, and the executioner, emphasized the "spiritual and other-worldly attitude" with which black prisoners (in their view) met their execution. The mayor of the city said of the Negro who prayed and "got religion" before his execution: "I saw one [Negro] hung that walked out singing and shouting that he was on his way to Heaven and they couldn't do anything to him as he was already on his way. Under the same conditions, a white man would probably have to be carried out, but they [Negroes] don't seem a bit afraid."[83] Davis further argued that the leaders of black churches supported the caste system of the South because of their fear of "physical terrorization," their training from childhood, and their having to rely on white benefactors for their church buildings.[84] In his review of sermons by black ministers, he found "no instance in which the Negro preacher attacked the economic and physical subordination of Negroes to whites on the plantation." Nor could he find "any instance in which a Negro minister advocated a modification of the economic system to aid the farm-tenant, the day laborer, factory worker, or small farmer."[85] In short, the central public figure in the black churches helped keep in place the caste system of black subordination to whites.

Davis contended that because the Negro Church was so constrained by the caste system, it was unable or unwilling to speak to other issues as it ought. Black ministers did not preach against illicit sexual relations between blacks, for example. Davis pointed to the "tremendously high rates of desertion and illegitimacy" that resulted in more than one-third of all black births out of wedlock in the city that he studied as evidence of the ineffectiveness of the Negro church to promote healthy sexual relationships and strong families.[86] The "ineffectivenesss of the Negro church in establishing sanctions to check the disorganization of family life among the great masses of lower class Negroes," he argued, "is largely attributable to the economic and social subordination of Negroes by whites, i.e., to caste."[87] Perhaps as a concession to "the Negro church," he acknowledged that "modes of behavior" that had developed within the black community led to family disruption (the result of slavery, segregation, and oppression) and "atypical family behavior" that was so embedded in the black community that they were "too strong for the Negro church to change."[88]

Yet Davis argued that the caste system so weakened the "sanctions of the Negro church" regarding the "aggressive behavior" of blacks toward other blacks that it did little to strengthen morals among lower-class blacks. He argued that because "white law" did not regard attacks on blacks as a serious crime, black neighborhoods often resembled battlefields where cuttings, shootings, sexual fights, and murders were common. Black preachers could therefore do little to prevent or hinder such aggressive behavior, so the black churches' influence was critically undermined by the arrangement of the racial caste system that devalued black life and promoted aggression against other blacks.[89]

As for the importance of the Negro Church within the black community, Davis had no interest in the older arguments about a racial temperament. He contended that with the lack of organization within the black community, most prominently in the disorganization of the family, and the exclusion of blacks from participation in most structures of society, the relative importance of the church increased. Churches provided opportunities for aggressive blacks to achieve "dominance and prestige" because they were excluded from participation or "roles of dominance" in most structures of the broader society, but churches also allowed the "average Negro" to participate in a "highly evaluated social organization." The Negro Church served as an "escape for its members from the caste role of subservience" and its various rituals, from baptism to the funeral ceremony, offered "each member a chance for social aggrandizement and personal dramatization."[90] Black churches also supplied a safer place to sublimate various forms of aggression by expending "fervor, competition, and intense activity" within the confines of the church. However, Davis regarded this intense competition for status and power within the churches as only partially successful in sublimating black anger because blacks often took out their anger on one another.[91]

A striking example of white images of black religion was provided in Davis's analysis of a religious pageant in song, "Heaven Is My Home," which was presented in the leading black church each year in the city he studied. The pageant was sponsored by the all-white Garden Club and portrayed the part that blacks played in the Old South. Though presented in a black church, whose members were chiefly upper and middle class, the position of the lower classes and that of the former slave was emphasized. It was presented to black and white audiences separately on different nights (it appears that its first presentation was in 1934). This plantation vision of blacks was apparently so popular among white audiences that the income garnered was quite good and allowed blacks to in part justify its success. Davis concluded that the pageant represented "the dogma of the spiritual and other-worldly Negro" and it emphasized "both the humility and the native genius for song of the Negro actors."[92] This was vividly illustrated when the white sponsors had black actors photographed by a newsreel company in front of an antebellum plantation house around which stood a group of blacks dressed in plantation clothes. An elderly black woman who played the role of a "mammy" proved to be the favorite of white audiences (newspapers emphasized that this woman was indeed a former slave).[93]

"Heaven Is My Home" was enthusiastically approved by most blacks in the community and in the church, although a few criticized the play. Davis noted that these "few aberrant individuals" condemned the play because it supported the subordination of blacks to whites. He quoted one "upper-middleclass Negro woman" who stated, "all it is, is white folks showing off their niggers. They really pack that church too."[94] Another upper-class Negro man, Mr. H., who had always been regarded as "queer" by blacks and whites because of his strong opposition to the pageant, stated that the play gave white people pleasure that they had once been "masters" of blacks and allowed whites to relive the power of "possessing Negroes" as they had in the "glorious past." Mr. H. was especially angered that blacks were "helping to degrade themselves" by supporting the play. Davis concluded that such overt expressions of hostility to the play represented "only a small group in the Negro caste."[95]

Davis's study is striking in the ways in which it broke from past accounts of black religion. Here was a detailed "thick" description of black life in all its varieties; emphasis on class, religious ritual, various "uses" of religion, and the social role or structure of religious institutions made for a sophisticated and vivid portrayal of black life that was rare for its day. However, the language of the Negro church still persisted despite the nuance in his depictions of black life.[96] It was perhaps to be expected that social scientists would be interested in churches as social institutions as most of them acknowledged themselves, and hence their use of phrases like the "Negro Church." But there was a deeper issue here than simply the question of methodology and conceptual tools. The pressing demands of the Great Depression and the extraordinary poverty and hardships of blacks often so overwhelmed and exasperated these interpreters that they felt forced to awaken the Negro church to its responsibilities or alert it to its complicity in sustaining black subordination to whites. Because many people attended the black churches, there had to be a way to help them realize how they could change things. Church leaders needed to be made aware of how they could contribute to the economic, political, and social elevation of blacks. For all of its strengths, it is clear that Davis's study hoped that black churches would no longer offer indirect support to the racial caste system of the South, even though no direct statements of this sort were made. His view of the "otherworldly" nature of black religion was also his gloss on the problem of religion in black communities. There is some indication that he regarded black churches as temporary institutions that would probably pass away once blacks gained some measure of political and economic power.

St. Clair Drake, a student of Warner and later professor of sociology at Roosevelt University, authored "The Negro Church and Associations in Chicago" in 1940 while he was in the process of preparing work for his groundbreaking book, Black Metropolis (1945), which was coauthored with Horace Cayton, a research assistant. Although Drake's manuscript for Myrdal's study had its distinctive emphases, perhaps most of its major arguments were taken up in Black Metropolis. Black Metropolis requires consideration for its development of the caste and class themes in a Northern and urban context (Chicago) and for its further complication of the issues raised by Davis's work on black churches in the South. The book was based on four years of research conducted by twenty students in various specialized fields. It had begun as an investigation of general social conditions surrounding the problem of juvenile delinquency on Chicago's South Side (Chicago's segregated black population). By employing the methods of sociologists and anthropologists, the authors focused on the culture of the black community in Chicago as a way of understanding the context within which the problem of delinquency could best be analyzed. Eventually delinquency was "subordinated" to the larger problem of the description and analysis of the structure and organization of the black community, both internally and in relationship to the larger Chicago environment of which it was a part.[97]

In his introduction to Black Metropolis, African American novelist Richard Wright, who had depicted graphically the conditions of black Chicago in Native Son (1940), argued that the fundamental sociological concepts employed in Drake and Cayton's work were industrialization, secularization, urbanization, and social differentiation (which showed social stratification and the development of social types).[98] Although all blacks had to wrestle with the problems of industrialization and urbanization in Chicago, secularization was given a detailed analysis within the context of social differentiation. Drake and Cayton described the institutions, social mores, and religious beliefs and practices of blacks in Chicago according to their place on the socioeconomic ladder (upper, middle, and lower class). They argued that the "real importance of the church can be understood only by relating it to the economic and social status of the various groups" in black Chicago.[99] In this painstaking investigation, a bewildering array of religious practices and ideas were described and rendered problematic any notion of the Negro Church.

Chicago was one of the most segregated urban areas in the North. In 1940, of the city's 337,000 blacks, over 90 percent lived in areas that were predominantly African American. A black belt had developed that was becoming increasingly more segregated and concentrated with the passage of time.[100] Drake and Cayton sought to capture the sights, sounds, smells, and feel of walking black Chicago's streets and to place their readers squarely in the middle of the pulsating activity and movement of black life in this urban metropolis. Amid hospitals, apartments, hotels, playgrounds, theaters, poolrooms, and taverns stood the black churches. Drake and Cayton counted about 500 churches in black Chicago, claiming over 200,000 members and distributed over thirty denominations.[101] Scores of storefront churches and colorfully extravagant names of various churches abounded. A sample of them follows: Hebrew Baptist Church, Baptized Believers' Holiness Church, Universal Union Independent, Church of Love and Faith, and United Pentecostal Holiness Church. Yet as conspicuous and nearly ubiquitous as the churches appeared, they were rivaled by "policy stations" (gambling houses), "reefer dens," buffet flats, and "call houses," all known to the residents of the underworld and their more "respectable" patrons.[102]

The taken-for-grantedness of the Negro Church was challenged in this diverse and changing environment. Drake and Cayton proclaimed, "The church is not the *center* of community life as it was in Midwest Metropolis before the Great Migration or as it is today in the small towns of the South."[103] The church was expected to help "advance the race" and therefore competed with the powerful black newspapers and other institutions in the city.[104] Like Fauset, Drake and Cayton viewed urbanization as crucial to the diminishing influence of black churches in African American communities. They noted that the continued migration of Southern blacks to Chicago contributed to a tradition of active church membership, even if the churches had to compete with a variety of secular organizations. But as Drake and Cayton argued, even as the church retained its central place among some blacks, it inevitably became a matter of public discussion, which subjected it to critical scrutiny.[105]

Drake and Cayton collected thousands of random comments from blacks to ascertain their feelings about a number of topics. The prevalence of "grumbling" against preachers and the church was the most striking finding. Both members and nonmembers were critical of the black churches. Drake and Cayton summarized the most frequent criticisms of black churches:

> (1) Church is a "racket," (2) Too many churches, (3) Churches are too emotional, (4) There's no real religion among members, (5) Churches are a waste of time and money, (6) Ministers don't practice what they preach, (7) Ministers don't preach against "sin," (8) Church places too much emphasis upon money, (9) Negroes are too religious.[106]

As Drake and Cayton observed, these charges were not necessarily new, but their frequency increased and was accompanied by an alternative vision of other institutions taking the place of the churches. There were those who lived without any formal relationship to the church in this sprawling urban world. The frustration and annoyance of blacks who were struggling to survive exacerbated the pressures placed on their churches.[107]

Black churches, Drake and Cayton insisted, still offered a variety of activities even though some members drifted away from them. Church services were "collective ceremonies" that lent a "certain rhythm to existence." Though theology was hardly emphasized, black churches contained a "mutually shared core of religious custom" that cut across denominational lines and allowed people to "feel at home." The sense of continuity with one's past was a feature of church life because many blacks who had grown up in the South were taught that they "ought to go to church." Non-"religious" reasons accounted for church attendance: The church supplied "good singing," "good speaking," and beautiful or "restful services."[108] After all, the black churches even in the North were located within a nearly self-contained segregated world, and outlets were limited for those who were taught that various activities outside the church were sinful. Ultimately, Drake and Cayton argued, the church gave large masses of black people the opportunity "to function in an organized group, to compete for prestige, to be elected to office, to exercise power and control, [and] to win applause and acclaim."[109] Though the churches were no longer the center of black life, they had the longest history, and they often gave the secular alternatives strong competition for the allegiance of blacks.

Drake and Cayton were particularly interested in the role of churches in maintaining social classes and in serving as markers of social mobility. Generally they found that Congregational and Episcopal churches were considered high status and holiness and spiritualist churches were regarded as low status.[110] Although *Black Metropolis* examined upper, middle, and lower classes among blacks in Chicago, because the lower classes comprised the vast majority of blacks (65 percent) in the city, they receive the bulk of attention that follows. This emphasis on the lower class can also be justified in part because Drake and Cayton devoted very little space to their coverage of religion among upper-class blacks, which they justified on the ground that the church had an "extremely limited" function among upper-class blacks and was not primarily a "religious institution" but a "status attribute." For upper-class blacks, the church granted social prestige and provided social and political connections that would not otherwise be available. Having a higher proportion of light-skinned church members, these were churches that the black masses had little connection with and labeled "high-toned" or "hifalutin."[111]

Among that vast number of blacks labeled the lower class by Drake and Cayton, the authors detected a world of storefront churches, secondhand clothing stores, cheap movies, dance halls, dilapidated houses, overcrowded kitchenettes, and taverns. They also found disorganized and broken families, whose lifestyles differed profoundly from the other black social classes. Alongside the delinquents and "minor" criminals (those who committed misdemeanors) were the "more stable group" of "church folks" and families (church and non-church) who were trying hard to make it. They existed side by side with the underworld—the pimps, prostitutes, thieves, pickpockets, drug addicts, and murderers. Drake and Cayton noted that despite their verbal protests, church folks had to live in close contact with the world of sin. They detected these different groups within the black lower class as a fluid and shifting population restricted by income and inadequate housing, making it impossible for the "church folks" and those who desired to be "respectable" to seal themselves off from their "shady neighbors."[112]

Of the 500 churches Drake and Cayton counted in the black belt, 300 of these were located in lower-class neighborhoods, but there were also 500 gambling houses, 80 pool rooms, 200 taverns, and scores of dives and buffet flats, most of which were located in the world of the lower class. During the evening hours, hymns, blues, and gospel songs and "low-down" music could be heard.[113] Drake and Cayton asserted that the "church-oriented" segment of the black lower class represented some stability in a "disordered milieu." This church world was a woman's world because less than a third of lower-class church members were men. These black women were generally, they insisted, an influence for stable family relations within their own social strata, though they complained of being "unequally yoked" with men who were "sinners" and who were devoted to gambling, extramarital sexual relations, and "big-timing" rather than church or religious life.[114]

Drake and Cayton wrote that over half of black Chicago's lower-class adults claimed to be church members, but only a "decided minority" would identify as "church people" (those actively involved in the churches), and fewer than a third were actually dues-paying members of any church. Fewer still "organized the greater part of their leisure time and their emotional life around the church and religion." In fact, Drake and Cayton found evidence of secular organizations such as the labor unions and radical political sects drawing away a segment of the lower-class black population in Chicago.[115] The "acids of modernity" were at work in black Chicago, which entailed the questioning of the necessity or efficacy of religion and a lower-class black world "in revolt against Heaven." Their vitriolic attacks against preachers and church members were, in Cayton and Drake's view, "part of the general secularization of life in the urban, industrial society."[116] Yet the nature of this revolt was not a rationalistic or intellectual critique of the foundations of religious belief or the Christian faith but a critique of the church's refusal to deal with the economic and social hardships of black life, the hypocrisy of ministers and church members, and the cupidity of church devotees. As the authors noted, even among blacks who criticized the church there was a feeling that they ought to be religious. The necessity of "good" preachers or "good" religion was affirmed alongside vehement denunciations of sin and evil committed by religious persons and church members. Most of these criticisms seemed to focus on personal problems of broken families, overworked single mothers, finding jobs, and having a decent place in which to live.[117]

But there was no doubt in Drake and Cayton's conclusions that this critique of the church was only vaguely related to the "insincerity" of church people. They detected the "centripetal pull of the urban milieu" as the reason behind such disaffection with religion and black churches. The explosion of churches in the North, the rise of the "new gods of the city" (so-called cult leaders), movies, ball games, social clubs, and gambling houses offered competing forms of participation and threw doubt on all "absolute conceptions of sin." Group controls of the small-town environment from which many black migrants came were absent or very weak. The prosperity of the "wicked," they observed, was a perpetual challenge to received notions of the desirability of being "poor saints." Religion therefore ceased to be the focus of lower-class black life, and the vast majority of lower-class blacks now organized their lives around having a "good time." The rhythm of daily life became geared to gambling and cheap forms of entertainment. No longer was the sentiment of the old-time religion—"take the world and give me Jesus"—uttered but rather, "What do I get out of it?"[118]

Similar to conclusions advanced in Fauset's study of blacks in Philadelphia, Drake and Cayton found that "when the old gods go," some lower-class blacks participated more actively in "racial movements," identified with the communist movement, joined the trade union and labor movements, and strove to "get ahead" in the traditional fashion of saving money, acquiring middle-class consumption patterns, getting more education, and participating in ward politics.[119] Some clung to the church as a "subsidiary center of interest," whereas others dropped all connections to the church and became "completely secularized except for fleeting moments of reverie or remorse."[120] This growing secularization was further evident in black newspaper reporting, which rarely covered church news as "big news," unless some sensational incident was involved. This was a significant shift, Drake and Cayton noted, from forty years prior when church news occupied a much greater proportion of newspaper space.[121]

Social scientists at the turn of the century had argued that blacks in their "natural environment" or apart from white supervision would revert to their natural selves. Superstition, innate religiosity and emotionalism were various ways of describing and diagnosing the religious condition (often regarded as a pathology) of blacks. Fauset, Drake and Cayton, and other black social scientists, however, indicated in their studies during World War II that religion was no longer taken for granted in black communities and black churches had to compete (often unsuccessfully) with secular organizations for the attention, time, and devotion of African Americans. The urban crucible was seen as the central factor in the drift away from religion. Secularization was viewed as a corollary of industrialization and urbanization.[122] To the extent that the proliferation of the black gods of the metropolis or the new religious movements were noticed, their presence was explained as ways that blacks relieved and released their psychological tensions, especially as they confronted for the first time the problems of the urban North. Religion was therefore a temporary mechanism that filled needs that would be met by secular institutions "under a different social order."[123] Theories of black innate religiosity therefore would have to be abandoned in light of developments in Northern cities.

Although Drake and Cayton focused on the particular issues that blacks faced in Chicago, perhaps no work on the general condition of blacks in America was as widely noted in the postwar period as Myrdal's *American Dilemma*. Myrdal's book reflected the author's concern with the social, political, and economic conditions of blacks, and his analysis of the race problem became the most influential interpretation of black life and the problems of race in American society from the end of World War II to the 1960s. Myrdal's interest in black churches was driven by his estimate of their value in fostering *protest* or *accommodation* to the caste subordination of blacks in America. Therefore his analysis dealt almost exclusively with how the Negro church functioned within the context of "power" and "power relations" vis-à-vis the white power structure. His work as a white liberal became the standard approach of those concerned with the Negro problem, especially the problems of the urban North as they affected race relations after World War II and into the 1960s. Myrdal had little interest in black churches as places of meaning or of community. Instead, he viewed the Negro Church as one social institution among many others.[124] His analysis was thus rather short and cursory, as well as uncompromisingly negative and harsh. He excoriated the Negro Church for its support of race patterns in the South and asserted that it kept blacks from fighting the caste system. This was why, he said, black churches garnered the goodwill of white Southerners who lauded the "old time religion" of blacks and attributed "particularly strong religious feelings" to them.[125]

Myrdal and African American sociologist E. Franklin Frazier were crucial interpreters in their analyses of black culture during the 1940s. Myrdal's project was in actuality the result of major collaboration, and Frazier's private papers indicate his indispensable assistance to the Swedish transplant's attempt to make sense of America's complicated race problem. Myrdal and Frazier rejected Herskovits's arguments about extensive African cultural retentions in black culture. Not surprisingly, Herskovits's cultural relativism reflected his uneasiness with comparing black culture only to the extent that it mirrored the culture of the white American majority. Myrdal and Frazier, however, regarded black culture as in serious need of reformation to facilitate assimilation. Myrdal carefully stated that he did not mean that "white American culture is 'higher' than other cultures in an absolute sense."[126] But he went on to state that this did not contradict his assumption that in the United States white "American culture is 'highest' in the pragmatic sense that adherence to it is practical for any individual or group which is not strong enough to change it."[127] In other words, he believed it was advantageous for blacks to acquire traits held in high esteem by the dominant white culture to facilitate their assimilation into the mainstream. This led him to argue that black culture was a "distorted development, or a pathological condition, of the general American culture."[128] Herskovits suggested that this devaluation of African cultural tenacity would inevitably lead to feelings of black inferiority on the part of blacks and racial prejudice on the part of whites.

Myrdal maintained that in general even the "the Northern Negro church has remained a conservative institution with its interests directed upon otherworldly matters and has largely ignored the practical problems of the Negroes' fate in this world."[129] Black youths were leaving the church because of their rising educational levels and "sophistication" and because of the "backwardness" of the black churches as manifested in their emotionalism and "puritanism." As younger blacks married and settled down, they joined a church, like whites, because they desired the respectability that church membership conferred. But the church they joined was likely to be "less attached to emotionalism and puritanism than the one attended by their parents." All of this meant that there was a general trend among black churches toward a "more intellectual and formal church service" as in white churches, except that blacks, along with a few whites in poor isolated areas, were "lagging about a half a century behind."[130]

Myrdal believed that the Negro church's chief weakness was its relatively inefficient status as an instrument of collective action to improve the condition of blacks in the broader society. Whereas in the South the black churches had rarely taken the lead in attacking the caste system or in bringing about even minor reforms, in the North, only occasionally had they been a strong force for social action. Black churches, Myrdal believed, were out of touch with "current social life in the field of morals," and their preaching of "traditional puritanical morals" had little effect on the ethical behavior of the masses of blacks. Most of the "real moral problems" of blacks were seldom considered in the church, he charged. Frequent divisions within the black churches weakened their institutional strength (here Myrdal is reminiscent of Woodson and Mays's critique of black churches). Rampant poverty made blacks dependent on white benefactors, leading to a deeper support of the caste system of racial subordination.[131]

In line with his basic belief that the concerns of blacks were "secondary reactions to more primary pressures from the side of the dominant white majority," Myrdal judged the black churches to be unoriginal and concluded that they were similar to white churches in their theology and church services.[132] Father Divine's Mission was the one exception to this rule, though he never indicated why he believed this. For Myrdal, the emotionalism in black churches was not much different from what one would find in lower-class

white Protestant churches. "Except for a slight slant in the direction of 'race,'"
there was nothing really distinct about black churches. Even God and the
angels were white in the imagination and fantasies of most blacks, he argued.[133] In light of such remarks, Myrdal's harsh summary judgment of the
Negro Church should come as no surprise:

> *the Negro Church fundamentally is an expression of the Negro community
> itself.* If the church has been otherworldly in outlook and indulged in
> emotional ecstasy, it is primarily because the downtrodden common
> Negroes have craved religious escape from poverty and other tribu-
> lations. If the preachers have been timid and pussy-footing, it is
> because the Negroes in general have condoned such a policy and
> would have feared radical leaders. The rivalry and factionalism, the
> organizational weakness and economic dependence of the Negro
> church, the often faltering economic and sexual morals of the
> preachers and their suspicion of higher education—all this reflects
> life as it is lived in the subordinate caste of American Negroes.[134]

In light of these views, when ideas of black cultural pathology were severely
criticized by black nationalists and social scientists in the 1960s, Myrdal's
sociological framework was at the top of the list.

Walter Jackson and David Southern have shown how Myrdal's work
played a major role in shaping a new racial liberalism for postwar America.
Jackson argues that together with the postwar generation of young sociologists,
"Myrdal believed that blacks desired complete assimilation into the mainstream white culture and that distinctive patterns of Afro-American culture
were a pathological vestige of slavery and segregation that would soon fade
away."[135] Southern suggests that Myrdal's book hindered deeper research on
black communities because it was widely thought that Myrdal had written the
definitive work on the race question. Paul B. Sheatsley, a longtime student of
racial attitudes, was asked in 1984 why so little study of black attitudes had
been done in the early postwar period. He replied, "It never occurred to us
when we wrote the questions in the Forties and Fifties to ask them of blacks
because Myrdal's dilemma was a white dilemma and it was white attitudes that
demanded study."[136] New works on race relations and black communities had
to be justified. Perhaps this explains why there were so few studies during the
1950s that went beyond the specific formulations of the works in the 1940s
about black churches and communities.

Frazier regarded Myrdal's *American Dilemma* as a tough-minded piece
of social analysis that was sorely needed, not surprisingly given Frazier's

major contributions to the work. He asserted that Myrdal "recognized the Negro community for what it was—a pathological phenomenon in American life." "Therefore, unlike many white Americans," he continued, Myrdal "did not indulge in a lot of foolish talk about the peculiar 'contributions' of the Negro and his deep 'spirituality.' "[137] Frazier thought that the traditional image of blacks had to be destroyed before it could be replaced, even if it meant regarding black culture as a pathological variant of white American culture. His agreement with Myrdal was particularly evident in his later insistence that the degree to which blacks failed to "measure up to the generally accepted standards" of American family life, church life, or moral behavior was not a result of a "racial inheritance" or an "African social heritage" but a product of social and economic factors.[138] For Frazier, Myrdal was absolutely right by not indulging in "overrating the achievements of the Negro and the ability and character of his leaders" because he realized that segregation had "handicapped" blacks intellectually and had a "bad effect" on their character. Social scientific analysis required honesty, he proclaimed, and freeing the study of blacks from "sentimentality" and "pathos."[139] From Frazier's perspective, if this meant pointing out what he regarded as the problems, frustrations, and pathologies of black life, then social scientists were obliged to conduct their work with frankness and forthrightness, even if it contradicted traditional images of blacks held by blacks and whites. He believed that this approach was necessary if blacks were to eventually have full participation in American society.

Frazier's implicit ideas about black religion became explicit in his 1953 lecture "The Evolution of Religion among American Negroes," delivered as the Sir James Frazer Lecture in Social Anthropology at the University of Liverpool (eventually published in 1963 as *The Negro Church in America*). Joe Feagin wrote in 1975 that Frazier's brief sociological essay "had become the last word on the subject" of black religion. Feagin argued that just as Myrdal saw the "black community and culture," including black churches, "as little more than a pathological reaction to white oppression," so did "subsequent researchers in the Myrdal tradition" include the "religion of blacks in a broad picture of ghetto pathology." He pointed to Frazier's work as having the most influence on "scholarly views of the black church." Frazier and "many subsequent analysts," Feagin contended, viewed the "black church" as a "major barrier standing in the wake of an inevitable trend toward assimilation and integration."[140]

As one of the most prominent black sociologists from the 1930s through the 1950s, Frazier did indeed become a leading interpreter of African American religion after War World II. He was interested primarily in "the broad problem of the relation of religion to social structure or, more specifically, the role of religion in the social organization of Negro life in the United States."[141] Frazier's theory about the history of blacks in the New World and the evolution of their social institutions in the United States was crucial to his ideas about the Negro Church.[142] Contra Herskovits, he denied African cultural survivals for blacks in the United States. Rather, he contended that slavery stripped blacks of their religious worldview and the social structures of African kinship and community. The religion of the slave owners became the new social world of the slaves. The various shocks of the slave trade, the Civil War, Emancipation, and the migration of blacks to Southern and Northern cities led to a massive disorganization of black life, leaving the family most vulnerable and divided (Frazier also argued that a new form of social and economic organization took place in the urban North, which made for increasing integration into the mainstream of American society).[143] As the family became increasingly disorganized, and as blacks were shut out of political and social intercourse in the broader society, the church assumed a broader role. It became a surrogate for the family, for business, and for politics. But with the increasing differentiation of the black community, especially in the urban North, the church was losing its power as an instrument of social control, even though among the masses it still held a significant sway. Not for the good, Frazier declared, the church had become "the most important institutional barrier" to assimilation because it was anti-intellectual and contributed to the backwardness of blacks, preventing their integration and assimilation into the mainstream culture. He held out hope that the black church was losing its grip; schools, businesses, and other institutions would socialize blacks into the broader culture and liberate them from the stifling influence of the black church, although he reiterated time and again that black church leaders had a vested interest in segregation and would not easily yield to integration because of their precarious position of leadership in the black community.[144]

Frazier and other social scientists espoused a variant of secularization theory for the black churches, making minor concessions to the salience of race and economic disparity when compared to white churches. Under this rubric, they viewed urbanization and the differentiation of social institutions as processes that were leading to the lessening of the influence of churches and religious beliefs and practices. In particular he argued that black churches in the urban North were becoming more secular by abandoning the old otherworldly emphasis and focusing on the problems of blacks in this world. Black churches were gradually giving up such strictures as banning card playing, dancing, and theatergoing, Frazier and others pointed out—all signs of secu-larization.[145] Furthermore, as these same social scientists began to deny the importance or continuing influence of African culture in the cultural practices of American blacks, there was a growing trend in the 1950s and 1960s that regarded the culture of urban blacks as pathological. Anthropologist Charles Keil described such studies in his book, *Urban Blues* (1966):

> a much more dangerous revision of it [the myth that blacks did not have a past] current today is that the Negro has no culture or at least no viable culture worthy of attention. Yesterday's rural Negro may have had something like a folk culture, so the myth goes, but today's urban Negro can be found only in a set of sociological statistics on crime, unemployment, illegitimacy, desertion, and welfare payments. The social scientists would have us believe that the Negro is psy-chologically maladjusted, socially disorganized and culturally de-prived. Others tell us that any Negro way of life that may exist is nothing more than a product of poverty and fear.[146]

It is difficult to deny the influence of Frazier's thought on the social sci-entists and public policy experts of the 1960s who combed the corners of the urban ghetto and found the pathology of which Keil wrote. Frazier's assess-ments of the black family and the black church set the theoretical groundwork for the kinds of works that emphasized social pathology in the 1960s (most of which had very little to say about African American religion, as if to confirm Frazier's views about the declining influence of the Negro Church).[147] Keil listed several works that in his words were "concerned primarily with the pathological side of Negro life."[148] These included Abram Kardiner and Lionel Ovesey's *Mark of Oppression* (1951), Nathan Glazer and Daniel Patrick Moyni-han's *Beyond the Melting Pot* (1963), and Charles Silberman's *Crisis in Black and White* (1964). Keil was especially critical of these and other authors for devoting more attention to "what whites have done to Negroes" than to what blacks had done for themselves. He was troubled that the "downgrading of the Negro church" reflected an "understandable but misdirected Marxist-Freudian dis-gust with the 'opiate of the masses.'"[149] Keil was observing what had become the dominant paradigm in social science literature on blacks in the urban North. Frazier's emphasis on black pathology and his insistence that blacks get rid of their cultural "peculiarities" to enter the cultural mainstream was be-coming the leading perspective on black culture, especially black religion, after World War II and would reach its culmination in social scientific works in the 1960s on urban blacks.

Urbanization as a Challenge to Innate Religiosity

Social scientific studies on black life during and after War World II noted a growing "race consciousness" accompanied by rising militancy. One study indicated that an outgrowth of this race consciousness was an appearance of a nationalistic consciousness among Negroes. For some blacks, this meant the rejection of Christianity and the invention of another religion that gave support to the ideals and values of the black community.[150] Not everyone was happy with these developments, however. With urbanization came new problems for blacks and the nation at large. Riots during the war were taken as evidence of growing anger among blacks, especially in the urban North. Race riots in Detroit and Harlem in 1943 were particularly notable, though these were by no means the only cities that experienced such violence.[151] The continued migration of blacks to cities in the North prompted greater interest in and studies of blacks, who were gathering in increasingly segregated pockets of this urban environment. In 1940, 23 percent of blacks in the United States were living in the North and West; by 1960, at the end of a second wave of migration, that figure rose to 40 percent, with nearly three-quarters of all American blacks living in cities—roughly the same percentage who had lived in rural areas (mostly in the South) at the start of the century.[152] Continued migration left some whites with a distinct fear of the masses of blacks who moved to the North and changed the national landscape. Desires and longings for a simple past fused with images of rural black religion.

While the nation was in the thick of World War II, two of the worst riots in the country's history broke out in Detroit and Harlem. In the three years preceding 1943, 50,000 African Americans had come to Detroit. The migration of massive numbers of blacks to the North and West in search of jobs raised new concerns about the patterns of race relations in cities of the North.[153] Writing from Cambridge, Massachusetts, in 1944, Willard Sperry, dean of Harvard Divinity School, was especially troubled by the violence in Detroit. Sperry noted that "northern cities do not know how to assimilate this unexpected flux" of blacks.[154] This massive urbanization of blacks was creating problems not only for whites but for blacks as well, who had to wrestle with their inherited religious traditions in a new alien environment. Sperry argued that the newly emancipated Negro of the North, like the "modernist Protestant," was now attempting to "restate his hope of heaven in the terms of an earthly Utopia." In his view, many urban blacks had become anticlerical and irreligious, thus going beyond the "golden mean of modernism." Therefore, the "conventional fabric of democracy," Sperry feared, "is in more danger from this type of man than is the sanctity of that southern womanhood which dares not walk abroad alone at night."[155] By rejecting the "old anodyne of heaven offered the slave as an opiate," he lamented, radical urban blacks found themselves released and alienated from the faith of their ancestors and thus from moral restraint.[156] Though Sperry agreed that secularization was taking place among blacks in the urban North, he did not regard it as the pathway that led to assimilation (as Frazier hoped).

All of the older images of black innate religiosity that Frazier and others ridiculed found a welcome presence in Sperry's work. Sperry contended that there was reality and feeling in traditional black religion that neither the black radical nor the white "modernist Protestant" had captured. For the mass of black believers, he argued, Jesus was real, not a "cold Christ in a tangled Trinity, much less an ethical teacher."[157] It was as though, from his perspective, blacks in such rural Southern contexts did not have to struggle to believe. "Neither the theologian nor the moralist," he proclaimed, "can ever quite feel the imperious forces of the simple summons, 'Steal away, steal away, steal away home to Jesus.'"[158] Negro spirituals confronted death in a way that was unknown to liberal Protestantism. There was a power to these serene and moving spirituals that seemingly escaped the modern believer. Sperry confessed that black religion could perhaps save barren souls form their doubts and thus make simple belief possible again (at least imaginatively):

> It is at this point that the Negro spirituals are perhaps our most moving statement of an inescapable fact and serene hope. Somehow, not even our classic hymns of heaven have the untroubled conviction of the spiritual. . . . I have read countless books and lectures on the immortality of the human soul. Nothing which I have ever read moves me and reassures me as does Paul Robeson's rendering of "Deep River, I'm goin' to cross over into camp ground." This may be sheer sentimentality; I can merely record the fact. . . . More than one American finds, therefore, in these simple lyrics about camp ground an expression for doubts and hopes and longings which the conventions forbid his mentioning to others, if not even conceding to himself. He allows himself this furtive theological self-indulgence on the grounds that all such sentiments are just Negro spirituals, nothing more.[159]

When Sperry mentioned his sorrow over urban blacks' rejection of Uncle Tomism, he was heartened by the fact that most blacks, in his view, retained the "old-time patient dignity" of their traditional faith. This patience was a rebuke

and an example to "much of the well-meant, but short-sighted ethical impatience of our white world." He noted that it was black ministers, not police or
military, who most effectively calmed their people during the Detroit riot. As
the "most silent and non-resistant of people" when insulted or injured, blacks
had proven that they had a lesson for America.[160]

Conclusion

It was as though Sperry mirrored the sentiment expressed in the conclusion of
Marc Connelly's *Green Pastures*. Mercy is learned through suffering was one of
the central messages of the play. Sperry praised blacks for being nonresistant,
noting that blacks had waited so long for their rights that waiting had become
"second mental and moral nature" to them. Waiting and suffering in silence,
he argued, had become their most distinctive trait. White "admirers" of blacks
like Sperry seemed content to simply invest blacks with heroic, godly qualities
as long as they were patient and silent and could teach a certain lesson to
barren and confused Americans.

Frazier was deeply concerned about the psychic satisfaction that traditional
images of black religion, as depicted by Sperry, provided whites and was relieved that urbanization removed the veil of black satisfaction and contentment
in a racist society. Although critics have often linked Myrdal and Frazier together in their respective emphases on pathology, a more nuanced reading of
Frazier leads us to conclude that he welcomed urbanization as a step toward
economic and social equality, which he regarded as crucial to assimilation. It is
true that he provided a scathing critique of black churches and had difficulty in
depicting the "softer" dimensions of black life compared to his emphasis on
economics, social structure, and demographic shifts. Yet Frazier's problem
with Herskovits and older theories about black innate religiosity reflected a
more profound concern about the place of blacks in the nation. As he wrote in
his unpublished review of Herskovits's *Myth of the Negro Past*, "The reviewer
cannot agree with the author that to establish the fact that the Negro had a
'cultural past' and that the Negro's 'cultural past' still influences his behavior
will alter his status in American life."[161] Frazier thought it rather naive of
Herskovits to assume that attention to an African past would suddenly cause
white Americans to change their estimate of blacks. Frazier gloomily concluded
his review with a question that encapsulates the hazards of this debate: "When
Professor Herskovits says that the Negro problem is psychological (that African
patterns of thought prevent the complete acculturation of the Negro) as well as
economic and sociological, is he not saying that even more fundamental bar-

riers exist between blacks and whites than are generally accepted?"[162] Claims of black innate religiosity had become a liability to blacks and a hindrance to assimilation. Social scientists like Frazier were eager to be done with these images of blacks. They welcomed the end of the naturally religious black in the urban centers of the North.

Epilogue

As a result of the massive changes taking place in black life during the 1940s, John Eubanks, in his 1947 University of Chicago doctoral dissertation, detected four trends in black religion:

1. A "modernist movement" that sought social reform and maintained that social problems cannot be separated from religion
2. A "secularist movement" shaped by the findings of modern science and modern thought that attempted to achieve social reforms without making any appeal to religious ideals or concepts
3. A cluster of groups outside the churches that made use of religious ideals and concepts[1]
4. Individual writers and movements such as the "cults" in which racism had become a religion for the redemption of the oppressed[2]

Eubanks regarded this latter movement as a "pathological condition" because the cults, in his view, stressed "race values" to the exclusion of "universal human values." By putting in the place of a transcendent deity the personality of a human being, the cults had adopted a radical position that was not healthy to religious life. The cults were, from Eubanks's perspective, "inadequate expressions of Christianity and democracy" because they made the basis of participation too narrow and served as a threat and challenge to

Christians to "practice the Christian Fatherhood of God and the Brotherhood of Man in all the relationships of our culture."[3]

In the resolve to find "cultural determiners" of African American religion, social scientists placed much less emphasis on the meaning of religion to black people or on how religion figured in their day-to-day lives.[4] So much attention was given to the ability of the larger environment to shape and mold African American culture that sociologist William Fontaine, in a debate with E. Franklin Frazier, asked, "Does not overstressing of environment as determinative of human conduct unduly minimize the creative power of humans in general and of blacks in particular?"[5] With the authority of the Myrdal-Carnegie findings behind them, black and white social scientists continued to focus their energies on what they saw as the cultural pathologies of black culture, stressing the need for such problems to be addressed so blacks could enter the mainstream. In their book *The Mark of Oppression* (1951), for example, based on their case studies of twenty-five urban blacks in Harlem, Columbia University professors of psychiatry Abram Kardiner and Lionel Ovesey listed in unsparing detail the "psychological scars" the caste system in America had inflicted on its hapless black victims. They were careful to note that they blamed the source of the pathologies in black culture on the society that tolerated oppression and racial discrimination. Although their call for the ending of oppression was made at the very end of the book, it is difficult to assess the extent to which such a call was lost or heard because it followed an unrelieved description of the "wretched internal life" of blacks.[6]

Similarly, African American psychologist Kenneth Clark, whose work was influential as a basis for some of the social scientific reasoning that underlay the Supreme Court decision of *Brown v. Board of Education* (1954), reported on the pathologies of the black ghetto in his *Dark Ghetto* (1965). Yet neither Kardiner and Ovesey nor Clark had much to say about African American religion. For Kardiner and Ovesey, black churches were places of escapism and a fantasy world where oppressed and psychologically deprived blacks sought answers to their many problems. But alas, they lamented, religion "does not answer their needs" and "hence they are constant prey to new religious adventurers."[7] They argued, however, that black churches did provide "emotional release," a minimal form of social cohesion, and a vehicle for the dissemination of political and social ideas among the black lower classes.[8] They contended that Father Divine's Peace Mission (a religious movement that was especially active in Harlem during the 1930s) furnished lower-class black women with "an idealized male figure who really acts as a provider and protector."[9] Because blacks had come from so many broken homes, Kardiner and Ovesey asserted, Father Divine's movement addressed their "frustrated dependency longings."[10] They also noted that Divine's was the only truly indigenous Negro social movement, but it was a "protest fantasy only" and a "grotesque flight into unreality" that denied the actual condition of blacks and sought to find "new values in a make-believe world."[11] Divine's movement was therefore deemed to be a hindrance to the ultimate goal of blacks' complete and equal integration into American society.[12]

In a chapter devoted to the "Power of the Church," Kenneth Clark examined black churches to the extent that they were able "to stimulate and direct constructive social change." The churches played a "cathartic role," in his view. Yet they also provided blacks with personal affirmation and self-esteem. Clark noted that among the Negro Church's most conspicuous weakness was its tendency to be "dissipated by preoccupation with trivia, competitiveness, suspiciousness, and a desperate struggle for the empty status, bombast, and show of the ghetto world."[13] He believed that black churches were generally hesitant about desegregation because they had historically functioned as havens for personal worth and bulwarks of protection from the pervasive racism of the broader society.[14] This left the black churches in a weakened position because black intellectuals were alienated from them for not dealing with the hard economic and racial realities of blacks. Such a situation made possible the rise of the black Muslims, Clark maintained. The Nation of Islam appealed to marginal groups, he asserted, and was a symptom "of the profound frustration, despair, and impatience found at all levels of Negro life . . . which have come to surface in recent years."[15]

Although social scientists were generally agreed from the 1940s to the early 1960s that there were significant problems in black culture in the urban North (most notably family disorganization, crime, juvenile delinquency, violence, and despair), they were not impressed with the efforts of the Nation of Islam to reach out to the urban masses. The Nation of Islam first came to the attention of white Americans with the production of the television documentary "The Hate That Hate Produced" in 1959.[16] After this production, newspaper articles and magazine reports on the "black Muslims" proliferated.[17] The most important scholarly studies were sociologist C. Eric Lincoln's *Black Muslims in America* (1961) and political scientist E. U. Essien Udom's *Black Nationalism in America* (1962).[18] In their own self-representation and in media portrayals, members of the Nation of Islam stood as the symbolic end of the naturally religious Negro. By their vehement denunciations of Uncle Tomism and black Christianity and their recruitment of and identification with blacks in the urban ghettoes of the North, the Nation of Islam stood as the antithesis of the naive and religious Southern black.

Gunnar Myrdal had noted the cultural traits that whites associated with blacks, which were, in his view, the "peculiarities" of the *average Negro* that would have to be addressed if intimate contact between the two groups was going to occur. These included aggressiveness; spontaneous good humor; "dumbness"; lying; love of the gaudy, bizarre, and ostentatious; eating habits that included such foods as chicken, watermelon, corn pone, pork chops, and opossum; lack of poise; superstitiousness; peculiar speech patterns (Negro dialect); and criminality.[19] Interpreters of the Nation of Islam noted the group's prohibitions against eating cornbread, pork, collard greens, and many other foods common to the diet of blacks in the South, which led white historian August Meier to assert that "Black Muslims are as much anti-Negro-lower-class values, and anti-Negro-middle-class complacency and opportunism as they are anti-white injustice."[20] Meier contended further that the Nation of Islam was trying not only to emphasize hard work, thrift, economic accumulation, and "Puritan morality" for members but also to paint an image of whites that was the reverse of the image that whites had of blacks, as inferior beings, lazy, sexually immoral, dirty, and criminal.[21] From this perspective, the Nation of Islam was, in his words, "trying to make Negroes over into the old-fashioned middle-class American image."[22] But for the Nation, acquiring personal habits of morality, cleanliness, and ritual purity were not seen as the means of gaining entry into the white mainstream but as the basis of self-esteem, group dignity, and a new identity for blacks.[23]

The image of the accommodating Christian Negro has long had probative value as a justification of racial oppression and segregation. Even black critics of the "Negro Church" expressed deep resentment of the Christian emphasis on the afterlife, which allegedly averted attention from the real problems of this world. The "emotionalism" of African American religion was pointed to by white critics as characteristic of a "primitive" people who lacked the capacity for a "rational" exposition of the faith.[24] Observers, however, noted that the Nation of Islam frowned on intemperate singing, loud laughing, and shouting.[25] In his visit to a temple of the Nation, Lincoln observed that there were no "happy" people among those gathered. There was no foot-thumping and head-wagging amens. Self-control, discipline, and composure were manifest.[26] Scholar and lawyer C. Haywood Burns noted that the Nation of Islam repudiated the doctrine of an afterlife or heaven because it was used as a tool to subjugate blacks.[27] So it appeared that the Nation of Islam stood as the figurative end of the stereotypical image of the naturally religious Negro and all that for which the Uncle Tom trope stood.

Yet for all their denunciations of Christianity and "white devils," the Nation of Islam and Malcolm X in particular held a special interest for whites even as the movement troubled liberal black leaders. Meier noted that by 1965 there was an "incredible fascination" with the Nation of Islam by whites and that there had emerged a "posthumous near-sanctification of Malcolm X by many naïve whites" and even some blacks.[28] White journalists were enchanted with Malcolm X and his personal religious journey. Yet one black interpreter of the Nation of Islam grudgingly conceded its religious status. Lincoln argued that the Nation's religious values were of secondary importance. He assured his audience that if white Americans attacked the diseases of racism and discrimination at their roots, then there would be no Nation of Islam. Lincoln explicitly proposed a functionalist understanding of the Nation of Islam to convince whites that their fears of the movement could only be relieved by addressing the more fundamental causes of the movement's origins.[29] So it would be too tidy to proclaim that the Nation of Islam, whatever its self-image, represented the end of the Uncle Tom trope and associated notions of romantic racialism.

Historian James M. McPherson argues that the tradition of romantic racialism survived in the "black aesthetic" or "soul" tradition of the late 1960s.[30] Romantic racialism was about more than black religion, and yet religion has been a central part of this cultural image of blacks. On the one hand, McPherson's claims are to be doubted because the black nationalists, the Nation of Islam, and Christian advocates of black theology explicitly rejected the Uncle Tom image and the long-standing assertions of black innate religiosity. But important similarities between the older romantic racialism and the black aesthetic movement of the 1960s are indeed apparent, because both included claims about religious spontaneity and warmth that was said to be unique to blacks. In 1969, African American church leader Gayraud S. Wilmore Jr. wrote that black people possessed a rich artistic and emotional freedom called "soul" that had its roots in the African heritage of communalism (though reformed and reshaped by the ghettos of America, he was careful to add). This soul quality was "opposite to the style of life formed by the structured, unfeeling, scientific rationality of white Western civilization."[31] Anthropologist Charles Keil in *Urban Blues* (1966) lauded the ecstatic elements of black religion, such as speaking in tongues, healing, trance, frenzied dancing, and hand clapping. He argued that such aspects of worship in black urban communities were far removed from the "staid and stolid Puritanism that has dominated the American [that is, white] Protestant tradition."[32] His work introduced the concept of soul as a serious scholarly discussion of black life.[33]

The notion of black "soul" was a reaction to portrayals of black urban areas as sites of cultural pathology. The immediate catalyst for these types of discussions of black urban life was the publication of Daniel Patrick Moynihan's *Negro Family* (1965), which found a "tangle of pathology" and a family structure among lower-class blacks in urban areas of the North that was "approaching complete breakdown."[34] Moynihan was then assistant secretary of Labor for the Lyndon B. Johnson administration and found himself at the center of controversy after this work became public. Although his work was not about religion, he did note that black urban youth were alienated from the values of middle-class whites and that the "Negro churches have all but lost contact with men in the Northern cities." This lack of contact with religion was perhaps a "normal condition of urban life," he argued, even though there was "a considerable number of lower class Negro males" who were being enlisted by the Nation of Islam, "a movement based on total rejection of white society, even though it emulates whites."[35] Moynihan recommended that the federal government implement policies that that would enhance the stability and resources of the black family.[36]

Sociologists Lee Rainwater and William L. Yancey argued that *The Negro Family*'s findings were consistent with earlier studies on black life conducted by Allison Davis, John Dollard, Horace Cayton and St. Clair Drake, and other social scientists.[37] Moynihan did indeed make considerable use of the works of E. Franklin Frazier and Kenneth Clark in his conclusions about the disorganization of the black family. But whatever the source of his ideas, his findings were viewed as an attack on the integrity of black culture more generally. Although delivered in February 1965, the full report gained widespread attention after *Newsweek* provided a summary of its main points on August 9, several days before the riot in Watts, a Los Angeles ghetto of a quarter of a million African Americans. The Watts riot was one of the most destructive race riots that had occurred in over two decades in the urban North. Newspaper and magazine articles that discussed the riot concentrated on black family disorganization, crime, venereal disease, hopelessness, and unemployment, among other topics, and increased attention was paid to Moynihan's conclusions.[38]

Reactions to Moynihan's report, however, reflected a much broader trend of growing disillusionment among black leaders and some liberal white political activists with attempts to integrate blacks into the white mainstream and disappointment with the Myrdalian framework of shedding the "peculiar" traits of black culture to find acceptance in a white world.[39] Harvard psychologist William Ryan regarded the report as part of a "new ideology" that made it "seem that unemployment, poor education and slum conditions result from family breakdown, 'cultural deprivation', and lack of 'acculturation' of Southern rural migrants."[40] James Farmer, a civil rights activist, complained that Moynihan failed to suggest that there may be "something wrong in an 'orderly and normal' white family structure that is weaned on race hatred and passes the word 'nigger' from generation to generation."[41] Although not all black leaders and social scientists reacted negatively to the report or questioned its conclusion, they had to confront the concerns about black cultural pathology and the relationship between black and white culture in America.[42]

Keil's *Urban Blues* represented one attempt to extol black ghetto culture against an affluent white American culture that allegedly suffered from spiritual impoverishment and its own forms of cultural deprivation.[43] Keil was deeply distressed by what he regarded as a dominant social scientific ideology that denied that blacks had any culture that needed to be guarded or protected.[44] He believed that blacks "reshaped, nurtured, and magnified in response to slavery and post-slavery conditions" what he regarded as "basic African predispositions governing religion and esthetics" in black life.[45] Although he affirmed what he called the "ecstatic elements" in black religion and the auditory and tactile expression of "Negro ghetto culture," he argued that the Nation of Islam, one of the most active religious groups in the urban North, was too faithfully wedded to the Protestant ethic in its emphasis on thrift, sobriety, "inner-directedness," sexual morality, and respectability.[46] The Nation of Islam and the "soul movement" were both revitalization movements, in his view, in that they were seeking self-respect for blacks, although they had very different means of doing so.[47] The soul movement embraced the folkways of lower-class blacks: collard greens, pork, and various other aspects of soul culture were the very things that sustained blacks through slavery and were thus seen as a source of strength. Both the soul movement and the Nation of Islam were seeking an answer to problems of identity and solidarity within black communities.[48] For the soul people, an attempt to articulate the distinctiveness of black culture was something that they shared with romantic racialists, particularly in their attraction to racial essentialism.[49]

McPherson, then, is only partially correct when he asserts that the soul movement and the "black aesthetic" tradition were a continuation of romantic racialism in their affirmation of a unique and special quality to black culture.[50] The advocates of "soul" and a black aesthetic were ambivalent about religion, particularly black Christianity, and they certainly rejected the notions of black religiosity advanced by the romantic racialists. Perhaps what the soul movement and the black aesthetic represented was a form of what John Bracey, August Meier, and Elliot Rudwick referred to as a "nationalist sentiment" that has emerged at various historical junctures in the black community.[51] This impulse tends to be most pronounced when blacks have experienced deep disillusionment after a period of heightened expectations or during historical moments of declining socioeconomic status. As Bracey, Meier, and Rudwick note, such attitudes of racial solidarity may be expressed in the form of cultural, religious, or economic nationalism.[52] Two most prominent examples would be the revival of the colonization movement in the 1850s after disappointment with the *Dred Scott* decision and the urban riots of the late 1960s partly because of slow economic progress for the black masses.

Here the peculiar burden of black religion is revealed in that a repudiation of those religious and cultural practices deemed singularly "Negro" provoked criticism for being a betrayal of blackness. To embrace such ideas, on the other hand, was viewed by others as an affirmation of the "natural" expression of the primitive and emotional passions of an essential blackness. It is true that such images and expectations of blacks have changed considerably during the nineteenth and twentieth centuries. Yet from Uncle Tom to the emergence of the discourse of the Negro Church in the twentieth century, the desire that "black religion" should play a special and unique role in American culture has been implicitly and explicitly expressed. It was also more often than not wrapped up in notions of intellectual inferiority and unassimilability. The idea of innate religiosity, although understood by the mid-nineteenth-century romantic racialists as feeling and emotions, which the "white man" putatively lacked, took on new meaning in the imagination of whites in the late nineteenth century as the unrestrained emotionalism of uncivilized blacks of the South, reverting to their natural African ancestry. Black leaders tried to salvage the older and seemingly benign image of blacks, urging them to conserve their spiritual gifts and view themselves as those people especially endowed by God with spiritual and emotional qualities that would soften the harshness and materialism of American society. All the while leading white social scientists medicalized and pathologized black religion at the end of the nineteenth century and located their emotionalism in defective bodies. Biology had replaced the environmentalist notion of a "degraded" culture as an explanation of black distinctiveness and the vicious African savage in the white mind returned with force.

Throughout the twentieth century, attempts to understand the meaning and place of black religion were crucial to concomitant endeavors to seek blacks' place in the nation and their distinctive contribution to American culture. Ironically, social scientific studies on the "defects" of black culture in the 1940s and emphasis in the social science literature on integration from *Brown v. Board of Education* to the early 1960s have been regarded in hindsight as contributing to notions of a damaged black psyche and urban pathology, even as critics concede that social science in the Myrdalian framework was crucial to debunking notions of the racial inferiority of blacks.[53] Although black religion did not figure prominently in these discussions about black culture and assimilation, especially as they related to public policy proposals, they inevitably raised questions about black religion and the Negro Church. African American religion, as noted in chapter 7, played a central part in the broader debate between anthropologist Melville Herskovits and sociologist E. Franklin Frazier in the 1940s about the continuity of elements of African culture in the New World.[54]

Black religion entered the polemical literature of the 1960s that denounced middle-class black bourgeois culture as inauthentic and untrue to blackness. Valorization of *urban* black culture was viewed by some as an affirmation of what was distinctively black (as in the 1920s and 1930s when whites offered sentimental images of rural Southern blacks). Criticisms of middle-class white and black culture by the Nation of Islam, black nationalists, and Christian advocates of black theology were often coupled with the claim that Christianity was the white man's religion and was therefore an escapist fantasy foisted on unsuspecting blacks during years of slavery and oppression. James Cone, the leading proponent of black theology in the late 1960s and early 1970s, relates how his talk about black Christianity at a workshop of the Congress of African People held in Atlanta, Georgia, in 1970 caused a storm of protest by all 100 participants, who denounced Christianity as the white man's religion that deserved no place at an African Congress.[55]

The celebration of working-class black culture by blacks and whites during the 1960s was reminiscent of the celebration of the primitive by blacks and whites during the 1920s.[56] There were very specific reasons for this extolling of black working-class urban culture in the 1960s. Ulf Hannerz, an anthropologist at the University of Stockholm, argued that in "much social science writing, ghetto dwellers have only been 'cases'—of crime, juvenile delinquency, mental disorder, [and] public assistance."[57] Hannerz did field work in the Winston Street black neighborhood of Washington, D.C., from 1966 to 1968. His research was conducted in conjunction with the Urban Language Center for Applied Linguistics and through personal conversations with civil rights activist John Lewis. Hannerz proposed anthropology as a "form of consciousness" that could give a more insightful picture of ghetto life than the other social sciences. This "human side" of the ghetto would include a discussion of willfulness, endurance, and strength, he argued, and bring to light the "soul" of blacks.[58] Hannerz and other social scientists sensed a need to move beyond depictions of black urban culture as pathological. They were influenced by increasing efforts among blacks themselves to rehabilitate their image. Yet the social scientists, though incorporating notions of a black aesthetic rather uneasily into their methodology, had virtually abandoned any discussion of black religion. Hannerz, for example, argued that churches had lost their influence among blacks in the urban ghettos. Yet he regarded black "soul" as the folk conception of the "national character" of black people in America.[59] Though historically a religious term, in the context of discussions of black culture in the

1960s, "soul" came to occupy a meaning that was similar to that of traditional cultural images of blacks and resembled romantic racialist notions. Black music, speech, sociability, and fashions were now seen as laudable features of black culture rather than harmful deviations from the mainstream culture.[60]

However, to the extent that black religion or, more generally, black culture encouraged morality, self-control, deferred gratification, or any other values that were deemed white middle-class, it was regarded as suspect in the writings of black leaders who rejected widespread negative images of black urban culture (as noted by Hannerz). The specter of whiteness haunted black attempts to formulate conceptions of the good and the beautiful and their endeavors to find and to value the distinctive features of their culture.[61] In his *Blues People* (1963) Amiri Baraka (born LeRoi Jones), black poet, novelist, and political activist, wrote that the "cruelest psychological and cultural imposition of all" on black people was the "inculcation of this Puritan ethos on a people whose elegant traditions were the complete antithesis of it."[62] Having lived among white bohemians in New York's Greenwich Village and Lower East Side from 1957 to 1962, perhaps it is not surprising that Baraka's views were similar to those of whites and blacks in Greenwich Village and Harlem who in the 1920s lauded the "natural" spontaneity, primitivism, and emotional freedom of blacks over the sterility and stiffness of whites.[63] To be sure, this cultural image of blacks was broader than religion, but the assertions of black distinctiveness and authentic blackness as a rejection of white or black middle-class restrictions continued.

This appreciation of a "black aesthetic" was also an attempt at cultural rehabilitation among blacks who had grown weary of trying to measure up to what they regarded as the values and mores of white middle-class Americans. With the growing influence of television, even blacks in segregated urban areas could not isolate themselves from exposure to the dominant values and customs of America.[64] In 1966, Keil predicted that because "Negro culture" in the urban ghettoes was primarily auditory and tactile, the "high powered auditory forces" of an increasingly electronic or "post-literate" age would give this culture a big technological boost.[65] So the influence of black culture on the white mainstream would likely increase even as physical segregation between blacks and whites in the North deepened. Precisely at the historical juncture when the social scientists were noticing an appreciable decline of the influence of black churches, especially in the urban North, one could observe growing white recognition of black contributions in music, entertainment, and other areas that were made more marketable by technological advances in radio, television, and other media (and these aspects of black culture would eventually be safely separated from their economic, political, and social context through the medium of television, allowing the viewer to enjoy an alienated "product" of a social world mostly created by a system of racial oppression). The soul movement and advocates of a black aesthetic seemed to have come full circle with similar claims of romantic racialists who argued that blacks would make peculiar contributions in many of the same areas that both groups identified.

Meier wrote in 1965 that white Americans found King's talk of Christianity, love, and nonviolence reassuring.[66] Similarly, David Chappell argues that black churches actively involved in the civil rights movement supplied what white liberals lacked. Black leaders like King brought, according to Chappell, a basis for solidarity and self-sacrifice (rooted in an emotional religious tradition) and a prophetic religious realism that made possible a cultural revolution in America.[67] Although Chappell is rather too eager to present blacks as supplying a religious quality to social reform that white liberals lacked (especially his overly confident assertions about prophetic realism and emotional revivalism), we cannot dismiss the later perception of the "righteousness" of the civil rights movement and the laudation (by whites and blacks) of King's religiously infused vision of the good society, which testified to a specific contribution of religious faith and moral vision that blacks in particular had made to the nation. Healthy skepticism is always useful to counter making hasty connections between various periods in history, but surely there is some family resemblance and historical resonance between the various positive and hostile responses to King's role in the civil rights movement and the earlier romantic racialist debates about how a sacrificial Uncle Tom figure, representative of blacks in general, could through a nonviolent and deeply grounded biblical faith absorb the racial and other evils of American society.[68] Was this something similar to that softening element that would "make itself felt as an element of the national character" to which reformer Robert Dale Owens referred in 1864 in his recommendations to President Lincoln about the future course of the freed persons?[69] The sacrifice that King and blacks made to bring about change in American culture makes one wonder if this was something that Harriet Beecher Stowe had in mind when she envisioned a deeply religious and heroic Uncle Tom who would teach America to live up to its ideal values more fully. I raise this in an ironic sense, with an acute awareness that Stowe's notion of Uncle Tom was very different than what the term came to mean among blacks by the 1960s.

Perhaps in no area of academic studies has the desire for a usable past been more pressing and urgent than in the historiography of African American religion. The emphasis on the accommodation/protest dichotomy, the persistent claims of the so-called otherworldliness, the escapist mentality or the compensatory nature of black religion, and the incessant debates about the political role of "the black church" testify to the issues at stake and the normative agenda of continuing constructions of the black church. What historian Barbara Savage writes about the 1930s and 1940s is surely relevant to later discussions of African American religion: "Implicit in many of these criticisms is a set of expectations that the church was called to be all things to all people, to be the savior institution at a time when the institutional infrastructure of the African American community—economic, political, and social—was so very limited."[70] The telling of the story of the black church for contemporary agendas and attempts to enlist the black churches in movements of social reform were not unique to historians and social scientists analyzing black religion, but the vehemence of the debates about black religion and the issues at stake were far greater for blacks because of their exclusion from so many other facets of the broader society and because of their forced reliance on internal voluntary institutions, such as the churches.[71] The weight of the past, mostly negative or simplistic representations of black religion in the broader culture, and the contemporary economic, social, and political problems of the black community placed a peculiar burden on those who sought to write about black history, especially black religion. Apologetic literature to defend "the race," critiques of "the Negro church," efforts to undermine notions of innate religiosity or primitive emotionalism, and calls for black churches to become more politically and socially active become more understandable, though not necessarily defensible, in this light. Church historian Robert T. Handy put his finger on this when he observed in 1968 that feelings of guilt troubled socially progressive white historians as they sought to come to terms with the fuller meaning of what white Christians had done to blacks in the past and present. More important, Handy detected a "touchiness" in discussions of the religious and church life of blacks and observed that the "immediacy and the connections with present problems are much in evidence."[72] The heaviness of the past hovered like the sword of Damocles over the heads of those who sought to write on this painful topic.

But the image of African American religion had wider ramifications than the specific expectations of blacks regarding the role of actual black churches. Sociologist Philip Rieff, reflecting on the prospects of the civil rights movement during the 1960s, wondered if Martin Luther King Jr. and other black religious leaders allied with a white Christian cultural elite could "save the United States from a barbarism long evident in the conduct of their own churches' members, in ordinary American commercial activity, and in the extraordinary incivilities of the American social manner."[73] After further reflection, Rieff argued that there was "little power" in the movement of black protest not so much because he believed that blacks were lacking the will to carry through this attempt at a cultural revolution but because for so long they had been "a focus for *releasing* images in the dominant white culture."[74] Blacks as a symbol of release from the unpleasant side of American culture functioned as a weak basis for a constructive work of cultural renewal. Because the image of blacks in America has historically been one of freedom from the alleged stifling or constricting demands of white culture, the notion of blacks as the "others" who did not belong in the nation or the imagined opposite of the stable white citizen became a natural corollary to this image.[75]

The opposite of this "releasing" image has been that of the brute or savage who threatened to undermine all that was good or moral, precisely that from which white critics of the culture sought escape by means of such projections of blacks. The representation of African American religion has figured prominently in these broader cultural images of blacks and has often revealed more about what whites desired in blacks and what whites hoped to reclaim as their own through their projected images of blacks. How else to explain the popularity of *The Green Pastures* during years of economic depression and social hardship? In these same years, savage lynchings of blacks continued (mostly in the rural South), and yet black activists, with a few white allies, could not get Congress to pass an antilynching bill. The very site of violence and the brutal exploitation of blacks, the rural South, was idealized into a heavenly place where whites could admire the simplicity and religious depth of poor blacks untouched by the problems of modern civilization. If the "Negro-hating" rural white South could produce such lovable and religious people, what other marvels could white oppression engender? The sentimentalist conception of blacks as naturally religious or the image of blacks as a release from the constraints of bourgeois morality contained no mechanism for dealing with real blacks seeking jobs and living space in the adjoining neighborhood.

All the tensions and expectations about black religion that have been examined in this book drove the production and structure of one of the most important works that came out of the ferment of the 1960s—Albert Raboteau's *Slave Religion* (1978). Questions about innate religiosity, African survivals, the role of the "black Church," otherworldliness, and the distinctiveness of black culture shaped and formed this work and these issues have occupied scholarship on African American religion since that time. As Raboteau rejuvenated the Herskovits-Fauset-Frazier debate about the nature of black religion, he remained trapped in the dichotomy of the political implications of assertions of natural religiosity. When Fauset criticized Herskovits's view of black religion, he, like Raboteau, scrutinized the particular assertion that black people, more so than other oppressed groups, turned to religion. The fear was that once one grants the claim that blacks were "naturally religious" or differed fundamentally from whites in their religious practices, they were either complicit in their enslavement or were adherents to a religion that did not spur resistance and self-assertion in the face of racial oppression.[76] So unlike the earlier critics of assertions of black innate religiosity, the worry was no longer that black religiosity would be a hindrance to assimilation into white American culture. Assimilation is precisely what was rejected by a number of black nationalists, and Raboteau's work gives evidence of his enthusiastic acceptance of black and white religious differences, whatever their presumed causes.[77] The major concern for Raboteau (and other interpreters of black religion in the post-1960s context) was the extent to which one explained black religion as a viable alternative in a new cultural situation that demanded black pride and a religion that supported black liberation.[78] The long-standing Marxist critique of religion as the opiate of the masses that deadened the pain of economic and political exploitation had garnered significant support from black intellectuals who criticized what they regarded as the nearly ubiquitous presence of religiosity among the black masses. So long as a significant number of blacks continued to practice Christianity, which was received at the hands of whites, though reworked and reinterpreted for their circumstances, black leaders struggled to come to terms with this fact, which implied partial acceptance of their oppression at the hands of whites.

Black theologian James Cone astutely noted this dilemma when he argued in 1976 that African American college students equated Christianity with the "white man's religion" and often identified such religion as the opiate of the people. For Cone, however, the issue could not be so easily resolved by a rejection of Christianity because this was the religion that he saw his father practice when he rejected the system of Jim Crow during the 1950s. Yet it was precisely because his father was defiant, referring to whites as "sons of bitches," that Cone could hold on to *that kind* of Christianity. So Cone, the radical and outspoken black theologian of the 1970s, urged blacks not to abandon Christianity so hastily because the black Church was not "primarily compensatory or otherworldly in any negative sense."[79] Although he insisted that black religion was a source of pride and affirmation of black worth in a racist society, this rather psychological rendering of the function of religion seemed hardly sufficient to satisfy the kind of activist faith that his students were demanding.

Now is a moment of great dissatisfaction with these particular issues. For one thing, we are beginning to historicize such questions to understand how they emerged in the first place and why they became so pressing to African American leaders. We have enough distance from them that we are able to stand back and ask other, more interesting questions. Now questions of meaning, culture, and practice have captured our attention. Cultural anthropologist Marla Frederick, for example, writes that her recent work, *Between Sundays: Black Women and Everyday Struggles of Faith* (2003), began out of intellectual frustration because social science often reduced religion to a "series of signs, symbols, rituals, and structures" and because the literature on black religion has been fixated on a functionalist interpretation that views it as compensatory or otherworldly. Frederick argues that the "accommodation" and "resistance" paradigm fails to capture the complexity of the everyday lives of religious practitioners, especially black women. She examines the "spirituality" of African American women in eastern North Carolina, focusing on how black women embody their faith and practice their religion in everyday situations outside of the churches.[80] Yet even she feels compelled to demonstrate that African American women resisted "structures of oppression." In her critique of the accommodation/protest paradigm, Frederick seeks to insert additional categories like gender, while leaving it basically intact. Though she acknowledges the limitations of this approach and notes that it does not take into account the "prosaic and constant struggle" of black people for survival and empowerment, she labors to show that faith, religion, spirituality, or the black church can be or has been a source of political strength. It seems too that she is responding to interpretations of black religion that reflected a progressive or activist approach, which tended to deemphasize the quiet and everyday work of building, sustaining, and reaffirming a culture.[81] Her work, then, is a rich study that moves beyond traditional studies in its attention to the varied aspects of black women's lives, especially in her astute analysis of the impact of televangelist ministries, black and white, on black women. Yet it still seems that the weight of past interpretations lies heavily on anyone who enters a discussion of African American religion with little interest in furthering these older debates.

As Frederick argues, we do not wish to leave behind entirely these older issues and questions, but we need not be unduly constrained by a historical debate that no longer resonates with our current situation. Assessing the political function of the black church, for example, has restricted the focus of the historiography of African American religion by obscuring the varied religious motives and activities of black religious persons, something that Frederick gets at in her work. It also implies a unity that is not there and it implicitly regards as backward or escapist those black religious groups or persons who are not involved in progressive political causes. As R. Laurence Moore writes, we must realize that to call certain religious positions escapist or unrealistic because they failed to encourage political activity that promised relief to downtrodden groups conceals how little many people have gotten from politics.[82] Robert Orsi rightly warns us to adopt a "more chastened view of culture generally and of religion in particular, one that steers clear of words like *empowerment* [and] *agency* (simply)" and to move instead in the register of the tragic, limited, and constrained.[83] This warning is all the more urgent in view of the difficult and long history that blacks have endured in America, which should caution scholars against overly robust notions of agency in light of the difficult and constricting social spaces in which Africans Americans have practiced their religions. Perhaps heeding Orsi's warning will help release us from the dichotomous interpretations of black religion that continue to be driven by past debates and enable us to be a bit more modest in our appraisal of how people work within a culture that is always working on them. Newer work must move beyond the black church and free up scholars to construct more interesting and empirically grounded narratives, thereby partially lifting the burden that has weighed so heavily on histories and interpretations of African American religion.[84]

Notes

INTRODUCTION

1. Proctor, *Between Black and White* (Boston: Pilgrim Press, 1925), 40, 45–46, 49.

2. Ibid., 49–53.

3. See Ralph Luker, *The Social Gospel in Black and White: American Racial Reform, 1885–1912* (Chapel Hill: University of North Carolina Press, 1991), 170–171, 184–187.

4. Proctor, *Between Black and White*, 52–53.

5. Allison Dorsey, *To Build Our Lives Together: Community Formation in Black Atlanta, 1875–1906* (Athens: University of Georgia Press, 2004), 73. The published autobiography of Proctor in 1925 rendered these statements as though they were his contemporary opinions of blacks and their distinctive contributions.

6. On the clergymen being "forced by the circumstance of racial slavery in America" to defend Christianity as a means of social control, see Winthrop Jordan, *Black over White: American Attitudes toward the Negro, 1550–1812* (Chapel Hill: University of North Carolina Press, 1968), 191.

7. *An Appeal in Favor of That Class of Americans Called Africans* (1833); reprint, *Against Slavery: An Abolitionist Reader*, ed. Mason Lowance (New York: Penguin Books, 2000), 171.

8. Elizabeth B. Clark, " 'Sacred Rights of the Weak': Pain, Sympathy, and the Culture of Individual Rights in Antebellum America," *Journal of American History* 82 (September 1995): 477.

9. James M. McPherson, "A Brief for Equality: The Abolitionist Reply to the Racist Myth, 1860–1865" (1965), in *Blacks in White America before 1865: Issues and Interpretations*, ed. Robert V. Haynes (New York: David

McKay, 1972), 529. Proctor asserted that his time period (1890s) was dominated by the enterprise, energy, vigor, and thrift of the Saxons and hoped that perhaps in the future Africans would have their day and would bring their unique gifts to the broader world. See Proctor, *Between Black and White*, 51.

10. The exception would be among whites, North and South, in the post–Civil War context and in the late nineteenth and early twentieth centuries, who regarded black religion as emotionalism lacking in morality and who proposed either the overthrow of black churches or the disciplining of black life through industrial labor and the punitive power of the state.

11. Two examples are Eugene Genovese's *Roll, Jordan, Roll* (1972) and Lawrence Levine's *Black Culture and Black Consciousness* (1978). My point here is to place these texts in a historical context, not to reduce the complexity of their arguments and historical research. For insight into the changing shape of the historical profession's approach to the study of African American history in the 1960s and 1970s, see Peter Novick, *That Noble Dream: The "Objectivity Question" and the American Historical Profession* (Cambridge: Cambridge University Press, 1988), 472–491.

12. The first two issues roughly correspond to the first two chapters of Raboteau's book, "The African Diaspora" and "Death of the Gods," and the last two correlate with chapter 6, "Religion, Rebellion, and Docility." A careful reading of the entire book, however, led me to distill these four issues as central. See Albert J. Raboteau, *Slave Religion: The "Invisible Institution" in the Antebellum South* (New York: Oxford University Press, 1978), 3, 43, 289, 329. Raboteau's own view of the historical and personal circumstances that led to his writing this text confirm some of my views about the central issues with which he wrestles in the book. See the afterword to the updated edition of Raboteau, *Slave Religion: The "Invisible Institution" in the Antebellum South* updated edition (New York: Oxford University Press, 2004), 323–334. Black natural religiosity was discussed in *Slave Religion* in the context of Raboteau's intervention in the debate between E. Franklin Frazier and Melville Herskovits about African cultural retentions among American blacks. Raboteau devoted only a paragraph refuting the claim of blacks' alleged innate religiosity by restating Arthur Fauset's critique of Herskovits's claim that blacks possessed a deep religious bent. See Raboteau, *Slave Religion*, 55–56. In the context of the social climate of the 1960s and 1970s, the political role of black churches, shedding images of an otherworldly docile slave religion, and emphasis on the connection to an African past were the most relevant and lively topics of debate.

13. McPherson, "A Brief for Equality," 529.

14. Stanley Harrold, *American Abolitionists* (London: Longman, 2001), 54–55.

15. George M. Fredrickson, *The Black Image in the White Mind: The Debate on Afro-American Character and Destiny, 1817–1914* (Middleton, Conn.: Wesleyan University Press, 1987 [1971]), 125.

16. See Wilson Jeremiah Moses, *The Golden Age of Black Nationalism, 1850–1925* (New York: Oxford University Press, 1988 [1978]), 46–47.

17. Milton Sernett, *Bound for the Promised Land: African American Religion and the Great Migration* (Durham, N.C.: Duke University Press, 1997), 242–243.

CHAPTER 1

1. Although I assert that the defense of slavery became more self-conscious and systematic by the 1830s, I am not arguing that slavery was posited as a "positive good" only *after* the 1830s by Southerners. More recent scholarship traces the defense of slavery to the eighteenth century and also notes the support of Northern defenders. See Larry E. Tise, *Proslavery: A History of the Defense of Slavery, 1701–1840* (Athens: University of Georgia Press, 1987). See also Jeffery Robert Young, *Domesticating Slavery: The Master Class in Georgia and South Carolina, 1670–1837* (Chapel Hill: University of North Carolina Press, 1999); Jeffery Robert Young, ed., *Proslavery and Sectional Thought in the Early South, 1740–1829* (Columbia: University of South Carolina Press, 2006); and Paul Finkelman, ed., *Defending Slavery: Proslavery Thought in the Old South: A Brief History with Documents* (Boston: Bedford Books, 2003). The following work hints at this newer scholarship: Elizabeth Fox-Genovese and Eugene D. Genovese, *The Mind of the Master Class: History and Faith in the Southern Slaveholders' Worldview* (Cambridge: Cambridge University Press, 2005), especially part four ("A Christian People Defend the Faith").

2. Audrey Smedley, *Race in North America: Origin and Evolution of a Worldview*, 2nd ed. (Boulder, Colo.: Westview Press, 1999), 28.

3. For a sample of some of the enormous scholarship on race and slavery in the nineteenth century, see Drew Gilpin Faust, ed., *The Ideology of Slavery: Pro-slavery Thought in the Antebellum South, 1830–1860* (Baton Rouge: Louisiana State University Press, 1981); Matthew Frye Jacoboson, *Whiteness of a Different Color: European Immigrants and the Alchemy of Race* (Cambridge, Mass.: Harvard University Press, 1998); Paul Goodman, *Of One Blood: Abolitionism and the Origins of Racial Equality* (Berkeley: University of California Press, 1998); Stanley Harrold, *The Abolitionists and the South, 1831–1861* (Lexington: University of Kentucky Press, 1995); and Stanley Harrold, *American Abolitionists* (London: Longman, 2001). A form of cultural environmentalism, which explained the differences between Europeans and Africans as a product of their natural habitat and climate, was one of the major historical developments of the second half of the eighteenth century. Environmentalism was appealing to Americans in the Revolutionary era because it confirmed the logic of natural rights and the assertion that all men were created equal. See Winthrop Jordan, *White over Black: American Attitudes toward the Negro, 1550–1812* (Chapel Hill: University of North Carolina Press, 1968), 287–288. Some historians doubt the prevalence of environmentalism during this time period, arguing instead for a limited "extremely environmentalist posture" that attributed skin color to the direct effects of climate, the state of society, and a people's manner of living. Yet even those who hold this view acknowledge that the idea that the mental, moral, and psychological characteristics of blacks were the result of environment persisted and that this notion was not effectively challenged as a "respectable ethnological doctrine" until the 1830s. See George M. Frederickson, *The Black Image in the White Mind: The Debate on Afro-American Character and Destiny, 1817–1914* (Middleton, Conn.: Wesleyan University Press, 1987 [1971]), 1–3. There were certainly variations in assertions of the

commonality of humans and different bases on which these claims were made. The point is that the religious and scientific aspects of claims about Africans' capacities and destiny in the New World changed over time, often depending on what system of thought and practice (science or religion) held the greatest cultural authority.

4. Jon Butler, "Enlarging the Bonds of Christ: Slavery, Evangelism, and the Christianization of the South, 1690–1790," in *The Evangelical Tradition in America*, ed. Leonard I. Sweet (Macon, Ga.: Mercer University Press, 1997 [1984]), 109. See also Butler, *Awash in a Sea of Faith: Christianizing the American People* (Cambridge, Mass.: Harvard University Press, 1990), 129–151.

5. For a helpful distinction between abolitionists and those opposed to slavery or its extension into Western territories, see Harrold, *American Abolitionists*, 3–9.

6. On the religious and cultural context of appeals to sympathy on behalf of slaves, see Elizabeth B. Clark, " 'The Sacred Rights of the Weak': Pain, Sympathy, and the Culture of Individual Rights in Antebellum America," *Journal of American History* 82 (September 1995): 463–493.

7. Harrold, *American Abolitionists*, 52–53.

8. Fredrickson, *Black Image*, 127.

9. Jordan, *White over Black*, 190. For a recent and brief attempt to read Jordan's classic text in light of some of the vast body of work on race that has accumulated since its original publication, see James Campbell and James Oakes, "The Invention of Race: Rereading *White over Black*," *Reviews in American History* 21 (March 1993): 172–183. For a general overview of European travelers' and missionaries' views of African cultures from the sixteenth to the eighteenth century, see Michael Adas, *Machines as the Measure of Men: Science, Technology, and Ideologies of Western Dominance* (Ithaca, N.Y.: Cornell University Press, 1989), 31–41, 65–68, 108–122.

10. On the monopoly of Anglicans in early attempts at slave conversion, see Sylvia R. Frey and Betty Wood, *Come Shouting to Zion: African American Protestantism in the American South and British Caribbean to 1830* (Chapel Hill: University of North Carolina Press, 1998), 63.

11. Albert Raboteau, *Slave Religion: The "Invisible Institution" in the Antebellum South* (New York: Oxford University Press, 1978), 126.

12. Ibid., 101–103.

13. Young, *Proslavery and Sectional Thought*, 68–69.

14. *Three Letters from the Reverend Mr. G. Whitefield* (1740; reprint, Young, *Proslavery and Sectional Thought*), 71–72.

15. Samuel Davies, *The Duty of Christians to Propagate Their Religion among the Heathens, Earnestly Recommended to the Masters of Negroe Slaves in Virginia* (1758; reprint, Young, *Proslavery and Sectional Thought*), 101.

16. Ibid., 111.

17. Ibid.

18. Ibid., 111–112.

19. Jeffrey Young argues that missionaries were not successful in the eighteenth century in their attempts to convince slave owners that Christianity made slaves more

docile and did not lead to rebellions or insurrections. See Young, *Domesticating Slavery*, 143–144.

20. See *Thomas Jefferson: Writings*, ed. Merrill D. Peterson (New York: Library of America, 1984), 264–270, 901–902, 90; and Jordan, *White over Black*, 430–455, 498–511. Reflecting the common sense moral philosophy of Dugald Stewart and others, Jefferson indicated to his nephew that our Creator "would have been a pitiful bungler if he had made the rules of our moral conduct a matter of science" (901). On the importance of the "moral sense" for American Protestant theological formulations in Jefferson's time, see Mark A. Noll, *America's God: From Jonathan Edwards to Abraham Lincoln* (New York: Oxford University Press, 2002), 110–113. Bruce Dain argues that Jefferson did not insist on the fundamental humanity of blacks when he asserted that they possessed a moral sense. Dain contends that Jefferson and contemporaries in the Scottish moral sense tradition who influenced his thought did not define "humanity" based on the moral sense. See Dain, *A Hideous Monster of the Mind: American Race Theory in the Early Republic* (Cambridge, Mass.: Harvard University Press, 2002), 35, 274 (note 78). If Dain is correct, it is difficult to make sense of Jefferson's comments to his nephew that the moral sense "is as much a part of man as his leg or arm" (901). By arguing that all, even the least intelligent, possess a moral sense over against the few who understood the rules and methods of "science," Jefferson was affirming the moral sense both as the common trait of humanity and the quality without which no society could be constructed and maintained. For these reasons, I do not agree with Dain's assessment, though my disagreement is in no way intended to understate Jefferson's low view of blacks, especially his jarring remarks that the "Oranootan" preferred to mate with black women rather than with his own species!

21. Jordan, *White over Black*, 454–455. See also James T. Campbell, *Songs of Zion: The African Methodist Episcopal Church in the United States and South Africa* (Chapel Hill: University of North Carolina Press, 1998), 16–29. Whether "scientific" or other achievements of blacks were being offered as specimens of their humanity, Jefferson grew irritated with the whole enterprise. Later, he dismissed the work of Benjamin Banneker, a black mathematician, as unoriginal (and thus, in his view, resembling the imitative and noncreative limitations of the black mind). Whatever Jefferson may have thought of blacks, Jordan's claim that the separation of morals from intellect had important implications for the evaluation of black capacities still seems plausible in light of the types of persons whom abolitionists seized on as evidence of black equality. For one of the most penetrating analyses of Jefferson's racial thought, again see Jordan, *White over Black*, 450–455.

22. *Thomas Jefferson*, 265–270. See also, Paul Finkelman, *Slavery and the Founders: Race and Liberty in the Age of Jefferson*, 2nd ed. (Armonk, N.Y.: M. E. Sharpe, 2001), 129–196.

23. Jordan, *White over Black*, 481.

24. Fredrickson, *Black Image*, 97–98. I have followed Fredrickson's narrative closely in my summary in this paragraph, and I am indebted to his analysis in

much that follows, but I have offered a different reading of some of the documents he cites. I also bring his work into conversation with additional secondary sources and my own analysis of African American leaders' participation in this discussion.

25. Frederickson, *Black Image*, 98; Jacobsen, *Whiteness of a Different Color*, 43–44.

26. James Freeman Clarke, "Slavery in the United States," sermon delivered in Armory Hall, on Thanksgiving Day, November 12, 1842, in *Essays and Pamphlets on Antislavery* (Westport, Conn.: Negro Universities Press, 1970), 1–15.

27. Ibid., 98–99; Jordan, *White over Black*, 287–289, 533–538. See also Thomas Gossett, *Race: The History of an Idea in America* (New York: Oxford University Press, 1997), 84–93; and Jacobson, *Whiteness of a Different Color*, 39–47.

28. Theodore Parker, "On Anglo-Saxon and African" (1854; reprint, *Racial Thought in America: From the Puritans to Abraham Lincoln, a Documentary History*, ed. Louis Ruchames [Boston: University of Massachusetts Press, 1969]), 367–369.

29. Theodore Parker, "The Races of America," in *Racial Thought*, 369–372.

30. George Frederickson has called for a deeper study of Parker's racial views. He argues that Parker was an extreme racist when he discussed black views in the abstract, but a militant egalitarian on questions of racial policy. See Frederickson, *Black Image*, 119–120, where he notes Parker's acceptance of common views of the sexual immorality and looseness of black women.

31. Frederickson, *Black Image*, 101.

32. Tilton is cited in Fredrickson, *Black Image*, 114–115.

33. Harrold, *Abolitionists and the South*, 48–49.

34. Hollis Read, *The Negro Problem Solved; Or, Africa as She Was, as She Is, and as She Shall Be* (New York: A. A. Constantine, 1864).

35. Fredrickson, *Black Image*, 108–109.

36. Albert Taylor Bledsoe, a professor of mathematics at the University of Virginia, and Charles Hodge, a prominent theologian at Princeton Seminary, interacted rather extensively with Channing in the essays that they contributed to the massive *Cotton Is King* anthology in 1860.

37. William Ellery Channing, *Slavery* (Boston: James Munroe, 1835), 100–101.

38. Ibid., 126. See also Fredrickson, *Black Image*, 103; and Daniel Walker Howe, *The Unitarian Conscience: Harvard Moral Philosophy, 1805–1861* (Middleton, Conn.: Wesleyan University Press, 1998 [1970]), 286–294. Howe writes that Channing never really dealt with the arguments of Southern anthropologists that blacks were inferior to whites and especially suited to slavery.

39. Fredrickson, *Black Image*, 116–117. The connection between colonizationist sentiment and romantic racialism is further strengthened when one closely examines Channing's feelings about free blacks. Though Channing made an eloquent public critique of slavery, his personal and private opinions indicated deep emotions of prejudice against blacks, particularly free blacks. He also believed that phrenology (the science of head shapes and temperaments) proved that blacks had smaller brains and more limited intellect than whites. For more on Channing from the viewpoint of English traveler Edward Abdy, who arrived in the United States in 1833

and later wrote of his conversations with Americans on a number of issues, including their views on blacks and slavery, see Goodman, *Of One Blood*, 240–243.

40. See Henry Noble Sherwood, "Early Negro Deportation Projects," *Mississippi Valley Historical Review* 2 (March 1916): 484–508; P. J. Studenraus, *The African Colonization Movement, 1816–1865* (New York: Columbia University Press 1961), 1–22; and Floyd J. Miller, *The Search for a Black Nationality: Black Emigration and Colonization, 1787–1863* (Urbana: University of Illinois Press, 1975), 3–4.

41. By the 1820s, white wage laborers in the North feared that black advancement would come at their expense. Racial violence became common in the North as a result of these fears and those of wealthy white "gentlemen of property and standing" who perceived immediate abolition to be a threat to the social order. See Harrold, *American Abolitionists*, 51–52.

42. Leon F. Litwack, *North of Slavery: The Negro in the Free States, 1790–1860* (Chicago: University of Chicago Press, 1961), 20–23.

43. Studenraus, *African Colonization Movement*, 20.

44. Jordan, *White over Black*, 550.

45. Hugh Thomas, *The Slave Trade: The Story of the Atlantic Slave Trade: 1440–1870* (New York: Touchstone, 1999), 270.

46. Leonard I. Sweet, *Black Images of America, 1784–1870* (New York: W. W. Norton, 1976), 23–28.

47. Miller, *Search for a Black Nationality*, 45; and Sweet, *Black Images*, 36.

48. Henry Noble Sherwood, "The Formation of the American Colonization Society," *Journal of Negro History* 2 (July 1917): 224.

49. "Address to the National Convention of 1834," in *Pamphlets of Protest: An Anthology of Early African American Protest Literature, 1790–1860*, eds. Richard Newman, Patrick Rael, and Phillip Lapsansky (New York: Routledge, 2001), 112.

50. Sherwood, "Formation of the American Colonization Society," 224.

51. Goodman, *Of One Blood*, 19.

52. "American Colonization Society: A Memorial to the United States Congress," in *Civil Rights and African Americans*, eds. Albert P. Blaustein and Robert L. Zangrando (Evanston, Ill.: Northwest University Press, 1991 [1968]), 70. For an argument that grounds the formation of the American Colonization Society in fears about free blacks as a violent and permanent laboring class, see Douglas R. Eagerton, " 'Its Origin Is Not a Little Curious': A New Look at the American Colonization Society," *Journal of the Early Republic* 5 (winter 1985): 463–480. Eagerton claims that fears about blacks becoming a violent and troubling underclass drove colonizationist sentiment more than religion or reform-oriented benevolence. Although it is certainly plausible that these worries may have been central factors in the origin of the movement, I want to maintain that religious rhetoric and Christian missionaries' concerns about Christianizing Africans were also crucial components in the *evolution* of colonizationists' efforts, whether or not they were *the* central impetus in the formation of the American Colonization Society.

53. Alexander Kinmont, *The Natural History of Man and the Rise and Progress of Philosophy* (Philadelphia: J. B. Lippincott, 1891), 170–193, 212–223.

54. Ibid., 91.

55. Ibid.

56. Ibid., 91–93.

57. Ibid., 186.

58. Ibid., 170–193, 212–223.

59. Ibid., 190–91, 195, 211–12.

60. Ibid., 186, 191, 215. Kinmont wrote that "the Negro and the European belong to distinct races of men . . . such as cannot be shown to be bred out of any combination of causes, natural or artificial, with which we are acquainted: and the causes, then, or the things which produced those original distinctions, I aver that I know nothing of,—they are *obscure*" (193; emphasis in original).

61. Clark, "Sacred Rights of the Weak," 477.

62. Ibid. See also David Brion Davis, "What the Abolitionists Were up Against," in *The Antislavery Debate: Capitalism and Abolitionism as a Problem in Historical Interpretation*, ed. Thomas Bender (Berkeley: University of California Press, 1992), 22–24.

63. In sorting through these changes about feminine emotions and the role of women in the spread of these ideas, I have found the following works helpful: Clark, "Sacred Rights of the Weak"; Gayle Kimball, *The Religious Ideas of Harriet Beecher Stowe: Her Gospel of Womanhood* (New York: Edwin Mellen Press, 1982); and Jane Tompkins, *Sensational Designs: The Cultural Work of American Fiction, 1790–1860* (New York: Oxford University Press, 1985).

64. Robert H. Abzug, *Cosmos Crumbling: American Reform and the Religious Imagination* (New York: Oxford University Press, 1994), 199–200.

65. *A Lydia Maria Child Reader*, ed. Carolyn L. Karcher (Durham, N.C.: Duke University Press, 1997), 137.

66. *An Appeal in Behalf of That Class of Americans Called Africans* (1833; reprint, Mason Lowance, ed. *Against Slavery: An Abolitionist Reader* [New York: Penguin Books, 2000]), 171.

67. *An Appeal*, in Karcher, *Lydia Maria Child Reader*, 171.

68. *An Appeal*, in Ruchames, *Racial Thought*, 316.

69. Ibid., 330.

70. Karcher, *Lydia Maria Child Reader*, 415.

71. Ibid., 214.

72. Ibid., 213.

73. Ibid, 214. George Fredrickson argues that Child also aired her speculations in 1842 that blacks and whites were "spiritually" and "physically" different. Although she denied that such differences had always existed, she insisted that they were the effects of "spiritual influences" operating on human character over an extended period of time. Child argued for "variety without inferiority" and asserted that whites should not tyrannize blacks or others even if they were different than blacks and possessed a superior intellect. See Frederickson, *Black Image*, 107. I have not been able to locate the exact source of Child's and Kinmont's quotations from Swedenborg's writings. Regarding one of his visions into heaven, Swedenborg wrote, "Among the heathen in heaven the Africans are most beloved, for they receive the

goods and truths of heaven more readily than others." *Heaven and Hell* (West Chester, Penn.: Swedenborg Foundation, 1995 [1758]), no. 326. In another place, he talks about Africans surpassing others in powers of inward judgment and in their deeper faith in God. *The True Christian Religion* (London: Swedenborg Society, 1988), nos. 835, 837. One author writes: "The life of the African nations, according to Swedenborg, most closely resembles life in the celestial kingdom. When Africans die they form communities and live much the same way they did on earth. Africans 'think interiorly' and follow their religion and its laws because of love, while Europeans (representatives of the spiritual kingdom) are merely born into their religion and follow its doctrine only because of its authority. In heaven, the highest angelic communities resemble those Swedenborg believes were African—naked, primitive, anarchic, and spontaneous." For quotation, see Erland J. Brock, ed., *Swedenborg and His Influence* (Bryn Athyn, Penn.: Academy of the New Church, 1988), 320.

74. On the possible influence of Kinmont, see Joan Hedrick, *Harriet Beecher Stowe: A Life* (New York Oxford University Press, 1994), 209–210; and Fredrickson, *Black Image*, 110–115.

75. The general and very well-known story line, plot, and setting of the novel need not concern us here. I am only interested in those sections of her work that deal with blacks as naturally religious and racially distinctive.

76. *The American Evangelicals, 1800–1900*, ed. William G. McLaughlin (New York: Harper and Row, 1968), 14.

77. See Hedrick, *Harriet Beecher Stowe*, 278–279.

78. Harriet Beecher Stowe, *Uncle Tom's Cabin or, Life among the Lowly* (Cambridge: Cambridge University Press, 1886), 82.

79. Ibid., 107.

80. Ibid., iv, 1–5, 161. For a broader analysis of the literary and social uses of "Uncle Tom," see Wilson Jeremiah Moses, *Black Messiahs and Uncle Toms: Social and Literary Manipulations of a Religious Myth* (University Park: Pennsylvania State University Press, 1982).

81. See Kinmont, *Natural History of Man*, 211.

82. On this point, see Arthur Riss, "Racial Essentialism and Family Values in 'Uncle Tom's Cabin'," *American Quarterly* 46 (December 1994): 513–544. Riss contends that "Stowe's commitment to racial difference is precisely what enables her denunciation of slavery" (514). However, he seems to be on safer ground when he asserts that "the most effective way Stowe elicits sympathy for Negroes is by giving them an essentially Christian character" (517). This point, in my view, is crucial to an understanding of the image of blacks as naturally religious. By locating religion (with Christian traits) within the biology or racial heritage of slaves, Stowe sought to draw sympathy for them, as if to ask how can Christian-professing people enslave persons naturally endowed with these admirable religious qualities?

83. Stowe, *Uncle Tom's Cabin*, 200; emphasis in original.

84. Riss, "Racial Essentialism and Family Values," 535–536.

85. Stowe, *Uncle Tom's Cabin*, 200, 441. In his review of the book, William Lloyd Garrison criticized Stowe on this point. See *William Lloyd Garrison and the Fight*

against Slavery: Selections from the Liberator, ed. William E. Cain (New York: Bedford Books, 1994), 127–131. Garrison expressed his regret to see the book concluding with "objectionable sentiments respecting African colonization." He also queried Stowe as to whether she was espousing Christian nonresistance only for blacks. Garrison wanted to know if there were two Christs, one who authorized whites to overthrow tyranny by violence and bloodshed, and another who required that blacks be patient, harmless, long-suffering, and forgiving. No doubt he was deeply troubled by the implications of the submissive Uncle Tom who meekly submits to being brutally beaten to death at the hands of the vicious Simon Legree. Garrison seems never to have entertained the views of the romantic racialists (his rejection of colonization and its associated rhetoric were no doubt factors), and thus expressed little sympathy for Stowe's fear that Garrison's radicalism would "take from poor Uncle Tom his Bible, and give him nothing in his place." As Garrison wrote to Stowe, "If the infernal cruelty of Legree could not shake his trust in his God and Saviour, do you really think a full discussion of the merits of the Bible, pro and con, might induce him to throw that volume away" (137). Perhaps Garrison's perspective on the Bible reminded Stowe too much of the Cicero whose head was filled with so many troubling questions that they unsettled his faith rather than established it. Tom's faith, after all, was simple and unquestioning. Garrison's approach to the Bible demanded that "neither of us accept any more of it than we sincerely believe to be in accordance with reason, truth, [and] eternal right."

86. See Hedrick, *Harriet Beecher Stowe,* chap. 20; and Thomas Graham, "Harriet Beecher Stowe and the Question of Race," *New England Quarterly* 46 (December 1973): 619–620.

87. See Robert C. Fuller, *Mesmerism and the American Cure of Souls* (Philadelphia: University of Pennsylvania Press, 1982), 48–82.

88. *Key to Uncle Tom's Cabin* (1853; reprint Joan D. Hedrick, ed., *The Oxford Harriet Beecher Stowe Reader* [New York: Oxford University Press, 1999]), 421.

89. Ibid., 418.

90. Ibid., 421–422.

91. For one prominent Southern clergyman's assertion that slave owners did not have authority over the slave's soul, see William W. Freehling, "James Henley Thornwell's Mysterious Antislavery Moment," *Journal of Southern History* 57 (August 1991): 383–406.

92. See also Philip D. Curtin, *The Image of Africa: British Ideas and Action, 1780–1850,* vol. 2 (Madison: University of Wisconsin Press, 1973), 376–377. Curtin notes that several British and continental authors (for example, W. R. Greg and Gustave Klemm) made distinctions between active and passive races. Greg, for example, contrasted vehement, proud, and energetic Europeans to the natural Christian submissiveness of Africans.

93. Thomas R. R. Cobb, "What Is Slavery, and Its Foundation in the Natural Law," reprint, *Defending Slavery, Pro-slavery Thought in the Old South: A Brief History With Documents,* ed. Paul Finkelman (Boston: Bedford Books, 2003), 143–156. Other

essays in the Finkelman collection were used to provide the summary of views of black character in proslavery writings. See also Faust, *The Ideology of Slavery*; and *Antebellum Writings of George Fitzhugh and Hinton Rowan Helper on Slavery*, ed. Harvey Wish (New York: Capricorn Books, 1960).

94. Kenneth Paul O'Brien, "The Savage and the Child in Historical Perspective; Images of Blacks in Southern White Thought, 1830–1915" (Ph.D. diss., Northwestern University, 1974), 31–33.

95. John W. Blassingame, *Slave Community: Plantation Life in the Antebellum South* (New York: Oxford University Press, 1979), 230.

96. Cobb, "What Is Slavery?," 143–156.

97. Ibid., 155; Albert Taylor Bledsoe, "Liberty and Slavery: Or, Slavery in the Light of Moral and Political Philosophy," in *Cotton Is King and Pro-Slavery Arguments*, ed. E. N. Elliott, part 1 (1860; reprint Adamant Media, 2003), 416.

98. Nehemiah Adams, *The Sable Cloud: A Southern Tale, with Northern Comments* (Boston, 1861), quoted in Riss, "Racial Essentialism and Family Values," 520.

99. William Stanton, *The Leopard's Spot: Scientific Attitudes toward Race in America, 1815–1859* (Chicago: University of Chicago, 1960), 18. In a close analysis of the work of Samuel Stanhope Smith, president of the College of New Jersey and one of the most important theorists of race in early America, Bruce Dain points out that even racial environmentalism was riddled with tensions about whether blackness was a moral defect or a temporary state on the way to whiteness. See Dain, *Hideous Monster*, chap. 2.

100. See Stanton, *Leopard's Spot*, for a discussion of the precise nature of these conflicts.

101. Smedley, *Race in North America*, 28.

102. Jacobson, *Whiteness of a Different Color*, 32.

103. James O. Farmer Jr., *The Metaphysical Confederacy: James Henley Thornwell and the Synthesis of Southern Values* (Macon, GA: Mercer University Press. 1999 [1986]), 87–109.

104. See *Slavery Defended: The Views of the Old South*, ed. Eric L. McKitrick (Englewood Cliffs, N.J.: Prentice Hall, 1963), 126–127.

105. Curtin, *Image of Africa*, 372.

106. Frederick Douglass, "The Claims of the Negro Ethnologically Considered," in Philip S. Foner, ed. *Frederick Douglass: Selected Speeches and Writings*, abridged and adapted by Yuval Taylor (Chicago: Lawrence Hill Books, 1999), 282–297.

107. Nancy Leys Stephan and Sander L. Gilman, "Appropriating the Idioms of Science: The Rejection of Scientific Racism" in *The "Racial" Economy of Science: Toward a Democratic Future*, ed. Sandra Harding (Bloomington: Indiana University Press, 1993), 175–176.

108. Fitzhugh, *Sociology for the South or the Failure of Free Society* (1854; reprint, Wish, ed., *Antebellum Writings of George Fitzhugh*), 89, 95.

109. Sweet, *Black Images*, 110–117. See also, Campbell, *Songs of Zion*, 20, who contends that the rise of independent black churches marked a crucial juncture in the

history of black nationalism that should not be confused with the idea that blacks shared an essential, racial genius (as later advanced by Alexander Crummell and W. E. B. Du Bois).

110. Wilson Jeremiah Moses, *The Golden Age of Black Nationalism, 1850–1925* (New York: Oxford University Press, 1988 [1978]), 32–47. See also *Black Nationalism in America*, eds. John H. Bracey Jr., August Meier, and Elliott Rudwick (Indianapolis: Bobbs-Merrill, 1970), xxv–xxxviii.

111. See *Dred Scott v. Sanford: A Brief History with Documents*, ed. Paul Finkelman (Boston: Bedford Books, 1997), 1–10, 61. On the political climate of the late 1850s, see John Hope Franklin and Alred A. Moss Jr., *From Slavery to Freedom: A History of African Americans*, 8th ed. (Boston: McGraw-Hill, 2000), 214–219.

112. For Stowe's remarks, see *Uncle Tom's Cabin*, 493.

113. Sweet, *Black Images*, 39–40.

114. Benjamin Quarles, *Black Abolitionists* (New York: Oxford University Press, 1969), 4–6; and Carol V. R. George, *Segregated Sabbaths: Richard Allen and the Rise of Independent Black Churches, 1760–1840* (New York: Oxford University Press, 1973), 135–136.

115. Campbell, *Songs of Zion*, 68.

116. Miller, *Search for a Black Nationality*, viii.

117. Ibid., ix.

118. *Liberator* (November 20, 1852; reprint, Carter G. Woodson, ed., *The Mind of the Negro as Reflected in Letters Written During the Crisis, 1800–1860* [New York: Russell and Russell, 1969 (1926)]), 282–283.

119. William Cooper Nell, an African American who was involved in efforts to integrate Boston public schools, indicated in a letter to Garrison that a large number of "colored citizens of New Bedford" was deeply troubled by the contents of Mann's letter. However, Nell was sure that such criticisms did not detract from Mann's "quota of applause" because he had done too much on behalf of blacks in his work against slavery. Nell commended the New Bedford blacks for their passion for freedom and their staunch opposition to any suggestion of colonization. See his comments in *Liberator* (December 1852) in Woodson, *Mind of the Negro*, 336.

120. Douglass to Harriet Beecher Stowe, March 8, 1853, in Foner, *Frederick Douglass*, 216–217.

121. Delany to William Lloyd Garrison, in *Liberator* (May 21, 1852) in Woodson, *Mind of the Negro*, 292–293.

122. Delany to Frederick Douglass in *Frederick Douglass' Paper*, April 29, 1853, in *Martin R. Delany: A Documentary Reader*, ed. Robert S. Levine (Chapel Hill: University of North Carolina Press, 2003), 233.

123. Ibid., 232; emphasis in original.

124. There were also protests against the admission of a woman during this academic year. The female student, on the advice of the faculty, withdrew her application. See "Martin R. Delany and the Harvard Medical School," in *Blacks at Harvard: A Documentary History of African-American Experience at Harvard and Radcliffe*, eds.

Werner Sollers, Caldwell Titcomb, and Thomas A. Underwood (New York: New York University Press, 1993), 19–20, 22–31.

125. Martin Delany, *The Condition, Elevation, Emigration, and Destiny of the Colored People of the United States* (1852; reprint, *Negro Social and Political Thought, 1850–1920: Representative Texts*, ed. Howard Brotz [New York: Basic Books, 1966]), 50.

126. *North Star*, January 16, 1849. On Delany's and other free Northern blacks' struggle with religion in the lives of slaves and its relation to blacks' situation in the nation in the mid-nineteenth century, see Eddie S. Glaude Jr., *Exodus! Religion, Race, and Nation in Early Nineteenth-Century Black America* (Chicago: University of Chicago Press, 2000), 19–43.

127. *North Star*, February 16, 1849. The claim that religious fatalism was widespread in black communities, as Delany argued, was also made in the writings of Thomas Wentworth Higginson. Higginson, an abolitionist and Unitarian, served in 1863 as colonel of First South Carolina Volunteers, a regiment of freed slaves. His journal notes of his experiences were later published as *Army Life in a Black Regiment* (1869), which became widely known for its collection of slave spirituals. Higginson wrote: "No matter how reckless in bearing they might be, those negroes were almost fatalists in their confidence that God would watch over them; and if they died, it would be because their time had come." See "The Black Troops: 'Intensely Human,'" in *The Magnificent Activist: The Writings of Thomas Wentworth Higginson (1823–1911)*, ed. Howard N. Meyer (New York: Da Capo Press, 2000), 188. Higginson's musings about the differences and similarities of the "Irish" or Celtic race, the Anglo-Saxon race, and the African race confirm the findings of "whiteness" studies about the fluidity of racial categories and the attribution of "racial" traits to ethnic and cultural groupings. Higginson believed that blacks and the Irish had several attributes in common: warmth of heart, open demonstrativeness, and a "religious element" that was characterized by an almost fatalistic dependence on God. He argued that these were attractive qualities that made each group "intensely human." He also affirmed that the Irish and blacks were more similar to Western recruits than to the "more reticent and self-controlled New England men" (187–188).

128. Delany, *Condition and Destiny of the Colored Race*, 54.

129. Ibid., 51. Delany also wrote: "We must therefore become a business, money-making people. Prayer and praise only fill one's soul with emotion, but can never fill his mouth with bread, nor his pocket with money. Whilst colored people are HOPING, the white man is DOING. We must also DO, if we desire the same enjoyments and possessions of this life." See *North Star*, March 23, 1849. Delany claimed that he was not denigrating Christianity, nor was he casting aspersions against God (though his writings give evidence of his struggles with God's providence and goodness in light of black oppression at the hands of whites, whom he deemed to have done far more evil than blacks). But he was trying to wean blacks away from what he saw as fatalistic reliance on providence and a failure to exert themselves to improve their earthly existence. Delany also urged blacks to stop "believing any interpretation that our oppressors may give the word of God." In his view, blacks had

been duped by the theology of slaveholders and white Christians who wanted to make them accept their enslavement.

130. "Political Destiny of the Colored Race on the American Continent" (1854), in Newman, Rael, and Lapsansky, *Pamphlets of Protest*, 231.

131. Ibid., 232.

132. "The Races of America," in Ruchames, *Racial Thought*, 371–372. See also, Mia Bay, *The White Image in the Black Mind: African American Ideas about White People, 1830–1925* (New York: Oxford University Press, 2000), 72–73, who argues that "aggression and masculinity were at a premium in American society" at this time. A reputation for gentle virtues and a "soft" Christianity did not stand blacks in good stead. These debates would become more acute as arguments about blacks' fitness for fighting emerged during the Civil War. On the radical abolitionist call to arms, most prominently in John Brown's raid of Harper's Ferry, see John Stauffer, *The Black Hearts of Men: Radical Abolitionists and the Transformation of Race* (Cambridge, Mass.: Harvard University Press, 2001), chap. 1.

133. Harrold, *The Abolitionists and the South*, 48–53; George M. Fredrickson, *The Inner Civil War: Northern Intellectuals and the Crisis of the Union* (Urbana: University of Illinois Press, 1993 [1963]), 36–43; and Fredrickson, *Black Image*, 119–121.

134. Moses distinguishes between white conservatives who were sympathetic to black Americans and hoped to see them a free and prosperous people far from the shores of America (the benevolent conservatives) and those who were hostile to black freedom and flourishing and simply wanted to dump free blacks into Liberia or some other location. This latter group was deeply opposed to antislavery and abolitionist activity. See Moses, *Golden Age of Black Nationalism*, 33.

135. Read, *Negro Problem Solved*, iv–v.

136. Ibid., v–vii.

137. See Stowe, *Uncle Tom's Cabin*, 200.

138. Read, *Negro Problem Solved*, iv.

139. Ibid., 347–348, 350–351. On this point of the presence of religion in black communities over against the commercial values of whites, Read's views were remarkably similar to those of Martin Delany.

140. Ibid., 332–333.

141. Ibid., 333–337. See also Edward Wilmot Blyden, "The Call of Providence to the Descendants of Africa in America," in Brotz, ed., *Negro Social and Political Thought*, 122–126. On Blyden's call for an indigenous form of African Christianity that conformed to what he called an "African personality," see Kwame Bediako, *Christianity in Africa: The Renewal of a Non-Western Religion* (Maryknoll, N.Y.: Orbis Books, 1997), 6–16.

142. Read, *Negro Problem Solved*, 397.

143. Owen was also the son of Robert Owen, who had founded the communitarian society at New Harmony, Indiana.

144. Robert Dale Owen, *The Wrong of Slavery; The Right of Emancipation; and The Future of the African Race in the United States* (New York: Kraus Reprint, 1969 [1864]), 220–221; emphasis added. See also, Fredrickson, *Black Image*, 116–117, 124.

145. Discussions of the place of blacks in the nation invariably involved analyses of "racial traits." One of the most common claims for blacks' and whites' ability to live together or benefit from the other was the assertion of black "imitativeness." Linked to this notion was a comparison of blacks with Indians, who were regarded as incapable of adapting to the rapid advances of Anglo-Saxon civilization and who would therefore eventually die out under the breath of European dominance. Gilbert Haven, Methodist bishop of Massachusetts, claimed that "eminent physiologists" affirmed that blacks were superior to Indians. Blacks possessed a grander nature, a more original and divine character, and superior manly qualities. Blacks excelled over Indians and whites in imitation and humor. See Haven, *National Sermons: Sermons, Speeches and Letters on Slavery and Its War: From the Passage of the Fugitive Slave Bill to the Election of President Grant* (Boston: Lee and Shepard, 1869), 128–131. Blacks favorably compared themselves to Indians, often at the latter's expense. To prove that blacks could adapt to civilization and imitate the virtues of Anglo-Saxons, Frederick Douglass asserted: "His tawny brother, the Indian, dies, under the flashing glance of the Anglo-Saxon. *Not* so the Negro; civilization cannot kill him. He accepts it—becomes part of it. In the Church, he is an Uncle Tom, in the State, he is the most abused and least offensive. All the facts in his history mark out for him a destiny, united to America" (emphasis in original). See Douglass, "The Claims of the Negro Ethnologically Considered," 297. For a brief but suggestive comment on black images of Indians, see Sweet, *Black Images*, 86–88.

146. Lawrence N. Powell, "Introduction," in Frederick Law Olmstead, *The Cotton Kingdom: A Traveller's Observations on Cotton and Slavery in the American Slave States*, ed. Arthur M. Schlesinger (New York: Modern Library, 1984 [1861]), xiv–xxiv.

147. Olmsted, "Letters on the Productions, Industry and Resources of the Southern States," *New York Daily Times*, June 21, 1853, in *The Papers of Frederick Law Olmsted: Slavery and the South, 1852–1856*, vol. 2, eds. Charles E. Beveridge and Charles Capin McLaughlin (Baltimore, Md.: John Hopkins University Press, 1981), 166.

148. Ibid., 167.

149. Ibid., 168. Olmsted summed up this argument by stating that slavery was "at war with progress, with enlightenment, [and] with Christianity" and that the "native manly spirit and capacity of the savage is but poorly compensated for by the pseudo-religion and civilization of the slave" (168).

150. Nat Turner's revolt occurred in Virginia in 1831, and it was well known that Turner was a precocious youth who was deeply immersed in the Scriptures and attributed his revolt to divine urgings.

151. Olmsted, *Cotton Kingdom*, 467.

152. On Olmsted's assertions of the basic humanity of slaves, see his "Letters on the Productions, Industry and Resources of the Southern States," *New York Daily News*, June 30, 1853, in *Papers of Olmsted*, 177–178.

153. Olmsted, *Cotton Kingdom*, 467.

154. Ibid., 240–242.

155. Ibid., 242. See also Blassingame, *Slave Community*, 131. Blassingame cites a white missionary who in 1863 observed the "wonderful sympathy between the [black]

speaker and the audience." See also Eugene Genovese, *Roll, Jordan, Roll: The World the Slaves Made* (New York: Vintage Books, 1974), 270, who argues that Olmsted believed that the congregation's response to the black preacher was a response to "his total performance rather than to the words of the formal sermon."

CHAPTER 2

1. Thomas Gossett, *Race: The History of An Idea in America* (New York: Oxford University Press, 1997), 261–62.

2. See Higginson, "To the Editor of *The Nation*," April 30, 1874, in *The Magnificent Activist: The Writings of Thomas Wentworth Higginson (1823–1911)*, ed. Howard N. Meyer (New York: Da Capo Press, 2000), 131.

3. James M. McPherson, *The Abolitionist Legacy: From Reconstruction to the NAACP* (Princeton, N.J.: Princeton University Press, 1995 [1975]), 62.

4. Eric Foner, *Reconstruction: America's Unfinished Revolution, 1863–1877* (New York: Harper and Row, 1988), 146. Generally, Northern whites continued, as throughout the antebellum period, to assert that slavery had debased and degraded blacks, and that a massive effort of reeducation and instruction in civilized life was required to move them along. Southern whites, as the proslavery apologists, contended that slavery was a school where savage blacks were introduced to civilized behavior through work and discipline. This line of reasoning was particularly appealing to those who asserted that blacks were reverting to African savagery without the "beneficent" supervision of slavery. For an extended analysis of white Southerners' views of blacks over a broad time period, see Kenneth Paul O'Brien, "The Savage and the Child in Historical Perspective: Images of Blacks in Southern White Thought, 1830–1915" (Northwestern University, Ph.D. diss., 1974).

5. Edward J. Blum, *Reforging the White Republic: Race, Religion, and American Nationalism, 1865–1898* (Baton Rouge: Louisiana University Press, 2005), 6.

6. Lawrence W. Levine, *Black Culture and Black Consciousness: Afro-American Folk Thought from Slavery to Freedom* (New York: Oxford University Press, 1977), 140.

7. Sandra E. Small, "The Yankee Schoolmarm in Freedmen's Schools: An Analysis of Attitudes," *Journal of Southern History* 45 (August 1979): 382.

8. Levine, *Black Culture*, 140.

9. McPherson, *Abolitionist Legacy*, 168. I do not deny the actual achievements of this generation of whites and blacks who worked among blacks in the Reconstruction period, though my attention to their failures will be obvious. As McPherson writes, the abolitionist legacy is a story of "frustration, disillusionment, and failure," but it is also one of "persistence against odds, of continuing faith and activism, of notable accomplishments, especially in the field of black education" (ix). No one doubts the enormous work that was required to help millions of people who were released from slavery and who continued to live among hostile whites who never intended to treat them as freed persons. My emphasis here is on the negative Northern characterizations of black religion and their relationship to beliefs about black prospects in the new nation.

10. Charles Stearns, *The Black Man of the South and the Rebels; Or, The Characteristics of the Former, and the Recent Outrages of the Latter* (New York: American News, 1872), xi, 16, 62–65, 365.

11. Ibid., 365–366.

12. Ibid., 345, 367.

13. Ibid., 345, 365.

14. Ibid., 372.

15. See McPherson, *Abolitionist Legacy*, 62, where the author argues that Stearns's book was quoted by racists, though McPherson does not list any names.

16. Stearns, *Black Man*, 326–344.

17. Stearns's statement about the Ku Klux Klan is consistent with Foner's argument that one of the Klan's central goals was to reestablish control of the black labor force. See Foner, *Reconstruction*, 425–426.

18. Elizabeth Kilham, "Sketches in Color," *Putman's Magazine* 15 (March 1870): 304.

19. Ibid., 305.

20. Ibid., 308.

21. Ibid., 309.

22. Ibid., 310. The dour view of Stearns and Kilham about the religious practices of blacks demonstrates that "persistent interracial contact" was no guarantee that whites would change their more negative assessments of black religion. These and other examples of white interpretations of black religion challenge Blum's argument that prolonged interracial contact tended to melt whites' initial prejudices and stereotypes of blacks. See Blum, *Reforging the White Republic*, 63.

23. Kilham, "Sketches," 310.

24. Ibid., 310–311.

25. Ibid., 308.

26. Ibid., 311.

27. "Fetish Follies," *American Missionary Magazine* (January 1875): 17.

28. "A Negro Camp-Meeting in the South," *Harper's Weekly* (August 10, 1872): 623.

29. "On Negro Schools," *Harper's New Monthly Magazine* 49 (September 1874): 463.

30. Bennett, "The Religion of the Negro," *Independent*, July 15, 1875.

31. Ibid.

32. Ibid.

33. Leon Litwack, *Been in the Storm So Long: The Aftermath of Slavery* (New York: Vintage Books, 1980 [1979]), 458; and William E. Montgomery, *Under Their Own Vine and Fig Tree: The African American Church in the South, 1865–1900* (Baton Rouge: Louisiana State University, 1993), 84–85.

34. Turner, *Christian Recorder*, June 23, 1865.

35. Cited in Levine, *Black Culture*, 141.

36. Tanner, "Religion of the Negro," *Christian Recorder*, July 15, 1875. Tanner included the following excerpt from the May 6, 1875, issue of the *Independent* in his article: "The frightful fact stares us in the face on every side that the great bulk of the

Negroes in the Gulf States have no education, no religion, and no conscience.
They have what passes for religion, but no pretense of education or conscience. They
have churches in abundance, excited singing and shouting; *but no religion in the
sense in which we use the word*. The Gulf States are filled with colored Baptists and
Methodist churches in which drunkenness, theft, and whoredom are no bar to acceptable membership and communion. We have in our own land—not on heathen
shores, but in these United States—millions of citizens—Protestants we call them—
whose character is as little affected by their lacquer of religion as that of Sicilian
bandits, who murder a traveler with a prayer to the Virgin" (emphasis added). Bennett
responded to this article and others like it in the essay cited. Tanner cited the testimony of several black ministers who had spent months (and years in one case) among
blacks in the South to challenge the dour analysis of black religious life offered by the
Independent. He argued that the witness of blacks on their own behalf was simply
ignored by white critics, whom he regarded as purveyors of a "vast amount of mis-
information in regard to the religious status of the Southern colored man."

37. Paul H. Buck, *Road to Reunion, 1865–1900* (Boston: Little, Brown, 1937), 133.

38. Ibid., 131.

39. Edward King, *The Southern States of North America: A Record of Journeys*
(London: Blackie and Son, 1875), 779.

40. Ibid., 780.

41. Ibid., 781. King's exact statement on fetishism is the following: "A clever
Northerner, who has for many years dwelt in the South, once told me that he
considered the Christianity of the negro as Fetichism with a Christian cloak on." It is
almost certain that the "clever Northerner" to whom King referred was Frederick
Law Olmsted, the noted landscape architect who spent some time in the South
studying conditions during the 1850s. Olmsted had written in 1861 that religious
instruction of the slaves had merely resulted in furnishing a "delusive clothing of
Christian forms and phrases to the original vague superstition of the African savage."
See Olmsted, *The Cotton Kingdom* (New York: Random House, 1984 [1861]), 462.
Both King and Olmsted had doubts about the extent to which slavery had lifted blacks
beyond the "savagery" and the "low and bestial condition" of their African past.
Yvonne Chireau states that the "European term 'fetish' was widely used as a concept
to describe one of the most salient features of African spirituality: the construction
and use of sacred charms and other supernatural artifacts." See Chireau, *Black Magic:
Religion and the African American Conjuring Tradition* (Berkeley: University of California Press, 2003), 40. When used to describe black religious practices in the
South, *fetishism* meant "superstition" and various religious practices that were seen as
antithetical to "true Christianity." Even among those like Olmsted who had abandoned traditional or orthodox forms of Christianity, there was a certainty that black
Southerners did not have the real thing (that is, "real Christianity").

42. King, *Southern States*, 781–82.

43. On the creation and influence of *The Nation* under the leadership of the
journalist Edwin Godkin, see John G. Sproat, *"The Best Men": Liberal Reformers in the
Gilded Age* (Chicago: University of Chicago, 1982 [1968]), 18–23.

44. Higginson, "To the Editor of *The Nation*," April 30, 1874, in Meyer, ed. *The Magnificent Activist*, 131–132.

45. Buck, *Road to Redemption*, 133. William Montgomery asserts that Northern whites were primarily responsible for creating the impression that the freed persons were demoralized. See Montgomery, *Under Their Own Vine and Fig Tree*, 264. It is true that Northern missionaries often portrayed grave and seemingly insuperable difficulties among blacks in the South, in part to elicit money and support for their efforts. And certainly Northern whites, both religious and secular observers, decried the superstition, emotionalism, and degradation that they claimed to find among blacks in the South. In my view, however, claims about demoralization are not common in many such reports. Rather, missionaries often criticized blacks for being too assured of their salvation or perfectly happy with their religious practices. The central issue was an attempt to elicit sympathy for white Southerners who had to deal with a population whose religion putatively did little to foster work habits, moral behavior, and civic responsibilities that were central to the formation and mainte- nance of a nation. For a balanced assessment of the work of the AMA among blacks in the South, see Joe M. Richardson, *Christian Reconstruction: The American Missionary Association and Southern Blacks, 1861–1890* (Athens: University of Georgia Press, 1986).

46. I have found several works to be very useful in sorting through this im- portant period of transition. See especially Buck, *Road to Reunion*; C. Vann Woodward, *Origins of the New South, 1877–1913* (Baton Rouge: Louisiana University Press, 1971 [1951]); Nina Silber, *The Romance of Reunion: Northerners and the South, 1865– 1900* (Chapel Hill: University of North Carolina Press, 1993); David W. Blight, *Race and Reunion: The Civil War in American Memory* (Cambridge, Mass.: Harvard Uni- versity Press, 2001); Heather Cox Richardson, *The Death of Reconstruction: Race, Labor, and Politics in the Post–Civil War North, 1865–1901* (Cambridge, Mass.: Harvard Uni- versity Press, 2001); and Blum, *Reforging the White Republic*.

47. Herbert Gutman, *The Black Family in Slavery and Freedom, 1750–1925* (New York: Vintage Books, 1976), 531–532.

48. Haygood, *Our Brother in Black: His Freedom and His Future* (New York: Phillips, 1881), 221.

49. Joel Williamson, *The Crucible of Race: Black-White Relations in the American South Since Emancipation* (New York: Oxford University Press, 1984), 87.

50. Leon Litwack, *Trouble in Mind: Black Southerners in the Age of Jim Crow* (New York: Vintage Books, 1998), 184–185.

51. George R. Stetson, *The Negro As He Is* (1877; reprint, *The "Benefits" of Slavery: The New Proslavery Argument*, ed. John David Smith [New York: Garland Publishing, 1993], 54).

52. Williamson, *Crucible of Race*, 111. Williamson makes distinctions between more moderate Southerners, who were by no means racial liberals, and the radical racists of the 1880s onward. The radical racists often justified lynching, disfran- chisement, and segregation vocally and proudly. They unhesitatingly affirmed that America was a "white man's country."

53. Gutman, *Black Family*, 533–534; and Gardiner H. Shattuck Jr., *Episcopalians and Race: Civil War to Civil Rights* (Lexington: University Press of Kentucky, 2002), 15.

54. Shattuck, *Episcopalians and Race*, 12–13.

55. Neil R. McMillen, *Dark Journey: Black Mississippians in the Age of Jim Crow* (Urbana: University of Illinois Press, 1990), 258–261.

56. Shattuck, *Episcopalians and Race*, 15.

57. Joseph L. Tucker, *The Relations of the Church to the Colored Race* (1882; reprint Smith, *"Benefits" of Slavery*), 75.

58. Ibid., 76.

59. Ibid., 77.

60. Ibid., 79.

61. Ibid., 83.

62. Ibid., 84.

63. Ibid.

64. Ibid., 91. See George M Fredrickson, *The Black Image in the White Mind: The Debate of Afro-American Character and Destiny, 1817–1914* (Middleton, Conn.: Wesleyan University Press, 1987 [1971]), 228, 240–241; and Ralph E. Luker, *The Social Gospel in Black and White: American Racial Reform, 1885–1912* (Chapel Hill: University of North Carolina Press, 1991), 31. Fredrickson and Luker point to the findings of Edward W. Gilliam, a Baltimore physician and novelist, whose February 1883 article sparked widespread debates and concern about the growth of the black population in the South. Gilliam felt that the "superior fecundity" of the African, based on his reading of the 1880 U.S. census, would lead to a sweltering mass of blacks in the South. This concern with the Africanization of the South connoted black political domination. Gilliam proposed colonization, but Tucker and others were more resigned to having blacks in their midst and figuring out ways to minimize their influence. Michael Perman notes the shift in the language from "Negro rule" used by opponents of Reconstruction and black suffrage to "Negro domination," a slogan that "became nearly universal by the 1890s" (which ironically coincided with claims that the black population would become extinct in the struggle for racial existence after various readings of the 1890 U.S. census). Tucker's fears about the Africanization of the South reflected broader concerns of Southern whites about blacks as a constant force in any public arena. On the meanings of Negro domination in the white mind and the implications for the disfranchisement of blacks in the South, see Michael Perman, *Struggle for Mastery: Disfranchisement in the South, 1888–1908* (Chapel Hill: University of North Carolina Press, 2001), 22–36.

65. Tucker, *Relations of the Church*, 85. Tucker did make a distinction between town and country blacks. He asserted that in recent history (since the Civil War) "town negroes" have emancipated themselves from these varied superstitions, though "country negroes" were still actively attached to the "old race traditions."

66. Ibid., 85.

67. Ibid.

68. Ibid., 89.

69. Ibid., 97–98. Tucker desired a form of industrial education for blacks, modeled after the Hampton Institute, but one that was "stronger, more positive, more radical in its teachings concerning religion" (26). He told a story about his work among blacks in 1866 before he entered the ministry. He wrote that he opened a school on a plantation and invited blacks from the surrounding area to join in this endeavor. Three times a week and on Sunday afternoons blacks were taught to read and heard the Bible read and explained. For about a month or so, all went well, Tucker recalled, until one Sunday he read and explained very carefully the meaning of the ten commandments. Immediately, the school broke up. Tucker attributed this breakup to the outspoken and indignant black women who would have no "impersition" of the white man's religion in their lives. For Tucker, this was a classic case of the belief among blacks that religion had absolutely nothing to do with conduct. We do not know which parts of the Bible he taught for the month or so prior to the school's breakup, but we may presume that his teaching style was altered after he began to feel that blacks were not living according to his interpretation of Christian morality (89–90).

70. See Louis R. Harlan, *Booker T. Washington: The Making of a Black Leader, 1856–1901* (New York: Oxford University Press, 1972), 52–64.

71. Ibid., 95.

72. Tucker, *Relations of the Church*, 95.

73. W. B. W. Howe, Episcopal bishop of the diocese of South Carolina, made this point rather bluntly in his endorsement of Tucker's speech. He wrote: "Slavery was a schoolmaster to the black man, but when the school master was turned out of doors and there was no longer any fear of his rod, there very naturally came along with the first years of emancipation a return to many of the vices which belonged to a recent barbarism. I think we had to look for this. But there is a factor at work for the improvement of the negro which must not be over-looked though it is not often considered. I refer to the laws of the States and their proper administration. These now stand to some extent where formerly the master did. The negro is beginning to learn that citizenship has duties as well as rights. Though he will not pay respect to Moses yet he will to the law which says, that a man who is guilty of stealing his neighbors' cattle shall not have a vote. There is more force in such a law than in sermons. Schools must do their part, the Church must do its part, but there will be great moral power in the State holding the negro to the responsibilities of citizenship." See "Endorsements" in Smith, *"Benefits" of Slavery*, 108.

74. Tucker wrote, "In the midst of prayer I have known them to steal from each other, and on the way home from a prayer meeting they will rob any hen-roost that lies conveniently at hand; and this without any thought of sin against God, and even without any perception of an incongruity. The most pious negro I know is one confined in a penitentiary for an atrocious murder, who can see no especial sin against God in his crime, though he acknowledges an offense against man." Tucker, *Relations of the Church*, 91.

75. "Endorsements" in Smith, *"Benefits" of Slavery*, 127.

76. Ibid., 128.

77. On Crummell, see Wilson Jeremiah Moses, *Alexander Crummell: A Study of Civilization and Discontent* (New York: Oxford University Press, 1989). Crummell later exerted a profound influence on the young scholar W. E. B. Du Bois, who included a moving chapter on Crummell in his classic *The Souls of Black Folks* (1903).

78. This church developed under Crummell's care into a center of black activity. See J. R. Oldfield, ed., *Civilization and Black Progress: Selected Writings of Alexander Crummell on the South* (Charlottesville: University Press of Virginia, 1995), 9.

79. Crummell, "Defence of the Negro Race," in *Civilization and Black Progress*, 85.

80. Ibid., 79.

81. Ibid.

82. William Wells Brown, *My Southern Home: Or, The South and Its People* (1880, reprint, *African American Religious History: A Documentary Witness*, 2nd ed, ed. Milton C. Sernett [Durham, N.C.: Duke University Press, 1999], 255–260).

83. See Michael W. Harris, *Rise of the Gospel Blues: The Music of Thomas Andrew Dorsey in the Urban Church* (New York: Oxford University Press, 1992), chap. 1; Evelyn Brooks Higginbotham, *Righteous Discontent: The Women's Movement in the Black Baptist Church, 1880–1920* (Cambridge, Mass.: Harvard University Press, 1993), chap. 2; Paul Harvey, *Redeeming the South: Religious Cultures and Racial Identities Among Southern Baptists, 1865–1925* (Chapel Hill: University of North Carolina Press, 1997), chap. 4; and Candy Gunther Brown, *The Word in the World: Evangelical Writing, Publishing, and Reading in America, 1789–1880* (Chapel Hill: University of North Carolina Press, 2004), 208–212. Each of these works details the various ways in which Northern blacks wrestled with a "vernacular spirituality" among blacks in the South and the growing desire among more educated blacks for respectable churches that emphasized decorum and propriety in worship. The growth of an educated black elite, constant white criticisms of black religion, black leaders' desire for assimilation into the white mainstream, class differences, and visions of standardization and modernization in black rural Southern culture were all salient issues in these debates.

84. Crummell, "Defence of the Negro Race," 89.

85. Ibid., 95.

86. Ibid., 95–97.

87. For a broader social and historical context of Cooper's work, particularly as it dealt with defending black women against charges of sexual immorality, see Paula Giddings, *When and Where I Enter: The Impact of Black Women on Race and Sex in America* (New York: Quill William Morrow, 1984). On the work of black Baptist women during this time, see Higginbotham, *Righteous Discontent*.

88. Anna Julia Cooper, "Womanhood: A Vital Element in the Regeneration and Progress of a Race" (1886; reprint, *The Voice of Anna Julia Cooper Including A Voice from the South and other Important Essays, Papers, and Letters*, eds. Charles Lemert and Esme Bhan [Lanham, Md.: Rowman and Littlefield, 1998], 65). The speech was included in her more well-known work, *Voice from the South* (1892).

89. Ibid., 65–67.

90. Rayford W. Logan, *The Betrayal of the Negro: From Rutherford B. Hayes to Woodrow Wilson* (New York: Da Capo Press, 1997 [1965]), 268.

91. John David Smith, *An Old Creed for the New South: Proslavery Ideology and Historiography, 1865–1918* (Athens: University of Georgia Press, 1991 [1985]), 173–174.

92. Gutman, *Black Family*, 535.

93. See Giddings, *When and Where*, 27, 31; and Gutman, *Black Family*, 534–538, for Bruce's negative views of black women and black families.

94. Philip A. Bruce, *The Plantation Negro as a Freedman: Observations on His Character, Condition, and Prospects in Virginia* (Northbrook, Ill.: Metro Books, 1972 [1889]), 93.

95. Ibid., 93–94.

96. Ibid., 101.

97. *Thomas Jefferson: Writings*, ed. Merrill D. Peterson (New York: Library of America, 1984), 269.

98. Ibid., 269, 901.

99. Ibid., 901.

100. Ibid., 101.

101. Ibid., 102–103. Elaborating on this theme of lack of religious skepticism, Bruce wrote: "The deficiency of the negro in original capacity is revealed in his total lack of any turn for speculation. His mind is never quickened and invigorated by skepticism; he seems to have no desire to penetrate beyond what is merely visible; the outer surface obstructs his mental as well as his ocular vision" (156).

102. Ibid., 103–104.

103. Ibid., 97–98.

104. Ibid., 108.

105. Ibid.,114, 124. At certain points in his work, Bruce noted the works (without citing them) of ethnologists who believed in the transmission of "inherited instincts." The language of Anglo-Saxonism is also apparent at several junctures. In his developmental schema of human populations, he compared blacks to white children in that they were said to be immature, needed supervision, lacked moral judgment, and had little understanding of the future. Ibid., 139–141.

106. Ibid., 243.

107. Ibid., 243–245, 247–248.

108. Ibid., 261. Paul Buck has written about the importance of depictions of blacks in fictional literature in the South beginning in the 1880s. So as claims about the degeneration of black culture were being promulgated in books, essays, and writings on the current Negro problem, fictional works created an imagined Old South where contented blacks faithfully adhered to their duties and served their benevolent white masters. This image was often intentionally set against depictions of free blacks in the contemporary South as lascivious, violent, and completely lost in their emancipated state. Buck suggests that this portrayal of the faithful black slave was in many ways a mirror image of Uncle Tom in the writings of such men as Thomas Nelson Page. In this type of literature, Buck avers, "the Negro was primarily a

device by which a white philosophy of race relations was advanced." See Buck, *Road to Reunion*, 203–210. David Blight shows that by the mid-1880s and throughout the 1890s, American culture was "awash in sentimental reconciliationist literature," a large part of which depicted blacks as slaves. Blight argues that literature was a "powerful medium for reuniting the interests of Americans from both North and South." An exotic Old South became the object of "enormous nostalgia." Urbanization, growing immigration, and labor unrest created huge audiences for a "literature of escape." So thousands of Southern and Northern readers were taken on "sentimental, imaginative journeys Southward and into idealized war zones, guided and narrated by faithful slaves." Blacks in this literature became the chief spokesmen of the old regime. Blight writes: "The freedpeople and their sons and daughters were the bothersome, dangerous antithesis of the noble catastrophe that the Confederacy's war increasingly became in reminiscence and fiction. Omnipresent, growing instead of vanishing, Southern blacks had to have their place in the splendid disaster of the war, emancipation, and Reconstruction." See Blight, *Race and Reunion*, 216, 210, 221. But even the use of the faithful slave in literature had additional negative implications. Although fans expressed affection for the slave, the use of the African American voice was in part muted by its "picturesque dialect." As Janet Gabler-Hover notes, "use of dialect was invariably patronizing in an age that equated grammaticality with social and moral stature." See Janet Gabler-Hover, "The North-South Reconciliation Theme and the 'Shadow of the Negro' in *Century Illustrated Magazine*," in *Periodical Literature in Nineteenth-Century America*, eds. Kenneth M. Price and Susan Belasco Smith (Charlottesville: University Press of Virginia Press, 1995), 247.

109. Frederick Douglass, "I Denounce the So-Called Emancipation as a Stupendous Fraud" (1888), in Philip S. Foner, ed., *Frederick Douglass: Selected Speeches and Writings*, abridged and adapted by Yuval Taylor (Chicago: Lawrence Hill Books, 1999), 714.

110. Ibid.

111. "The Colored Ministers of the South—Their Preaching and Peculiarities," *AME Church Review* (hereafter *AMECR*) (October 1884): 140.

112. This journal was the leading academic and scholarly journal of the African Methodist Episcopal Church, though it was not limited to articles by members of this denomination. It was founded in 1884.

113. "Development," *AMECR* (January 1887): 210–211.

114. "The Colored Ministry: Its Defects and Needs," in *The Booker T. Washington Papers*, ed. Louis R. Harlan, vol. 3 (Urbana: University of Illinois Press, 1974), 71–73.

115. See Willard B. Gatewood, *Aristocrats of Color: The Black Elite, 1880–1920* (Fayetteville: University of Arkansas Press, 2000 [1990]), 296–297.

116. "The Defects of Our Ministry, and the Remedy," *AMECR* (October 1888): 154–156.

117. Higginbotham, *Righteous Discontent*, 44.

118. *Fifty Years in the Gospel Ministry from 1864 to 1914*, AME Book Concern, 1921, 216; available online at docsouth.unc.edu/church/steward/menu.html. See also Albert G. Miller, *Elevating the Race: Theophilus G. Steward, Black Theology, and the*

Making of an African American Civil Society, 1865–1924 (Knoxville: University of Tennessee Press, 2003), 10–11.

119. Patricia A. Schechter, *Ida B. Wells-Barnett and American Reform, 1880–1930* (Chapel Hill: University of North Carolina Press, 2001), 64–65.

120. See also Higginbotham, *Righteous Discontent*, 42–46, 67–80.

121. Louis R. Harlan, *Booker T. Washington: The Wizard of Tuskegee, 1901–1915* (New York: Oxford University Press, 1983), chap. 6.

122. August Meier, *Negro Thought in America, 1880–1915* (Ann Arbor: University of Michigan Press, 1988 [1963]), 88.

123. Booker T. Washington, *Up from Slavery* (New York: Dover, 1995 [1901]), 26–28.

124. James D. Anderson, *The Education of Blacks in the South, 1860–1935* (Chapel Hill: University of North Carolina Press, 1988), 53.

125. Louis Harlan offers a plausible interpretation of Washington's relationship with Armstrong when he suggests that Washington found in Armstrong the "white father figure" he perhaps had been unconsciously looking for. Harlan contends that Washington's years at Hampton became the "central shaping experience" of his life and that Armstrong's social philosophy and personal example "became the beacon that guided Washington throughout the rest of his life." Harlan, *Booker T., Black Leader*, 52. In his autobiography, Washington tenderly relates how Armstrong spent the last six months of his life in Washington's home at Tuskegee, and how Armstrong, despite the loss of control of his body and his voice and his partial paralysis, continued to work indefatigably "for the cause to which he had given his life," the uplift of the Negro. See Washington, *Up from Slavery*, 26–27.

126. Meier, *Negro Thought*, 102–103; and Harlan, *Booker T., Black Leader*, chaps. 6 and 7.

127. On Washington's many stories and anecdotes, and their tendency to reinforce whites' stereotypes of blacks, see Harlan, *Booker T., Black Leader*, 234–235.

128. Harlan, *Booker T., Black Leader*, 194.

129. "The Colored Ministry," 71–73. Ida B. Wells congratulated Washington in an editorial for the *Christian Index* on his "manly criticism of our corrupt and ignorant ministry" in his role as leader at Tuskegee. See Schecter, *Ida B. Wells-Barnett*, 65. She made a distinction between his criticism of blacks within the black community and his criticism of blacks before white audiences. Later Wells wrote: "It was a wrong thing for him to have that criticism in a white paper [the *Christian Register* in Boston] so far away from home. When the people needed such criticism, I felt he ought to have done as we did—tell them about it at home rather than tell our enemies abroad. Of course I said as much in an editorial." See Wells, *Crusade for Justice: The Autobiography of Ida B. Wells*, ed. Alfred M. Duster (Chicago: University of Chicago Press, 1970), 41.

130. "The Colored Ministry," 73. James Anderson attributes this story in its original telling to Samuel Armstrong. Anderson, *Education of Blacks*, 53. Washington made it his own, and repeated it, along with other "darky" stories, endlessly before white audiences.

131. "The Colored Ministry," 73.

132. Ibid.

133. Ibid., 74.

134. Daniel Alexander Payne to Booker T. Washington, November 3, 1890, in *Washington Papers*, 97–98. On Payne's vigorous quest for an educated ministry, see James T. Campbell, *Songs of Zion: The African Methodist Episcopal Church in the United States and South Africa* (Chapel Hill: University of North Carolina Press, 1998), 53–60.

135. "A Speech before the National Unitarian Association," September 26, 1894, *Washington Papers*, 477.

136. Ibid., 477–478.

137. See his "Speech Delivered before the Women's New England Club," January 27, 1889, and "Speech before the New York Congregational Club," January 16, 1893, in *Washington Papers*, 25–23, 279–289.

138. "Extracts of an Address before the Men and Religion Forward Movement," April 21, 1912, in *Booker T. Washington Papers*, eds. Louis R. Harlan and Raymond W. Smock, vol. 11 (Urbana: University of Illinois Press, 1981), 527.

139. "The Religious Life of the Negro" (July 1905), in *The Booker T. Washington Papers*, eds. Louis R. Harlan and Raymond W. Smock, vol. 8 (Urbana: University of Illinois Press, 1979), 333–334.

140. Ibid., 335. I have not found the phrase "the Negro Church" in Washington's writings of the 1890s. His usage may have been influenced by his work with Du Bois and readings in social scientific literature on black religion.

141. Ibid.

142. Anderson, *Education of Blacks*, 72–73.

143. Henry Field, *Bright Skies and Dark Shadows* (1890; reprint, *Plessy v. Ferguson: A Brief History with Documents*, ed. Brook Thomas (Boston: Bedford Books, 1997), 112.

144. Blight, *Race and Reunion*, 220.

145. Nathan Irvin Huggins, *Harlem Renaissance* (New York: Oxford University Press, 1971), 62.

146. For a brilliant explication of the difficulties black Methodists (AME) faced in this endeavor during the antebellum period, see Campbell, *Songs of Zion*, chap. 1.

147. Crummell, "The Social Principle among a People and Its Bearing on Their Progress and Development," in *Civilization and Progress*, 37–38. This speech was not published until the 1880s.

148. Meier, *Negro Thought*, 35.

149. "Why Negro Churches Are a Necessity," *AMECR* (October 1877): 154–156.

150. *History of the African Methodist Episcopal Church* (1891; reprint, *Black Nationalism in America*, eds. H. Bracey Jr., August Meier, and Elliott Rudwick [New York: Bobbs-Merrill, 1970]), 11.

151. Ibid., 11–13.

152. Crummell, "Piety, Moralism, and Enthusiasm" (1890; reprint, *Destiny and Race: Selected Writings, 1840–1898*, ed. Wilson Jeremiah Moses [Amherst: University of Massachusetts Press, 1992]), 140–145.

153. Moses, *Destiny and Race*, 14.

154. "Hope for the Negro Race in America" (1895), in *Civilization and Black Progress*, 179.

155. Ibid., 180.

156. Ibid., 181–184.

CHAPTER 3

1. George W. Stocking Jr., *Race, Culture, and Evolution: Essays in the History of Anthropology* (New York: Free Press, 1968), 113–116.

2. Ibid., 300–301. On the use of psychological tests that claimed to demonstrate that intelligence was inherent and asserted that blacks were mentally or intellectually inferior to whites, see Carl N. Degler, *In Search of Human Nature: The Decline and Revival of Darwinism in American Social Thought* (New York: Oxford University Press, 1991), chap. 7. See also Thomas Gossett, *Race: The History of an Idea in America* (New York: Oxford University Press, 1997), 373–377. For black responses to this literature, see William B. Thomas, "Black Intellectuals on IQ Tests," in *The Bell Curve Debate: History, Documents, Opinions*, eds. Russell Jacoby and Naomi Glauberman (New York: Times Books, 1995), 510–541.

3. William H. Tucker, *The Science and Politics of Racial Research* (Urbana: University of Illinois Press, 1994), 72. Tucker offers an interesting conjecture about why psychologists began emphasizing the measurement of intelligence throughout the 1920s. He suggests that intellectual and moral traits were believed to be highly correlated in psychological thought, thus the emphasis on intelligence presupposed that more intelligent people would be more just, kind, and decent. Even so, Tucker acknowledges that intelligence became a basic index of human value in the psychology of the 1920s and that other discrete qualities (such as justice, decency, and kindness) were regarded as having less significance as measures of human worth (because they were associated with intelligence anyway).

4. Ann Taves, *Fits, Trances, and Visions: Experiencing Religion and Explaining Experience from Wesley to James* (Princeton, N.J.: Princeton University Press, 1999), 261. When using the term *naturalistic* I mean a nondogmatic interpretation of religion that provided a theory of human or psychological evolution to account for contemporary religious practices. The terms *natural* or *naturalized* in the context of this chapter refer to the attempts of theorists of African American religion to explain black culture by reference to biological or "racial" foundations. Generally, environmentalist explanations were eschewed in favor of a racial African past or a theory of the mind that posited innate African traits. Studies, for example, like those of Hall, "naturalized" the harsh conditions of blacks in the South by pointing to their supposed African traits rather than white racism or political or economic oppression. Hall and other white interpreters of lynching asserted a biological propensity for blacks' alleged frequent raping of white women and further claimed that sexual licentiousness was part of blacks' African heritage.

5. Frederick L. Hoffman, "The Race Traits and Tendencies of the American Negro," *Publications of the American Economic Association* 11 (January–March–May 1896): 310–312, 328–329.

6. Richard Hofstadter, *Social Darwinism in American Thought*, 2nd ed. (Boston: Beacon Press, 1955), 33, 34.

7. Ibid., 41, 43, 46.

8. Stocking, *Race, Culture*, 117.

9. For a broader treatment of Spencer's views on race and sociocultural evolution, see Stocking, *Race, Culture*, 126–128; John S. Haller Jr., *Outcasts from Evolution: Scientific Attitudes of Racial Inferiority, 1859–1900* (Carbondale: Southern Illinois University Press, 1995 [1971]), chap. 5; and Lee D. Baker, *From Savage to Negro: Anthropology and the Construction of Race, 1896–1954* (Berkeley: University of California Press, 1998), 28–31.

10. Herbert Spencer, *The Principles of Sociology*, vol. 1 (New York: D. Appleton, 1925 [1885]), 23.

11. Spencer, *Principles*, 72. This apparently meant that representative democracy had an analogy in the very mind of civilized man that was lacking in the primitive mind.

12. Written for the *African Methodist Episcopal Church Review* (hereafter *AMECR*) (October 1893): 325.

13. "Lessons of the Hour," *AMECR* (July 1894).

14. Ibid., 125. On the arrangement of the fairgrounds and its meaning for race and culture, see Robert W. Rydell, *All the World's a Fair: Visions of Empire at American International Expositions, 1876–1916* (Chicago: University of Chicago Press, 1984), 58–68. See also, David F. Berg, *Chicago's White City of 1893* (Lexington: University Press of Kentucky, 1976).

15. Rydell, *All the World's a Fair*, 64, 55.

16. For a perceptive analysis of Douglass, see Robert W. Rydell, " 'Darkest Africa': African Shows at America's World Fairs, 1893–1940," in *Africans on Stage: Studies in Ethnological Show Business*, ed. Berth Lindfors (Bloomington: Indiana University Press, 1999), 142. On Jubilee Day, August 24, 1893, Douglass said, "Look at the progress the Negro has made in thirty years. We have come out of Dahomey into this. Measure the Negro. But not by the standard of the splendid civilization of the Caucasian. Bend down and measure him—measure him—from the depths out of which he has risen." Douglass, "The World in Miniature," *Indianapolis Freeman*, September 2, 1893. This was precisely one of the anthropological lessons of the fair!

17. Kenten Druyvesten, "The World's Parliament of Religion" (Ph.D. diss., University of Chicago, 1976), 5–6.

18. Richard Seager, *The World's Parliament of Religions: The East/West Encounter, Chicago, 1893* (Bloomington: Indiana University Press, 1995), xxviii–xxix.

19. John P. Burris, *Exhibiting Religion: Colonialism and Spectacle at International Expositions, 1851–1893* (Charlottesville: University of Virginia Press, 2001), xiv–xix.

20. William R. Hutchison, *Religious Pluralism in America: The Contentious History of a Founding Ideal* (New Haven, Conn.: Yale University Press, 2003), 112.

21. For general treatments of blacks at the fair, besides the works of Rydell, see Elliot Rudwick and August Meier, "Black Man in the 'White City': Negroes and the Columbian Exposition, 1893," *Phylon* 26 (fourth quarter, 1965): 354–361; and Christopher Robert Reed, *"All the World Is Here!": The Black Presence at White City* (Bloomington: Indiana University Press, 2000). Rydell notes the importance of Herbert Spencer's presence at the Congress of Evolution and his general ideas of racial and material progress along evolutionary lines. See Rydell, *All the World's a Fair*, 68.

22. See James T. Campbell, *Songs of Zion: The African American Episcopal Church in the United States and South Africa* (Chapel Hill: University of North Carolina Press, 1998), 262–263, where Campbell asserts that though "largely forgotten today, Arnett in his time may have been the most influential black man in America."

23. "In Behalf of Africa," in *Neely's History of the Parliament of World Religions and Religious Congresses at the World's Columbian Exposition,* 4th ed., ed. Walter R. Houghton (Chicago: Neely Publishing, 1894), 70.

24. Paul Carus, "The Dawn of a New Religious Era," *Forum* (November 1893): 389–390.

25. "Origin of the Parliament of Religion," in Houghton, ed., *Neely's History,* 27.

26. Ibid., 70, 71. The summary of Arnett's speech that I have given is based on the edited version in *Neely's History.* A considerably longer version is found in the journal of Arnett's denomination, the *AME Church Review.* John Burris shows how that even in John Henry Barrow's massive collection of papers from the Parliament all of Arnett's negative comments about the role of Christianity in slavery are edited out. See Burris, *Exhibiting Religion,* 161.

27. "Africa and the Descendants of Africa," *AMECR* (July 1894): 231–238. The *AMECR* version of Arnett's address makes no mention of the favorable remark about the providential role of slavery. Burris indicates that the *Daily Inter-Ocean,* a newspaper that reported on all aspects of the Parliament, did not even mention Arnett's address. See Burris, *Exhibiting Religion,* 162.

28. "Editorial: Across the Continent," *AMECR* (October 1893): 325.

29. "Christianity and the Negro," in *The Dawn of Religious Pluralism: Voices from the World's Parliament of Religions, 1893,* ed. Richard Hughes Seager (LaSalle, Ill.: Open Court, 1993), 138–139.

30. Ibid., 140.

31. "What Can Religion Further Do to Advance the Condition of the American Negro?," in Seager, ed., *Dawn of Religious Pluralism,* 142–150. Williams was also one of six African American women selected to speak before the World's Congress of Representative Women in May 1893. Further evidence of her attempt to distance American blacks from Africa *and* to assert the naturalness of religion to blacks (which was assumed to be a good thing) can be found in this speech. Speaking of blacks in the South as viewed by white missionaries, presumably after the Civil War, she wrote: "It has always been a circumstance of the highest satisfaction to the missionary efforts of the Christian church that the colored people are so susceptible to religion that marks the highest point of blessedness in human history. Instead of finding witchcraft, sensual fetishes, and the coarse superstitions of savagery possessing our

women, Christianity found them with hearts singularly tender, sympathetic, and fit for the reception of its doctrines. Their superstitions were not deeply ingrained, but were of the same sort and nature that characterize the devotees of the Christian faith everywhere." Fannie Barrier Williams, "The Intellectual Progress of the Colored Women of the United States Since the Emancipation Proclamation," in *The World's Congress of Representative Women*, ed. May Wright Sewall (1894; reprint, *Lift Every Voice: African American Oratory, 1787–1900*, eds. Philip S. Foner and Robert James Branham [Tuscaloosa: University of Alabama Press, 1998]), 763.

32. Burris, *Exhibiting Religion*, 161.

33. Ibid., 160.

34. Seager, *World's Parliament of Religions*, 45.

35. Burris, *Exhibiting Religion*, 163.

36. Ibid., 176.

37. Cited in Rydell, *All the World's a Fair*, 53.

38. Joseph Tillinghast, *The Negro in Africa and America* (New York: Macmillan, 1902), 25–27.

39. Ibid., 58.

40. Ibid., 59.

41. Ibid., 91–94.

42. Spencer, *Principles*, 90–91.

43. Philip Bruce, *The Plantation Negro as Freedman: Observations on His Character, Condition, and Prospects in Virginia* (Northbrook, Ill.: Metro Books, 1972 [1889]), 156–157.

44. G. Stanley Hall, "The Negro in Africa and America," *Pedagogical Seminary* 12 (September 1905): 14. At a particularly heated discussion at the American Social Science Association held at Washington, D.C., in 1901, one speaker spoke on this question and offered a dissenting view. He stated: "No anthropologist or psychologist who has examined the subject with any degree of scientific accuracy, and in any unprejudiced way, has evolved anything to show that in the public schools, during the life of childhood, there is any difference between white and colored children. It is the universal testimony that there is no difference appreciable here. They do say, however, that a little later on, at the age of puberty, or of adolescence, if you please, there does seem to be a difference. It seems that colored children fall back, and do not make such rapid progress. But they do not give the reason. The problem is simply this: The republic of childhood is essentially a democracy. The colored child goes to school the same as the white child. He has not learned any difference, and neither has the white child.... As soon as the colored boy reaches the age of puberty, and begins to look upon the world and sees it in his larger view, he finds that he has left some time ago the republic of childhood, which is essentially democracy, and has come into the world, which is practically an aristocracy. He finds that a great many of the positions which he dreamed of in his childhood are not open to him." Mr. Moore, "Discussion," *Journal of Social Science* 39 (November 1, 1901): 136. John Haller provides evidence of post–Civil War studies on the brain and cranium that posited that the central frontal sutures in the brains of blacks closed at puberty and prevented or

hindered further intellectual development. See Haller, *Outcasts from Evolution*, 34–36.

45. John Corrigan, *Business of the Heart: Religion and Emotion in the Nineteenth Century* (Berkeley: University of California Press, 2002), 241.

46. Tillinghast, *Negro in Africa and America*, 97–98.

47. Ibid., 96, 98–101.

48. Ibid., 136.

49. Ibid., 148.

50. Ibid., 149.

51. Ibid., 150.

52. Ibid., 156.

53. Ibid., 194.

54. Ibid., 195.

55. Ibid., 197.

56. Ibid., 200.

57. Ibid., 203.

58. Ibid., 203–204.

59. Ibid., 205.

60. Ibid., 205.

61. Ibid., 206.

62. Ibid., 207.

63. Ibid., 208.

64. Haller, *Outcasts from Evolution*, 205.

65. W. E. B. Du Bois, Review of *The Negro in Africa and America* by Joseph Alexander Tillinghast, *Political Science Quarterly* 18 (December 1903): 695.

66. Ibid., 696–697.

67. Walter Fleming, Review of *The Negro Church* by W. E. Burghardt Du Bois, *Political Science Quarterly* 19 (December 1904): 703. Fleming was also irked because he read Du Bois to be suggesting that blacks did not need to be "prepared to receive Christianity."

68. John Bassett, "The Negro's Inheritance from Africa," *South Atlantic Quarterly* (April 1904): 99–107.

69. Bassett was not a radical in his views of race. He eventually left the South, in part because of his struggles for academic freedom there. His positive comments about Booker T. Washington's "greatness" caused a furor, with many asking for Bassett's resignation. Yet even "moderate" figures like him were not progressive in their views of race. See Joel Williamson, *The Crucible of Race: Black-White Relations in the American South since Emancipation* (New York: Oxford University Press, 1984), 261–271. Williamson calls Bassett a "conservative" with respect to his views on race compared to radical racists who found little place for blacks in the nation. My use of the term *moderate* refers to his broader views of politics, culture, and the place of blacks in the nation.

70. Although black historians in the late nineteenth century held ideas about ancient Africa that affirmed racial pride and the achievements of blacks, they saw little

to be proud of in contemporary African life. Many of them shared the negative views of Africa held by their white contemporaries. See Dickson D. Bruce Jr., "Ancient Africa and the Early Black American Historians, 1883–1915," *American Quarterly* 36 (Winter 1984): 686–699.

71. Taves, *Fits, Trances, and Visions*, 261. There is some evidence of the influence of psychological theories of conversion in the writings of members of the African Methodist Episcopal church. A. C. Garner debated the merits of religious revivals among black Methodists and argued for their usefulness in specific situations. Showing awareness of psychological theories that posited temperamental and racial differences between blacks and whites, Garner had no sympathy for such theories when they regarded the Negro "as a peculiar being." The "explosiveness" of black religion, he averred, was borrowed from white people in the early days of revivalism and was "in no sense characteristic of the Negro in his African home." But Garner was insistent that blacks not get carried away in their revival methods so as to give the impression that they were "peculiar" in their religious practices. Contrary to those who believed that "excitements," visions, and "strange phenomena" were central to conversion, he pointed to the evidence of psychologists "who tell us that these marvels of power can be accounted for by the ordinary laws of mind." So blacks should desist from any revivals that lasted late into the night and realize that "animalism" and "great physical agitation" were simply extraneous phenomena to true religious experience. See "The True and the False in the Revival Methods of the Race," *AMECR* (October 1902): 489, 492–993.

72. George Barton Cutten, *The Psychological Phenomena of Christianity* (New York: Charles Scribner's Sons, 1912 [1908]), 171.

73. *American Christianity: An Historical Interpretation with Representative Documents*, eds. H. Shelton, Robert T. Handy, and Leffert A. Loetscher (New York: Charles Scribner's Sons, 1963), 233.

74. Charles W. Eliot, *The Religion of the Future* (Boston: American Unitarian Association, 1909), 4–8.

75. Robert A. Orsi, *Between Heaven and Earth: The Religious Worlds that People Make and the Scholars Who Study Them* (Princeton, N.J.: Princeton University Press, 2005), 186.

76. Kilgore, "Our Duty to the Negro," *South Atlantic Quarterly* (October 1903): 372.

77. Robert Bennett Bean, "Some Racial Peculiarities of the Negro Brain," *American Journal of Anatomy* 5 (September 1, 1906): 379. For a criticism of Bean's work by Franz Boas, see Vernon J. Williams Jr., *Rethinking Race: Franz Boas and His Contemporaries* (Lexington: University Press of Kentucky, 1996), 20–21.

78. Hall, "The Negro in Africa and America," 10. Dorothy Ross has argued that despite Hall's contributions in psychology, child development, and other areas, his thinking on race belonged to the era of biological determinism. See Ross, *G. Stanley Hall: The Psychologist as Prophet* (Chicago: University of Chicago Press, 1972), 415–416.

79. Williamson, *The Crucible of Race*, 224–225. Originating in Mississippi by a constitutional convention in 1890, the disenfranchisement of blacks in other South-

ern states was accomplished by rewriting state constitutions and other measures and was virtually complete in the South by 1910. See C. Van Woodward, *Origins of the New South, 1877–1913* (Baton Rouge: Louisiana State University Press, 1971 [1951]), 321.

80. George T. Winston, "The Relation of the Whites to the Negroes," *Annals of the American Academy of Political and Social Science* 18 (July 1901): 105, 109.

81. Ibid., 117–118.

82. See John David Smith, *An Old Creed for the New South: Proslavery Ideology and Historiography, 1865–1918* (Athens: University of Georgia Press, 1991 [1985]), 105, 112–116.

83. Quotations are from Eric Foner, *Reconstruction: America's Unfinished Revolution, 1863–1877* (New York: Harper and Row, 1988), 609. See also Kenneth M. Stamp, "The Tragic Legend of Reconstruction," in *Reconstruction: An Anthology of Revisionist Writings*, eds. Kenneth M. Stamp and Leon F. Litwack (Baton Rouge: Louisiana State University, 1969), 3–8. The studies of Dunning and his colleagues were far more extensive and complicated than my analysis suggests. My intent is to show how both conservative Southerners and "liberal" reformers were often united in their negative views of black capacities.

84. Wilson Jeremiah Moses, *Alexander Crummell: A Study of Civilization and Discontent* (New York: Oxford University Press, 1989), 259.

85. John L. Love, "The Disfranchisement of the Negro," *American Negro Academy Occasional Paper* 6 (1899; reprint, New York: Arno Press, 1969), 9.

86. Ibid., 13–14.

87. Walter F. Willcox, "Negro Criminality," *Journal of Social Science* 37 (1899): 81. For broader institutional structures and their support of works that promoted scientific racism, with particular attention to the role of Willcox, see Mark Alrich, "Progressive Economists and Scientific Racism: Walter Willcox and Black Americans, 1895–1910," *Phylon* 40 (first quarter 1979): 1–14; and William Darity Jr., "Many Roads to Extinction: Early AEA Economists and the Black Disappearance Hypothesis," *History of Economics Review* 40 (Winter 1994): 47–64.

88. Hall, "Negro in Africa and America," 10.

89. On the broader context of scientific racism in the various disciplines, see I. A. Newby, *Jim Crow's Defense: Anti-Negro Thought in America, 1900–1930* (Baton Rouge: Louisiana University Press, 1965), especially chaps. 1 and 2.

90. Hall, "The Negro in Africa and America," 16, 17. On the process of disenfranchisement in Virginia, see Williamson, *Crucible of Race*, 234–241.

91. Hall, "The Negro in Africa and America," 1, 7. Hall cited Du Bois's *Souls of Black Folk* in this section, though Du Bois's comment about the "tropical imagination" was not developed in the way that Hall emphasized emotionalism as the basis of black religion.

92. *Adolescence: Its Psychology and Its Relations to Physiology, Anthropology, Sociology, Sex, Crime, Religion, and Education*, vol. 1 (New York: D. Appleton, 1904), 266.

93. "The Negro in Africa and America," 14.

94. *Adolescence: Its Psychology and Its Relations to Physiology, Anthropology, Sociology, Sex, Crime, Religion, and Education*, vol. 2 (New York: D. Appleton, 1905), 676.

95. Ibid.; "Negro in Africa and America," 14.

96. Ibid.

97. Ibid., 14–15.

98. Ibid., 7.

99. Ibid., 8. The expression "lower type" appears to be a reference to poor blacks in the rural South.

100. Ibid., 19–20.

101. Ibid., 19. For an interesting study of Hall's ideas of culture, gender, and race, see Gail Bederman, *Manliness and Civilization: A Cultural History of Gender and Race in the United States, 1880–1917* (Chicago: University of Chicago Press, 1995), chap. 3.

102. Taves, *Fits, Trances, and Visions,* 261–263.

103. Frederick Morgan Davenport, *Primitive Traits in Religious Revivals: A Study in Mental and Social Evolution* (New York: Macmillan, 1905), vii–viii.

104. The chapter was originally published as a separate article in the September 1905 issue of *Contemporary Review.*

105. Taves, *Fits, Trances and Visions,* 295.

106. Davenport, *Primitive Traits,* 15–17.

107. Ibid., 21.

108. Ibid., 369–370.

109. Ibid., 45, 46.

110. Ibid., 67–68, 305–306. Davenport wrote: "The vice of religious, political, and industrial democracy is emotionalism in the wide sense of that term." His critique of emotionalism was added to his advice to missionaries. He counseled them to change the emotional and superstitious religion of the natives.

111. Ibid., 301.

112. Ibid., 205.

113. Ibid., 292–293.

114. Ibid., 58.

115. See Davenport, "The Religion of the American Negro," *Contemporary Review* 82 (September 1905): 375.

116. *Social and Mental Traits of the Negro* was published as one volume in the Columbia University series Studies in History, Economics and Public Law.

117. See Morton Sosna, *In Search of the Silent South: Southern Liberals and the Race Issue* (New York: Columbia University Press, 1977), 42–45; and Daniel Joseph Singal, *The War Within: From Victorian to Modernist Thought in the South, 1919–1945* (Chapel Hill: University of North Carolina Press, 1982), 115–119.

118. Howard Odum, *Social and Mental Traits of the Negro: Research into the Conditions of the Negro in Southern Towns, A Study in Race Traits, Tendencies, and Prospects* (New York: Columbia University, 1910), 5.

119. Ibid., 13.

120. Ibid., 54, 162–163, 208–210.

121. Ibid., 88.

122. The sexual connotation usually attached to the latter word is relevant because, as John Haller notes, the alleged "sexual madness" and religious emotionalism

of blacks were seen as marks of the "innate character of the African." Some social scientists argued that the stimulation and emotional release that occurred in black religious worship services were equivalent to physical release during sexual orgasm. Indeed, the very center of the black temperament, argued the social scientists, was an intense emotionalism, which sought expression in sexual abandon and wild religious frenzies. See Haller, *Outcasts from Evolution*, 54; and Hall, "The Negro in Africa and America," 14.

123. Odum, *Social and Mental Traits*, 88.

124. Ibid., 89.

125. Ibid., 239.

126. Many white social scientists accepted that not only were black males out of control and raping white women in great numbers in the South but there was a physiological and psychological basis to such heinous crimes. Ida B. Wells emphatically rejected such claims. She insisted that individual black men "commit crimes the same as do white men, but that the Negro race is peculiarly given to assault upon women, is a falsehood of the deepest dye." Her research on lynchings indicated that less than one-sixth of blacks lynched were even charged with rape. See *Southern Horrors and Other Writings: The Anti-Lynching Campaign of Ida B. Wells, 1892–1900*, ed. Jacqueline Jones Royster (Boston: Bedford Books, 1997), 207. W. E. B. Du Bois, who was a recognized expert on various aspects of the so-called Negro problem, laid out several reasons for the increase of crime among blacks in the South. His list became the standard moderate view against claims that blacks were criminal by nature. Du Bois argued that (1) Emancipation was a social revolution that was bound to place strains on the black population and produce competition for jobs, poverty, and moral challenges that led to more crime. (2) The convict-lease system "harvested" criminals. Under this system, criminals were leased to private corporations or individuals. The criminal became a source of revenue for the states. Thousands of Southern men and women, mostly black, labored in mines or swamps under atrocious conditions. (3) The unfairness of the Southern courts, which treated whites leniently compared to blacks (the Southern criminal justice system, obviously brutal in its treatment of blacks, was one of the harshest in the industrialized world). (4) The lawlessness and barbarity of mobs, which directly encouraged crime because they shattered blacks' faith in the justice system and transformed horror at crime into sympathy with victims (some of whom were burned alive after several body parts were surgically removed). (5) The unnatural separation of the best class of blacks and whites, which deprived them of sympathy for one another because there was no mutual understanding or common meeting of the mind. See "The Negro and Crime," *Independent* (May 18 1899; reprint, *Writings by W. E. B. Du Bois in Periodicals Edited by Others*, vol. 1, ed. Herbert Aptheker [Millwood: Kraus-Thomson, 1982]), 57; and Du Bois, *The Philadelphia Negro: A Social Study* (Philadelphia: University of Pennsylvania Press, 1996 [1899]), 282–284. On the convict-lease system and crime in the South, see Woodward, *Origins of the New South*, 212–215; and Edward L. Ayers, *Vengeance and Justice: Crime and Punishment in the 19th Century American South* (New York: Oxford University Press, 1984), chap. 6.

127. Odum, *Social and Mental Traits*, 188; emphasis added.

128. Ibid., 165.

129. Ibid., 259.

130. Ibid., 260.

131. George Stocking argues that as early as 1894 Boas took Spencer to task on a number of Spencer's claims about primitives based on Boas's field experience with Indians. See Stocking, *Race, Culture*, 219.

132. Franz Boas, "The Mind of Primitive Man," *Journal of American Folklore* 14 (January–March 1901): 1–11.

133. On the critique of "universalizing assumptions" in Boasian anthropology, see Richard Handler, "Boasian Anthropology and the Critique of American Culture," *American Quarterly* 42 (June 1990): 254–255.

134. G. Stanley Hall, "Point of View toward Primitive Races," *Journal of Race Development* 1 (1910): 5.

135. Bederman, *Manliness and Civilization*, 77.

136. Hall, "Point of View," 5–7.

137. Alexander Francis Chamberlain, "The Contribution of the Negro to Human Civilization," *Journal of Race Development* (April 1911): 482–502. Chamberlain was also the editor of the *Journal of American Folklore* from 1900 to 1908 and had written several articles on blacks and Africa.

138. Ronald LaMarr Sharps, "Happy Days and Sorrow Songs: Interpretations of Negro Folklore by Black Intellectuals, 1893–1928" (Ph.D. diss., Washington University, 1991).

139. Baker, *From Savage to Negro*, 143–147.

140. Hall, "The Negro in Africa and America," 19–20.

141. Odum, *Social and Mental Traits*, 66–68.

142. "The Artistic Gifts of the Negro" (1908; reprint, *Race Adjustment/The Everlasting Stain* [New York: Arno Press, 1968]), 232–242. James Weldon Johnson, a writer and poet, wrote in 1915 that ragtime had "swept the world" and that attempts to rob blacks of the credit for originating it were afoot. See Johnson, "The Poor White Musician," in *James Weldon Johnson: Writings*, ed. William L. Andrews (New York: Library of America, 2004), 619.

143. William H. Ferris, *The African Abroad or His Evolution in Western Culture: Tracing His Development under Caucasian Milieu*, vol. 1 (New Haven, Conn.: Tuttle, Morehouse and Taylor Press, 1913), 24–45. Ferris was a graduate of Harvard and Yale. He later cast his lot with the Garvey movement. See S. P. Fullinwider, *The Mind and Mood of Black America: 20th Century Thought* (Homewood, Ill.: Dorsey Press, 1969), 22–25; and William Toll, *The Resurgence of Race: Black Social Theory from Reconstruction to the Pan-African Conferences* (Philadelphia: Temple University Press, 1979), 138–139.

144. August Meier, *Negro Thought in America, 1880–1915* (Ann Arbor: University of Michigan Press, 1988 [1963]), 267.

145. The beginnings of an appreciation for a distinctive "black beauty" had taken place in the early twentieth century, and this tradition was built on in the works of

black poets and writers in the period leading up to World War I. See Bruce Dickson, *Black American Writing in the Nadir: The Evolution of a Literary Tradition, 1877–1915* (Baton Rouge: Louisiana State University Press, 1989), 222.

146. For a general overview of cultural changes in these years, see Stanley Corben, "The Assault on Victorianism in the Twentieth Century," in *Victorian America*, ed. Daniel Walker Howe (Philadelphia: University of Pennsylvania Press, 1984), 160–181.

147. "The Passing Tradition and the African Civilization," *Journal of Negro History* 1 (January 1916): 35, 41. See also, Williams, *Rethinking Race*, 66–67.

148. Richard Clark Reed, "A Sketch of the Religious History of Negroes in the South," *Papers of the American Society of Church History* 4 Second Series (New York: G. P. Putnam's Sons, 1914). The period between these two works is exceedingly extended, but because so few papers or books on black religion by the American Society of Church History exist from this time period, these two rather different works seemed useful to compare. Sweet did not have African American religion in mind, but the construction of and changing attitudes toward emotionalism were relevant to conceptions of black religion.

149. *Revivalism in America: Its Origin, Growth and Decline* (New York: Charles Scribner's Sons, 1944), xiii.

150. Ibid., 181.

CHAPTER 4

1. W. E. B. Du Bois, *Dusk of Dawn* (New York: Schocken Books, 1968 [1940]), 51.

2. *The Reminiscences of W. E. B. Du Bois* (Ithaca, N.Y.: Oral History Collection of Columbia University, 1963), 122.

3. *The Souls of Black Folk*, ed. Farah Jasmine Griffin (New York: Barnes and Noble Classics, 2003 [1903]), 99.

4. *Reminiscences*, 122.

5. Du Bois, *Dusk of Dawn*, 54.

6. Robert A. Orsi, *Between Heaven and Earth: The Religious Worlds People Make and the Scholars Who Study Them* (Princeton, N.J.: Princeton University Press, 2005), 188.

7. "The Problem of Amusement" (1897; reprint, *W. E. B. Du Bois: On Sociology and the Black Community*, eds. Dan S. Green and Edwin D. Driver [Chicago: University of Chicago Press, 1978]), 228.

8. By a "Puritan" conception of a purified church, I mean an implicit normative model of religion or a churchly sphere of activity that Du Bois used to judge black churches.

9. Du Bois, *Dusk of Dawn*, 42–43.

10. *Reminiscences*, 133.

11. This conclusion was greeted with some relief by those who had read the work of novelist and physician Edward W. Gilliam, who argued that the 1880 census indicated that the South would be "Africanized" because of the superior fecundity of

blacks. Gilliam proposed that blacks be colonized to avert racial warfare. See George M. Fredrickson, *The Black Image in the White Mind: The Debate on Afro-American Character and Destiny, 1817–1914* (Middleton, Conn.: Wesleyan University Press, 1971 [1987]), 249.

12. Frederick L. Hoffman, *Race Traits and Tendencies of the American Negro* (New York: Macmillan, 1896), 311.

13. Ibid., 312.

14. Ibid., 327.

15. Fredrickson, *Black Image*, 249–250.

16. Hoffman, *Race Traits*, 133.

17. Ibid., 310.

18. Du Bois, Review of *Race Traits and Tendencies of the American Negro* by Frederick L. Hoffman, *Annals of the American Academy of Political and Social Science* 9 (January 1897): 127.

19. John S. Haller Jr., *Outcasts from Evolution: Scientific Attitudes of Racial Inferiority, 1859–1900* (Carbondale: Southern Illinois University Press, 1995 [1971]), 60.

20. Lee D. Baker, *From Savage to Negro: Anthropology and the Construction of Race, 1896–1954* (Berkeley: University of California Press, 1998), 79.

21. Green and Driver, *Du Bois*, 6.

22. English translation, "The large- and small-scale management of agriculture in the Southern United States, 1840–1890." Du Bois spent the winter of 1893 in Neustadt, Germany, studying the mores and living standards of twenty peasant families. Under Schmoller's suggestion, he compared their lives to African Americans from the backcountry of Tennessee. See David Levering Lewis, *W. E. B. Du Bois: Biography of a Race, 1868–1919* (New York: Henry Holt, 1993), 137.

23. Green and Driver, *Du Bois*, 6–7.

24. Du Bois, *Dusk of Dawn*, 51.

25. Du Bois, "The Study of the Negro Problems" (1897), in Green and Driver, *Du Bois*, 83.

26. Ibid., 79.

27. Barbara Dianne Savage, "W. E. B. Du Bois and 'the Negro Church'," *Annals of the American Academy of Political and Social Science* 568 (March 2003): 236.

28. Du Bois, "Study of Negro Problems," 82.

29. Ibid., 78.

30. Ibid., 81.

31. Du Bois, *Dusk of Dawn*, 67.

32. Lewis, *W. E. B. Du Bois*, 226.

33. Du Bois, "The Problem of Amusement," in Green and Driver, *Du Bois*, 226.

34. Ibid., 226.

35. Ibid., 226–227.

36. Ibid., 228.

37. Ibid., 230.

38. Ibid., 232–233.

39. Ibid. 233.

40. Ibid., 234.

41. W. E. B. Du Bois, "The Religion of the American Negro" (1900), in Green and Driver, *Du Bois*, 220.

42. On the particular problems that blacks faced in the urban North at the turn of the century, see Du Bois, *The Black North in 1901: A Social Study*, in Green and Driver, *Du Bois*, 140–153. Gilbert Osofsky argues that black churches were founded in some of the most unsavory parts of New York City late in the nineteenth and early twentieth centuries. See Osofsky, *Harlem: The Making of a Ghetto: Negro New York, 1890–1930*, 2nd ed. (New York: Harper and Row, 1971), 12–14. Yet public amusements, sports events, cabarets, and other attractions of the city did compete, as Du Bois argued, for the attention and loyalty of increasing numbers of black migrants to the Northern cities in the 1890s. See Seth M. Schreiner, "The Negro Church and the Northern City, 1890–1930," in *Seven on Black: Reflections on the Negro Experience in America*, eds. William G. Shade and Roy C. Herrenkohl (Philadelphia: J. B. Lippincot, 1969), 105.

43. Du Bois, "The Religion of the American Negro," 225.

44. W. E. B. Du Bois, *The Souls of Black Folk* (New York: Library of America, 1990 [1903]), 123.

45. Ibid., 147.

46. For the claim that crime was increasing among blacks in Northern cities, see Willcox, "Negro Criminality," 79. When he wanted to point out the problems of crime and vice in black communities, Willcox quoted extensively from Du Bois's studies. For a more detailed study of the social context of and social scientific debates about black crime in urban Northern areas, see Khalil G. Muhammad, " 'Negro Stranger in Our Midst': Origins of African American Criminality in the Urban North, 1900–1940" (Ph.D. diss., Rutgers University, 2004).

47. Du Bois, *Souls of Black Folk*, 149. For a convincing argument that Du Bois believed that black spirituality was a counter to white materialism and a distinctive virtue for blacks, see Bruce Dickson Jr., *Black American Writing in the Nadir: The Evolution of a Literary Tradition, 1877–1915* (Baton Rouge: Louisiana State Press, 1989), 206–207. David Levering Lewis argues that Du Bois was convinced that the old, quasi-feudal South was being swamped by new classes "thrown up by industrial exploitation." For Lewis, this reflected Du Bois's earlier antidemocratic mindset because Du Bois not only lamented the passing of the planters but asserted that democracy unleashed the "full savagery" of the profit motive, which was restrained in the past by hierarchy and paternalism. See Lewis, *Biography of a Race*, 284.

48. Du Bois, *The Souls of Black Folk*, 14, 180–181.

49. Du Bois, "The Conservation of Races," in Green and Driver, *Du Bois*, 241, 245, 247; emphasis in original.

50. W. E. B. Du Bois, ed., *The Negro Church* (1903; reprint, with introduction by Phil Zuckerman, Sandra L. Barnes, and Daniel Cady [Walnut Creek: AltaMira Press, 2003]), vii.

51. Ibid., xiii.

52. Ibid., i.

53. Du Bois, "The Study of the Negro Problems" (1898), in Green and Driver, *Du Bois*, 78. Although Du Bois does not cite the source of his conclusions about Africa and the black churches, Lewis argues that he made use of the writings of German ethnographer Friedrich Ratzel. See Lewis, *Biography of a Race*, 222. For a critical evaluation of the attempt by Du Bois and others in the early twentieth century to develop a richer understanding of African cultures, and a fuller, more positive image of Africa, see Vernon Williams Jr., *Rethinking Race: Franz Boas and His Contemporaries* (Lexington: University Press of Kentucky, 1996), chaps. 3 and 4.

54. Du Bois, "The Negro Church," in *Du Bois on Religion*, ed. Phil Zuckerman (Walnut Creek: AltaMira Press, 2000), 110–112, 113. See also Lewis, *Biography of a Race*, 222–223.

55. Perhaps this may explain why, besides making use of the categories of social science, Du Bois referred to black churches as the "Negro Church." Because it had become in his view an almost "natural" organism or unit as the family, then it should be so designated.

56. Du Bois, *Philadelphia Negro*, 205–206. Between 1898 and 1905, Du Bois provided a number of studies on the industrial history of blacks in the South at the request of Carroll Davidson Wright, who from 1885 to 1905 was the (first) commissioner of the U.S. Bureau of Labor. See *The Correspondence of W.E.B. Du Bois Selections, 1877–1934*, vol. 1, ed. Herbert Aptheker (Amherst: University of Massachusetts Press, 1973), 40–41.

57. Aptheker, *Correspondence*, 41–42.

58. Du Bois, "Study of Negro Problems," in Green and Driver, *Du Bois*, 78.

59. Elijah Anderson, ed., *The Philadelphia Negro: A Social Study* (Philadelphia: University of Pennsylvania Press, 1996 [1899], xviii.

60. Ibid., 58–59.

61. Ibid., 2–3.

62. *Report of the Industrial Commission on Education* 15 (Washington, D.C.: U.S. Industrial Commission Reports, 1900–1902), 171.

63. "The Atlanta Conferences," in Green and Driver, *Du Bois*, 54.

64. Du Bois, *Souls of Black Folk*, 7.

65. Ibid., 12–13.

66. Ibid., 4.

67. Du Bois to Walter Francis Willcox, March 29, 1904, in Aptheker, *Correspondence*, 74.

68. Ibid., 75.

69. Walter Fleming, Review of *The Negro Church, Political Science Quarterly* 19 (April 1904): 703.

70. "The Religious Life of the Negro," in *The Booker T. Washington Papers*, vol. 8, eds. Louis R. Harlan and Raymond W. Smock (Urbana: University of Illinois Press, 1979), 333.

71. Lewis, *Biography of a Race*, 171–174.

72. "Conservation of Races," 244.

73. C. G. Woodson to W. E. B. Du Bois, February 18, 1908, in Aptheker, *Correspondence*, 140.

74. On the influence of Hegel on Du Bois's thought, see Shamoon Zamir, *Dark Voices: W. E. B. Du Bois and American Thought, 1888–1903* (Chicago: University of Chicago Press, 1995), chap. 4. I not agree with Zamir's argument that Du Bois's account of double consciousness in *Souls of Black Folk* is a reference to the black middle class rather than the "black folk" as a "homogenized collectivity." It seems to me that it is a reference to both rather than one or the other.

75. Joel Williamson, *The Crucible of Race: Black-White Relations in the American South Since Emancipation* (New York: Oxford University Press, 1984), 402–403.

76. Du Bois, "Conservation of Races," in Green and Driver, *Du Bois*, 243.

77. Du Bois, *Souls of Black Folk*, 139.

78. Ibid., 140.

79. Ibid., 146.

80. Savage, "Biblical and Historical Imperatives: Towards a History of Ideas about the Political Role of Black Churches," in *African Americans and the Bible: Sacred Texts and Social Texture*, ed. Vincent L. Wimbush (New York: Continuum International, 2000), 369.

81. Du Bois, "The Negro Church," in Zuckerman, *Du Bois on Religion*, 46.

82. Ibid.

83. Du Bois, "Religion as the Solvent of the Race Problem" (1908; reprint, *Race Adjustment/The Everlasting Stain* [New York: Arno Press, 1968]), 133–134.

84. Ibid., 140.

85. Ibid., 150–151. This view was promoted by Henry Hugh Proctor, a black pastor in Atlanta. See my remarks in the introduction.

86. Ibid., 149–150. Miller used terms such as "Anglo-Saxon" and "Teuton" interchangeably.

87. Faduma later served as a pastor of a church in the all-black town of Boley, Oklahoma, and was involved in a back to Africa scheme in 1914, which reflected the drift of some members of the academy towards African emigration. See Wilson Jeremiah Moses, *The Golden Age of Black Nationalism, 1850–1925* (New York: Oxford University Press), 203–204; and Moses, *Alexander Crummell: A Study of Civilization and Discontent* (New York: Oxford University Press, 1989), 296–297. Faduma had written a sympathetic article on the religious beliefs and practices of the Yorubas in West Africa. See his "Religious Belief and Worship of the Yorubas in West Africa," *African Methodist Episcopal Church Review* (July 1895): 150–158. Faduma adopted his African name by combining the names of Orisha and Tukeh, two Yoruba divinities.

88. Quotation from Moses N. Moore, *Orishatukeh Faduma: Liberal Theology and Evangelical Pan-Africanism, 1857–1946* (Lanham, Md.: Scarecrow Press, 1996), 105.

89. Ibid.

90. Dickson D. Bruce Jr., *Archibald Grimké: Portrait of a Black Independent* (Baton Rouge: Louisiana State University, 1993), 117.

91. Faduma, "The Defects of the Negro Church," *American Negro Academy Occasional Papers* 10 (1904; reprint [New York: Arno Press, 1969]), 3–4, 6, 8, 13, 14.

92. Ibid., 4–5.

93. Ibid., 6–7.

94. Washington had a similar assessment of rural blacks in the 1880s, though perhaps not as harsh as Faduma's. He wrote of a whole family sleeping in one room and the lack of privacy in such homes. Harlan argues that such scenes offended the deeply imbibed "Puritanism" that Washington acquired from his time at Hampton. See Louis R. Harlan, *Booker T. Washington: The Making of a Black Leader, 1856–1901* (New York: Oxford University Press, 1972), 119–120; and Washington's *Up from Slavery* (New York: Dover Publications, 1995 [1901]), 54–55. Du Bois's portrayal of blacks he visited in rural Tennessee in the 1880s and his reactions to their culture are detailed in his *Autobiography of W.E.B. Du Bois: A Soliloquy on Viewing My Life from the Last Decade of the It's First Century*, chap. 8 [Online] May 1, 2005; available from www .alexanderstreet4.com.ezp1.harvard.edu/cgi-bin/asp/bltc/getdoc.pl?/projects/artfla/ databases/asp/bltc/fulltext/IMAGE/.2884. See also Lewis, *W. E. B. Du Bois*, 67–72.

95. Faduma, "Defects of the Negro Church," 9–10.

96. Ibid., 11–13.

97. Moore, *Orishatukeh Faduma*, 62–63. For a detailed study of the new theology, see William R. Hutchison, *The Modernist Impulse in American Protestantism* (New York: Oxford University Press, 1976), chap. 3.

98. Faduma, "Defects of the Negro Church," 11–12. Moore's claim that the new theology's influence on Faduma's thought is not as evident as Moore suggests in Faduma's critique of the black church. After all, Henry Hugh Proctor (mentioned in the introduction to the book) studied at Yale around the same time that Faduma did and he did not share these very negative views of African American religion. These criticisms can be found in other writings of the period that show little direct influence from the new theology. The general trend of social and intellectual thought on race and the broader discourse on the dangers of emotionalism to civilization and self-control are crucial in our efforts to understand these criticisms of black religion.

99. Ibid., 14.

100. Ibid. Faduma pointed to the findings of a Dr. Graham at the "last meeting" of the British Association for the Advancement of Science, who apparently argued that there was less insanity among Roman Catholics than Protestants in Ireland. The Protestants of Ireland, according to Faduma's reading of this study, were intensely morbid and ascetic in their Calvinism. Faduma speculated that similar results would be found if such investigations were pursued in America. He conjectured that there were fewer "maniacs" among Presbyterians and Congregationalists than among Baptists and Methodists (most blacks belonged to the latter two denominations).

101. Ibid., 15.

102. Ibid., 15–16. Faduma concluded his talk with these words: "When reason is overfed in the exercise of religion, the result is a dry and barren rationalism. When the emotions are overfed the result is a wild and sickly sentimentalism, a neurotic religion" (17). On the meaning of manliness at the time of Faduma's writing, see Gail Bederman, *Manliness and Civilization: A Cultural History of Gender and Race in the United States, 1880–1917* (Chicago: University of Chicago Press, 1995).

103. Miller, "Religion as the Solvent of the Race Problem," 140–142.

104. *Black Protest and the Great Migration: A Brief History with Documents*, ed. Eric Andersen (Boston: Bedford Books, 2003), 1–2.

105. Milton Sernett, *Bound for the Promised Land: African American Religion and the Great Migration* (Durham, N.C.: Duke University Press, 1997), 4–5.

106. For examples of the recent literature on the Social Gospel, especially reinterpretations of black involvement, see Ronald C. White Jr., *Liberty and Justice for All: Racial Reform and the Social Gospel* (New York: Harper and Row, 1990); Ralph E. Luker, *The Social Gospel in Black and White: American Racial Reform, 1885–1912* (Chapel Hill: University of North Carolina Press, 1991); and Gary Scott Smith, *The Search for Social Salvation: Social Christianity and America, 1880–1925* (Lanham, Md.: Lexington Books, 2000).

107. Gilbert Osofsky, *Harlem: The Making of a Ghetto: Negro New York, 1890–1930*, 2nd ed. (Chicago: Ivan R. Dee, 1996 [1966]), chap. 4.

108. Luker, *Social Gospel*, chap. 7.

109. Sernett, *Bound for the Promised Land*, 116.

110. Robert Gregg, *Sparks from the Anvil of Oppression: Philadelphia's African Methodists and Southern Migrants, 1890–1940* (Philadelphia: Temple University Press, 1993), 98–100.

111. On institutional churches, see Luker, *Social Gospel*, 170–178.

112. Gregg, *Sparks from the Anvil*, 100–101.

113. Wright, "Social Work and Influence of the Negro Church," *Annals of the American Academy of Political and Social Science* 30 (November 1907): 81–93.

114. Du Bois, "The Negro Church," in Zuckerman, *Du Bois on Religion*, 45–46.

115. "The Atlanta Conferences" (1904), in Zuckerman, *Du Bois on Religion*, 58.

116. The coeditor was Augustus Granville Dill, associate professor of sociology at Atlanta University. The emphases were clearly Du Bois's, and the continuities between his earlier work are noticeable.

117. "Morals and Manners among Negro Americans," *Atlanta University Publications* 18 (1914; reprint [New York: Arno Press, 1968]), 4–8. On the work of the black women's club movement and the social outreach of the National Baptists, see Evelyn Brooks Higginbotham, *Righteous Discontent: The Women's Movement in the Black Baptist Church, 1880–1920* (Cambridge, Mass.: Harvard University Press, 1993), 150–164.

118. "Morals and Manners," 136; and "The New Negro Church," in *Against Racism: Unpublished Essays, Papers, Addresses, 1887–1961: W. E. B. Du Bois*, ed. Herbert Aptheker (Amherst: University of Massachusetts, 1985), 84–85.

CHAPTER 5

1. "The Power of the Negro Church," in *The Selected Writings of James Weldon Johnson: The New York Age Editorials (1914–1923)*, vol. 1, ed. Sondra Kathryn Wilson (New York: Oxford University Press, 1995), 146–147.

2. Robert A. Bone, *The Negro Novel in America*, rev. ed. (New Haven, Conn.: Yale University Press, 1965), 62–64.

3. See Jacqueline Googin, *Carter G. Woodson: A Life in Black History* (Baton Rouge: Louisiana State University Press, 1993).

4. Mays and Nicholson incorporated more current research, used sociological methodology, and emphasized more recent developments in black religion. Woodson's work treated long-term historical trends and focused on denominational developments. See Albert J. Raboteau and David D. Wills, "Retelling Carter G. Woodson's Story: Archival Sources for Afro-American Church History," *Journal of American History* 77 (June 1990): 183–199.

5. Carter G. Woodson, *The History of the Negro Church*, 2nd ed. (Washington: Associated Publishers, 1945), v.

6. Ibid., 226. Woodson's analysis came close to assertions of white Southerners who regarded slavery as a necessary restraint to prevent blacks from degenerating into "superstitious" and "barbarous" African religious traditions. Yet he seemed not to have any awareness of this.

7. Woodson, *History of the Negro Church*, 227.

8. Ibid., 228.

9. Ibid., 228–230.

10. Gilbert Osofsky, *Harlem: The Making of a Ghetto: Negro New York, 1890–1930* (New York: Harper and Row, 1966), 127–136.

11. Ibid., 14, 114–115. See also John William Kinney, "Adam Clayton Powell, Sr. and Adam Clayton Powell, Jr.: A Historical Exposition and Theological Analysis" (Ph.D. diss., Columbia University, 1979), 37–48, 106–107. Based on his analysis of black newspapers in New York City, Kinney argues that in spite of the social programs offered by Abyssinian and other institutional churches, there was extensive criticism of black churches in Harlem in the 1920s, which deepened in the 1930s.

12. "The Church in Social Work," in *The Opportunity Reader: Stories, Poetry, and Essays from Urban League's Opportunity Magazine*, ed. Sondra Kathryn Wilson (New York: Modern Library, 1999), 390–391.

13. Seth Scheiner, "The Negro Church and the Northern Ghetto, 1890–1930," in *Seven on Black: Reflections on the Negro Experience in America*, eds. William G. Shade and Roy Herrenkohl (Philadelphia: Lippincott, 1969), 100.

14. George E. Haynes, "Negro Migration: Its Effects on Family and Community Life in the North," in *Up South: Stories, Studies and Letters of this Century's African American Migrations*, ed. Malaika Adero (New York: New Press, 1993), 80–81. Haynes's article originally appeared in the journal of the Urban League, *Opportunity*, October 1924. For a later assessment of black religion by Haynes, see "The Negro Church and Social Progress," *Annals of the American Academy of Political and Social Science* 140 (November 1928): 264–271.

15. Mark Miles Fisher, "The Negro Church and the World War," *Journal of Religion* (September 1925): 483, 486–499.

16. Wilson Record, *The Negro and the Communist Party* (New York: Atheneum, 1971 [1951]), 16–22.

17. Walter Hawkins, "Too Much Religion," in *The Messenger Reader: Stories, Poetry and Essays from the Messenger Magazine*, ed. Sondra Kathryn Wilson (New York: Modern Library, 2000), 9.

18. Eugene Gordon, "A New Religion for the Negro" (1928), in *A Documentary History of the Negro People in the United States, 1910–1932*, ed. Herbert Aptheker (Seacus, N.J.: Citadel Press, 1973), 572, 574–575, 578–579.

19. Ibid., 579.

20. George S. Schuyler, "The Black Man's Burden—Religion," in Claude Barnett Papers (hereafter CBP), Lamont Library Microfilm. The essay is not dated, but was probably written around 1930, based on internal evidence.

21. Ibid. Both Gordon and Schuyler suggested that the predominance of black women was a major factor in the continuing influence of black churches. Schuyler was especially critical of ministers who he believed had illicit sexual relations with complicit black women who were the most loyal members of the churches. He claimed that the Negro Church's weakness was in part because it was a "woman's institution presided over by men."

22. Benjamin E. Mays, *The Negro's God as Reflected in His Literature* (Boston: Chapman and Grimes, 1938), 242.

23. Cardinal George W. Mundelein to Father J. A. Burgmer, S.V.D. (October 26, 1917; reprint, Joseph J. McCarthy, "History of Black Catholic Education in Chicago, 1871–1971" (Ph.D. diss., Loyola University of Chicago, 1973), 149–150.

24. See Robert E. L. Faris, *Chicago Sociology, 1920–1932* (Chicago: University of Chicago Press, 1967), 27–30; and Vernon Williams Jr., *Rethinking Race: Franz Boas and His Contemporaries* (Lexington: University of Kentucky Press, 1996), chap. 5.

25. For Park's view of blacks in the city, see Wallace Best, *Passionately Human, No Less Divine: Religion and Culture in Black Chicago, 1915–1952* (Princeton, N.J.: Princeton University Press, 2005), 27.

26. Robert E. Park, "The Conflict and Fusion of Cultures with Special References to the Negro," *Journal of Negro History* 4 (April 1919): 112.

27. Ibid.

28. Ibid., 129.

29. Ibid., 129–130. On theories of race in Park's day and their implications, particularly within the context of European immigration, see Matthew Frye Jacobson, *Whiteness of Different Color: European Immigrants and the Alchemy of Race* (Cambridge, Mass.: Harvard University Press, 1999).

30. Park, "Conflict and Fusion," 130.

31. For the exact references, see Harriet Beecher Stowe, *Uncle Tom's Cabin Or, Life among the Lowly* (Cambridge: Cambridge University Press, 1886), 107, 200; and Robert Dale Owen, *The Wrong of Slavery; The Right of Emancipation; and The Future of the African Race in the United States* (New York: Kraus Reprint, 1969 [1864]), 220–221.

32. Park, "Conflict and Fusion," 130.

33. Ibid., 116.

34. Ibid., 125

35. Ibid, 122.

36. Ibid., 113–115.

37. Ibid., 127–128.

38. Ibid., 130. For a contemporary study of slavery and slave conceptions of heaven, see G. R. Wilson, "The Religion of the American Negro Slave: His Attitude Toward Life and Death," *Journal of Negro History* 8 (January 1923): 41–71.

39. Park, "Conflict and Fusion," 112.

40. George Hutchinson, *The Harlem Renaissance in Black and White* (Cambridge, Mass.: Harvard University Press, 1995), 44–46.

41. Ibid., 185, 425–427. In defense of Barnes, Hutchinson writes, "Barnes did not come to black art as a result of European-inspired exotic primitivism; he came to European modernism by way of the aesthetic inspiration of black gospel singing, which melded with philosophical pragmatism" (45).

42. For Hall's views of blacks, see "The Negro in Africa and America," *Pedagogical Seminary* 12 (September 1905): 19.

43. David Joseph Singal, "Towards a Definition of American Modernism," *American Quarterly* 39 (spring 1987): 7; and John Jervis, *Transgressing the Modern: Explorations in the Western Experience of Otherness* (Malden, Mass.: Blackwell, 1999), 219.

44. Historian Gail Bederman writes that during the 1890s the natural man or the primitive in the context of race and gender discussions represented the antithesis of the civilized, self-restrained Victorian man. The natural man was regarded as violent, impulsive, and untouched by civilization. His "innate savagery" stood as a threat to civilization and was thought to be simmering in the hearts of modern men, but the natural man was also seen as possessing those qualities that modern men lacked. Bederman argues that at the turn of the century the figure of the violent and passionate natural man (particularly reflected in the increased interest in boxing) allowed Americans who were searching for an alternative vision of manhood to imagine a manhood that was powerful but uncivilized. See Bederman, *Manliness and Civilization: A Cultural History of Race and Gender in the United States, 1880–1917* (Chicago: University of Chicago Press, 1995), 73–74.

45. Jervis, *Transgressing the Modern*, 76–77.

46. Hutchinson, *Harlem Renaissance in Black and White*, 46.

47. Albert C. Barnes, "Negro Art and America," in *The New Negro: Voices of the Harlem Renaissance*, ed. Alain Locke (New York: Touchstone, 1992 [1925]), 19.

48. One is reminded of Phillip Bruce's and Howard Odum's arguments that the "current" of black emotions impelled them forward, rendering them unable to think of the actions that they took. The point here is not to imply equality of argument but to note the similarity of expression and the mental maps of the black mind, though the implications for black life of each theorist's ideas in their varying social and historical contexts were considerably different.

49. Barnes, "Negro Art and America," 19.

50. Ibid., 19–20.

51. Ibid., 20.

52. Ibid., 22–25.

53. Alain Locke, "Legacy of the Ancestral Arts," in *New Negro*, 254–255.

54. See Thomas Gossett, *Race: The History of an Idea in America* (New York: Oxford University Press, 1997 [1963]), 376. George Stocking argues that psychological intelligence testing "provided the most important single scientific buttress for the racism of the 1920s." See George R. Stocking Jr., *Race, Culture, and Evolution: Essays in the History of Anthropology* (New York: Free Press, 1968), 300–301.

55. Horace Mann Bond, "Temperament," in *The Crisis Reader: Stories, Poetry, and Essays from the NAACP's Crisis Magazine*, ed. Sondra Kathryn Wilson (New York: Modern Library, 1999), 378.

56. Ibid., 379.

57. Ibid., 378.

58. Ibid., 379.

59. Ibid., 380.

60. Ibid.

61. Ibid.

62. Ibid., 382–383.

63. E. Franklin Frazier, "Racial Self-Expression" (1927; reprint, *Black Protest Thought in the Twentieth Century*, 2nd ed., eds. August Meier, Elliott Rudwick, and Francis L. Broderick [New York: Macmillan, 1971]), 118.

64. Ibid., 118.

65. Wilson Jeremiah Moses, *Black Messiahs and Uncle Toms: Social and Literary Manipulations of a Religious Myth* (University Park: Pennsylvania State University Press, 1982), 119.

66. "Race Prejudice and the Negro Artist," in *James Weldon Johnson: Writings*, ed. William L. Andrews (New York: Library of America, 2004), 753–755.

67. David Levering Lewis, ed., *The Portable Harlem Renaissance Reader* (New York: Penguin Books, 1994), xiii–xiv.

68. Gerald Early, ed., *My Soul's High Song: The Collected Writings of Countee Cullen, Voice of the Harlem Renaissance* (New York: Anchor Books, 1991), 24–34.

69. Nathan I. Huggins, *Harlem Renaissance* (New York: Oxford University Press, 1971), 248, 299–300. I find Huggins's rather pessimistic analysis of the New Negro movement and white involvement to be closer to my own view than Lewis's and Hutchinson's interpretations. Huggins's trenchant critique of white projections of emotionally satisfying images of blacks is, in my estimation, a foundational starting point for an appreciation of black/white relations in American dramatic and literary productions.

70. Hutchinson, *Harlem Renaissance in Black and White*, 1–18, 185.

71. David Levering Lewis, *When Harlem Was in Vogue* (New York: Penguin Books, 1997 [1979]), 99.

72. George Houston Bass and Henry Louis Gates Jr., eds. *Mule Bone: A Comedy of Negro Life by Langston Hughes and Zora Neale Hurston* (New York: Harper Collins, 1991), 15.

73. Montgomery Gregory, "The Drama of Negro Life," in *The New Negro*, 159.

74. Sterling Brown, *Negro Poetry and Drama* (New York: Atheneum, 1971 [1937]), 125.

75. "Recollections of O'Neill's Plays," in *Opportunity Reader*, 353.

76. "The Dilemma of the Negro Author," in *Johnson Writings*, 746.

77. Ibid., 751–752.

78. "The Negro Artist and the Racial Mountain," in *Portable Harlem Renaissance Reader*, 94–95.

79. Ibid., 92–95.

80. Lewis, *When Harlem Was in Vogue*, xvii, xxi–xxii.

81. Harold Cruse, *The Crisis of the Negro Intellectual: From Its Origins to the Present* (New York: William Morrow, 1967), 23–24, 26–33.

82. Huggins, *Harlem Renaissance*, 102; and Bruce Kellner, *Carl Van Vechten and the Irreverent Decades* (Norman: University of Oklahoma Press, 1968), 195–199.

83. "The Caucasian Storms Harlem," in *Portable Harlem Renaissance Reader*, 110–117.

84. Huggins, *Harlem Renaissance*, 116.

85. Lewis, *When Harlem Was in Vogue*, xx.

86. "Race Prejudice and the Negro Artist," in *Johnson Writings*, 753.

87. Preface to *The American Book of American Negro Poetry*, in *Johnson Writings*, 688.

88. "Race Prejudice and the Negro Artist," 763–765.

89. "Our Negro Intellectuals," in *Crisis Reader*, 326–327.

90. Ibid., 326–327. Davis does not cite the work of Mencken that attacked black ministers. Barbara Dianne Savage, however, refers to an article written by Mencken in 1931 for *Opportunity* magazine in which he called black preachers "moron Negro theologians" and "bold and insatiable parasites." Mencken characterized black Christianity as "extraordinarily stupid, ignorant, barbaric and preposterous." See Savage, "Biblical and Historiographical Imperatives: Toward a History of Ideas about the Political Role of Black Churches," in *African Americans and the Bible: Sacred Texts and Social Textures*, ed. Vincent L. Wimbush (New York: Continuum, 2000), 375. This could not have been the same article that Davis had in mind because his essay was written in 1928. Apparently Mencken's attacks on black religion extended over several years.

91. "Our Negro Intellectuals," 330.

92. Ibid.

93. Quotations taken from Arnold Rampersad, *The Life of Langston Hughes: I, Too, Sing America*, vol. 1: 1901–1941 (New York: Oxford University Press, 1986), 140–141.

94. Davis listed Claude McKay, Countee Cullen, and James Weldon Johnson as writers who exploited the Harlem cabaret and primitive themes in their literature. Oddly, Davis referred to many of the writers in the Harlem Renaissance as "young" as if to disparage them on this account. When he wrote his essay, Davis was only twenty-six years old!

95. "Our Negro Intellectuals," 326–328. Those listed as representative of the jazz age in literature and art were Waldo Frank, F. Scott Fitzgerald, Miguel Covarrubias, Winold Reiss, Carl Van Doren, Max Rheinhardt, and Van Vechten.

96. "Our Negro Intellectuals," 327–328.

97. Ibid. 328.

98. Ibid., 328–329.

99. Ibid., 332.

100. Ibid.; emphasis in original.

101. Ibid.

102. Ibid., 330, 332.

103. "Letter from Langston Hughes," September 1928, in *The Collected Works of Langston Hughes*, vol. 9: *Essays on Art, Race, Politics, and World Affairs*, ed. Christopher De Santis (Columbia: University of Missouri Press, 2002), 627; available online at www.alexanderstreet4.com.ezp1.harvard.edu/cgi-bin/asp/bltc/getdoc.pl?/projects/artfla/databases/asp/bltc/fulltext/IMAGE/.1488.

104. "Negro Authors and White Publishers" (1929), in *Crisis Reader*, 262–264.

105. W. E. B. Du Bois, *The Gift of Black Folk*, in *Du Bois on Religion*, ed. Phil Zuckerman (Walnut Creek: AltaMira Press, 2000), 161, 165.

CHAPTER 6

1. Jordan Miller and Winifred Frazer, *American Drama between the Wars: A Critical History* (Boston: Twayne, 1991), 257.

2. Ibid., 259.

3. Ibid.

4. Thomas Cripps, "Introduction: A Monument to Lost Innocence," in *The Green Pastures*, ed. Thomas Cripps (Madison: University of Wisconsin Press, 1979), 11.

5. Ibid., 12.

6. Paula J. Massood, *Black City Cinema: African American Urban Experiences in Film* (Philadelphia: Temple University Press, 2003), 29.

7. Walter Lippmann, *A Preface to Morals* (New York: Life, 1957 [1929]), 9. One asks for permission to engage in rhetorical excess in making this judgment. We would have to know far more about the audiences to make this assessment with any degree of certainty. Socioeconomic status, regional variations, age, and a number of other variables would have to be taken into account before more confident generalizations about the audiences can be made, not to mention what the play's popularity meant in the broader culture. However, the long run of *The Green Pastures* and the confluence of relevant social factors discussed in the body of this chapter do allow us to make certain plausible inferences about why this play was so popular. Jack Poggi's work on theater in the United States has shown that "Broadway was in severe depression by the 1930–31 season." Even though ticket costs increased, the risks incurred to produce a play grew (a play that ran for fewer than a hundred performances in the 1920s was generally deemed to have lost money), and an increase occurred in competition from movies (which began using sound more widely by the 1930s), *The Green Pastures* was still a big hit. See Jack Poggi, *Theater in America: The Impact of Economic Forces, 1870–1967* (Ithaca, N.Y.: Cornell University Press, 1968), 55–56, 58, 71–75.

8. " 'Green Pastures' Reveals New Field for Dramatist," *World*, March 9, 1930, in Tuskegee Institute News Clippings, Lamont Library Microfilm (hereafter TINC).

9. Paul T. Nolan, *Marc Connelly* (New York: Twayne, 1969), 85.

10. The full article title was "Last Days for 'Uncle Tom': A Mainstay for Decade After Decade, the Play Has Given Way before Modernity," *New York Times*, July 12, 1931, in TINC.

11. W. Fitzhugh Brundage, *Lynching in the New South: Georgia and Virginia, 1880–1930* (Urbana: University of Illinois Press, 1993), 245.

12. Philip Dray, *At the Hands of Persons Unknown: The Lynching of Black America* (New York: Random House, 2002), 303.

13. Brundage, *Lynching in the New South*, 247–251.

14. These changes were by no means uniform in the South. Progress was tediously slow, and violence sometimes flared as a result of modernization, especially as New Deal programs were implemented that aimed at altering Southern agriculture. See Gunnar Myrdal, *An American Dilemma: The Negro Problem and Modern Democracy*, vol. 2 (New Brunswick: Transaction, 2002 [1944]), 565–566; and Jack Temple Kirby, *Rural Worlds Lost: The American South, 1920–1960* (Baton Rouge: Louisiana State University, 1987), 118–133.

15. For the period under consideration in this chapter (late 1920s to about 1935), I do not wish to overstate the number of blacks who left the South in comparison to those who remained. It is estimated that between 1915 and 1920, from 500,000 to 1 million African Americans left the rural South for the urban North. From 1920 to about 1930, another 700,000 to 1 million blacks moved to the North and West. Even so, as late as 1940, "only" 23 percent of blacks in the United States were living in the most urban North and West. Yet these numbers continued to increase between 1940 and 1960. See "The Great Migration," in *Africana: The Encyclopedia of the African American Experience*, eds. Kwame Anthony Appiah and Henry Louis Gates (New York: Perseus Books, 1999), 869–871. Fears of social interaction between blacks and whites, white Northerners' perceptions of being overrun by "Negro hordes" in urban neighborhoods, and fantasies of an ideal rural South uniquely suited for blacks were crucial to the social context of reactions to *The Green Pastures*. Because of obvious spatial distance, rural blacks were seen as less dangerous than urban blacks by some Northern whites, though the increase in lynchings reminded those who needed reminding that the happy-go-lucky rural black person in a serene Southern environment hardly conformed to the reality of violence that many blacks in the South encountered within and outside their communities.

16. On claims of authenticity by white producers of black films, see Judith Weisenfeld, *Hollywood Be Thy Name: African American Religion in American Film, 1929–1949* (Berkeley: University of California Press, 2007), 19–22, 52–58.

17. "Marc Connelly," *American National Biography*, vol. 5, eds. John A. Garrity and Mark C. Carnes (New York: Oxford University Press, 1999), 342–343.

18. Cripps, "Monument to Lost Innocence," 16–19; and Walter Prichard Eaton, "A Playboy Makes Good," *New York Herald Tribune*, March 23, 1930 in the Alexander Gumby Collection, Lamont Library Microfilm (hereafter AGC). See also Marc Con-

nelly, *Voices off Stage: A Book of Memoirs* (New York: Holt, Rinehart and Winston, 1968), 144–155.

19. " 'Green Pastures' Back in Gotham," March 14, 1935, and "Finis to 'Green Pastures,' " *New York Times*, March 8, 1936, in TINC.

20. Marc Connelly, "Green Pastures," in *A New Edition of the Pulitzer Prize Plays*, eds. Kathryn Coe and William H. Cordell (New York: Random House, 1940), 599.

21. Connelly, *Voices off Stage*, 148.

22. Ibid.

23. Ibid.

24. "New Negro Drama of Sublime Beauty," *New York Times*, February 27, 1930, in TINC.

25. "Loveliness of Drama Confusing," *New York Telegram*, March 1, 1930, in AGC.

26. *World*, March 1, 1930, in AGC.

27. *World*, March 15, 1930, in AGC.

28. "It Seems to Me," *New York Telegram*, February 27, 1930, in AGC.

29. William R. Hutchison, *The Modernist Impulse in American Protestantism* (New York: Oxford University Press, 1982 [1976]), 271–273.

30. "The End of Spiritual Comfort" (1927; reprint, *The Culture of the Twenties*, ed. Loren Baritz [New York: Bobbs-Merrill, 1970]), 360. The article by Krutch originally appeared as "The Modern Temper" in the *Atlantic Monthly*. It was expanded (with the same title) to book length in 1929.

31. "The End of Spiritual Comfort," 359; emphasis in original.

32. Ibid., 360.

33. Ibid., 364–365.

34. "Miracle," *Nation*, March 26, 1930, in TINC.

35. *Black and White Together: The Reminiscences of an NAACP Founder*, ed. Ralph Luker (New York: Feminist Press, 1995), 103–104.

36. Ibid., 104.

37. Ibid.

38. "Leaving the Southern Phase," *New York Times*, January 1, 1934, in TINC.

39. *Columbia Record*, March 1, 1930, in TINC.

40. *August Herald*, October 24, 1933, in TINC.

41. "The 'Green Pastures' Should Be Hissed off Stage, Says Preacher," *Pittsburgh Courier*, January 24, 1931, in TINC.

42. "Dramatis Personae," *Crisis*, May 1930, 162, 167.

43. Burrill's words were cited in Maine's *Lewiston Journal*, November 6, 1930 in TINC; emphasis in original.

44. Ibid. After concluding Burrill's words, the author of the article went on to reflect on the problem of religion in American society. The author expressed worries that the economic plight of blacks was making it possible for them to open up to proselytizing "anarchy." Such forces, the author feared, could take away the Negro's faith. The author stated, "Naturally of fervent religious emotion, he may perhaps be turned as emotionally against religion—such is the boring-in effect of Communism.

If the Negro is ever convinced that Heaven is a joke—as Communism preaches—and that work is demanded of him here on the false premise that he can loaf over there, there may be a real world-movement. Much depends on the Negro's conception of God." The depiction of the religious and simple Negro was a common and conveniently used symbol to compare with the radical, irreligious Negro who espoused socialism, communism, and other dangerous ideologies that demanded a radical transformation of the economic and political structure of the nation.

45. "The Hell in 'Green Pastures,'" *Black Dispatch*, January 1, 1934, in TINC.

46. Ibid.

47. George S. Schuyler, "Mr. Geo. Schuyler Says a Few Words," *Pittsburgh Courier*, October 8, 1930, in AGC.

48. Quotations and summary taken from Valerie Boyd, *Wrapped in Rainbows: The Life of Zora Neale Hurston* (New York: Scribner, 2003), 220.

49. Hurston to Charlotte Osgood Mason, September 25, 1931, in *Zora Neale Hurston: A Life in Letters*, ed. Carla Kaplan (New York: Double Day, 2002), 226.

50. Van Vechten to Langston Hughes, January 21, 1931, in *Remember Me to Harlem: The Letters of Langston Hughes and Carl Van Vechten, 1925–1964*, ed. Emily Barnard (New York: Knopf, 2001), 78. For a full analysis of the conflict surrounding the production of *Mule Bone* and why it was never produced in Hughes's and Hurston's lifetimes, see *Mule Bone: A Comedy of Negro Life by Langston Hughes and Zora Neale Hurston*, eds. George Houston Bass and Henry Louis Gates Jr. (New York: Harper Collins, 1991).

51. Connelly made two separate trips to the South, both lasting no more than two or three months.

52. Carter G. Woodson, *The Rural Negro* (Washington: Association for the Study of Negro Life and History, 1930), xv–xvi; Benjamin E. Mays and Joseph William Nicholson, *The Negro's Church* (Salem: Ayer, 1988 [1933]), v–vii, 295–313; and Mays, *The Negro's God*, vii–viii. See also Milton Sernett, *Bound for the Promised Land: African American Religion and the Great Migration* (Durham, N.C.: Duke University Press, 1997), 225–230.

53. Woodson, *Rural Negro*, 149–179, 227–241. For specific criticisms of rural churches, black and white, and the context of the debates, I have found the following helpful: Sernett, *Bound for the Promised Land*, chap. 8, James. H. Madison, "Reformers and the Rural Church, 1900–1950," *Journal of American History* 73 (December 1986): 645–668. See also the following two important primary sources on black rural churches: C. Horace Hamilton and John M. Ellison, *The Negro Church in Rural Virginia* Bulletin 273 (Blacksburg: Virginia Agricultural Experiment Station, 1929); and Harry V. Richardson, *Dark Glory: A Picture of the Church among Negroes in the Rural South* (New York: Friendship Press, 1947).

54. See W. Clark Gilpin, *A Preface to Theology* (Chicago: University of Chicago Press, 1996), 97–98.

55. Mathews was one of the leading defenders of liberal Protestantism and a social form of Christianity.

56. Gilpin, *A Preface to Theology*, 98, and Sernett, *Bound for the Promised Land*, 228–230.

57. See Mays and Nicholson, *The Negro's Church*, 59–93, 198–229; and Mays, *Negro's God*, vii. On the production of *The Negro's Church*, see Kim Leathers, "A Historical Survey of the Sociology of the Black Church" (Ph.D., diss., Howard University, 1999), 92–95.

58. Mays and Nicholson, *The Negro's Church*, 259–251.

59. Mays, *The Negro's God*, 1–97, 156–161, 245–255.

60. Ibid., 245–255.

61. *New York Times*, July 17, 1936.

62. Besides the standard works on religion and the many analyses of the cultural and social context of the 1920s, I have found the following two books especially helpful: Frederick J. Hoffman, *The 20s: American Writing in the Postwar Decade*, rev. ed. (New York: Free Press, 1962); and Lynn Dumenil, *Modern Temper: American Culture and Society in the 1920s* (New York: Hill and Wang, 1995).

63. Nathan I. Huggins, *Harlem Renaissance* (New York: Oxford University Press, 1971), 300–301.

64. George M. Frederickson, *The Black Image in the White Mind: The Debate about Afro-American Character and Destiny, 1817–1914* (Middleton: Wesleyan University Press, 1987 [1971]), 328–330.

CHAPTER 7

1. The following two texts have treated the formation of the Myrdal-Carnegie project and the various reactions to it quite thoroughly: David Southern, *Gunnar Myrdal and Black-White Relations: The Use and Abuse of "An American Dilemma," 1944–1969* (Baton Rouge: Louisiana State University, 1987); and Walter A. Jackson, *Gunnar Myrdal and America's Social Conscience: Social Engineering and Racial Liberalism, 1938–1987* (Chapel Hill: University of North Carolina Press, 1990).

2. Gunnar Myrdal, *An American Dilemma: The Negro Problem and Modern Democracy*, bol. 2 (New Brunswick, N.J.: Transaction, 2002 [1944]), 928. For those social scientists who were influenced by Myrdal's massive study, the language of black cultural pathology attained greater salience over time. For a broader historical view of social scientists and racial policy and claims about a damaged black psyche, see Daryl Michael Scott, *Contempt and Pity: Social Policy and the Image of the Damaged Black Psyche, 1880–1996* (Chapel Hill: University of North Carolina Press, 1997).

3. Margaret Brenman, "Minority Group Membership and Religious, Psychosexual and Social Patterns in a Group of Middle-Class Negro Girls," *Journal of Social Psychology* 2 (1940): 179–197, in Schomburg Collection of Negro Literature, Lamont Library Microfilm (hereafter SCNL). Some of Brenman's articles were used in the 1952 appendix to the appellants' brief to *Brown v. Board of Education* to support claims about the effects of racial prejudice and segregation on the personalities of black youth. See Brown v. Board of Education: *A Brief History with Documents*, ed. Waldo E. Martin (Boston: Bedford, 1998), 143–144.

4. Brenman, "Minority Group Membership," 144.

5. In 1931, R. A. Billings, a psychiatrist at Howard University, made this point. He wrote, "The Negro will continue to take his church seriously, just as long as he is handicapped economically, socially and psychically. When these handicaps have been removed there will be a great reduction in the Negro church membership, because the purpose it served and the psychic function it performed will no longer be necessary." See Billings, "The Negro and His Church," *Psychoanalytic Review* 8 (1931): 441.

6. Walter Jackson, "Mellville Herskovits and the Search for Afro-American Culture," in *Malinoski, Benedict and Others: Essays on Culture and Personality*, ed. George W. Stocking Jr. (Madison: University of Wisconsin, 1986), 95–126.

7. Melville J. Herskovits, *The Myth of the Negro Past* (Boston: Beacon Press, 1990 [1941]), 207.

8. Ibid.

9. Although historians, anthropologists, and sociologists have usually pitted Herskovits against Park because of the former's assertion of the durability of African cultures in the United States and the latter's denial of the persistence of specific African traditions in the United States, both social scientists used universalizing language about Africans and people of African descent. Park, like Herskovits, wrote of blacks as possessing and expressing certain qualities and attributes "everywhere and always." Similarly, he argued in grand terms about "the racial character of the Negro" exhibiting itself "everywhere in something like the role of the *wish* in the Freudian analysis of dream life." See Robert E. Park, "The Conflict and Fusion of Cultures with Special References to the Negro," *Journal of Negro History* 4 (April 1919): 129, 130.

10. Myrdal, *American Dilemma*, 753, 930. It is not clear to me why Myrdal uncritically used the even more demeaning term *amorality* rather than *immorality* to describe how blacks were viewed by whites. Perhaps his extensive conversations and debates with white Southerners at the time gave him more insight into the pervasive and virulent use of racist language.

11. Ibid., 930. Myrdal was critical of both Herskovits and black historian Carter G. Woodson because he believed that they selectively attributed negative traits such as crime and "amorality" among blacks to the pressures of living in a white, oppressive society, while they tended to attribute more positive features of black life to an African heritage. Walter Jackson also notes that Myrdal was deeply skeptical of the emphasis of Woodson, Herskovits, and others on the Africanness of American blacks because he felt it would play into the hands of racists such as Mississippi Senator Theodore Bilbo, who wanted to forcibly remove American blacks to Africa. Bilbo and his ilk had a deep fear of racial miscegenation and were adamantly opposed to the idea that blacks wanted to or could be assimilated into American culture. See Jackson, *Gunnar Myrdal*, 120.

12. Arthur Huff Fauset, *Black Gods of the Metropolis: Negro Religious Cults of the Urban North* (Philadelphia: University of Pennsylvania Press, 2002 [1944]), 96. Barbara Savage's excellent foreword to this edition deserves careful reading. Her work

sets Fauset's text within the context of his broader social and political activism. For Fauset's contributions in anthropology and folklore, see Lee D. Baker, *From Savage to Negro: Anthropology and the Construction of Race, 1896–1956* (Berkeley: University of California Press, 1998), 153–157. I have chosen not to provide a detailed retelling of the well-known debate between E. Franklin Frazier and Herskovits about the importance and presence of African cultural patterns among American blacks. The more basic issue for Frazier was assimilation. In his view, positing an African heritage or a racial temperament would lead whites to treat blacks as permanently different and perpetuate white justifications for segregation. As Jonathan Scott Holloway argues, "The debate was not so much about how culture can survive catastrophic human trauma as it was about two things: blacks' ability to assimilate into the white majority and the terms through which this assimilation would operate." See Holloway, *Confronting the Veil: Abram Harris, Jr., E. Franklin Frazier, and Ralph Bunch, 1919–1941* (Chapel Hill: University of North Carolina Press, 2002), 129. This emphasis on assimilation is not intended to minimize the importance to sociologists and anthropologists of such issues as the durability of culture, the relationship between European and African cultures, and racial capacities as they figured into the debate between Herskovits and Frazier. For a recent statement of current scholarly views on this issue, see Judith Weisenfeld, "On Jordan's Stormy Banks: Margins, Centers, and Bridges in African American Religious History," in *New Directions in American Religious History*, eds. Harry S. Stout and D. G. Hart (New York: Oxford University Press, 1997), 420–423, 439.

13. Fauset, *Black Gods*, 96.

14. Ibid., 97.

15. Oddly, Mays and Nicholson and Fauset did not find it necessary to offer any explanation as to why more black women than white women attended church. The figures cited by Fauset indicated that 46 percent of black men thirteen years old and older were church members, compared to 49 percent of white men. The comparable figures for black and white women were 73 and 62 percent, respectively. Although these statistics were used to demonstrate that blacks were not more religious than whites, one wonders why such a high percentage of women (black and white) attending church did not merit some explanation. See Fauset, *Black Gods*, 96–97; and Benjamin Elijah Mays and Joseph William Nicholson, *The Negro's Church* (1933; reprint, New York: Arno Press, 1969), 200–201.

16. Fauset, *Black Gods*, 97. I have not examined through comparison with other sources of data how reliable Mays and Nicholson's figures were. The important point is how Fauset used these statistics and what he hoped to demonstrate by employing them: that blacks could not be naturally religious if a smaller percentage of them attended church than whites (which partially rested on church attendance as a crucial measure of human religiosity).

17. Ibid., 97.

18. Ibid. 98.

19. Ibid., 99.

20. Ibid.

21. Ibid.

22. Ibid., 100.

23. Ibid.

24. Ibid., 98, 100–101. Herskovits denied that he asserted innate black religiosity. He argued that blacks had a cultural rather than a "natural" bent toward religion (though Fauset and other social scientists rightly noted that sections of his *Myth of the Negro Past* suggested otherwise). Herskovits was angry that Fauset attacked a "straw man" argument and that his efforts to fight racism were not sufficient for Fauset to understand his intentions and meaning. He appeared puzzled that black social scientists in particular would have such strenuous objections to his attempts to affirm the tenacity of African culture. See Melville J. and Frances S. Herskovits Papers, Box 38, Folder 372; Manuscripts, Archives, and Rare Books Division, Schomburg Center for Research in Black Culture, New York Public Library. That Herskovits had to appeal to his record against racism was an indication of the politicized nature of this debate.

25. Fauset, *Black Gods*, Ibid., 7.

26. Thelma Ackiss, "Changing Patterns of Religious Thought among Negroes," *Social Forces* 23 (December 1944): 212.

27. Ibid.

28. Ibid.

29. Eighty-eight students were females and twelve were males.

30. Ackiss, "Changing Patterns of Religious Thought," 213.

31. On the increase in church attendance and the social meaning attached to church membership in the United States during and after World War II, see Sydney E. Ahlstrom, *A Religious History of the American People* (New Haven, Conn.: Yale University, 1972), chap. 56. Will Herberg was critical of the link between institutional affiliation and social respectability and the importance that Protestants, Catholics, and Jews attached to "religious belonging" in the context of the postwar period. See Herberg, *Protestant-Catholic-Jew* (Garden City: Anchor Books, 1960), 257–262.

32. Ibid., 215. When Ackiss's study was conducted, Houston was then one of the foremost urban centers in the South in population and manufacturing. Because of the Houston Ship Channel, the city was exceeded only by New York and Philadelphia among American ports. See George B. Tindall, *The Emergence of the New South, 1912–1945* (Baton Rouge: Louisiana State University Press, 1967), 101–102.

33. Eugene Gordon, "A New Religion for the Negro," in *A Documentary History of the Negro People in the United States, 1910–1932,* ed. Herbert Aptheker (Secaucus, N.J.: Citadel Press, 1973), 579.

34. John Dollard, *Caste and Class in a Southern Town,* 3rd ed. (Garden City, N.Y.: Doubleday Anchor Book, 1957 [1937]), 267–268.

35. Billings, "The Negro and His Church," 426. Billings wrote that he visited the House of Prayer church and observed their worship services. He indicated that it was one of many churches that had been established by a "cult leader." Although Billings only provided a sketchy analysis of the group's identity, his descriptions suggested that this was a black Pentecostal church.

36. Ibid., 431.

37. Ibid.

38. Hortense Powdermaker, *After Freedom: A Cultural Study in the Deep South* (Madison: University of Wisconsin Press, 1993 [1939]), 247.

39. Dollard, *Caste and Class*, 263. This function of magic was similar to the role that other social scientists believed the black churches performed. Powdermaker argued that "folk superstitions" and the use of "voodoo doctors" were common among older blacks in Indianola, though she noted that some "educated young people" and those who were "devoutly religious" did not see a conflict between Christianity and voodoo. Powdermaker claimed that the voodoo doctors answered a need "felt particularly by illiterate peoples for magical and supernatural help in facing a hostile and mysterious world." She argued that blacks who practiced voodoo and conjure practices drew on European, African, and American Indian medicine and traditions, thus demonstrating the eclectic nature of their use of traditions to face the varied problems of pain, disease, and suffering in their lives. Powdermaker saw evidence that "superstition" was on the wane and was weakening faster than "religion" among blacks in Indianola. She averred that because superstition had no "prestige value" in white culture, it was likely to disappear among blacks as they gradually became acculturated to white standards and behaviors. See Powdermaker, *After Freedom*, 286–287, 295–296.

40. Dollard, *Caste and Class*, 263–264.

41. Myrdal, *American Dilemma*, 938.

42. Hortense Powdermaker, "The Channeling of Aggression by the Cultural Process," *American Journal of Sociology* 48 (May 1943): 754. For a broader analysis of studies on the personalities of blacks after World War II, with particular attention to anger and aggression, see Scott, *Contempt and Pity*, 71–91.

43. Powdermaker, "Channeling of Aggression," 755–757.

44. Ibid., 758.

45. Ibid. For another study that extended this analysis of the emotional health of blacks, though with less emphasis on religion, see Helen V. McLean, "The Emotional Health of Negroes," *Journal of Negro Education* 18 (summer 1949): 283–290.

46. "Are There Too Many Churches?" *Baltimore Afro-American*, February 1, 1930. See also, "Multiplicity of Negro Churches," December 28, 1929, in Tuskegee Institute News Collection, Lamont Library Microfilm (hereafter TINC).

47. "Schuyler's Attack on Negro Church Brings Sharp Reply from Minister," *Norfolk Journal and Guide*, April 9, 1932, in TINC.

48. Milton Sernett, *Bound for the Promised Land: African American Religion and the Great Migration* (Durham, N.C.: Duke University Press, 1997), 4–5.

49. Barbara Dianne Savage, "Carter G. Woodson and the Struggle for a 'United Black Church,'" *AME Church Review* (fall 2000): 15–16. The formation of the Fraternal Council of Negro Churches in 1934, a national organization representing all of the mainline black denominations as well as smaller groups of black churches, was seen as an alternative to the Federal Council of Churches, an ecumenical body of mostly white denominations founded in 1908. Bishop Reverdy Ransom in the AME

church was elected to preside over the group. On the work of the Federal Council of Churches and race relations, see David W. Wills, "An Enduring Distance: Black Americans and the Black Establishment," in *Between the Times: The Travail of the Protestant Establishment in America, 1900–1960*, ed. William R. Hutchison (Cambridge: Cambridge University Press, 1989), 168–192.

50. Cited in John T. McGreevy, *Parish Boundaries: The Catholic Encounter with Race in the Twentieth-Century Urban North* (Chicago: University of Chicago Press, 1996), 31.

51. "Kelly Miller Says," *Baltimore Afro-American*, November 27, 1925, in TINC. See also "Roman Catholic Church to Proselyte Negro in South as Means to Winning Dominant Place in American Religion," *New York Age*, April 3, 1926; and "Bidding for the Negro," *Southern Christian Advocate*, September 20, 1926, in TINC.

52. Miller had convened a conference in 1924 that stressed the need for a Negro Sanhedrin, which addressed how to deal with the particular problems that blacks faced and a way forward to greater unity. See *The Negro Sanhedrin: A Call to Conference* in *Black Nationalism in America*, eds. John H. Bracey Jr., August Meier, and Elliott Rudwick (Indianapolis: Bobbs-Merrill, 1970), 348–365.

53. Carter G. Woodson, "A United Negro Church," August 12, 1931, in Claude Barnett Papers, Lamont Library Microfilm (hereafter CBP).

54. Woodson, "Theology a Factor in Disunion of the Churches," September 30, 1931, in CBP. Other titles in CBP that reveal Woodon's desire for a unified black church are the following: "Superfluous Negro Preachers Prevent the Union of the Churches," October 7, 1931, and "Need for Union Emphasized by Recent Data of the Churches," October 14, 1931.

55. James Weldon Johnson, *Negro Americans, What Now?* (1934; reprint, *The Selected Writings of James Weldon Johnson: Social, Political and Literary Essays*, vol. 2, ed. Sondra Kathryn Wilson [New York: Oxford University Press, 1995]), 146–147.

56. Ibid., 147.

57. James Weldon Johnson, *Black Manhattan* (New York: Da Capo Press, 1991 [1930]), 163–165.

58. Johnson, *Negro Americans*, 147. Johnson's expression "conservation of power" is reminiscent of Du Bois's 1897 lecture title, "conservation of races," which emphasized race organizations and cooperative work among blacks.

59. Ibid.

60. Johnson, *Black Manhattan*, 167.

61. Ibid., 166.

62. Ibid., 167; Johnson, *Negro Americans*, 146.

63. Among other blacks who wrote for the series were poet and literary critic Sterling Brown, political scientist Ralph Bunch, sociologist Ira Reid, economist Abram Harris, and Woodson.

64. David Levering Lewis, *W.E.B. Du Bois: The Fight for Equality and the American Century, 1919–1963* (New York: Henry Holt, 2000), 422–424.

65. Alain Locke to W. E. B. Du Bois, November 29, 1936, in *The Correspondence of W.E.B. Du Bois: Selections, 1934–1944*, vol. 2, ed. Herbert Aptheker (Amherst: University of Massachusetts Press, 1976), 85.

66. Du Bois, W. E. B., *Dusk of Dawn: An Essay Toward an Autobiography of a Race Concept* (New York: Schocken Books, 1968 [1940]), 319.

67. Ibid., 304–305.

68. W. E. B. Du Bois, "The Negro and Social Reconstruction," in *Against Racism: Unpublished Essays, Papers, Addresses, 1887–1961*, ed. Herbert Aptheker (Amherst: University of Massachusetts Press, 1985), 104.

69. Ibid.

70. Ibid., 153–154.

71. David Levering Lewis asserts that Du Bois's plan for blacks at this time included "virtually no modern role assigned to the Negro church." Ideally, given Du Bois's growing antipathy to religion during the 1930s, this may have been so. But Du Bois could not ignore the importance of religion within the black community, and for pragmatic reasons he still offered his radical proposals for what he felt *ought* to be done with black religion. See Lewis, *W.E.B. Du Bois*, 306. On Du Bois's evolving approach to religion, see Edward J. Blum, *W. E. B. Du Bois: American Prophet* (Philadelphia: University of Pennsylvania, 2007).

72. Myrdal, *An American Dilemma*, lix.

73. See Jackson, *Gunnar Myrdal*, 11–27; and Southern, *Gunnar Myrdal*, 1–5.

74. Jackson, *Gunnar Myrdal*, 27–31; and Southern, *Gunnar Myrdal*, 4–5.

75. Jackson, *Gunnar Myrdal*, 28–35, 110–111.

76. St. Clair Drake coauthored with Horace Cayton the monumental *Black Metropolis* (1945), which was in part based on the research conducted by Drake for his manuscript on religion in Chicago for the Carnegie-Myrdal project.

77. See Vernon J. Williams Jr., *From a Caste to a Minority: Changing Attitudes of American Sociologists toward Afro-Americans, 1896–1945* (Westport, Conn.: Greenwood Press, 1989), 163–166.

78. Dollard, *Caste and Class in a Southern Town*, 61–87.

79. Davis later taught anthropology at the University of Chicago and was "said to be the first black man ever to attain full professorship at a major unsegregated university." See Richard Kluger, *Simple Justice: The History of* Brown v. Board of Education *and Black America's Struggle for Equality* (New York: Vintage Books, 1975), 557.

80. Allison Davis, "The Negro Church and Associations in the Lower South," iii, 36, in SCNL.

81. Ibid., 37.

82. Ibid., 40.

83. Ibid., 41. Such comments that sought to attribute racial grounds for actions or statements made under acute pain (whether administered by the lynch mobs or the state) obviously have to be taken with considerable caution and recognized for their polemical and rationalizing functions. Davis did not mention the many instances of

white lynch mobs denouncing blacks for their alleged criminality and lust for white women, all the while justifying lynching as a suitable punishment for such blacks who were putatively incapable of feeling pain or undeterred from criminal actions by "normal" threats and more "humane" forms of punishment.

84. Davis, "Negro Church and Associations," 44.

85. Ibid., 46.

86. Ibid., 57. Sometimes it is difficult to tell precisely which community Davis is discussing. He alternates between New Orleans and Natchez (and sometimes an unnamed city).

87. Ibid. Davis's ideas about the black family were very similar to those advanced by African American sociologist E. Franklin Frazier in many of his writings, most prominently in *The Negro Family in the United States* (1939).

88. Davis, "Negro Church and Associations," 57.

89. Ibid., 58.

90. Ibid., 59.

91. Ibid., 60.

92. Ibid., 68.

93. Ibid., 67-68.

94. Ibid., 69-70. Davis does not mention any connections between this pageant and the extraordinary popularity of the Broadway play *The Green Pastures*, which was contemporaneous with "Heaven Is My Home." Though further research would perhaps reveal more about the connection between the two, it is difficult to avoid the conclusion that this was a small-scale Southern version of *Green Pastures*. The image of blacks as naturally religious and docile, with the specific Southern nostalgia for a romanticized antebellum past, proved potent and had an enduring influence. For an astute analysis of the plantation image of blacks and fantasies of a white and glorious southern past, see Grace Elizabeth Hale, *Making Whiteness: The Culture of Segregation in the South, 1890–1940* (New York: Vintage Books, 1998), 85–119, 258–279.

95. Davis, "Negro Church and Associations," 69-70.

96. There were a few studies that began emphasizing ritual and class differentiation within black churches. They also expressed dissatisfaction with an exclusive focus on what happened within the churches. See Vattel Elbert Daniel, "Ritual and Stratification in Chicago Negro Churches," *American Sociological Review* 7 (June 1942): 352–361; and Vattel Elbert Daniel, "Negro Classes and Life in the Church," *Journal of Negro Education* 13 (winter 1944): 19–29.

97. St. Clair Drake and Horace Cayton, *Black Metropolis: A Study of Negro Life in a Northern City* (Chicago: University of Chicago Press, 1993 [1945]), xiii.

98. Ibid., xx.

99. Ibid., 388.

100. Ibid., 174.

101. Ibid., 412–413. The authors indicated that church membership rolls were not very reliable. Church rolls were seldom cleared when members left or attended infrequently. One church that boasted of 10,000 "members" included on its list persons who had shifted to other churches and even the dead (418)!

102. Ibid., 379–381.

103. Ibid., 418.

104. Ibid., 412.

105. Ibid.

106. Ibid. 419.

107. Ibid., 418–419, 420–421.

108. Ibid., 423.

109. Ibid., 423–424.

110. Ibid., 520.

111. Ibid., 537–540. In addition to Episcopalians and Congregationalists, Presbyterian churches made some headway among the black upper classes.

112. Ibid., 600. On the struggle of working-class black migrants to maintain a religious moral order and strict guidelines of gender roles and sexual conduct amid the fluid environment of the urban North, see Evelyn Brooks Higginbotham, "Rethinking Vernacular Culture: Black Religion and Race Records in the 1920s and 1930s," in *The House That Race Built: Black Americans, U.S. Terrain*, ed. Wahneema Lubiano (New York: Pantheon Books, 1997), 157–177.

113. Drake and Cayton, *Black Metropolis*, 611.

114. Ibid., 612.

115. Ibid.

116. Ibid., 617, 650.

117. Ibid., 617–618, 650–651.

118. Ibid., 653. Perhaps this attitude to religion by lower-class blacks would have pleased George Gordon, the black Marxist who lamented in 1928 that blacks were "rich in Jesus even if poor in the world."

119. Ibid., 653.

120. Ibid., 653.

121. Ibid., 418. In my own general analysis of black newspapers, I noticed a shift in design when a special section for "religion" was moved to a less prominent part of the newspaper or shrank in total words in the 1920s. This religion section was eliminated in some black newspapers by the 1940s.

122. Drake and Cayton argued that the "bewildering diversity of denominations" and the array of activities that operated apart from the influence of the church multiplied the choices available to blacks in the urban North. These developments led to a weakening of the influence of the churches because they cast doubt on singular absolute conceptions of good and evil. See *Black Metropolis*, 653. This argument anticipated, among others, sociologist Peter Berger's claim that pluralism in the form of competing religious denominations and nonreligious groups and "socially powerful rivals in the definition of reality" makes religion a "choice" or "preference" and therefore weakens its force because it limits or restricts religion to the private world or to the construction of "sub-worlds." Berger argued that a religious preference by its very nature can be abandoned as readily as it was first adopted. In this reading, secularization was a product of pluralism because the latter reduces religion to a choice among other options and therefore forces it to compete for allegiance as though

it were a product. Berger also argued that pluralism was a product of secularization in a dialectical process. See Berger, *The Sacred Canopy: Elements of a Sociological Theory of Religion* (New York: Anchor Books, 1990 [1967]), 134–138, 155–157.

123. Fauset, *Black Gods*, 87.

124. Myrdal, *American Dilemma*, 720, 858–859.

125. Ibid., 861–862.

126. Ibid., 929.

127. Ibid.

128. Ibid., 928.

129. Ibid., 863.

130. Ibid., 863–864.

131. Ibid., 873–874.

132. Ibid., lxxxiii.

133. Ibid., 866.

134. Ibid., 877; emphasis in original. Myrdal has been criticized for his emphasis on pathology in the black community. Stephan Thernstrom and Abigail Thernstrom argue that he was so "tone deaf to religion" that nothing in his work would have prepared readers for the role that black churches would play in the civil rights struggle of the 1950s and 1960s. See Thernstrom and Thernstrom, *America in Black and White: One Nation, Indivisible* (New York: Touchstone, 1999), 50–51. Walter Jackson also notes that Myrdal's perspective as a "rational, secular, functionalist social engineer" structured his assessment of African American religion as emotionalism. Jackson tells the story of Myrdal taking his family to visit Father Divine's Harlem church, where they were seated among the "angels" near the podium. Myrdal was so troubled by this church visit that later he could only recommend that African American religion be studied by the methods of abnormal psychology. See Jackson, *Gunnar Myrdal*, 107.

135. Jackson, *Gunnar Myrdal*, 240.

136. Cited in Southern, *Gunnar Myrdal*, 198.

137. E. Franklin Frazier, "Race: An American Dilemma," *Crisis*, April 1944, 106.

138. Frazier, "Problems and Needs of Negro Children and Youth Resulting from Family Disorganization," *Journal of Negro Education* 19 (summer 1950): 269–270.

139. "Race: An American Dilemma," 106.

140. Joe R. Feagin, "Book Review Essay: The Black Church: Inspiration or Opiate," *Journal of Negro History* 60 (October 1975): 537.

141. E. Franklin Frazier, *The Negro Church in America* (New York: Schocken Books, 1963), 8.

142. This point is helpfully developed in James Robert Young, "E. Franklin Frazier and His Critics: The Role of Religion in the Sociological Analysis of Race Relations in the United States" (Ph.D., diss., Boston University, 1984).

143. Frazier, *The Negro Church*, 9–23.

144. All of these remarks are summaries of various sections of *The Negro Church*.

145. Frazier, *The Negro Church*, 54–57.

146. Charles Keil, *Urban Blues* (Chicago: University of Chicago Press, 1966), 4–5.

147. See Scott, *Contempt and Pity*, 41–50. Scott insists that Frazier did not imply that black family disorganization, at least in its rural context, was pathological. Though relevant to discussions about Frazier's purported influence on discussions of pathology about black urban life in the 1960s, the specific details of Scott's argument do not challenge my analysis of Frazier's assessment of the Negro Church.

148. *Urban Blues*, 13.

149. Ibid., 5, 13, 41.

150. John Bunyan Eubanks, "Modern Trends in the Religion of the American Negro" (Ph.D. diss., University of Chicago, 1947), 16–18.

151. Herbert Shapiro, *White Violence and Black Response: From Reconstruction to Montgomery* (Amherst: University of Massachusetts, 1988), 310–337.

152. "The Great Migration," in *Africana: The Encyclopedia of the African American Experience*, eds. Kwame Anthony Appiah and Henry Louis Gates Jr. (New York: Perseus Books, 1999), 872.

153. Shapiro, *White Violence and Black Response*, 301; and John Hope Franklin and Alfred A. Moss, *From Slavery to Freedom: A History of African Americans*, 8th ed. (Boston: McGraw-Hill, 2000), 496–497.

154. Willard Sperry, *Religion in America* (New York: Macmillan, 1946), 183.

155. Ibid., 195. This callous allusion to one of the chief justifications of lynching, the alleged widespread raping of white women by black men, indicates how ominously Sperry viewed the new black migration to the North.

156. Ibid.

157. Ibid., 193. Sperry was among those postwar figures who adopted a neo-orthodox critique of Protestant liberalism. An interesting project would be to examine to what extent Sperry and colleagues like Perry Miller expressed their disappointment with theological liberalism by their imaginative and professional embrace of simpler societies (such as the Puritans in Miller's case). For the neo-orthodox critique of Protestant liberalism, see William R. Hutchison, *The Modernist Impulse in American Protestantism* (New York: Oxford University Press, 1976), chap. 9.

158. Sperry, *Religion in America*, 193.

159. Ibid., 194–195. Sperry quoted Mays's work, *The Negro's God* (1938), to point to the kind of "traditional, compensatory" religion that existed among the masses of blacks. This was the type of religion that he contrasted favorably to the radicalism of urban blacks, particularly those influenced by the Communist Party. Mays had a diametrically opposite evaluation of the value of otherworldly religion for blacks.

160. Sperry, *Religion in America*, 196–197. He added, "The Negro has to a marked degree a native dignity, which no affront or cruelty has ever destroyed. He is in this respect not unlike the American Indian, and here, if anywhere, the myth of the noble savage would seem to have a warrant in fact."

161. E. Franklin Frazier Papers, Box 131-78, Folder 14, Manuscript Division, Howard University.

162. Ibid.

EPILOGUE

1. John Bunyan Eubanks, "Modern Trends in the Religion of the American Negro" (Ph.D. diss., University of Chicago, 1947), 240.

2. Ibid., 241.

3. Ibid., 241, 221.

4. The term is found in Eubanks, "Modern Trends," 241. Eubanks concluded, like Benjamin Mays, that the "Negro's religion does not originate in any specula-tion about the origin of the universe, God, or the nature of evil." Theological and metaphysical issues hold no interest for an oppressed people. The root of their reli-gion lies in the "basic desire drives which seek fulfillment in the political, social, economic, and cultural life of the country." The "inexorable forces of culture" shaped the specific nature of black religion, and "cultural determiners" such as lynching and mob violence, segregation, discrimination, and denial of the ballot were re-sponsible for the precise expression of black religion in recent times.

5. William T. Fontaine, "'Social Determination' in the Writings of Negro Scholars," American Journal of Sociology 49 (January 1944): 311.

6. Abram Kardiner and Lionel Ovesey, The Mark of Oppression: Explorations of the Personality of the American Negro (Cleveland: Meridian Books, 1962 [1951]), xv, 81, 385–387. In the preface to the 1962 edition of this book, the authors were happy to report that blacks, though crushed when they wrote the work in 1951, had now come to life as a group, and were actively seeking their place in American society.

7. Ibid., 385. The authors agreed with Frazier's position about the impact of slavery on the black family. They argued that Africans' "original culture was smashed" (39).

8. Ibid., 353.

9. Ibid.

10. Ibid., 356.

11. Ibid., 358, 385.

12. Ibid., 359.

13. Kenneth B. Clark, Dark Ghetto: Dilemmas of Social Power (New York: Harper and Row, 1965), 174–175.

14. Ibid., 177.

15. Ibid., 177–178, 216. It is not clear what role Clark preferred that churches have. On one hand, he was critical of churches for not dealing with "real problems" of the masses, yet he was rather dismissive of groups such as the Nation of Islam, which he saw reaching out to the black lower classes. Clark also rejected Martin Luther King Jr.'s call for love of white oppressors because, in his view, this was "consistent with the stereotype of the Negro as a meek, long-suffering creature who prays for deliverance but who rarely acts decisively against injustices" (218–219). Though Clark found pathologies aplenty in the ghetto, the rising militancy and impatience of blacks in the urban North against racial injustice was preferable to what he saw as the accommodating ethos of the religious culture of blacks in the South (217–219).

16. Bruce Perry, *Malcolm X: The Life of a Man Who Changed Black America* (Barrytown, N.Y.: Station Hill Press, 1991), 174.

17. Claude Andrew Clegg III, *An Original Man: The Life and Times of Elijah Mohammed* (New York: St. Martin's Griffin, 1997), 125–128.

18. For an early study of the movement, though not apparent from the title of the essay, see Erdmann Doane Beynon, "The Voodoo Cult among Negro Migrants in Detroit," *American Journal of Sociology* 43 (May 1938): 894–907. White historian August Meier wrote a very insightful essay in 1963 on the Nation of Islam, which was in part based on his debate in 1962 with Malcolm X at Morgan State College in Baltimore, Maryland. See Meier, "The Black Muslims," in *A White Scholar and the Black Community, 1945–1965* (Amherst: University of Massachusetts, 1992), 127–136. See also the following report and collection of speeches by reporter Louis Lomax: *When the Word Is Given* (New York: Signet Books, 1963). Lomax co-wrote with Mike Wallace the CBS documentary "The Hate That Hate Produced."

19. Gunnar Myrdal, *An American Dilemma: The Negro Problem and Modern Democracy*, vol. 2 (New Brunswick, N.J.: Transaction, 2002 [1944]), 957–967.

20. Meier, "Black Muslims," 134. See also Lawrence L. Tyler, "The Protestant Ethic among the Black Muslims," *Phylon* 27 (first quarter, 1966): 5–14; C. Eric Lincoln, *The Black Muslims in America* (Boston: Beacon Press, 1961), 81; and E. U. Essien-Udom, *Black Nationalism: A Search for an Identity in America* (Chicago: University of Chicago Press, 1962), 15.

21. Meier, "Black Muslims," 134. Meier's comments about the Nation of Islam's emphasis on morality and middle-class values, though plausible, should also be taken in context of the author's own dislike of "bourgeois morality" and his generally negative characterization of religion among blacks. However, I am in general agreement with the sentiments of Meier, Essien-Udom, and Lincoln in their conclusions about the centrality of the specific cultural traits that were emphasized by the Nation of Islam. On one hand, I do not wish to underestimate the voices of those who joined the Nation as they talked about personal empowerment, a newer sense of dignity, and a feeling of control over their lives. On the other hand, the pervasive negative images of blacks and the various responses of black Americans, religious and otherwise, have to be taken together. There is a dialectical relationship between the two, with blacks of necessity *responding* to such dominant images even as they sought to define their own identity. My comments should not be construed as a contention that the religious beliefs, myths, and practices of the Nation were merely responses to white images of blacks. For a balanced analysis of religious practice among ordinary members of the Nation of Islam, see Edward E. Curtis, IV, *Black Muslim Religion in the Nation of Islam, 1960–1975* (Chapel Hill: University of North Carolina, 2007).

22. Meier, "Black Muslims," 134.

23. See Essien-Udom, *Black Nationalism*, 14–15; and W. Haywood Burns, *Voices of Negro Protest in America* (New York: Oxford University Press, 1963), 73.

24. Luther Clyde Carter Jr., "Negro Churches in a Southern Community" (Ph.D. diss., Yale University, 1955), 297.

25. Essien-Udom, *Black Nationalism*, 15.

26. Lincoln, *Black Muslims*, 119.

27. Burns, *Voices of Negro Protest*, 67–68. See also Essien-Udom, *Black Nationalism*, 136–138.

28. August Meier, "On the Role of Martin Luther King, Jr," *New Politics* (winter 1965), in *Reporting Civil Rights, Part Two: American Journalism, 1963–1973* (New York: Library of America, 2003), 456.

29. Lincoln, *Black Muslims*, 27, 255.

30. James M. McPherson, *The Abolitionist Legacy: From Reconstruction to the NAACP* (Princeton, N.J.: Princeton University Press, 1995 [1975]), 343.

31. Gayraud S. Wilmore Jr., "The Black Church in Search of a New Theology," in *Will the Church Lose the City?*, eds. Kendig Brubaker Cully and F. Nile Harper (New York: World, 1969), 140–141. At the time, Wilmore was chairman of the Division of Church and Race in the Board of Missions of the United Presbyterian Church in the U.S.A.

32. Charles Keil, *Urban Blues* (Chicago: University of Chicago Press, 1966), 7–8.

33. Lee Rainwater, "Introduction," in *Soul*, ed. Lee Rainwater (Chicago: Aldine, 1970), 8.

34. Daniel Patrick Moynihan, *The Negro Family: The Case for National Action*, in *The Moynihan Report and the Politics of Controversy*, eds. Lee Rainwater and William L. Yancey (Cambridge, Mass.: MIT Press, 1967), 51.

35. Ibid., 90–91.

36. Ibid., 94.

37. "Preface," in *Moynihan Report*, x.

38. "The Report Becomes Public," in *Moynihan Report*, 139–142. For the context of Watts in the broader struggle for political and economic advances in the urban North, see Harvard Sitcoff, *The Struggle for Black Equality, 1954–1992*, 2nd ed. (New York: Hill and Wang, 1993), 185–187.

39. Walter A. Jackson, *Gunnar Myrdal and America's Social Conscience: Social Engineering and Racial Liberalism, 1938–1987* (Chapel Hill: University of North Carolina Press, 1990), 302–306.

40. William Ryan, "Savage Discovery: The Moynihan Report," in *Moynihan Report*, 463.

41. "Newspaper Columns by James Farmer," in *Moynihan Report*, 410.

42. Martin Luther King Jr., for example, agreed with Moynihan's conclusions about the extent of breakdown among urban black families. King believed that city life was "ruinous for peasant people" and that the environment and conditions of the urban North had devastated the families of black migrants. Nearly all observers, including King, argued that a "matriarchal" female-headed household among blacks was the signal cause of dysfunction and continued poverty. He feared, however, that some would attribute this to "innate Negro weaknesses" and use such findings "to justify neglect and rationalize oppression." Yet even the preacher King had little to say about religion or its potential role in the urban North. He insisted that jobs, education, housing, and "access to culture" were those things that blacks needed "to

grow from within." See "An Address by Dr. Martin Luther King, Jr." in *Moynihan Report*, 402–409.

43. To the extent that Keil's work mirrored that of white admirers of *The Green Pastures* who compared favorably what they saw as the simple and spontaneous faith of the Negro masses to the overcivilized rationality of white Americans—which I maintain was a revived form of romantic racialism—then we may regard McPherson's assertion about the continuity between romantic racialism and the black soul movement as having some validity.

44. Keil, *Urban Blues*, 5.

45. Ibid.

46. Ibid., 7–8, 16.

47. Keil was indebted to anthropologist Anthony F. C. Wallace's notion of "revitalization movements." Keil was particularly interested in the disillusionment of blacks with trying to attain self-respect by salvaging aspects of their culture that were denigrated by whites and how the turn to the culture of the black masses, South and North, was a mark of attempts at cultural revitalization. He argued that "the soul ideology ministers to the needs for identity and solidarity" (165–166) and a genuine "cultural pluralism" would respect the integrity of a distinct Negro culture that brought its special contributions to America (194–197).

48. Keil, *Urban Blues*, 165–166, 186.

49. For a recent essay that examines one instance of the historical importance of how racial essentialism was used for "progressive" purposes, see Arthur Riss, "Racial Essentialism and Family Values in 'Uncle Tom's Cabin,'" *American Quarterly* 46 (December 1994): 513–544.

50. McPherson, *Abolitionist Legacy*, 343. Here I am focusing on the question of the similarities in the actual language and rhetoric that was used to describe blacks and their culture. I am aware of the vastly different issues that were being confronted in the 1830s compared to the 1960s. Furthermore, I take seriously George Fredrickson's critique of romantic racialism when he notes that it sometimes reflected "little more than a nagging sense, on the part of 'tender-minded' reformers, that their culture had its harsh and unattractive side and that white Americans lacked the disposition to conform fully to their own 'spiritual' values." See Fredrickson, *The Black Image in the White Mind: The Debate on African-American Character and Destiny, 1817–1914* (Middletown, onn.: Wesleyan University Press, 1987 [1971]), 125. With this in mind, we recognize the rhetorical uses to which such assertions of black religiosity were often put in various historical contexts without taking them at face value or as statements of what was thought to be historically true.

51. Hence the formal similarities between them and romantic racialism. Black portrayals of black religion and culture during moments of disillusionment with American culture at various historical junctures were similar to white depictions of blacks when whites became troubled by the materialism or harshness of American culture.

52. John H. Bracey Jr., August Meier, and Elliott Rudwick, eds., *Black Nationalism in America* (Indianapolis: Bobbs-Merrill, 1970), xxxvi.

53. Daryl Michael Scott, *Contempt and Pity: Social Policy and the Image of the Damaged Black Psyche, 1880–1996* (Chapel Hill: University of North Carolina Press, 1997), 119–136; and Waldo E. Martin, ed., *Brown v. Board of Education: A Brief History with Documents* (Boston: Bedford, 1998), 28–29, 37.

54. For how this debate continued in the 1960s, see R. L. Watson, "American Scholars and the Continuity of African Culture in the United States," *Journal of Negro History* 63 (October 1978): 375–386.

55. "Black Theology and the Black College Student," in James H. Cone, *Risks of Faith: The Emergence of a Black Theology of Liberation, 1968–1978* (Boston: Beacon Press, 1999), 120–121.

56. E. Franklin Frazier's criticisms of the black bourgeoisie in his *Black Bourgeoisie* (1957) as living in a world of "make-believe," suffering from intense feelings of inferiority, and slavishly imitating the white middle class were odd because Frazier was also known for his negative portrayals of urban black folk culture. On the critique of black middle-class culture as inauthentic, see Gary T. Marx, "The White Negro and the Negro White," *Phylon* 28 (second quarter, 1967): 168–177.

57. Ulf Hannerz, *Soulside: Inquiries into Ghetto Culture and Community* (New York: Columbia University Press, 1969), 14.

58. Ibid., 14. Hannerz regarded his work as building on books like Keil's *Urban Blues* that sought to counter social scientific depictions of urban blacks as merely case studies.

59. Ibid., 144–145.

60. William L. Van Deburg, *New Day in Babylon: The Black Power Movement and American Culture, 1965–1975* (Chicago: University of Chicago Press, 1992), 193.

61. I do not use the terms *good* and *beautiful* in an abstract philosophical sense, but I have in mind repeated attempts by black leaders in specific historical contexts to formulate and realize practices, habits, and social structures that would lead to the development of what they saw as a vibrant black culture that prospered economically and sustained psychological and moral well-being among black Americans.

62. Amiri Baraka, *Blues People: Negro Music in White America* (New York: Quill, 1999 [1963]), 126.

63. For a brief biography of Baraka, see "Introduction," in *The Leroi Jones/Amiri Baraka Reader by Amiri Baraka*, ed. William J. Harris (New York: Thunder's Mouth, 1991), xvii–xxx.

64. Hannerz, *Soulside*, 70, 200.

65. Keil, *Urban Blues*, 16–17.

66. Meier, "On the Role of Martin Luther King, Jr," in *Reporting Civil Rights, Part Two: American Journalism, 1963–1973* (New York: Library of America, 2003), 456.

67. David L. Chappell, *A Stone of Hope: Prophetic Religion and the Death of Jim Crow* (Chapel Hill: University of North Carolina Press, 2004), 3, 189–190.

68. Obviously, I am not saying that King was an Uncle Tom figure in the way that this term was pejoratively used in the 1960s. Yet I want to call attention to the particular criticisms and commendations of King's work and the implications of

the expectations each side held about the role of blacks in the nation. Though a pacifist, William Lloyd Garrison criticized Stowe for her depiction of the meek, forgiving, and Christ-like Uncle Tom. See his "Review of Harriet Beecher Stowe's *Uncle Tom's Cabin*," *Liberator*, (March 26, 1852; reprint, *William Lloyd Garrison and the Fight against Slavery: Selections from* The Liberator, ed. William E. Cain [Boston: Bedford Books, 1995]), 129, 131. Similarly, Malcolm X derided King's philosophy of nonviolence and any suggestion that blacks "love everybody." He had no desire that blacks become sacrificial lambs to redeem America. See *Martin Luther King, Jr., Malcolm X, and the Civil Rights Struggle of the 1950s and 1960s: A Brief History with Documents*, ed. David Howard-Pitney (Boston: Bedford Books, 2004), 134–135. See also Ronny E. Turner, "The Black Minister: Uncle Tom or Abolitionist?," *Phylon* 34 (first quarter, 1973): 86–95.

69. Robert Dale Owen, *The Wrong of Slavery; The Right of Emancipation; And the Future of the African Race in the United States* (New York: Kraus Reprint, 1969 [1864]), 221.

70. Barbara Dianne Savage, "Biblical and Historiographical Imperatives: Toward a History of Ideas about the Political Role of Black Churches," in *African Americans and the Bible: Sacred Texts and Social Textures*, ed. Vincent L. Wimbush (New York: Continuum, 2000), 380.

71. On attempts to find a usable past and for a critical analysis of the normative agendas of the writing of general American church and religious history, see R. Laurence Moore, *Religious Outsiders and the Making of Americans* (New York: Oxford University Press, 1986); Henry Warner Bowden, *Church History in an Age of Uncertainty: Historiographical Patterns in the United States, 1906–1990* (Carbondale: Southern Illinois University Press, 1991); and Thomas A. Tweed, "Narrating U.S. Religious History," in Thomas A. Tweed, ed., *Retelling U.S. Religious History* (Berkeley: University of California Press, 1997), 1–23.

72. Robert T. Handy, "Negro Christianity and American Church Historiography," in *Reinterpretation in American Church History*, ed. Jerald C. Brauer (Chicago: University of Chicago Press, 1968), 93.

73. Philip Rieff, *The Triumph of the Therapeutic: Uses of Faith after Freud* (Chicago: University of Chicago Press, 1987 [1966]), 23.

74. Ibid., 23; emphasis in original.

75. Rieff's use of "releasing symbols" reflects his belief that all cultures struggle with the tension between the "modalities of control and release" and that culture both organizes the moral demands humans make on themselves into a system of symbols that make their lives intelligible and "trustworthy" to each other and structures the "expressive remissions" by which humans release themselves, to some degree, from the strain of conforming to the controlling symbolic, "internalized variant readings of culture that constitute individual character." See Rieff, *The Triumph of the Therapeutic*, 232–233.

76. Albert Raboteau, *Slave Religion: The "Invisible" Institution in the Antebellum South* (New York: Oxford University Press, 1978), 56.

77. For an account of the social and political context in which his work was originally written, see Raboteau, *Slave Religion: The "Invisible" Institution in the Antebellum South,* updated edition (New York: Oxford University Press, 2004), 323–334.

78. An important and popular text that illustrates this point is Gayraud S. Wilmore's *Black Religion and Black Radicalism,* originally published in 1973.

79. James H. Cone, "Black Theology and the Black Student," in *Risks of Faith,* 121–123.

80. See Marla F. Frederick, *Between Sundays: Black Women and Everyday Struggles of Faith* (Berkeley: University of California Press, 2003), ix–x.

81. Ibid., 5–12, 210–220. My use of the phrase "everyday work" should not be confused with related terms used by James Scott's *Weapons of the Weak* (1985). I want to avoid the uses to which Scott's work has been put. I am not interested in reasserting claims of everyday forms of opposition to oppression in the lives of blacks. Perhaps it is time to rethink entirely religion among African Americans without resorting to the dichotomy of protest/accommodation, whether we view protest as prosaic and small-scale or as overtly political. For recent uses of Scott's work on the religious practices of African American women, see Evelyn Brooks Higginbotham, *Righteous Discontent: The Women's Movement in the Black Baptist Church, 1880–1920* (Cambridge, Mass.: Harvard University Press, 1993), 221; and Frederick, *Between Sundays,* 5–6, 223.

82. Moore, *Religious Outsiders and the Making of Americans,* 209.

83. Robert A. Orsi, *Between Heaven and Earth: The Religious Worlds People Make and the Scholars Who Study Them* (Princeton, N.J.: Princeton University Press, 2005), 170.

84. For one example of a rich work that moves beyond the dichotomies and functionalist interpretations of past studies of African American religion, see Wallace D. Best, *Passionately Human, No Less Divine: Religion and Culture in Black Chicago, 1915–1952* (Princeton, N.J.: Princeton University Press, 2005).

Selected Bibliography

PRIMARY SOURCES

ARCHIVES

Horace Bumstead Papers, Archives/Special Collections, Atlanta University Center, Robert Woodruff Library.

St. Clair Drake Papers, Manuscripts, Archives, and Rare Books Division, Schomburg Center for Research in Black Culture, New York Public Library.

E. Franklin Frazier Papers, Manuscript Division, Howard University.

Melville J. and Frances S. Herskovits Papers, Manuscripts, Archives, and Rare Books Division, Schomburg Center for Research in Black Culture, New York Public Library.

C. Eric Lincoln Papers, Archives/Special Collections, Atlanta University Center, Robert Woodruff Library.

Benjamin Mays Papers, Manuscript Division, Howard University.

Reminiscences of W. E. B. Du Bois, Oral History Collection, Columbia University.

Reminiscences of Marc Connelly, Oral History Collection, Columbia University.

Reminiscences of Frederick Morgan Davenport, Oral History Collection, Columbia University.

Reminiscences of Carl Van Vechten, Oral History Collection, Columbia University.

PERIODICALS

American Anthropologist
American Journal of Sociology

American Negro Academy Occasional Papers
American Sociological Review
Annals of the American Academy of Political and Social Science
Journal of American Folk-Lore
Journal of Negro Education
Journal of Negro History
Phylon
Social Forces
South Atlantic Quarterly

BOOKS, DISSERTATIONS, THESES, DOCUMENTARY COLLECTIONS,
AND SELECTED ARTICLES

Adero, Malaika, ed. *Up South: Stories, Studies, and Letters of This Century's African-American Migrations*. New York: New York Press, 1993.

Andersen, Eric, ed. *Black Protest and the Great Migration: A Brief History with Documents*. Boston: Bedford Books, 2003.

Andrews, William L., ed. *James Weldon Johnson: Writings*. New York: Library of America, 2004.

Angell, Stephen W. and Anthony B. Pinn, eds. *Social Protest Thought in the African Methodist Episcopal Church, 1862–1939*. Knoxville: University of Tennessee Press, 2000.

Aptheker, Herbert, ed. *A Documentary History of the Negro People in the United States, 1910–1932*. Seacus, N.J.: Citadel Press, 1973.

————, ed. *The Correspondence of W.E.B. Du Bois: Selections, 1877–1934*. Vol. 1. Amherst: University of Massachusetts Press, 1973.

————, ed. *The Correspondence of W.E.B. Du Bois: Selections, 1934–1944*. Vol. 2. Amherst: University of Massachusetts Press, 1976.

————, ed. *Against Racism: Unpublished Essays, Papers, Addresses, 1887–1961: W. E. B. Du Bois*. Amherst: University of Massachusetts, 1985.

Baritz, Loren, ed. *The Culture of the Twenties*. New York: Bobbs-Merrill, 1970.

Barnard, Emily, ed. *Remember Me to Harlem: The Letters of Langston Hughes and Carl Van Vechten, 1925–1964*. New York: Alfred A. Knopf, 2001.

Bass, George Houston and Henry Louis Gates Jr., eds. *Mule Bone: A Comedy of Negro Life by Langston Hughes and Zora Neale Hurston*. New York: Harper Collins, 1991.

Bean, Robert Bennett. "Some Racial Peculiarities of the Negro Brain." *American Journal of Anatomy* 5 (September 1, 1906): 353–432.

Beveridge, Charles E. and Charles Capin McLaughlin, eds. *The Papers of Frederick Law Olmsted: Slavery and the South, 1852–1856*. Vol. 2. Baltimore, Md.: Johns Hopkins University Press, 1981.

Blaustein, Albert P. and Robert L. Zangrando, eds. *Civil Rights and African Americans*. Evanston, Ill.: Northwest University Press, 1991 [1968].

Bracey, John H., Jr., August Meier, and Elliott Rudwick, eds. *Black Nationalism in America*. Indianapolis: Bobbs-Merrill, 1970.

Brotz, Howard, ed. *Negro Social and Political Thought, 1850–1920: Representative Texts.* New York: Basic Books, 1966.

Brown, Sterling. *Negro Poetry and Drama.* New York: Atheneum, 1971 [1937].

Bruce, Philip A. *The Plantation Negro as a Freedman: Observations on His Character, Condition, and Prospects in Virginia.* Northbrook, Ill.: Metro Books, 1972 [1889].

Cain, William E, ed. *William Lloyd Garrison and the Fight against Slavery: Selections from the* Liberator. New York: Bedford Books, 1994.

Chamberlain, Alexander Francis. "The Contribution of the Negro to Human Civilization." *Journal of Race Development* (April 1911): 482–502.

Channing, William Ellery. *Slavery.* Boston: James Munroe, 1835.

Clarke, James Freeman, "Slavery in the United States," in *Essays and Pamphlets on Antislavery.* Westport, Conn.: Negro Universities Press, 1970.

Cripps, Thomas, ed. *The Green Pastures.* Madison: University of Wisconsin Press, 1979.

Cutten, George Barton. *The Psychological Phenomena of Christianity.* New York: Charles Scribner's Sons, 1908.

Daniel, W. A. *The Education of Negro Ministers.* New York: Negro Universities Press, 1969 [1925].

Daniels, John. *In Freedom's Birthplace: A Study of the Boston Negroes.* New York: Arno Press, 1969 [1914].

Davenport, Frederick Morgan. *Primitive Traits in Religious Revivals: A Study in Mental and Social Evolution.* New York: Macmillan, 1905.

———. "The Religion of the American Negro." *Contemporary Review* 82 (September 1905): 369–375.

Davis, Allison, Burleigh B. Gardner, and Mary R. Gardner. *Deep South: A Social Anthropological Study of Caste and Class.* Chicago: University of Chicago Press, 1941.

Dollard, John. *Caste and Class in a Southern Town,* 3rd ed. New York: Doubleday Anchor Books, 1957 [1937].

Douglass, H. Paul. *The Metropolitan Pittsburgh Church Study.* Executive Committee of the Metropolitan Pittsburgh Church Study, 1948.

Drake, St. Clair and Horace R. Cayton. *Black Metropolis: A Study of Negro Life in a Northern City,* revised and enlarged edition. Chicago: University of Chicago Press, 1993 [1945].

Du Bois, W. E. B. *The Philadelphia Negro: A Social Study.* Philadelphia: University of Philadelphia Press, 1996 [1899].

———. *The Souls of Black Folk.* New York: Vintage Books, 1990 [1903].

———. *The Negro Church.* Atlanta: Atlanta University Press, 1903.

———. *Dusk of Dawn: An Essay toward an Autobiography of a Race Concept.* New York: Schocken Books, 1968 [1940].

Early, Gerald, ed. *My Soul's High Song: The Collected Writings of Countee Cullen, Voice of the Harlem Renaissance.* New York: Anchor Books, 1991.

Eliot, Charles W. *The Religion of the Future.* Boston: American Unitarian Association, 1909.

Elliot, E. N., ed. *Cotton is King and Pro-Slavery Arguments*. Adamant Media, 2003.

Eubanks, John B. "Modern Trends in the Religion of the Negro." Ph.D. diss., University of Chicago, 1947.

Fauset, Arthur Huff. *Black Gods of the Metropolis: Negro Religious Cults of the Urban North*. Philadelphia: University of Pennsylvania Press, 2002 [1944].

Faust, Drew Gilpin, ed. *The Ideology of Slavery: Proslavery Though in the Antebellum South, 1830–1860*. Baton Rouge: Louisiana State University Press, 1981.

Ferris, William H. Ferris, *The African Abroad or His Evolution in Western Culture: Tracing His Development under Caucasian Milieu*. Vol. 1. New Haven, Conn.: Tuttle, Morehouse and Taylor Press, 1913.

Finkelman, Paul, ed. *Dred Scott v. Sanford: A Brief History with Documents*. Boston: Bedford Books, 1997.

———, ed. *Defending Slavery: Proslavery Thought in the Old South: A Brief History with Documents*. Boston: Bedford Books, 2003.

Fisher, Mark Miles. "The Negro Church and the World War." *Journal of Religion* (September 1925): 483–499.

Foner, Philip S., ed. *Frederick Douglass: Selected Speeches and Writings*. Abridged and adapted by Yuval Taylor. Chicago: Lawrence Hill Books, 1999.

Foner, Philip S. and Robert James Branham, eds. *Lift Every Voice: African American Oratory, 1787–1900*. Tuscaloosa: University of Alabama Press, 1998.

Fox, William Kappen. "Experiments in Southern Rural Religious Development among Negroes." B.D. thesis, University of Chicago Divinity School, 1943.

Frazier, E. Franklin. *The Negro Church in America*. New York: Schocken Books, 1963.

Green, Dan S. and Edwin D. Driver, eds. *W. E. B. Du Bois: On Sociology and the Black Community*. Chicago: University of Chicago Press, 1978.

Hall, G. Stanley. *Adolescence: Its Psychology and Its Relations to Physiology, Anthropology, Sociology, Sex, Crime, Religion, and Education*. Vols. 1 and 2. New York: D. Appleton, 1904 and 1905.

———. "The Negro in Africa and America." *Pedagogical Seminary* 12 (September 1905): 350–368.

———. "Point of View toward Primitive Races." *Journal of Race Development* 1 (July 1910): 5–11.

Hamilton, C. Horace and John M. Ellison. *The Negro Church in Rural Virginia*. Bulletin 273. Blacksburg: Virginia Agricultural Experiment Station, 1929.

Harlan, Louis R., ed. *The Booker T. Washington Papers*. Vol. 3. Urbana: University of Illinois Press, 1974.

Harlan, Louis R. and Raymond W. Smock, eds. *Booker T. Washington Papers*. Vol. 8. Urbana: University of Illinois Press, 1979.

———. *Booker T. Washington Papers*. Vol. 11. Urbana: University of Illinois Press, 1981.

Haven, Gilbert. *National Sermons: Sermons, Speeches and Letters on Slavery and Its War: From the Passage of the Fugitive Slave Bill to the Election of President Grant*. Boston: Lee and Shepard, 1869.

Haygood, Atticus. *Our Brother in Black: His Freedom and His Future*. New York: Phillips, 1881.

Hedrick, Joan D., ed. *The Oxford Harriet Beecher Stowe Reader*. New York: Oxford University Press, 1999.

Herskovits, Melville J. *The Myth of the Negro Past*. Boston: Beacon Press, 1958 [1941].

Hoffman, Frederick L. *Race Traits and Tendencies of the American Negro*. New York: Macmillan, 1896.

Houghton, Walter R., ed. *Neely's History of the Parliament of World Religions and Religious Congresses at the World's Columbian Exposition*, 4th ed. Chicago: Neely Publishing, 1894.

Johnson, James Weldon. *Black Manhattan*. New York: Da Capo Press, 1991 [1930].

Kaplan, Carla, ed. *Zora Neale Hurston: A Life in Letters*. New York: Doubleday, 2002.

Karcher, Carolyn L, ed. *Lydia Maria Child Reader*. Durham, N.C.: Duke University Press, 1997.

Kinmont, Alexander. *The Natural History of Man and the Rise and Progress of Philosophy*. Philadelphia: J. B. Lippincott, 1891 [1839].

Klineberg, Otto, ed. *Characteristics of the American Negro*. New York: Harper and Brothers, 1944.

Lemert, Charles and Esme Bhan, eds. *The Voice of Anna Julia Cooper Including* A Voice from the South *and Other Important Essays, Papers, and Letters*. Lanham, Md.: Rowman and Littlefield, 1998.

Levine, Robert S., ed. *Martin R. Delaney: A Documentary Reader*. Chapel Hill: University of North Carolina Press, 2003.

Lewis, David Levering, ed. *The Portable Harlem Renaissance Reader*. New York: Penguin Books, 1994.

——, ed. *W.E.B. Du Bois: A Reader*. New York: Henry Holt, 1995.

Lewis, Hylan. *Blackways of Kent*. Chapel Hill: University of North Carolina Press, 1955.

Lewis, John Henry. "Social Service in Negro Churches." M.A. thesis, University of Chicago Divinity School, 1914.

Lippman, Walter. *A Preface to Morals*. New York: Life, 1957 [1929].

Locke, Alain, ed. *The New Negro: Voices of the Harlem Renaissance*. New York: Touchstone, 1992 [1925].

Lowance, Mason, ed. *Against Slavery: An Abolitionist Reader*. New York: Penguin Books, 2000.

Luker, Ralph, ed. *Black and White Together: The Reminiscences of an NAACP Founder*, by Mary Ovington. New York: Feminist Press, 1995.

Martin, Waldo E., ed. *Brown v. Board of Education: A Brief History with Documents*. Boston: Bedford, 1998.

Mays, Benjamin Elijah. *The Negro's God as Reflected in His Literature*. Boston: Chapman and Grimes, 1938.

Mays, Benjamin Elijah and Joseph William Nicholson. *The Negro Church*. New York: Institute of Social and Religious Research, 1933.

McKitrick, Eric L., ed. *Slavery Defended: The Views of the Old South*. Englewood Cliffs, N.J.: Prentice Hall, 1963.

McLoughlin, William G., ed. *The American Evangelicals, 1800–1900*. New York: Harper and Row, 1968.

Meier, August, Elliott Rudwick, and Francis L. Broderick, eds. *Black Protest Thought in the Twentieth Century*, 2nd ed. New York: Macmillan, 1971.

Meyer, Howard N., ed. *The Magnificent Activist: The Writings of Thomas Wentworth Higginson (1823–1911)*. New York: Da Capo Press, 2000.

Miller, Kelly. *Race Adjustment: Essays on the Negro in America*. New York, 1908.

Moses, Wilson Jeremiah, ed. *Destiny and Race: Selected Writings, 1840–1898*. Amherst: University of Massachusetts Press, 1992.

Myrdal, Gunnar. *An American Dilemma: The Negro Problem and Modern Democracy*. New York: Harper and Brothers, 1944.

Newman, Richard, Patrick Rael, and Phillip Lapsansky, eds. *Pamphlets of Protest: An Anthology of Early African American Protest Literature, 1790–1860*. New York: Routledge, 2001.

Odum, Howard W. *Social and Mental Traits of the Negro: Research into the Conditions of the Negro Race in Southern Towns: A Study in Race Traits, Tendencies, and Prospects*. New York: Columbia University Press, 1910.

Oldfield, J. R., ed. *Civilization and Black Progress: Selected Writings of Alexander Crummell on the South*. Charlottesville: University Press of Virginia, 1995.

Owen, Robert Dale. *The Wrong of Slavery; The Right of Emancipation; and The Future of the African Race in the United States*. New York: Kraus Reprint, 1969 [1864].

Peterson, Merrill D., ed. *Thomas Jefferson: Writings*. New York: Library of America, 1984.

Pinn, Anthony B., ed. *Making the Gospel Plain: The Writings of Bishop Reverdy C. Ransom*. Harrisburg, Penn.: Trinity International Press, 1999.

Powdermaker, Hortense. *After Freedom: A Cultural Study in the Deep South*. Madison: University of Wisconsin Press, 1993 [1939].

Proctor, Henry Hugh. *Between Black and White*. Boston: Pilgrim Press, 1925.

Read, Hollis. *The Negro Problem Solved; Or, Africa as She Was, as She Is, and as She Shall Be*. New York: A. A. Constantine, 1864.

Richardson, Harry V. *Dark Glory: A Picture of the Church among Negroes in the Rural South*. New York: Friendship Press, 1947.

Royster, Jacqueline Jones, ed. *Southern Horrors and Other Writings: The Anti-Lynching Campaign of Ida B. Wells, 1892–1900*. Boston: Bedford Books, 1997.

Rubin, Morton. *Plantation County*. Chapel Hill: University of North Carolina Press, 1951.

Ruchames, Louis, ed. *Racial Thought in America: From the Puritans to Abraham Lincoln, a Documentary History*. Boston: University of Massachusetts, 1969.

Schlesinger, Arthur M., ed. *The Cotton Kingdom: A Traveler's Observations on Cotton and Slavery in the American Slave States*, by Frederick Law Olmsted. New York: Modern Library, 1984 [1861].

Seager, Richard Hughes, ed. *The Dawn of Religious Pluralism: Voices from the World's Parliament of Religions, 1893*. LaSalle, Ill.: Open Court, 1993.

Sernett, Milton C., ed. *African American Religious History: A Documentary Witness*, 2nd ed. Durham, N.C.: Duke University Press, 1999.

Smith, John David, ed. *The "Benefits" of Slavery: The New Proslavery Argument*. New York: Garland, 1993.

Spencer, Herbert. *The Principles of Sociology*. Vol. 1, 3rd ed. New York: D. Appleton, 1925 [1888].

Sperry, Willard. *Religion in America*. New York: Macmillan, 1946.

Stearns, Charles. *The Black Man of the South and the Rebels; Or, The Characteristics of the Former, and the Recent Outrages of the Latter*. New York: American News, 1872.

Stowe, Harriet Beecher. *Uncle Tom's Cabin Or, Life among the Lowly*. Cambridge: University Press, 1886 [1852].

Sutherland, Robert. "An Analysis of Negro Churches in Chicago." Ph.D. diss., University of Chicago, 1930.

Sweet, William Warren. *The Story of Religions in America*. New York: Harper and Brothers, 1930.

———. *Revivalism in America: Its Origin, Growth and Decline*. New York: Charles Scribner's Sons, 1944.

Thomas, Brook, ed. *Plessy v. Ferguson: A Brief History with Documents*. Boston: Bedford Books, 1997.

Tillinghast, Joseph. *The Negro in Africa and America*. New York: Macmillan, 1902.

Trotter, Joe W. and Earl Lewis. *African Americans in the Industrial Age: A Documentary History, 1915–1945*. Boston: Northeastern University Press, 1996.

Wilson, Sondra Kathryn, ed. *The Selected Writings of James Weldon Johnson: The New York Age Editorials (1914–1923)*. Vol. 1. New York: Oxford University Press, 1995.

———, ed. *The Selected Writings of James Weldon Johnson: Social, Political and Literary Essays*. Vol. 2. New York: Oxford University Press, 1995.

———, ed. *The Crisis Reader: Stories, Poetry, and Essays from the NAACP's* Crisis *Magazine*. New York: Modern Library, 1999.

———, ed. *The Opportunity Reader: Stories, Poetry, and Essays from Urban League's* Opportunity *Magazine*. New York: Modern Library, 1999.

———, ed. *The Messenger Reader: Stories, Poetry and Essays from the* Messenger *Magazine*. New York: Modern Library, 2000.

Wish, Harvey, ed. *Antebellum Writings of George Fitzhugh and Hinton Rowan Helper on Slavery*. New York: Capricorn Books, 1960.

Woodson, Carter G. *The History of the Negro Church*, 2nd ed. Washington, D.C.: Associated Publishers, 1945 [1921].

———, ed. *The Mind of the Negro as Reflected in Letters Written during the Crisis, 1800–1860*. New York: Russell and Russell, 1969 [1926].

———. *The Rural Negro*. Washington, D.C.: Association for the Study of Negro Life and History, 1930.

Young, Jeffrey Robert, ed. *Proslavery and Sectional Thought in the Early South, 1740–1829*. Columbia: University of South Carolina Press, 2006.

Zuckerman, Phil, ed. *Du Bois on Religion*. New York: AltaMira Press, 2000.

SECONDARY SOURCES

BOOKS, DISSERTATIONS, THESES, AND SELECTED ARTICLES

Abzug, Robert H. *Cosmos Crumbling: American Reform and the Religious Imagination.* New York: Oxford University Press, 1994.

Adas, Michael. *Machines as the Measure of Men: Science, Technology, and Ideologies of Western Dominance.* Ithaca, N.Y.: Cornell University Press, 1989.

Anderson, James D. *The Education of Blacks in the South, 1860–1930.* Chapel Hill: University of North Carolina Press, 1988.

Angell, Stephen Ward. *Bishop Henry McNeal Turner and African-American Religion in the South.* Knoxville: University of Tennessee Press, 1992.

Ayers, Edward L. *Vengeance and Justice: Crime and Punishment in the 19th Century American South.* New York: Oxford University Press, 1984.

———. *The Promise of the New South: Life after Reconstruction.* New York: Oxford University Press, 1992.

Baer, Hans and Merrill Singer. *African-American Religion in the Twentieth Century: Varieties of Protest and Accommodation,* 2nd ed. Knoxville: University of Tennessee Press, 2002.

Baker, Lee D. *From Savage to Negro: Anthropology and the Construction of Race, 1896–1954.* Berkeley: University of California Press, 1998.

Barkan, Elazar. *The Retreat of Scientific Racism: Changing Concepts of Race in Britain and the United States between the World Wars.* Cambridge: Cambridge University Press, 1992.

Bay, Mia. *The White Image in the Black Mind: African American Ideas about White People 1830–1925.* New York: Oxford University Press, 2000.

Bederman, Gail. *Manliness and Civilization: A Cultural History of Gender and Race in the United States, 1880–1917.* Chicago: University of Chicago Press, 1995.

Bender, Thomas, ed. *The Antislavery Debate: Capitalism and Abolitionism as a Problem in Historical Interpretation.* Berkeley: University of California Press, 1992.

Best, Wallace D. *Passionately Human, No Less Divine: Religion and Culture in Black Chicago, 1915–1952.* Princeton, N.J.: Princeton University Press, 2005.

Blassingame, John W. *Slave Community: Plantation Life in the Antebellum South,* revised and enlarged edition. New York: Oxford University Press, 1979.

Blight, David W. *Race and Reunion: The Civil War in American Memory.* Cambridge, Mass.: Harvard University Press, 2001.

Blum, Edward J. *Reforging the White Republic: Race, Religion, and American Nationalism, 1865–1898.* Baton Rouge: Louisiana State University Press, 2005.

———. *W. E. B. Du Bois: American Prophet.* Philadelphia: University of Pennsylvania, 2007.

Bone, Robert A. *The Negro Novel in America,* rev. ed. New Haven, Conn.: Yale University Press, 1965.

Boyd, Valerie. *Wrapped in Rainbows: The Life of Zora Neale Hurston.* New York: Scribner, 2003.

Brundage, W. Fitzhugh. *Lynching in the New South: Georgia and Virginia, 1880–1930.* Urbana: University of Illinois Press, 1993.

Buck, Paul H. *Road To Reunion, 1865–1900.* Boston: Little, Brown, and Co., 1937.

Burns, W. Hayward. *Voices of Negro Protest in America.* New York: Oxford University Press, 1963.

Burris, John P. *Exhibiting Religion: Colonialism and Spectacle at International Expositions, 1851–1893.* Charlottesville: University of Virginia, 2001.

Butler, Jon. "Enlarging the Bonds of Christ: Slavery, Evangelism, and the Christianization of the South, 1690–1790." In *The Evangelical Tradition in America,* edited by Leonard I. Sweet. Macon: Mercer University Press, 1997 [1984].

———. *Awash in a Sea of Faith: Christianizing the American People.* Cambridge: Harvard University Press, 1990.

Campbell, James T. *Songs of Zion: The African Methodist Episcopal Church in the United States and South Africa.* Chapel Hill: University of North Carolina Press, 1998.

Campbell, James T., and James Oakes. "The Invention of Race: Rereading *White over Black.*" *Reviews in American History* 21 (March 1993): 172–183.

Carter, Luther Clyde. "Negro Churches in a Southern Community." Ph.D. diss., Yale University, 1955.

Chapell, David L. *A Stone of Hope: Prophetic Religion and the Death of Jim Crow.* Chapel Hill: University of North Carolina Press, 2003.

Chireau, Yvonne. *Black Magic: Religion and the African American Conjuring Tradition.* Berkeley: University of California Press, 2003.

Clark, Elizabeth. "'Sacred Rights of the Weak': Pain, Sympathy, and the Culture of Individual Rights in Antebellum America." *Journal of American History* 82 (September 1995): 463–493.

Clark, Kenneth B. *Dark Ghetto: Dilemmas of Social Power.* New York: Harper and Row, 1965.

Clegg, Claude Andrew III. *An Original Man: The Life and Times of Elijah Mohammed.* New York: St. Martin's Griffin, 1997.

Coben, Stanley. *Rebellion against Victorianism: The Impetus for Cultural Change in 1920s America.* New York: Oxford University Press, 1991.

Cole, Douglas. *Franz Boas: The Early Years, 1858–1906.* Seattle: University of Washington Press, 1999.

Corrigan, John. *Business of the Heart: Religion and Emotion in the Nineteenth Century.* Berkeley: University of California Press, 2002.

Curse, Harold. *The Crisis of the Negro Intellectual: From its Origins to the Present.* New York: William Morrow, 1967.

Curtin, Philip D. *The Image of Africa: British Ideas and Action, 1780–1850.* Vol. 2. Madison: University of Wisconsin Press, 1973.

Curtis, Edward E., IV. *Black Muslim Religion in the Nation of Islam, 1960–1975.* Chapel Hill: University of North Carolina, 2007.

Dain, Bruce. *A Hideous Monster of the Mind: American Race Theory in the Early Republic.* Cambridge, Mass.: Harvard University Press, 2002.

Degler, Carl N. *In Search of Human Nature: The Decline and Revival of Darwinism in American Social Thought*. New York: Oxford University Press, 1991.

Dickson, Bruce D. Jr. "Ancient Africa and the Early Black American Historians, 1883–1915." *American Quarterly* 26 (winter 1984): 686–699.

———. *Black American Writing from the Nadir: The Evolution of a Literary Tradition, 1877–1915*. Baton Rouge: Louisiana State University Press, 1989.

———. *Archibald Grimké: Portrait of a Black Independent*. Baton Rouge: Louisiana State University Press, 1993.

Dorsey, Allison. *To Build Our Lives Together: Community Formation in Black Atlanta, 1875–1906*. Athens: University of Georgia Press, 2004.

Dray, Phillip. *At the Hands of Persons Unknown: The Lynching of Black America*. New York: Random House, 2002.

Dumenil, Lynn. *Modern Temper: American Culture and Society in the 1920s*. New York: Hill and Wang, 1995.

Eagerton, Douglas. " 'Its Origins Is Not a Little Curious': A New Look at the American Colonization Society." *Journal of the Early Republic* 5 (winter 1985): 463–480.

Essien-Odum, E. U. *Black Nationalism: A Search for an Identity in America*. Chicago: University of Chicago Press, 1962.

Farmer, James O. Jr. *The Metaphysical Confederacy: James Henley Thornwell and the Synthesis of Southern Values*. Macon, Ga.: Mercer University Press, 1999 [1986].

Finkelman, Paul. *Slavery and the Founders: Race and Liberty in the Age of Jefferson*, 2nd ed. Armonk, N.Y.: M. E. Sharpe, 2001.

Foner, Eric. *Reconstruction: America's Unfinished Revolution, 1863–1877*. New York: Harper and Row, 1988.

Fox-Genovese, Elizabeth and Eugene D. Genovese. *The Mind of the Master Class: History and Faith in the Southern Slaveholders' Worldview*. Cambridge: Cambridge University Press, 2005.

Franklin, John Hope, and Alfred A. Moss Jr., *From Slavery to Freedom: A History of African Americans*, 8th ed. Boston: McGraw-Hill, 2000.

Frazier, Thomas Richard. "An Analysis of Social Scientific Writing on American Negro Religion." Ph.D. diss., Columbia University Press, 1967.

Frederick, Marla. *Between Sundays: Black Women and Everyday Struggles of Faith*. Berkeley: University of California Press, 2003.

Fredrickson, George M. *The Inner Civil War: Northern Intellectuals and the Crisis of the Union*. Urbana: University of Illinois Press, 1993 [1963].

———. *The Black Image in the White Mind: The Debate on Afro-American Character and Destiny, 1817–1914*. Middletown, Conn.: Wesleyan University Press, 1987 [1971].

Freehling, William H. "James Henley Thornwell's Mysterious Antislavery Moment." *Journal of Southern History* 57 (August 1991): 383–406.

Frey, Sylvia R. and Betty Wood. *Come Shouting to Zion: African American Protestantism in the American South and British Caribbean to 1830*. Chapel Hill: University of North Carolina Press, 1998.

Fuller, Robert C. *Mesmerism and the American Cure of Souls*. Philadelphia: University of Pennsylvania Press, 1982.

Fullinwider, S. P. *The Mind and Mood of Black America: 20th Century Thought.* Homewood: Dorsey Press, 1969.

Gatewood, Willard B. *Aristocrats of Color: The Black Elite, 1880–1920.* Fayetteville: University of Arkansas Press, 2000 [1991].

Genovese, Eugene D. *Roll, Jordan, Roll: The World the Slaves Made.* New York: Vintage Books, 1974.

George, Carol V. R. *Segregated Sabbaths: Richard Allen and the Rise of Independent Black Churches, 1760–1840.* New York: Oxford University Press, 1973.

Giddings, Paula. *When and Where I Enter: The Impact of Black Women on Race and Sex in America.* New York: Quill William Morrow, 1984.

Glaude, Eddie S. Jr. *Exodus! Religion, Race, and Nation in Early Nineteenth-Century Black America.* Chicago: University of Chicago Press, 2000.

Goggin, Jacqueline. *Carter G. Woodson: A Life in Black History.* Baton Rouge: Louisiana State University Press, 1993.

Goodman, Paul. *Of One Blood: Abolitionists and the Origins of Racial Equality.* Berkeley: University of California Press, 1998.

Gossett, Thomas F. *Race: The History of an Idea in America.* New York: Oxford University Press, 1997.

Gould, Stephen Jay. *The Mismeasure of Man,* rev. and expanded ed. New York: W. W. Norton, 1996.

Graham, Thomas. "Harriet Beecher Stowe and the Question of Race." *New England Quarterly* 46 (December 1973): 614–622.

Gregg, Robert. *Sparks from the Anvil of Oppression: Philadelphia's African Methodists and Southern Migrants, 1890–1940.* Philadelphia: Temple University Press, 1993.

Gutman, Herbert. *The Black Family in Slavery and Freedom, 1750–1925.* New York: Vintage Books, 1976.

Hale, Grace Elizabeth. *Making Whiteness: The Culture of Segregation in the South, 1890–1940.* New York: Vintage Books, 1998.

Haller, John S. Jr. *Outcasts from Evolution: Scientific Attitudes of Racial Inferiority, 1859–1900.* Carbondale: Southern Illinois University Press, 1995 [1971].

Harding, Sandra, ed. *The "Racial" Economy of Science: Toward a Democratic Future.* Bloomington: Indiana University Press, 1993.

Harlan, Louis R. *Booker T. Washington: The Making of a Black Leader, 1856–1901.* New York: Oxford University Press, 1972.

———. *Booker T. Washington: The Wizard of Tuskegee, 1901–1915.* New York: Oxford University Press, 1983.

Hannerz, Ulf. *Soulside: Inquiries into Ghetto Culture and Community.* New York: Columbia University Press, 1969.

Harris, Michael W. *The Rise of Gospel Blues: The Music of Thomas Andrew Dorsey in the Urban Church.* New York: Oxford University Press, 1992.

Harrold, Stanley. *American Abolitionists.* London: Longman, 2001.

———. *Abolitionists and the South, 1831–1861.* Lexington: University of Kentucky Press, 1995.

Harvey, Paul. *Redeeming the South: Religious Cultures and Racial Identities among Southern Baptists, 1865–1925.* Chapel Hill: University of North Carolina Press, 1997.

Haynes, Robert V., ed. *Blacks in White America before 1865: Issues and Interpretations.* New York: David McKay, 1972.

Haynes, Stephen R. *Noah's Curse: The Biblical Justification of American Slavery.* New York: Oxford University Press, 2002.

Hedrick, Joan D. *Harriet Beecher Stowe: A Life.* New York: Oxford University Press, 1994.

Higginbotham, Evelyn Brooks. *Righteous Discontent: The Women's Movement in the Black Baptist Church, 1880–1920.* Cambridge, Mass.: Harvard University Press, 1993.

Hoffman, Frederick J. *The 20s: American Writing in the Postwar Decade,* rev. ed. New York: Free Press, 1962.

Hofstadter, Richard. *Social Darwinism in American Thought,* 2nd ed. Boston: Beacon Press, 1955.

Holloway, Jonathan Scott. *Confronting the Veil: Abram Harris, Jr., E. Franklin Frazier, and Ralph Bunche, 1919–1941.* Chapel Hill University of North Carolina Press, 2002.

Howe, Daniel Walker. *The Unitarian Conscience: Harvard Moral Philosophy, 1805–1861.* Middleton, Conn.: Wesleyan University Press, 1998 [1978].

Huggins. Nathan. *Harlem Renaissance.* New York: Oxford University Press, 1971.

Hutchinson, George. *The Harlem Renaissance in Black and White.* Cambridge, Mass.: Harvard University Press, 1995.

Hutchison, William R. *The Modernist Impulse in American Protestantism.* New York: Oxford University Press, 1976.

Hyatt, Marshall. *Franz Boas—Social Activist: The Dynamics of Ethnicity.* New York: Greenwood Press, 1990.

Jackson, Walter A. "Melville Herskovits and the Search for Afro-American Culture." In *Malinoski, Benedict and others: Essays on Culture and Personality,* edited by George W. Stocking Jr. Madison: University of Wisconsin, 1986.

———. *Gunnar Myrdal and American Social Conscience: Social Engineering and Racial Liberalism, 1938–1987.* Chapel Hill: University of North Carolina Press, 1990.

Jacobson, Matthew Frye. *Whiteness of a Different Color: European Immigrants and the Alchemy of Race.* Cambridge, Mass.: Harvard University Press, 1998.

Janken, Kenneth Robert. *Rayford W. Logan and the Dilemma of the African-American Intellectual.* Amherst: University of Massachusetts Press, 1993.

Jervis, John. *Transgressing the Modern: Explorations in the Western Experience of Otherness.* Malden: Blackwell, 1999.

Jordan, Winthrop. *White over Black: American Attitudes toward the Negro, 1550–1812.* Chapel Hill: University of North Carolina Press, 1968.

Kardiner, Abram and Lionel Ovesey. *The Mark of Oppression: Explorations of the Personality of the American Negro.* Cleveland: Meridian Books, 1962 [1951].

Kimball, Gayle. *The Religious Ideas of Harriet Beecher Stowe: Her Gospel of Womanhood.*
    New York: Edwin Mellen Press, 1982

Kinney, John William. "Adam Clayton Powell, Sr. and Adam Clayton Powell, Jr.:
    A Historical and Theological Analysis." Ph.D. diss., Columbia University, 1979.

Kirby, Jack Temple. *Rural Worlds Lost: The American South, 1920–1960.* Baton Rouge:
    Louisiana State University Press, 1987.

Kluger, Richard. *Simple Justice: The History of* Brown v. Board of Education *and Black
    America's Struggle for Equality.* New York: Vintage Books, 1975.

Leathers, Kim. "A Historical Survey of the Sociology of the Black Church." Ph.D. diss.,
    Howard University, 1999.

Levine, Lawrence W. *Black Culture and Black Consciousness: Afro-American Folk
    Thought from Slavery to Freedom.* New York: Oxford University Press, 1977.

Lewis, David Levering. *When Harlem Was in Vogue.* New York: Penguin Books, 1997
    [1981].

———. *W.E.B. Du Bois: Biography of a Race, 1868–1919.* New York: Henry Holt, 1993.

———. *W.E.B. Du Bois: The Fight for Equality and the American Century, 1919–1963.*
    New York: Henry Holt, 2000.

Lincoln, C. Eric. *The Black Muslims in America.* Boston: Beacon Press, 1961.

Lincoln, C. Eric and Lawrence H. Mamiya. *The Black Church in the African American
    Experience.* Durham, N.C.: Duke University Press, 1990.

Litwack, Leon. *North of Slavery: The Negro in the Free States, 1790–1860.* Chicago:
    University of Chicago Press, 1961.

———. *Been in the Storm So Long: The Aftermath of Slavery.* New York: Vintage Books,
    1980.

———. *Trouble in Mind: Black Southerners in the Age of Jim Crow.* New York: Vintage
    Books, 1998.

Logan, Rayford W. *The Betrayal of the Negro: From Rutherford B. Hayes to Woodrow
    Wilson,* new ed. New York: Da Capo Press, 1997 [1965].

Luker, Ralph. *The Social Gospel in Black and White: American Racial Reform, 1885–1912.*
    Chapel Hill: University of North Carolina Press, 1991.

Madison, James H. "Reformers and the Rural Church, 1900–1950." *Journal of
    American History* 73 (December 1986): 645–668.

Masood, Paula J. *Black City Cinema: African American Urban Experiences in Film.*
    Philadelphia: Temple University Press, 2003.

McCarthy, Joseph J. "History of Black Catholic Education in Chicago, 1871–1971."
    Ph.D. diss., Loyola University of Chicago, 1973.

McGreevy, John T. *Parish Boundaries: The Catholic Encounter with Race in the Twentieth
    Century Urban North.* Chicago: University of Chicago Press, 1996.

McKivigan, John R. and Mitchell Snay, eds. *Religion and the Antebellum Debate over
    Slavery.* Athens: University of Georgia Press, 1998.

McPherson, James M. *The Abolitionist Legacy: From Reconstruction to the NAACP.*
    Princeton, N.J.: Princeton University Press, 1995 [1975].

Meier, August. *Negro Thought in America, 1880–1915.* Ann Arbor: University of
    Michigan Press, 1988 [1963].

Miller, Albert G. *Elevating the Race: Theophilus G. Steward, Black Theology, and the Making of an African American Civil Society, 1865–1924*. Knoxville: University of Tennessee Press, 2003.

Miller, Floyd J. *The Search for a Black Nationality: Black Emigration and Colonization, 1787–1863*. Urbana: University of Illinois Press, 1975.

Miller, Jordan Y. and Winifred L. Frazer. *American Drama between the Wars: A Critical History*. Boston: Twayne, 1991.

Miller, Randall M., Harry S. Stout, and Charles Reagan Wilson, eds. *Religion and the American Civil War*. New York: Oxford University Press, 1998.

Montgomery, William E. *Under Their Own Vine and Fig Tree: The African American Church in the South, 1865–1900*. Baton Rouge: Louisiana State University Press, 1993.

Moore, Moses N. *Orishatukeh Faduma: Liberal Theology and Evangelical Pan-Africanism, 1857–1946*. Lanham, Md.: Scarecrow Press, 1996.

Moses, Wilson Jeremiah. *The Golden Age of Black Nationalism, 1850–1925*. New York: Oxford University Press, 1988 [1978].

———. *Black Messiahs and Uncle Toms: Social and Literary Manipulations of a Religious Myth*. University Park: Pennsylvania State University Press, 1982.

———. *Alexander Crummell: A Study of Civilization and Discontent*. New York: Oxford University Press, 1989.

Muhammad, Khalil G. " 'Negro Stranger in Our Midst': Origins of African American Criminality in the Urban North, 1900–1940." Ph.D. diss., Rutgers University, 2004.

Newby, I. A. *Jim Crow's Defense: Anti-Negro Thought in America, 1900–1930*. Westport, Conn.: Greenwood Press, 1980 [1965].

Noll, Mark A. *America's God: From Jonathan Edwards to Abraham Lincoln*. New York: Oxford University Press, 2002.

Novick, Peter. *That Noble Dream: The "Objectivity Question" and the American Historical Profession*. Cambridge: Cambridge University Press, 1988.

O'Brien, Kenneth Paul. "The Savage and the Child in Historical Perspective; Images of Blacks in Southern White Thought, 1830–1915." Ph.D. diss., Northwestern University, 1974.

Orsi, Robert A. *Between Heaven and Earth: The Religious Worlds that People Make and the Scholars who Study Them*. Princeton, N.J.: Princeton University Press, 2005.

Osofsky, Gilbert. *Harlem: The Making of a Ghetto: Negro New York, 1890–1930*. New York: Harper and Row, 1966.

Perman, Michael. *Struggle for Mastery: Disfranchisement in the South, 1888–1908*. Chapel Hill: University of North Carolina Press, 2001.

Perry, Bruce. *Malcolm X: The Life of a Man Who Changed Black America*. Barrytown, N.Y.: Station Hill Press, 1991.

Pinn, Anthony B. *Why, Lord? Suffering and Evil in Black Theology*. New York: Continuum, 1995.

Quarles, Benjamin. *Black Abolitionists*. New York: Oxford University Press, 1969.

Rabinowitz, Howard N. *Race Relations in the Urban South, 1865–1890.* Urbana: University of Illinois Press, 1980.

Raboteau, Albert J. *Slave Religion: The "Invisible" Institution in the Antebellum South.* New York: Oxford University Press, 1978.

Raboteau, Albert J. and David D. Wills. "Retelling Carter G. Woodson's Story: Archival Sources for Afro-American Church History." *Journal of American History* 77 (June 1990): 183–199.

Rainwater, Lee and William L. Yancey, eds. *The Moynihan Report and the Politics of Controversy.* Cambridge, Mass.: MIT Press, 1967.

Rainwater, Lee, ed. *Soul.* Chicago: Aldine, 1970.

Rampersad, Arnold. *The Life of Langston Hughes: I, Too, Sing America.* Vol. 1. New York: Oxford University Press, 1986.

Record, Wilson. *The Negro and the Communist Party.* New York: Atheneum, 1971 [1951].

Reed, Christopher Robert. *"All the World Is Here!": The Black Presence at White City.* Bloomington: Indiana University Press, 2000.

Richardson, Heather Cox. *The Death of Reconstruction: Race, Labor, and Politics in the Post–Civil War North, 1865–1901.* Cambridge, Mass.: Harvard University Press, 2001.

Richardson, Joe M. *Christian Reconstruction: The American Missionary Association and Southern Blacks, 1861–1890.* Athens: University of Georgia Press, 1986.

Riss, Arthur. "Racial Essentialism and Family Values in 'Uncle Tom's Cabin,'" *American Quarterly* 46 (December 1994): 513–544.

Rydell, Robert W. *All the World's A Fair: Visions of Empire at American International Expositions, 1876–1916.* Chicago: University of Chicago Press, 1986.

Savage, Barbara Dianne. "Biblical and Historiographical Imperatives: Toward a History of Ideas about the Political Role of Black Churches." In *African Americans and the Bible: Sacred Texts and Social Textures,* ed. Vincent L. Wimbush. New York: Continuum, 2000.

———. "W.E.B. Du Bois and 'the Negro Church.'" *Annals of the American Academy of Political and Social Science* 568 (March 2000): 235–249.

———. "Carter G. Woodson and the Struggle for a 'Unified Black Church.'" *A.M.E. Church Review* (fall 2000): 13–20.

Schechter, Patricia A. *Ida B. Wells-Barnett and American Reform, 1880–1930.* Chapel Hill: University of North Carolina Press, 2001.

Scheiner, Seth M. *Negro Mecca: A History of the Negro in New York City, 1865–1920.* New York: New York University Press, 1965.

———. "The Negro Church and the Northern Ghetto, 1890–1930." In *Seven on Black: Reflections on the Negro Experience in America.* ed. William G. Shade and Roy Herrenkohl. Philadelphia: Lippincott, 1969.

Scott, Daryl Michael. *Contempt and Pity: Social Policy and the Image of the Damaged Black Psyche, 1880–1996.* Chapel Hill: University of North Carolina Press, 1997.

Sernett, Milton C. *Bound for the Promised Land: African-American Religion and the Great Migration.* Durham, N.C.: Duke University Press, 1997.

————. *African American Religious History: A Documentary Witness*, 2nd ed. Durham, N.C.: Duke University Press, 1999.

Sharps, Ronald Lamar. "Happy Days and Sorrow Songs: Interpretations of Negro Folklore by Black Intellectuals, 1893–1928." Ph.D. diss., Washington University, 1991.

Sherwood, Henry Noble. "Early Negro Deportation Projects," *Mississippi Valley Historical Review* 2 (March 1916): 484–508.

————. "The Formation of the American Colonization Society," *Journal of Negro History* 2 (July 1917): 209–228.

Silber, Nina. *The Romance of Reunion: Northerners and the South, 1865–1900.* Chapel Hill: University of North Carolina Press, 1993.

Singal, Daniel Joseph. *The War Within: From Victorian to Modernist Thought in the South, 1919–1945.* Chapel Hill: University of North Carolina Press, 1982.

Sitkoff, Harvard. *The Struggle for Black Equality, 1954–1992*, 2nd ed. New York: Wang and Hill, 1993.

Small, Sandra E. "The Yankee Schoolmarm in Freedmen's Schools: An Analysis of Attitudes." *Journal of Southern History* 45 (August 1979): 381–402.

Smedley, Audrey. *Race in North America: Origin and Evolution of a Worldview*, 2nd ed. Boulder: Westview Press, 1999.

Smith, Gary Scott. *The Search for Social Salvation: Social Christianity and America, 1880–1925.* Lanham, Md.: Lexington Books, 2000.

Smith, John David. *An Old Creed for the New South: Proslavery Ideology and Historiography, 1865–1918.* Athens: University of Georgia Press, 1991 [1985].

Snay, Mitchell. *Gospel of Disunion: Religion and Separatism in the Antebellum South.* Chapel Hill: University of North Carolina Press, 1993.

Sousna, Morton. *In Search of the Silent South: Southern Liberals and the Race Issue.* New York: Columbia University Press, 1977.

Southern, David W. *Gunnar Myrdal and Black-White Relations: The Use and Abuse of an American Dilemma 1944–1969.* Baton Rouge: Louisiana State University Press, 1987.

————. *John LaFarge and the Limits of Catholic Interracialism, 1911–1963.* Baton Rouge: Louisiana State University Press, 1996.

Spear, Allan H. *Black Chicago: The Making of a Negro Ghetto.* Chicago: University of Chicago Press, 1967.

Stanton, William. *The Leopard's Spot: Scientific Attitudes toward Race in America, 1815–1859.* Chicago: University of Chicago Press, 1960.

Stauffer, John. *The Black Hearts of Men: Radical Abolitionists and the Transformation of Race.* Cambridge, Mass.: Harvard University Press, 2001.

Stocking, George W. Jr. *Race, Culture, and Evolution: Essays in the History of Anthropology.* New York: Free Press, 1968.

Stowell, Daniel W. *Rebuilding Zion: The Religious Reconstruction of the South, 1863–1877.* New York: Oxford University Press, 1998.

Studenraus, P. J. *The African Colonization Movement, 1816–1865.* New York: Columbia University Press, 1961.

Sweet, Leonard I. *Black Images of America, 1784–1870.* New York: W. W. Norton, 1976.

Taves, Ann. *Fits, Trances, and Visions: Experiencing Religion and Explaining Religion from Wesley to James.* Princeton, N.J.: Princeton University Press, 1999.

Tindall, George B. *The Emergence of the New South, 1912–1945.* Baton Rouge: Louisiana State University Press, 1967.

Tise, Larry E. *Proslavery: A History of the Defense of Slavery in America, 1701–1840.* Athens: University of Georgia Press, 1987.

Toll, William. *The Resurgence of Race: Black Social Theory from Reconstruction to the Pan-African Conferences.* Philadelphia: Temple University Press, 1979.

Tompkins, Jane. *Sensational Designs: The Cultural Work of American Fiction, 1790–1860.* New York: Oxford University Press, 1985.

Trotter, Joe William Jr., ed. *The Great Migration in Historical Perspective: New Dimensions of Race, Class, and Gender.* Bloomington: Indiana University Press, 1991.

Tucker, William H. *The Science and Politics of Racial Research.* Urbana: University of Illinois Press, 1994.

Turner, Richard Brent. *Islam in the African American Experience.* Bloomington: Indiana University Press, 1997.

Van Deburg, William L. *New Day in Babylon: The Black Power Movement and American Culture, 1965–1975.* Chicago: University of Chicago Press, 1992.

Watts, Jill. *God, Harlem, USA: The Father Divine Story.* Berkeley: University of California, 1991.

Weisbrot, Robert. *Father Divine and the Struggle for Racial Justice.* Urbana: University of Illinois Press, 1983.

Weisenfeld, Judith. "On Jordan's Stormy Banks: Margins, Centers, and Bridges in African American Religious History." In *New Directions in American Religious History*, ed. Harry S. Stout and D. G. Hart. New York: Oxford University Press, 1997.

———. *Hollywood Be Thy Name: African American Religion in American Film, 1929–1949.* Berkeley: University of California Press, 2007.

White, Ronald C. Jr. *Liberty and Justice for All: Racial Reform and the Social Gospel.* New York: Harper and Row, 1990.

Williams, Vernon Jr. *From a Caste to a Minority: Changing Attitudes of American Sociologists toward Afro-Americans, 1896–1945.* Westport, Conn.: Greenwood Press, 1989.

———. *Rethinking Race: Franz Boas and His Contemporaries.* Lexington: University Press of Kentucky, 1996.

Williamson, Joel. *The Crucible of Race: Black-White Relations in the American South since Emancipation.* New York: Oxford University Press, 1984.

Wilson, Charles Reagan. *Baptized in Blood: The Religion of the Lost Cause, 1865–1920.* Athens: University of Georgia Press, 1980.

Wood, Betty. *Come Shouting to Zion: African American Protestantism in the American South and British Caribbean to 1830.* Chapel Hill: University of North Carolina Press, 1998.

Woodward, C. Vann. *Origins of the New South, 1877–1913*. Baton Rouge: Louisiana State University Press, 1971 [1951].

———. *The Strange Career of Jim Crow*, 3rd rev. ed. New York: Oxford University Press, 1974.

Young, James O. *Black Writers of the Thirties*. Baton Rouge: Louisiana State University Press, 1973.

Young, James Robert. "E. Franklin Frazier and His Critics: The Role of Religion in the Sociological Analysis of Race Relations in the United States." Ph.D. diss., Boston University, 1984.

Young, Jeffrey Robert. *Domesticating Slavery: The Master Class in Georgia and South Carolina, 1670–1837*. Chapel Hill: University of Carolina Press, 1999.

Zamir, Shamoon. *Dark Voices: W. E. B. Du Bois and American Thought, 1888–1903*. Chicago: University of Chicago Press, 1995.

Index